Singapore Teachers

Narratives of Care, Hope and Commitment

Singapore Teachers

Narratives of Care, Hope and Commitment

Yanping Fang

Aristotle Motii Nandy   David Liew   Huey Min Sun   Say Pin Tan   Sonia Khan

WS education

A Subsidiary of **World Scientific**

NEW JERSEY · LONDON · SINGAPORE · BEIJING · SHANGHAI · HONG KONG · TAIPEI · CHENNAI · TOKYO

Published by

World Scientific Publishing Co. Pte. Ltd.

5 Toh Tuck Link, Singapore 596224

USA office: 27 Warren Street, Suite 401-402, Hackensack, NJ 07601

UK office: 57 Shelton Street, Covent Garden, London WC2H 9HE

Library of Congress Cataloging-in-Publication Data

Names: Fang, Yanping.

Title: Singapore teachers : Narratives of care, hope and commitment / Yanping Fang,
    National Institute of Education, Nanyang Technological University, Singapore.

Description: New Jersey : World Scientific, [2015] | Includes bibliographical references.

Identifiers: LCCN 2015011290| ISBN 9789814678254 (hardcover : alk. paper) |
    ISBN 9789814678261 (pbk. : alk. paper)

Subjects: LCSH: Teachers--Singapore.

Classification: LCC LB2832.4.S5 F36 2015 | DDC 371.1095957--dc23

LC record available at http://lccn.loc.gov/2015011290

British Library Cataloguing-in-Publication Data

A catalogue record for this book is available from the British Library.

In-house Editors: Shreya Gopi/Elizabeth Lie

Typeset by Stallion Press

Email: enquiries@stallionpress.com

This book is dedicated to celebrating the resilience of Singaporean teachers whose stories are worth being told...

These stories are richly deposited in the rocks that form the foundation of Singapore's education system. Through narratives and inquiry they emerge from the rocks' fissures making visible teachers' embedded learning and emotions, their beliefs of education, their identity formation... Through the telling and retelling of these stories, care, hope and commitment are shared and strengthened....

Prologue

Yanping FANG

The teacher narratives and the study of these narratives included in this book were written by and derived from teacher participants and the instructors in a post-graduate course taught at the National Institute of Education (NIE), Singapore. Narrative inquiry has been used in this course to help teachers to make meaning of their personal and professional learning and growth trajectory.[1] Here, narratives are autobiographical or self-narratives told and retold in more structured and purposeful ways to inquire into the meaning of one's own life and work experience (Bruner, 1990). The authors' courage to confront the vulnerability that arises when examining and reliving their emotional encounters in their teaching journeys, and making their personal learning public, is what makes this book possible. They spread this courage and passion to more teachers in Singapore.

More than being a mere summary of teacher narratives, the Overviews of each of the six Parts of the book, written by the editorial team after many rounds of reading and re-reading, tease out

---

[1] Thanks to Dr. Eisuke Saito and Mr. John Yeo who co-taught the course with me in 2010 and 2011 and to Dr. Jiang Heng who co-taught it with me in 2012. Their contributions are deeply appreciated.

patterns to usher readers into the narratives contained in each Part in more informative and reflective ways. The final Part with two reflective essays and one research paper explores more systematically the narrative experiences of the course participants, while the Epilogue records the instructor's own journey in developing a narrative inquiry pedagogy in teacher education. The book is expected to benefit teacher educators at NIE, future course participants and local teachers as a resource for teaching and professional development, and inform researchers and policy makers who are interested in understanding the lived experiences of teachers in Singapore to create better teacher engagement in schools.

The final editing of the narratives and the writing of the Overviews were made possible by a small Start-Up Grant (SUG 26/12 FYP) awarded by the Office of Educational Research of NIE.[2] Despite its size, the fund played an important role in putting together an editorial team made up of five former course participants who have contributed in different ways to bringing the book to fruition. I am indebted to their encouragement and hard work. The book, in many ways, represents the outcome of the creative endeavour of teachers.

Last but not least, my gratitude to David Yean Sin Liew for illustrating the book covers. Currently a freelance artist, David was a former course participant and member of the editorial team as well as a former Junior College (JC) art and history teacher, and a lecturer in art at Republic Polytechnic.

Reference

Bruner, J. (1990). *Acts of meaning*. Harvard: Harvard University Press.

---

[2] Editing was partly funded with a Start-Up Grant from the Office of Education Research of NIE under the Grant No. SUG 26/12 FYP. The ideas and opinions in this book are those of the editors, the editorial team, as well as the contributing authors. They do not represent those of the funding agency.

Foreword:
Inside Singapore Schools

F. Michael Connelly

Yanping Fang contacted me over narrative inquiry during my 2011 preparations for a Visiting Professorship at the National Institute of Education in Singapore in 2011. My visit had nothing to do with narrative inquiry and I was unaware of any faculty interest in the Curriculum, Teaching and Learning Department which would be my visitor's home. I was, in fact, somewhat surprised at her interest in narrative inquiry because establishing academic respect and credibility for narrative inquiry was a continuing struggle for those of us working in the area, almost all of whom were working in what we imagined to be less structured and rigorous environments than was thought to prevail in Singapore. Freema Elbaz once remarked that in her opinion narrative inquiry flourished in Canada during its development phase because of the relaxed Canadian educational environment. In 2011, Singapore was frequently discussed in comparative international achievement terms as one of the lead nations worldwide. In general, outsiders such as me imagined the educational system to be strongly oriented to national goals, carefully structured in terms of curriculum policy, and heavily monitored for teaching and learning. It was difficult to imagine narrative inquiry gaining a foothold in teacher education and post graduate instruction under those imagined circumstances. Since then, of course, the excellent "insiders" book on Singapore education, *Globalization and the Singapore Curriculum: From Policy to Classroom*, edited by Zongyi Deng, S. Gopinathan and Christine Lee has provided a much more realistic nuanced view of Singapore education. The Singapore education of our imagination is still there but looking beneath this formalised outline revealed practical variations. Still, even in the light of this new book Yanping Fang's interest in narrative inquiry remains somewhat surprising. Yanping Fang was then an untenured junior professor. During my doctoral studies one of my Committee members received tenure at the University of Chicago about which he said "Now I can do what I want." Working in a comparatively decentralised educational environment, my own work in narrative inquiry began post-tenure. Yanping Fang's interest, and teaching, developed in a vastly different educational environment than my own in Canada and she did it while academically vulnerable. These conditions help this book transcend its narrative inquiry methodology to shed a riveting, concrete and detailed, light on the workings of education in Singapore. This book moves beyond the aforementioned Singapore education book to the inner workings of schools and classrooms.

There are versions of narrative inquiry worldwide which are better suited to therapy than to curriculum; and there are versions so structured and defined as to be indistinguishable from a standard teacher-directed lesson structure. But I discovered in my conversations with Yanping Fang, what readers of this book will readily see, that she, and her former student collaborators, are exploring new territory not in the least familiar to her curricular environment and yet highly relevant to it. One thing led to another in our discussions and we ended up planning a full day workshop to be run as a teleconference between the National Institute of Education in Singapore and the School of Teacher Education at Southwest University in Chongqing China where my colleague Shijing Xu was a visitor and acted as Southwest University seminar coordinator.

The seminar was run in such a way that Shijing Xu and I presented what one might think of as the theory of narrative inquiry, and Yanping Fang and colleagues, some of whom are represented in this book, presented real life narrative material developed and written in her graduate classes. The workshop clinched it! Professor Yanping Fang's work was original. She was clearly making a contribution to Singapore teacher education and to Singapore curriculum and instruction, and she was taking her place on an international stage in which her work contributed to the evolving field of narrative inquiry. Following the seminar she hinted that she wanted to draw things together in the form of a book. This is it.

The book grows out of several years of teaching a National Institute of Education graduate course in teacher education and is based on over 200 student narratives. The book is organised around six themes or general ideas that emerged in the narratives. Each theme is introduced by one or more authors who reflect on the set of papers relative to the theme developed. The six parts are:

1. Working with students: The calling of teachers' work.
2. Working with colleagues: Source of energy or wear or tear?
3. What shapes a teacher?
4. What shapes a leader?
5. Teacher identity and self.
6. Research on the narrative inquiry practice by course participants and instructors.

Each of the first five parts is made up of an overview and a set of narrative chapters. The sixth part makes a transition from narrative to narrative inquiry though I confess this is my interpretation and may not quite square with Fang's intentions. Part 6 turns from what Polkinghorne (1995) called *narrative analysis* — the analysis of events in narrative terms — to *analysis of narrative* — the application of Bruner's (1986) paradigmatic inquiry to narrative material. In addition to this fascinating, somewhat jolting, narrative turn the turn is taken gradually as if one were driving a sweeping freeway bend in the road. Two chapters are written as the group member analyses of a set of narratives written by group members. The twists and turns of their group inquiries are revealing. The final chapter is flat out *analyses of narrative*, written by Yanping Fang and her colleague John Yeo, and is a superb example of using narratives as data in traditional (paradigmatic) inquiry. I know of no other publication where *narrative analysis* and *analyses of narrative* are juxtaposed so intimately. This feature alone warrants wide use of the book in qualitative methodology courses.

The chapters in the Parts 1 through 5 are genuine narrative and as such open the door to a host of interpretations unlike, for example, a document built largely of numerical data tables. There are, of course, interpretive possibilities for such tables but the interaction of a narrative text with a reader's narrative generates seemingly endless possibilities. I want to comment briefly on these chapters while restricting myself to three interpretive points: How recognisable Singapore education is in the narratives presented; How unique and nuanced Singapore education appears in the narratives presented; and the fundamental narrative point that narrative observations are not so much facts of the case as they are invitations to inquiry.

With respect to my first and second points I found it significant that Yanping Fang defines the lives that teachers live in terms of *care, hope* and *commitment*. These are universal human qualities and, in various ways, interpenetrate the literature of teacher education. Teachers are expected to care, to have hope for the future and to be committed to their calling. One of my first significant international educational ventures was with the International Association for the Evaluation of Educational Achievement (IEA). As I visited schools in different parts of the world I remember being struck by my former colleague comparative educator Joseph Farrell's observation that, "Schools are recognisable anywhere in the world." So while Yanping Fang appears, somewhat surprisingly, to be doing narrative inquiry in an environment one might not think supportive of it we see the universals of educational thought coming forward in the narrating. Story after story throughout the five parts brings forward recognisable, telling, events in teachers lives. There is the "mousy Malay girl with the deadbeat dad and the mother holding two jobs" (Ch. 2); the gifted student who makes life miserable for the average teacher (Ch. 3); the support of the supervisor who guides a beginning teacher (Ch. 10); the problem of minorities and lowered expectations (Ch. 28) and many others. These, and many many more concrete events, people and circumstances show the Singapore system as it is experienced by teachers. These stories with their description of events, people and circumstances cut through the stereotypes and expectations of Singapore education. They cut through the popular imagination on what constitutes Singapore education. This book gives a close, face against the glass, picture of Singapore education. This is a recognisable education but is also a unique and special education. For me, having read the Deng *et al.* book, I find that this book of narratives brings life to the nuanced policy picture provided in the Deng book. These two books should be read together by anyone interested in trying to grasp a sense of the practice of Singapore education to compliment the imaginary sense of Singapore education emerging from mesmerised international traveller reports and standardised achievement results. This book does as it intends and provides a picture of educational life in Singapore.

My third point has to do with the importance of narrative observation to inquiry. This point is front and center, though not named as such, in Aristotle Motii Nandy's overview to Part 1: *Working with students: The calling of teachers' work* and in the narratives that follow. This section beautifully illustrates the importance to narrative inquiry and for that matter to life in general, of never taking things at face value but always asking "Why? What are the narrative origins of this observation?" An apparently lazy student is shown to have home difficulties; an apparently obnoxiously gifted student has an abusive father. Almost all the stories in this book whether they are about students, or administrators, or teachers, deal with insights gained from the narrative inquiry exploration of observations easily taken, and thereby dismissed, as factual descriptions of the world. The taken-for-granted factual observations are often narrative inquiry's starting point. This questioning of the "obvious" is one of the book's shaping metanarratives.

Before turning to my final section I want to make an observation about the book's authorship. The cover page shows six authors with Yanping Fang's name in large font. This design signals Yanping Fang's central leading role while acknowledging the extraordinary writing and interpretive section introductions by others, all of whom were student members in Yanping Fang's graduate courses where the narratives that form the book were originally crafted. No doubt there was a great deal of editing by the authors, and editorialising by Yanping Fang, to convert the raw course narratives into this polished, telling book on the classroom workings of Singapore education. It would be easy to overemphasise Yanping Fang's role at the expense of the associated student authors. Their contribution is massive. It would also be easy to overlook the extraordinary collegiality Yanping Fang created in her teaching. How did she manage to get a group of students who probably began their course experience thinking it was all a bit offbeat and odd to commit to the huge amount of work needed to pull this kind of book together? In part it no doubt had to do with her teaching. But it also had to do with her students. The mere fact of this collegiality tells readers something about the educational spirit at work in Singapore education.

Finally, a Question?

Not long ago I wrote the Foreword to *Narrative Inquiries into Curriculum Making in Teacher Education* edited by Julian Kitchen, Darlene Ciuffetelli Parker and Debbie Pushor in which junior professors talked about the difficulties faced with their classes and with their institutions in undertaking narrative inquiry teaching. The entire book is devoted to describing and understanding the struggles confronted by these newly minted professors working in a newly minted area. When I opened Yanping Fang's book, I expected to see a text more along the lines of the authors in the Kitchen *et al.* book. But Yanping Fang gets on with it. She hints at the issues discussed in the other book when she comments that there were "numerous challenges" and an "arduous learning journey". But there is nothing equivalent to the discussion of difficulties in the other book. Notwithstanding my modified insights into Singapore education, I am inclined to think that Yanping Fang may have had a less accepting environment to teach narrative inquiry than did many of those in the Kitchen *et al.* book. Moreover her three part course structure in which people wrote narratives, reflected on them, and then wrote group reflections would, in my experience, exacerbate difficulties that may have arisen during the first narrative task, writing the narrative. In my own graduate teaching I used a two course sequence to move from Yanping Fang's Part I to her Part II. As a long time teacher of narrative inquiry I am in awe that she accomplished what she did with her compressed course structure.

I am curious as to how she was able to bring off so successfully what she has done in this book. I would like to know not only some of her "difficulties" and what made the journey "arduous" but also somewhat more detail on the actual assignments given to students. What were students asked to do in and out of class and what was the response to these requests? How did she finally chart a course in which the students' expectations and hers emerged in a course plan and outline? My request, I think, is that Yanping Fang write a small book, or perhaps a standard academic journal article, on these matters. Perhaps she could write a review of Kitchen *et al.* book in which she juxtaposes her experience with that of the book's authors.

Meanwhile the book is a treasure and provides insight into teachers lives, into Singapore education, and into education more generally. This book provides a solid frame for Yanping Fang's intention of producing a Singapore, and East Asian Education, book series.

References

Bruner, J. (1986). *Actual minds, possible worlds.* Massachusetts: Harvard University Press.

Deng, Z., Gopinathan, S., & Lee, C. K.-E. (Eds.). (2013). *Globalization and the Singapore curriculum: From policy to classroom.* New York: Springer.

Kitchen, J., Parker, D. C., & Pushor, D. (Eds.). (2010). *Narrative inquiries into curriculum making in teacher education*. Bingley, United Kingdom: Emerald Group Publishers.

Polkinghorne, D. E. (1995). Narrative configuration in qualitative analysis. In J. A. Hatch & R. Wisniewski (Eds.), *Life history and narrative*. Washington, D.C.: The Falmer Press.

Introduction: Lives of Singapore Teachers — Narratives of Care, Hope and Commitment

Yanping FANG

People lead storied lives and it is through telling and retelling our stories that we make meaning of our lives (Bruner, 1990; Connelly & Clandinin, 1990). As teachers, we tell our own stories to understand ourselves and, in doing so, to also "understand the power of story in the lives of the students we teach" (Connelly & Clandinin, 1994, p. 150). Integral to any inquiry and in learning to teach, teachers too undergo numerous challenges and emotional turmoil in journeying through life and work. Yet, through narrative writing and group deliberation processes, they can get reconnected with a stronger sense of commitment to the caring of their students and have a renewed sense of hope and purpose. Hence, the title of the book: *Singapore Teachers — Narratives of Care, Hope and Commitment.* The narratives included in this book are from more than 200 narratives written by teachers of all subject areas across different career stages who had attended a postgraduate course at the National Institute of Education (NIE) (see more details about reflections on designing and teaching the course in the Epilogue). They give voice to Singapore teachers as to what shapes their day-to-day work lives, how they define their identity and their sense of self and purpose as educators. They also bring to our attention teachers' dynamic learning experiences and personal practical knowledge.

Overview of the Book

The selected narratives are grouped into five Parts, each representing the dominant theme depicted by the narratives within that Part: working with students, working with colleagues, what shapes a teacher, what shapes a school leader, and teacher identity and self. Part 6 looks back at the individual and collaborative narrative experiences of the participants in the above-mentioned postgraduate course. The editorial team members carefully read and edited the narratives placed under their purview and looked for patterns across the narratives in writing the Overview for their designated Part. The Overviews were each written to reflect the editorial members' own teacher or teacher researcher perspectives and styles, with some in prose and others more academic. Summarised below is each Part in a nutshell, followed by a few highlights across all six Parts.

In Part 1, the authors lead readers into the inner worlds of students while recounting episodes in their teaching journeys. The teacher narratives show how students lead significantly different home lives than their own. By drawing on their teaching experiences with a diverse range of students, they demonstrate increasing awareness of the important roles they play in supporting these students and begin advocating for their needs and rights. While doing so, however, they were left vulnerable by their limited power to intervene in their students' personal lives. The emotional nature of working with students and their families and knowing about the lives of students beyond the classroom permeates the narratives in this publication.

Part 2 offers a peek into the complex world of human relationships at the workplace, in particular the power and politics in interacting with colleagues and supervisors. These narratives show that collegiality in the work setting can cheer teachers up and add meaning to their work by reducing isolation and stress, while power struggles can wear away their spirit, sap their energy and force them to transfer schools or even leave the profession entirely. Thus, working with colleagues and supervisors may either make or break a teacher. It is evident that the notion of clear and honest communication, and the ability to balance the personal and the professional, beg our attention as education professionals. It also makes us aware of the tension and stress caused by a hierarchical system and the bureaucratic ranking practices which can be detrimental to teachers' mental health and wellbeing.

In addition to interactions with students, colleagues and superiors, there are a multitude of other factors that shape teachers personally and professionally, as manifested in the narratives in Part 3. These factors can vary from teachers' upbringing, their early schooling experience, their motivations to enter teaching, their work assignments and so on. Such factors can impact teachers' beliefs positively or negatively. Through "restorying", teachers are found to have reconnected with their fundamental education beliefs and reignited their passion for teaching.

Narratives in Part 4 are written by a few school leaders, ranging from leaders newly promoted to leadership positions, to leaders towards the end of their service. Despite the diverse range in experience, what they have in common is the capability to reflect on their career trajectory and roles as leaders as well as their impact on the teaching staff and local communities. Their narratives help us see these school leaders through both their strengths and vulnerability as human beings engaged in learning and reflection.

Part 5 refocuses on teacher identity and self as the authors take an inward gaze at the meaning- and decision-making junctures of their career. In the process, they ask significant questions such as whether to leave a leadership role to resume a teacher role; what the roles and responsibilities imply when faced with competing tensions; how a new sense of self emerges as a result of change in work context; whether to emphasise teaching for character or to just transmit book knowledge given the constraints of time; and how the ethnic identity as a minority teacher pans out in a multiracial and predominantly Chinese society. Again, the narratives offer a kaleido-scopic view of the diverse factors shaping teacher identity and self in the local school context and in a multicultural society that is uniquely Singapore.

Part 6 presents three studies on the narrative experiences of teacher participants in the postgraduate course. The first two are written by David and Sonia, who attended the course in 2012 and 2013 respectively. They reflect in different ways the restorying experience in their Group Projects. As a course component, group members read, provide feedback to and analyse each other's narratives with a goal to co-construct meaning of the group's narrative writing experience in light of the course readings. The third piece, written by the course instructors as a narrative inquiry research paper, examines the narratives written by a cohort of 33 course participants. It focuses on the emotional work of teachers in interacting with students.

The Epilogue shares the course instructor's journey in developing a "narrative inquiry pedagogy" in teacher education (Conle, 2000) through continuous experimenting and improving. She believes that teacher and student narratives should be capital-ised on as powerful resources for personal and professional learning and knowledge-building (Golombek & Johnson 2004; Johnson & Golombek, 2011).

Together, this collection depicts the "narrative truth" of the dynamic everyday lived experiences of a group of teachers in and out of school buildings. They reveal the dynamic tensions and emo-tions underneath as well as the joy of the individuals undergoing learning and growth in daily school life. When these lived experi-ences are paused, recorded, shared and examined collectively and publicly, they help reinforce the educative power of teacher narra-tives as stressed by Day & Leitch (2001), "… to neglect the stories of teaching and the narratives of teachers' experiences may be to collude in oversimplification or distortion" (p. 407) of the realities of teachers' lives and their inner worlds.

References

Bruner, J. (1990). *Acts of meaning*. Cambridge, MA: Harvard University Press.

Connelly, F. M., & Clandinin, D. J. (1990). Stories of experience and narrative inquiry. *Educational Researcher,* 19 (5), 2–14.

Connelly, M., & Clandinin, D. J. (1994). Telling teaching stories. *Teacher Education Quarterly,* 21 (1), 145–158.

Conle, C. (2000). Narrative inquiry: Research tool and medium for professional development. *European Journal of Teacher Education,* 23 (1), 49–63.

Day, C., & Leitch, R. (2001). Teachers' and teacher educators' lives: The role of emotion. *Teacher and Teacher Education,* 17 (2), 4, 403–415.

Golombek, P. R., & Johnson, K. E. (2004). Narrative inquiry as a mediational space: Examining emotional and cognitive dissonance in second language teachers' development. *Teachers and Teaching: Theory and Practice,* 10 (3), 307–327.

Johnson, K.E., & Golombek, P. R. (2011). The transformative power of narrative in second language teacher education. *Tesol Quarterly,* 45 (3), 486–509.

Contents

Prologue vii
Yanping FANG

Foreword: Inside Singapore Schools ix
    F. Michael Connelly

Introduction: Lives of Singapore Teachers —
      Narratives of Care, Hope and Commitment xvii
    Yanping FANG

Part 1: Working with Students:
      The Calling of Teachers' Work 1

  Overview 3
  Aristotle Motii NANDY

1. The Bull and the Leopard: Teacher Authority
    and Student Personal Space 9
    Joyce Lixiang ONG

2. Courage, Tenacity and Care — Inspirations from
    Working with Low Ability Upper Primary Pupils 19
    Marianne Ee Lyn HA

3. Learning to Teach and Understand Gifted Students   29
   Chen Chen TEO

4. "Caring Teacher Award" or "Caring Student Award":
   Teachers' Experiences — Shaping Beliefs   47
   Sivagouri KALIAMOORTHY

5. Confessions of an Accidental Teacher   61
   Bernard Kim San SIT

6. Growing and Learning from Teaching Different
   Students in the Context of Change   69
   Lawrence LAU

**Part 2: Working with Colleagues — Source of Energy
   or Wear or Tear?**   79

   Overview   81
   Aristotle Motii NANDY

7. Attributing My Professional Growth
   to My Mentor and My Students   87
   Vimi D SAMBWANI

8. "The Looking Glass Self" — Locating My Professional
   Identity from Interactions with Students and Colleagues   101
   Sheikh Luqmahn Bin AHMAD

9. Leadership: The Hardware versus the Heartware   117
   Fatimah OTHMAN

10. Sunshine after the Rain — A Reflection
    on My Teaching Career   133
    Melanie

11. To Stand on My Own Two Feet   145
    Ting Ting LEE

12. The Accidental Leader   157
    Hwei Fang SONG

Part 3: What Shapes a Teacher? **167**

Overview 169
Huey Min SUN

13. Being Tested 177
Li Meng GOH

14. My Germination Process 193
Annie SENG

15. Leaders that Make or Break Your Career 207
Jackie Chye Chen ANG

16. Chapters of My Teaching Career 219
Siti Aisha SAID

17. I Teach Because I was Taught — A Teacher's Story 229
Anu RADHA

18. A Journey to Designing Student-Centred Learning
    in a Problem-Based Learning Environment 243
Rachel ONG .

Part 4: What Shapes a Leader? **257**

Overview 259
Say Pin TAN and Sonia KHAN

19. A Tale of Two Schools: Leadership, Perceptions,
    Perspectives 265
Huey Min SUN

20. Journey of Growth to be a Teacher and School Leader 281
Siew Khim TEO

21. New Beginnings: An Educator's Journey through
    the Door of Mentorship 295
Aristotle Motii NANDY

22. Managing Stereotypes in a Diverse Educational
    Landscape — A Teacher's Journey towards
    Self-discovery   309
    Nur SABARIAH Mohamed Ibrahim

23. The Passing of a Day   319
    Say Pin TAN

24. Becoming My Own Heroes   335
    Thiam Chuan YAP

Part 5: Teacher Identity and Self   351

   Overview   353
   Yanping FANG and Sonia KHAN

25. The Heart of a Teacher   359
    Tin Hong HON

26. An "Upgraded" Consciousness   373
    CHC

27. Beyond Passing Them Knowledge and Skills —
    The Moral Dimension of a Teacher's Work   383
    Andy TAN

28. Regardless of Race, Language and Religion —
    My Identity as a Malay Teacher   395
    N. B. MIZZY

29. Re-Evaluating My Professional Trajectory: A Journey
    in Search of My Identity   411
    Rina MIZZY

30. My Life in (Jigsaw) Pieces   427
    Vivian RODRIGUES

Part 6: **Research on the Narrative Inquiry Practice**
of Course Participants and Instructors **443**

Overview 445

Yanping FANG

31. The Collegial Factor in Narrative Inquiry — How Group
Meaning-Making Helps Let Go Deep-Seated Traumas 449

David Yean Sin LIEW

32. Five Brooks One Purpose 457

Sonia KHAN

33. Understanding the Emotional Work of Singapore
Teachers in Interacting with Students 475

Yanping FANG and John YEO

Epilogue: **Narrative Inquiry for Teacher Education and**
Professional Development — An Instructor's
Journey **503**

Yanping FANG

Index 513

Part 1:
Working with Students:
The Calling of Teachers' Work

Overview

Aristotle Motii NANDY

Part 1 includes the personal narratives of six teachers of events in their professional journeys. It points to the various reasons for which different individuals decided to join teaching. Their reasons may be myriad — for satisfaction, to accommodate finances and seek scholarship, to change the system, to fill the void in their lives, or in search of self — but while reading the stories in this section, one realises that their purposes converge on the well-being of their students (Grimmett & MacKinnon, 1992). Further, these purposes have been achieved through varied means, each of which has unveiled a hidden corner of the teaching world. However, in this entire process — a process of understanding, realisation, action, inaction, awakening and change — teachers are not the sole entity; they are but a part of a larger context — the school, the families of students, the society and the nation. The context has played a major part in shaping their teaching, their beliefs and their identity (Bruner, 1990; Connelly & Clandinin, 1990).

These narratives also shed light into the often times unknown waters of working with students. The experiences of interacting with students are as varied as the social and cultural backgrounds of the students, teachers' beliefs about their personal and professional roles as educators and the contexts in which the teacher–student relationship plays out. However, from all the narratives presented, it is evident that the rudder that keeps teachers on course in their teaching voyage is the tenacity of their beliefs as educators. As teachers interact more regularly and connect more deeply with their students, they discover more about the inner or other worlds in which their students live, and, especially in cases of challenging situations where their emotions are strongly churned, they are inexorably led to reflect upon their underlying motivations for entering the profession.

The stories also bring to the fore the unpleasant dimensions of some teachers' work in the professional milieu when working with students. Due to the fear of facing difficult students or students with difficulty, teachers may ignore reading the underlying signs of trouble, show lack of empathy, and even try to prove themselves right; and in the process, they may lose sight of the purpose of their becoming a teacher and in doing so move away from the noble and larger task at hand.

As one reads through the stories, one shall find rare awakenings. In "Courage, Tenacity and Care — Inspirations from Working with Low Ability Upper Primary Pupils", Marianne observed that a student in her class was inattentive and lazy, only to find dark clouds lingering over the nine-year old girl. It dawned upon her that "everyone has a story and that there is so much more than meets the eye." In another class, she observed that a student leader who was well-known for his charisma and endearing personality was actually suffering in silence, unbeknownst to any of his teachers and friends. Citing the two examples, Marianne discovered that the high correlation between socio-economic status and academic performance was due to the cultural capital of the child, which spurred her to be more determined to become a "pillar of strength" for herself and her students.

In the story "Learning to Teach and Understand Gifted Students", Chen Chen shares her understanding of gifted students and the assumptions that teachers harbour about them. Because such students are gifted, that is, intellectually more capable, it is assumed that all about them is perfect including their familial situation. However, this may not be the case and thus such generalisation may ill afford any help to the teacher. Fortunately, she observed a minute problem which revealed a deeper malady — why a gifted student who had been doing remarkably well in class could not cope with work assigned to be completed at home. The story also highlights some of the far-reaching social impacts of economic downturn and unemployment. It also puts the spotlight on the unawareness of the boy's teachers of the predicament faced by him. At the heart of the matter is the notion of the role of a teacher, the grave implications on the nature of a teacher's relationship with students and how it impacts students' growth and development.

Joyce, in "The Bull and Leopard", reflects on her struggle with the professional milieu and also highlights teachers' fears in handling rebellious students. Having struck a positive cord with a student, she listened carefully to the problems that her colleagues had with the student with a view of coming up with a resolution. How she struck a balance, what difficulties she faced and what realisation she was left with are worth taking note. Many a time we, as teachers, ignore basic courtesies that our students are entitled to and infringe upon their sensitivities, not realising the effects it may have on them and also on our relationships with them.

Bernard's story, "Confessions of an Accidental Teacher", too, hints at a similar story where a student is considered a cause of trouble to teachers and to whom teachers fear to teach. However, the story also reveals the genuineness of one teacher that caused the student to open up and let the teacher into his world of experiences, thoughts and feelings and helped effect a dramatic turnaround in the student's behaviour and academic performance. This affirms that positive teacher-student interaction influences learning and development of students, and forms an important aspect of adolescent development. The story stresses the utility of the support system in the form of annual medical checks that have been well placed by the Ministry to help students and how such a system can help detect a problem at an early stage and help provide a solution.

Another teacher, Lawrence, carried lofty notions of being able to "change the world" at the onset of his teaching career but had a reality check when he was assigned to teach a Secondary Three (Normal Academic) class. The whole experience proved to be a culture shock to him. The story takes one to a journey of an "emotionless teacher" to a teacher who let go his "'cold professional' façade", thus reflecting upon the change in his belief about his role and identity as a teacher.

In "'Caring Teacher Award' or 'Caring Student Award' — A Tamil Language Teacher", Sivagouri, the teacher, struggled to deal with her own emotions when she found out that one of her students who had been absent from school had been sexually assaulted by a family "friend", and that she, as the little girl's teacher, had been completely unaware of this. The story also shed some light on the indifference of some teachers towards their students.

In conclusion, the emotional nature of a teacher's interactions with students (Hargreaves, 2000; Day & Leitch, 2001) is highly visible in all the narratives in this section. The narratives show that for effective teaching and learning to take place, it is imperative that teachers not merely be competent in the mastery of the subject matter they teach, but more importantly learn to build good working relations with students. This entails taking up the opportunity to start conversations with students, develop an interest in them, and be aware of any signs or indications in their work or behaviour that may be of concern. It is also essential that teachers develop a reflective and reflexive disposition, which would help them continually review themselves, in particular with their interactions with their students.

References

Bruner, J. (1990). *Acts of Meaning*. Cambridge: Harvard University Press.

Connelly, F. M. & Clandinin, D. J. (1990). Stories of experience and narrative inquiry. *Educational Researcher*, 19 (5), 2–14.

Day, C. & Leitch, R. (2001). Teachers' and teacher educators' lives: The role of emotion. *Teacher and Teacher Education*, 17 (2), 4, 403–415.

Grimmett, P. P. & MacKinnon, A. M. (1992). Craft knowledge and the educatin of teachers. *Review of Research in Education*, 18, 385–456.

Hargreaves, A. (2000). Mixed emotions: Teachers' perceptions of their interactions with students. *Teaching and Teacher Education*, 16, 811–826.

Chapter 1

The Bull and the Leopard: Teacher Authority and Student Personal Space

Joyce Lixiang ONG

"Want to cane me, cane now! Stop wasting my time! I want to go back to class for lessons!" said Ryan to the Principal rudely.

This was his fourth session in the Principal's office. Sitting in the Principal's office with his fists clenched, Ryan appeared to be agitated and tired. Ryan's parents and aunt arrived in the school once again because of his discipline case. It was clear that Ryan's parents and aunt wanted to "end the emotional misery" for their son/nephew.

Sitting beside Ryan, I felt helpless. I looked at him. In my eyes, he had not changed much since I first knew him in Secondary Two. Flashbacks of past years' encounters began to blur my eyes.

The Bull

Ryan was a Secondary Four Express student who had a reputation for being rude towards teachers whom he disrespected. Two days ago, he had gotten himself into trouble again by being openly defiant towards a National Institute of Education (NIE) trainee who had relieved his class during Physics lessons.

Recalling the time when he was in Secondary One, I had heard many instances of him behaving rudely towards his subject teachers, often causing them to complain about him in the staffroom. Every time his name was mentioned, groups of teachers would either exclaim "That Ryan again!" or shake their heads and sigh aloud. Many colleagues who had taught Ryan would have rather not taught him if they had a choice. Some kept minimal contact with him, for fear of getting into disputes or anger management issues. Most of the teachers were convinced that this boy was prone to getting himself into discipline cases and had a big anger management problem. He was also labelled "the bull", someone who was not only stubborn but also considered a handful, by some of the teachers.

My Fears

Ryan was banded into the strongest Secondary Two Chinese Language class because of his proficiency in the Chinese language, and I became his Chinese Language teacher. Having heard so much about him from the other teachers in the staffroom, I was apprehensive about teaching him at first. As a beginning teacher, I was scared. I feared that I would be incapable and not equipped with the classroom management strategies needed to deal with him!

On the first day of lessons, although I specifically told myself not to be unduly worried, I still could not help feeling a sense of uncertainty about teaching this boy. As I walked along the corridor towards the classroom, ideas and strategies of how to avoid and manage confrontation, disputes, and upfront defiance crossed my mind. Till today, I still remember his nonchalant face as he sat in the front row of the class, getting ready for lessons to begin. The coldness and awkward meeting made me feel uneasy. Throughout that first lesson, he stared at me with a blank face, as if he was analysing and reading my words, sentences and actions. I felt uneasy. I felt like I was being monitored and scrutinised closely. I did not enjoy my lessons with this class. In fact, I dreaded going into class and I often asked myself, "Why am I so unlucky to have to teach this class?" Each time the bell rang for class dismissal, I felt a great sense of relief.

Slowly, it dawned on me that I should not be overly worried about his presence in class. I had to look into the needs of the other students as well. Being affected by Ryan's cold stares would only cause me to lose focus in my teaching and adversely impact the other students' learning. Subsequently, I learnt to look at his cold face with an open mind. I began to enjoy my lessons.

Look Beyond

It did not take me long to realise that Ryan was in fact a bright boy who had so much potential academically. In class, I observed that he was always the first student to finish the assignments and the tasks I assigned, after which he would take the initiative to complete other work given by his subject teachers. Although I was walking around the classroom, checking and answering questions posed by other students, I was often curious about what he was doing. Occasionally, he would also tutor his classmates when they had doubts.

Our very first conversation started two weeks into the semester. I recall him finishing his work earlier than the rest, and working on a mathematics question on algebra. He looked frustrated after a while. I walked over, wanting to find out what was actually wrong, for fear that it might balloon into an anger management issue. I spotted a careless mistake that he had made but I was hesitant to point it out to him immediately. I merely asked him to redo that particular question. Eventually, that indirectly allowed him to spot his own mistake and solve the mathematics question. And to my pleasant surprise, he actually looked up and said, "Thank you!" with a boyish smile. Instantly, I felt good. I sensed the goodness in him. Somehow, I felt he was different from what the teachers had made him out to be.

Subsequently, Ryan and I started engaging in small conversations in class while waiting for the other students to finish their assignments. Every chitchat session with him was enjoyable and I got to see him in a different light. As he rattled on about being an entrepreneur or a businessman when he grew up, his eyes lit with such great hope and drive! He was in fact a teenager with his own thoughts and ideals.

"Concerned" Colleagues

It was interesting how some teachers who had issues with Ryan would drop by my desk to check if he was already creating any problems in my class. Initially, I thought it was nice of them to be concerned and perhaps they had some good advice to offer, but I slowly realised that they were not genuine about it. Whenever I heard teachers complaining about him, I would go forward and share my good experiences with them, suggesting to them to give him more time to change. These teachers stared at me in disbelief when they heard me speaking up for him. It was as if I was spouting nonsense. Some even mentioned I had not seen his true colours and there would come a time where I would complain about him to them. I was dumbfounded. I knew at once I had to move myself away from these colleagues. I had to battle forward alone, and I felt a growing sense of ownership and responsibility for Ryan. I wanted to shield him from all this prejudice.

Shelter of Refuge (For Both Teachers and Student)

When Ryan got into trouble, I would call him the next day to find out his side of the story and try to rationalise with him about the possible consequences for his actions. As a result, Ryan often looked to me for advice and help whenever he had issues with his teachers. Soon, word spread across the staffroom that I was the one to look for whenever there were matters pertaining to Ryan. Some colleagues looked surprised when they heard that. I was, after all, neither his form teacher nor his co-form teacher. Some were simply glad there was "someone" to handle their cases. Others questioned why I even bothered for such a student. I knew that explaining myself to them was fruitless, so I chose to smile it off; but in my heart, I exclaimed, "If you do not care, allow me to take care of Ryan!"

Foundation of Trust

In the following year, Ryan was again banded into the strongest class for Chinese Language. I, on the other hand, was no longer teaching that band. My new class consisted of students who had a much lower proficiency level as compared to Ryan. His aunt, whom I had also heard much about previously, called my then Subject Head to request for either a change of teacher for the strongest band or the possibility of transferring Ryan into my Chinese Language class. To be honest, it came to me as a surprise and I was truly flattered by her actions. It was also a huge sense of relief for the other teacher (teaching the strongest band) who had sighed at the first instance when she thought she would be Ryan's teacher for the year. I gladly agreed to the arrangement of having him transferred to my class, but nonetheless, I was also worried that this might affect his progress in the language.

Ryan was in high spirits when he stepped into my class. I had a chat with him after class to convey my concerns.

"Don't worry, I will make sure I improve even further!" he said brimming with full confidence.

At that moment, I was speechless. I did not really know how to react to this boy's firm belief in himself. I thought to myself, "Here I have a student who has so much belief in himself and in me. And yet, as a teacher, I have doubts about my own capacity and will to help him scale greater heights in the language."

Even till today, that conversation keeps me motivated. I want to be the best teacher I can be for my students. Trusting myself and believing in my students empowers me to contribute more to their learning.

The Agony of being "Aunt Agony"

In Secondary Three, Ryan continued to be involved in minor discipline cases and I became his and other teachers' shelter of refuge. After class, teachers would come to me and complain about Ryan. They indirectly asked me to punish him on their behalf or hoped to ruin the good relationship I had with Ryan. Some pressed me for answers and solutions to their problems. I felt myself suffocating under their eagle eyes. On the other hand, Ryan would come to me for "time-out" sessions, where I would hear his frustrations about how teachers were impatient and insensitive towards his feelings. Every word from him sounded so real, with no intent of pretence. Often I found myself asking — "Was it a 'time-out' session for Ryan or a welcome relief for me to catch a breather from the tense atmosphere in the staffroom?"

Needless to say, I was constantly entangled between some of the teachers and Ryan. I had to double up as "Aunt Agony" for both parties, providing suggestions and making sure that the relationship between them would not be strained. It was frustrating for me. I had to be politically right to my colleagues, and at the same time be a nurturing and understanding figure to Ryan. I felt as if I had a split personality! I became frustrated at myself for being useless, for being unable to pacify both parties, for getting myself involved in their problems. I often questioned, "Why did I get myself into this?" "Why didn't I choose to just teach like everyone else?"

It took some time before I felt that my commitment to Ryan became worthwhile when I noticed that Ryan and his teachers began to view their problems from different perspectives. I had made that happen for them! In the process, though frustrating, the experience had moulded me into a more understanding and patient teacher. I realised that everyone learns in his or her own time — some are faster than others, and we should never give up. Giving up is never an option for us.

Can a Leopard Change its Spots?

When Ryan progressed to Secondary Four, teachers seldom complained about him. I figured he had either matured over the years or was simply tired of getting himself into constant trouble.

I still recall asking him jokingly after one lesson, "What happened to you? What happened to all the nonsense you often got yourself into for the past years?" And to my amazement, this boy replied with a shy smile, "No lah, ma'am. This year is my "O"-Level year leh... Must study hard. Cannot get into trouble like previous years lah." I laughed at his innocent response but was pleased with his truthful answer.

When he walked past me and headed towards the canteen for his recess, I was still thinking about that short casual conversation. I then realised that this boy, whom I had known since Secondary Two, had matured over the years.

While many teachers figured that it would not be long before Ryan got himself into trouble again, I remained optimistic that he had truly changed for the better. However, the peace was short-lived.

Just as some subject teachers started singing praises about how focussed he was in preparing for the "O"-Levels, I received news one morning that a student named "Ryan" had gotten himself into serious trouble with a trainee teacher from NIE. My heart sank. I asked, "Which Ryan? Ryan from Class 4G?" The answer broke me.

In the staffroom, teachers were talking and discussing about the incident loudly with one another. Soon, everyone had heard about it in many different variations. I was standing, in the midst of them all, observing and listening to the different variations and assumptions made. I could hear my heart beating faster and my mind asking only one question, "What exactly happened?"

I knew that I had to hear from him. I walked briskly out of the staffroom, wanting to find him for clarification, hoping he would tell me that all I had heard were rumours and that none of that had happened. I found him in his class and requested to talk to him. He was not surprised to see me. In fact, he knew I would come and look for him. I looked at him and asked in a low tone, "Tell me exactly what happened."

He let out a sigh and went on to narrate, "Today we had our Physics test. Our Physics teacher did not come. An NIE teacher came in instead. I finished my test, and it was two more minutes to the end of paper. While waiting, I took out my small mirror to check myself. The teacher came forward and snatched my mirror away without any warning. I stood up and asked him to return my mirror.

He refused and accused me of wanting to use the mirror to cheat on the test."

At this point, Ryan had his fists clenched. He continued the rest of his story in an agitated manner. "I defended myself and explained why I was using the mirror but he did not accept my explanation at all. I shouted, 'Teacher, so what? That does not mean you can simply snatch away my things.' He still refused to return my mirror and rebutted 'What can you do about it?' Than he walked away. Out of anger, I went forward and spat on his shoes. My classmates came forward and pulled me back to my seat for fear I would get into a fight with the teacher."

After hearing him out, I rationalised with Ryan and laid out the implications and consequences for using a mirror during a test, and asked if the whole incident could have been avoided. Ryan admitted that it was wrong and stupid of him to use the mirror before the end of the test. At this point, I thought to myself, "My chance has come. Now that he admitted it was his fault, persuade him to apologise to the teacher."

Following my plan, I went on to persuade Ryan to apologise to the teacher for being disrespectful. But he refused! He was insistent that it was the teacher who had provoked him by not returning his mirror and had challenged him. Standing firm in his belief that the teacher should not have simply snatched his mirror away without his permission, he said in an angry tone, "Why should I apologise to him? He is a teacher, so what? He did not respect me first!" By then, his face had already turned red. I tried explaining to him repeatedly that there was no need to flare up into a rage over this matter. Ryan remained adamant. This was the first time I felt helpless handling him. It seemed that nothing I said could change his mind. There was absolutely no way in getting this boy to apologise to the teacher. It was obvious that our conversation was going in circles. We were getting nowhere. Visibly tired and disappointed, I asked him, "Why are you so stubborn? Why can't you just apologise?" He remained silent. I walked away.

I walked straight into the nearest toilet. I needed a quiet place to think; I needed to be away from everyone. I felt helpless. I could feel my face burning and my sight blurring. My mind was frantically searching for the answers needed. I did not know how else to help him. All I knew was that he stood a high chance of being suspended or caned. And all the teachers in the staffroom would probably laugh their heads off and drown me in their sarcasm. I could imagine them saying, "Ryan will never change! A leopard can never change its spots! Give up!"

Ultimately, I regained my composure and decided to approach the trainee teacher to hear his side of the story, hoping to find a way to solve the case amicably. The NIE trainee looked surprised to see me and was a bit puzzled about my interest in the case. As he narrated his side of the story, I could not help but disagree with the way he had dealt with the situation. But I did not speak a word. I thanked him for sharing. Before walking off, I took another look at the trainee and wondered, "How would he have felt if the roles had been switched?"

Now, I was more convinced that Ryan was not entirely to be blamed for the whole incident. It was an intrusion of personal space and he had the rights to flare up to defend himself. I finally understood why he was so reluctant to apologise to the teacher. If it were me, I might not apologise as well. It was frustrating to me because the teacher was also wrong but he was let off because he was merely disciplining the student. On the other hand, the poor child had his mirror snatched away from him, provoked, and was left to defend himself. As a teacher myself, I could not openly stand on Ryan's side. I had the obligation to uphold values and support my own colleagues. I needed to be politically right. I felt small in comparison to Ryan's bravery in standing up to his beliefs. The thought of escaping from the case crossed my mind. Perhaps being ignorant (not getting involved) would make me a happier person? I did not know.

Long Tussle

It was an emotionally stressful week for Ryan, his parents, his aunt and myself. My Principal was kind enough to grant me two days to persuade Ryan to apologise for his actions. I was optimistic about the task at first. I tried speaking to Ryan repeatedly, persuading him to consider apologising for his actions (and not to the teacher) so that the case could be closed as soon as possible. But time after time, I was disappointed. However, I was also aware that every disappointment I felt at the end of each conversation magnified Ryan's strong beliefs, which he held so dearly to himself. Sighing in resignation, I went to the Principal's office, and handed the case back to the Principal. Ryan's aunt and parents thanked me for my time and patience. I smiled out of courtesy. There was no sense of relief. My heart was heavy.

In the end, Ryan was still adamant about not apologising to the teacher. He was later given the choice of either to be caned or home suspended. Even when Ryan chose to be caned, he made a commotion in the Principal's office. I will never forget his words just before the caning was administered in the Principal's office.

"Want to cane me, cane now! Stop wasting my time! I want to go back to class for lessons!"

The door closed. And three strokes of the cane were heard shortly after.

In my heart, I applaud Ryan for standing firm in his beliefs and I say this with mixed feelings. To be frank, in his case, setting aside his anger management problems, were his principles misplaced? Did I do the right thing in getting him to apologise for his actions (but not to the trainee teacher)? Constantly, I find myself seeing teachers using their authoritative power to "legitimately" step into students' personal space without permission. For Ryan, I say with conviction, "I did my best for him." From him, not only have I learnt to see things from the students' perspectives, but also find myself frequently challenging and questioning my personal values and beliefs. Moving on to my fourth year of teaching, I am now certainly more confident when handling students, more mature in my thoughts and more careful with my words. Frankly, I await the next "Ryan-like" student to come my way. And I want to be that positive figure in his or her life.

Students today yearn to be heard. They wish to be understood. And they are crying out for the need to be respected silently!

Chapter 2

Courage, Tenacity and Care — Inspirations from Working with Low Ability Upper Primary Pupils

Marianne Ee Lyn HA

My journey as a teacher unofficially began in 2003, when I had left my job of four years as a Public Relations Consultant to join the world of education. It was not that I did not enjoy my previous job; I was working for a large multinational public relations consultancy, got to travel a fair bit and worked on numerous exciting, challenging projects. However, as I toiled through the years, working to please bosses, clients and media, I began to develop a sense of dissatisfaction and emptiness. I resented how "corporate" my scope of work and impact were; I often asked myself: Who am I benefitting? All this hard work ... for what? To put more money into other people's pockets? I resented the fact that what I was doing was not benefitting the people who really needed help, hence my foray into teaching.

I managed to secure a six-month relief teaching position at a convent school in the east. I had opted for a longer relief teaching period so that I could ascertain if teaching was really something I wanted to sign on to. I was pretty excited about being posted to that school; it was an all-girls school, predominately made up of middle class, English-speaking Chinese pupils. Coming from a similar background, I felt that I would be able to relate better to such a profile of children.

I was assigned a Primary Three class and everything was going fairly smoothly. There was one mousey little Malay girl, Nurul*, one of the two Malay girls in class, who frustrated me though. She was always daydreaming in class and seemed so unfocused — "inattentive" was the adjective teachers would commonly accord such students. She would often be tardy in handing her assignments, despite repeated reminders. One day, I stayed back after school (we were in the morning session) due to a meeting. It was almost time for the afternoon session dismissal. I was walking towards the school gate and bumped into Nurul, who was in her home clothes. I was naturally surprised and asked her why she had come back to school. She replied that she was there to pick up her younger sister, who was in Primary One in our school. I sat down and talked to her as we waited for the Primary One and Two pupils to be dismissed, and I began to find out more about her background. Despite being only nine years old, she was the eldest of three. Her dad was a deadbeat who had left the family a few years ago, and her mom was holding down two jobs. Because of this, not only did Nurul have to look after her younger siblings, she also had to do the household chores. I was aghast when I found out her daily routine included cooking and cleaning until late, about 10 pm, when most of her peers were tucked into bed and sound asleep. I now knew the reason for her behaviour in school — her distractedness in class and her tardiness in handing up work. This epiphany opened my eyes to a world I had never personally encountered before — that of the underclass. The truth began to unravel — pupils that we would ordinarily have written off as "lazy" or "unmotivated"; there were underpinning reasons for their behaviour. It dawned on me that everyone has a story and that there is so much more than meets the eye.

Since then, my teaching journey has inadvertently landed me in close contact with students of a similar profile. After obtaining my Postgraduate Diploma in Education at the National Institute of Education, I was posted to Redwood* Primary School. I started off with a mixed-ability Primary Four class, but within six months I was given a low-ability Primary Five class, "the last class" as it would be referred to by many. I have been teaching "the last class" of Primary Fives and Sixes for six years now and, as I had stated in my profile on a Master's class blog, "I am touched every day by my pupils and their personal journeys, many of whom inspire me with their courage and tenacity."

These words are not empty platitudes; the stories of my pupils truly hold deep and profound meaning for me. The story that has impacted me most is that of a boy named Rafiz*. Small in size but big in personality, he was one of those boys who had a magnetism and charisma that everyone was drawn to. He was easily one of the most popular boys in school, among both pupils and teachers. Even though he might not have excelled academically, he was very diligent and he always tried. He had so many strengths: he was a natural leader, he was witty and would be the one contributing quips in class and enlivening the atmosphere, he was always enthusiastic and would motivate his peers, he was a great mediator and would be the one bridging differences in group disputes. But above all, he had an amazing character. In his journal (a private communication log between teacher and pupil), he had written about his close relationship with his mom and how much he cared for her. His mom was the sole breadwinner and so Rafiz would help support the household by taking over his grandmother's cleaning duties (his grandmother earned money by cleaning houses). In his journal, he wrote that he would slip the money he earned into his mom's handbag because she would not accept the money otherwise. I was also aware that Rafiz helped to take care of his younger sister because he occasionally could not make it for after-school activities such as his Student Council meetings as he had to babysit. Once, during a meet-the-parents session, he was wheeling his sister around in her stroller and playing with her while I was talking to his mom. It melted my heart to see this "cool" adolescent boy being so sweet and caring towards a little two-year-old girl.

In response to a journal question about what we had to be thankful for, Rafiz wrote that he was thankful his mom never bought him a PlayStation Portable (PSP) because, in his words, "if not, [he] won't be studying and [his] eyes will be fixed on the PSP 24/7". He elaborated on the back story to this PSP saga. He once begged his mom to buy him a PSP but his mom always retorted, "Will you die if you don't have a PSP?" He reflected on his mom's words and saw the truth in them. This quiet maturity struck me; so many of my other boys were fixated on their computer and video games and here was a boy who had the good sense and sensibility not to get sucked into that vortex. There were so many remarkable little anecdotes that made me like and respect Rafiz even more, but it is perhaps this incident, that I am going to share, that left the deepest impression.

Rafiz lived in a housing estate quite near school, so he would cycle to school every morning. As a Student Councillor, he was usually punctual as he had morning duties to serve. However, there were two days when he arrived late for school. He gave the reason of having woken up late; he did look tired and his eyes were puffy. I figured that to be the case so I let him off with a warning. On the third consecutive morning he was late, I caught him walking towards the stairs to the school hall where we were having morning assembly. He looked exhausted; he must have overslept again, I thought. I began chiding him and I was midway through my sermon on responsibility and self-discipline when he suddenly broke down. He crouched on the floor and sobbed into his shirt sleeve. I was stunned; I had never seen him sad, let alone in such a fragile and vulnerable state. I immediately asked him what was wrong. He looked up and, in between sniffles, explained that his back hurt so he could not cycle properly. Naturally I asked him what had caused the back pain. He stared at me, not wanting to continue. He had this incredible look of sorrow etched on his face; I knew it was a grave matter. Upon further coaxing, he finally said he would tell me, but begged me not to report back to his mom. Ordinarily we can make no such promises as we have to inform the children's parents if their safety is at risk, but he had such a look of desperation and worry in his eyes I relented and assured him that our conversation would be kept confidential. It was then that he opened up, and I learnt that it was his father who had hit his back with a *rotan*. It was then that I learnt that he was hit by his father while trying to defend his mother and that his mother and siblings had been physically and verbally abused by their father for years. I could not believe that this boy, who put up such a confident and unwavering front in school, was harbouring such hurt and fear inside him.

There were many things I took away from that incident, and what was to follow. I discovered the intricacies of handling cases of family disputes and violence and the boundaries and constraints we as teachers have. On a more philosophical level, I reflected on my role as a teacher, "If this 12-year-old boy can possess such strength and courage, what more me as his teacher?" Later that morning after my episode with Rafiz, as I sat at my teacher's table and gazed out at my students, I realised that I needed to be their strength, I needed to be the one to give them courage. It was something that had always been instinctive but had never been explicitly articulated, but from that day forward, I made a promise to myself and to my students to be their pillar of strength.

There are so many other stories that have given me new insights and perspectives. There's Shahrul*, who is taken care of by two "mothers", i.e. a legal guardian and her partner. Shahrul was given up by his biological mother when he was a baby, and these two "mothers" have raised him since. Shahrul's "mothers" dote on him and, even though they do not earn much, they make it a point to provide for him the best they can. While I am quite liberal in my beliefs, having personal knowledge of such a family has taught me to be non-judgmental towards same-sex couples. Shahrul has a far better life than many other children; he has two mothers who care deeply for him and would do anything for him, which is more than what I can say for some of my other students from traditional, nuclear families. My experience with Shahrul, though, has made me question the legitimacy of our curriculum. Whenever a family is represented, it will comprise one father, one mother and the children. Shahrul has actually expressed his embarrassment about his family make-up during a lesson on the drawing of the family tree. Should he feel ashamed just because his family structure is different? Our curriculum reproduces social norms that beget the questions: Whose norms? Those of the dominant elite? How inclusive are we really?

Apple's (1990) questions resonate clearly with me every time I examine the legitimacy of knowledge intended in a curriculum:

When and how are particular aspects of a collective culture represented in schools as objective, factual knowledge?

How concretely may official knowledge represent the ideological configurations of the dominant interests in a society?

How do schools legitimise these limited and partial standards of knowing as unquestioned truths?

Then, there is Simon*, a repeat student who failed the Primary School Leaving Examinations (PSLE) once. He is a smart boy, but lacks guidance and affirmation. His father is in the Drug Rehabilitation Centre (DRC) and I found out from our school counsellor that his father used to take drugs in the presence of Simon and his younger sister, affecting them emotionally. He is doing much better academically this year, but has fallen into a bad crowd outside of school, primarily because he feels lost and alone without a father figure in his life. And there is Gaytri*, a sweet, diligent girl who puts in great effort in her studies. She comes from a poor family, and her parents put immense pressure on her to do well in her studies so as to help break them out of the poverty cycle. Gaytri sometimes gets so stressed by the ambition her parents place on her that she has contemplated suicide on several occasions, and has even resorted to self-mutilation. Thank goodness Gaytri sought help, and came to me about her problems, and the school counsellor and I are currently trying to help her and her family work through her problems.

When I reflect on all these stories, two central themes come to me: Care and Social Inequality. Let me first elaborate on the theme of care.

The central theme of Care has come to the forefront for me in terms of my curriculum and pedagogical approaches. A key thinker in this area is Noddings (2002), whose argument is that care is basic in human life — that all people want be cared for. Noddings (1995) goes on to argue that "in an age when violence among school-children is at an unprecedented level, when children are bearing children with little knowledge of how to care for them, when the society and even the schools often concentrate on materialistic messages, it may be unnecessary to argue that we should care more genuinely for our children and teach them to care." This seems to ring especially true for my students, the children in the underclass, and I am sure that the same can be said for all children as our world continually evolves into a more mercenary and banausic one.

Through my interactions with my students over the years, and from readings such as Noddings', my personal beliefs about teaching and education have evolved. They used to be about "imparting knowledge, skills and attitudes" (an excerpt from my personal statement in school), but now I realise the heart of it all is to care for the children and to teach them to care.

Noddings' (1995) words sum up how I feel about this topic: "... caring is not just a warm, fuzzy feeling that makes people kind and likable. Caring implies a continuous search for competence. When we care, we want to do our very best for the objects of our care. To have as our educational goal the production of caring, competent, loving and lovable people is not anti-intellectual. Rather, it demonstrates respect for the full range of human talents. Not all human beings are good at or interested in mathematics, science, or British literature. But all humans can be helped to lead lives of deep concern for others, for the natural world and its creatures, and for the preservation of the human-made world. They can be led to develop the skills and knowledge necessary to make positive contributions, regardless of the occupation they may choose." This is my desire, and my hope, for the students who pass through my classes.

The other central theme when I reflect upon the many students I have met throughout my young but rich teaching career is that of Social Inequality.

It is, perhaps, unsurprising that all the students I have mentioned in this narrative paper are under the Ministry of Education's

Financial Assistance Scheme (FAS).[1] I did not pick these children to talk about because they are under the FAS, I picked them out and subsequently realised the common thread. In fact, 18 students in my class are under the FAS, compared to an average of four students in each of the other Primary Six classes.

There is no doubt that socioeconomic status (SES) and academic achievement are correlated. Sirin (2005) conducted a meta-analysis which reviewed all literature on SES and academic achievement in journal articles published between 1990 and 2000 and found a medium to strong SES-achievement relation. He also discovered that the relationship increased significantly with each school level.

What I wonder about is whether policymakers acknowledge that, with families of low SES, we are dealing with an underclass that faces not just financial woes but a whole host of other related social issues. There is also the matter of the effects of one's cultural capital, defined by Bourdieu (1977) as the knowledge, skills, education and advantages that a person has that enable social mobility. In a study by Lareau (1986) on the importance of cultural capital in home–school relationships, she found that "social class position and class culture become a form of cultural capital in the school setting ... although working class and middle class parents share a desire for their children's educational success, social location leads them to construct different pathways for realising that success." DiMaggio (1982) also confirmed that cultural capital has an impact on school grades that is "highly significant". Furthermore, parents' educational qualifications and material resources increase with social class, thus making the playing field even more uneven for students from the lower social class.

That being the case, is it enough to merely offer handouts or are there systems and structures that reproduce these class distinctions? Let us examine the existing systems in place that favour the middle and upper classes.

---

[1]MOE's FAS is made available to pupils in households with a gross income of less than S$1,500 per month (one or two children) or S$1,800 per month (3 or more children).

The fact that kindergarten education is not compulsory[2] means that, as in McLaren's (2007) analogy of a race, disadvantaged students get ready at the starting line while the more affluent students get ready at the other end of the track just a few metres from the finish line. Let us look at the Primary One registration system, where the initial registration phases give priority to those living within a close proximity of the school (and we note that the elite schools are largely located in the affluent districts), alumni or members of the School Advisory Committee and parents who have the time to clock in 40 hours of voluntary work at the school of choice. Once the child has made it into the school, there is streaming. If we are to observe characteristics in classes that have been streamed, we would most definitely notice patterns of social stratification emerging. Gamoran (1992) states that "the more rigid the tracking system, the more research studies have found no benefits to overall school achievement and serious detriments to equity." In Singapore, as the students move along their "pathways" into secondary school or vocational institutes, the gap between social classes grows.

Jean Anyon, a critical thinker in education, has researched extensively on social class and schools. In her paper "Social Class and School Knowledge" (1981), she concluded that "there [were] profound differences in the curriculum and curriculum-in-use" in the working class and executive elite schools. The key differences were that the curriculum in the working class schools emphasised mechanical behaviours, and neglected to teach about the history of the working class. It was found that the executive elite schools, however, offered cultural capital to their students by teaching them about the history of the ruling groups and rule by wealth and aristocracy as rational. The parallel in Singapore would be the Gifted Education Programme and elite schools with their Integrated Programmes which offer more enrichment activities and a curriculum meant to stretch the individual, compared to the Normal (Technical) stream where students pick up technical skills.

---

[2]Taken from http://www.moe.gov.sg/education/preschool/faq/.

Confucius once said in his Analects that "in teaching, there should be no distinction of classes." With such structures in place, the systematically disadvantaged are trapped, casting great doubt on Singapore's renowned system of meritocracy. When I reflect on my students and their circumstances, I wonder if I could have achieved the same "success" I have now if I had been born into a different family. I wonder what my students can do in such an education system, and if they truly are competing on the same level as their peers from more affluent backgrounds. These thoughts propel me to want to do something, starting from the school-level to hopefully policy-level, that addresses the needs of the socially disadvantaged in and through education.

*Pseudonym used.

References

Anyon, J. (1981). Social class and school knowledge. *Curriculum Inquiry*, 11 (1), 3–42.

Apple, M. W. (2000). Can critical pedagogies interrupt right policies? *Educational Theory*, 50 (2), 229–258.

DiMaggio, P. (1982). Cultural capital and school success: The impact of status culture participation on the grades of US high school students. *American Sociological Review*, 47 (2), 189–201.

Gamoran, A. (1992). Synthesis of research: Is ability grouping equitable? *Educational Leadership*, 50 (2), 11–17.

Lareau, A. (1987). Social class differences in family–school relationships: The importance of cultural capital. *Sociology of Education*, 60 (2), 73–85.

McLaren, P. (2007). *Life in Schools: An Introduction to Critical Pedagogy in the Foundation of Education*. USA: Allyn and Bacon.

Noddings, N. (1995). Teaching themes of care. *Phi Delta Kappan*, 76 (9), 675–680.

Noddings, N. (2002). *Educating Moral People: A Caring Alternative to Character Education*. USA: Teachers College Press.

Sirin, R. S. (2005). Socioeconomic status and academic achievement: A meta-analytic review of research. *Review of Educational Research*, 75 (3), 417–453.

Chapter 3

Learning to Teach and Understand Gifted Students

Chen Chen TEO

Introduction: Gifted Students — "A Misunderstood Race"?

Hoge & Renzulli (1993) stated that controversies and ambiguities exist with respect to the conceptualisation and measurement of the giftedness construct as the definitions of this construct vary from those with a narrow focus on highly exceptional intellectual capacities to those based on a broad range of intellectual, motivational, and artistic dimensions. However, in recent years, there has been a move away from IQ as the accepted gauge of "giftedness" with a concomitant embracement of multiple concepts of talent as there is a shift amongst educators to view human potential in a more humane and democratic light (Morelock, 1996). Morelock highlighted two emergent strands of gifted education with two differing metaphors: gifted achiever and gifted child. Dai & Renzulli (2000) elaborated that educators who believe in the "gifted achiever" strand develop educational agendas with an eye to bringing up the next generation of leaders, scientists, professionals and so forth, while educators rooting for the "gifted child" strand focuses on the social–emotional needs of gifted children and advocates an education that nurtures the growth of the self, instead of an education for success.

From my observation and personal interaction with colleagues from the mainstream, it is evident that most teachers are still subscribing to the "gifted achiever" strand. They believe in the myth that the primary goal for gifted student development is to develop perfectly well rounded students (Cross, 2002). Hence, many of my colleagues share the common misconception that our gifted students are perfect well-rounders who achieve in all subject areas; are highly intellectual and therefore, highly motivated; and are individuals with a drive to succeed. They assume that gifted students are near perfection and do not deem them as a cause of concern for teachers. What they fail to understand is that precisely because our gifted students are highly intellectual and highly knowledgeable beyond their years; their social-emotional needs are more complex and more demanding than their non-gifted peers. Silverman (1997) highlighted the challenges gifted children face as their emotional development is qualitatively different from their agemates due to the impact of their greater cognitive awareness and their heightened emotions. She drew the analogy of a vulnerable young child having a mental maturity of a 14-year-old while trapped in the body of an 8-year-old. Silverman attributed this to the asynchronous development of gifted children in terms of their intellectual capacity and their emotional development.

This out-of-sync development may at times end up working against the gifted children. At their worst, our gifted students may engage in a not-so-moral tendency of benign chicanery, where they may evolve into manipulative individuals. Such gifted students would use their intelligence to avoid disagreeable tasks and to get their own way with their peers, their parents and their teachers. (Hollingworth cited in Griffin, 2001). To further deepen these existing misconceptions, teachers would often assume that our gifted students have fully supportive parents who are of equal intellect, and hence are from families of elite professions with high social economic status. Sadly, the truth is far from this.

Having taught gifted students for the past eight years, I have come to accept and appreciate some of the idiosyncrasies of my gifted students. I have learnt much about them and from them. I am taking this opportunity to share my experience of working with gifted children and how it has heightened my beliefs in the importance of a gifted education in meeting their learning needs; how it has impacted me to change my perception and ways of working with them; how it has changed the ways I build relationships with them and how it has eventually left me disillusioned about the role of a teacher.

Presentation of lessons

In this segment of the chapter, three stories from different parts of my teaching experience will be narrated to illustrate the critical lessons from my gifted students which led me to self-discovery and greater self-awareness. The first lesson was an encounter in my first year as a gifted education teacher. I was initially very much intimidated by the daunting thought of teaching a class of 25 with an average IQ score way higher than mine. It was this encounter which helped me to reconcile my fears and made me understand my role as a gifted education teacher. The second lesson took place when I was into my fourth year with the Gifted Education Programme (GEP). By then, I had become a parent myself and hence the incident tugged at my heart strings more than ever. It also made me realise that it is so easy to be caught in the school system and to lose sight of my students as individuals. The third lesson which I have selected to write about is a painful one. There was some internal struggle before I decided to include it. It is a current situation which I am working on and trying to manage. It has put me in a great dilemma, and many times I had to question and to justify the intention of my actions in handling the situation.

Lesson 1: Who is that rude and arrogant boy?

I taught for two years in a neighbourhood primary school before I was invited to join GEP as a gifted education teacher. I was apprehensive at first, as the information I gathered from my senior colleagues about gifted students and gifted education teachers was not too comforting. I was told that gifted education teachers were a selfish bunch who guard their resources warily from others and that gifted students were worse as they thrive on embarrassing their teachers and reducing them to tears to prove that they are the stronger race. Fearful though I was, I took up the challenge when I was offered the position to teach Primary Science as I was intrigued by this "mysterious" programme which I knew very little of. Now eight years on, I can only dispel the information I have received earlier from my well-meaning colleagues as urban myths which hold little truth and I have not looked back since.

In my first year, I was assigned to teach two classes of Primary Four Gifted Education Science in my new school — a school with a rich Chinese culture and heritage. As students nation-wide are selected to join the GEP at Primary Three, the successful candidates would join us from different primary schools at Primary Four. On the first day of school, I remember this scruffy-looking, chubby, bespectacled boy with unkempt hair very well. He was hard to miss as he often spoke up loudly and did not mince his words. During the orientation tour around the school, he commented very loudly that the school looked more like a Chinese temple than a school. Some students sniggered, perhaps agreeing with what he had said but had more politeness to keep that comment to themselves. When we attended the assembly talk in the hall, he pointed out equally loudly every single grammatical error and mispronounced word made by the speaker. The speaker was our well-respected Principal who had received formal Chinese education from days of the past. Our Head of Department called the boy to the side to highlight his inappropriate behaviour, but he was adamant that he had done nothing wrong and argued till the end, refusing to acknowledge that his action was inappropriate. I certainly was not looking forward to the end of the one-week orientation programme, when I had to start teaching him and start speaking perfect Queen's English.

I started out being intimidated and fearing this boy, who unfortunately has a great passion for Science, especially Physics — my area of weakness. He was always ready to ask a few thousand "whys" in my lessons and, in order to beat him at all his "why" questions, I read up furiously and did further research beyond the expected curriculum to arm myself with sufficient ammunition to defend myself against his numerous rounds of firing. I always left the classroom exhausted and often with a bruised ego as I was not really his match. I feared the day when I would have to suffer the humiliation of saying "I don't know the answer" and I feared the day when my students would respect me less when they realised I was not as "knowledgeable" as they thought I was. Then, there was this one occasion when the boy I feared refused to budge and continued asking me "why?" for the 100th time, and was trying hard to convince his classmates that the answer I had given was unacceptable. The rest of his classmates had long given up on their arguments with him and were ready to go for their recess. In his frustration of not being heard, he actually started sobbing. I was taken aback; at that moment, I did not see the boy I feared. I saw a small child, passionate in Science, crying in disappointment. This boy has a wealth of knowledge and has such great ideas but is still a child no doubt. He made me realise that I cannot be the sole provider of knowledge in a gifted classroom and that I am not in class to prove that I am the authority of knowledge and therefore my students had to listen to me. This boy made me learn that saying, "I don't know, why don't you share your idea with the class?" does not make me any less respectable to my students. I found that when I admit "I don't know … let's try to figure this out together", it made me more human to my students and they learnt too that it is alright for them to admit that there are things they do not know though they have been identified as gifted.

I came to a better understanding that my role in a gifted classroom is to facilitate my students' learning by imparting skills to enable them to be aware of their own thinking and skills to apply the vast amount of knowledge they bring with them. I need to create opportunities for them to stretch their minds to feel and to understand issues from different perspectives. Each of these students in my class has their own areas of strengths and weaknesses. When we work together, we are able to build on each other's strengths and work on each other's weaknesses to become better individuals. The boy who taught me this simple yet important lesson is Shunren*. Though I grew to be fond of him later on, I had to teach him a few hard lessons at first, especially about self-governance in being respectful towards others. Eventually, I could actually enjoy and appreciate the mental sparring he provided during my lessons.

Lesson 2: Losing sight of the "gifted child"

I was into my fourth year in the programme when I was tasked to shoulder the heavy responsibility of preparing our students for the high-stakes national assessment, the Primary School Leaving Examination (PSLE), with three other colleagues. We were to ensure that our students live up to the great expectation the school and their parents had of them. All 52 of them were expected to produce close to a 100% A* in all four subjects. Hence, one can imagine the immense pressure and stress the teachers were faced with in the uphill task of moving our students towards this unwritten expectation from the school and the parents.

By Term Two, most of our students had resigned to fate, knowing that they needed to put in real effort in order to score a relatively high aggregate score for the PSLE. They were motivated to do well and believed that they were capable of doing well when they put in their fair share of hard work. However, as usual, there would be a few hard core cases where the students remained unmotivated and unmoved by all the intense revision and preparatory work happening around them. Many of them would only start cooperating with us after we resort to forfeiting their recess breaks or their Physical Education lessons, while others needed us to take more drastic measures of meeting up with their parents to discuss about their progress in school.

There was this particularly indifferent boy, Mengwei*, with whom we tried almost all the tricks we had up our sleeves and we were nearing our wits' ends in this losing battle. There was nothing we could do to convince him the slightest to start working hard for himself. We tried punishing and threatening, which led to the threat of being held back after school hours being carried out eventually. We tried coaxing and appealing but his reaction was always the same; he would give us a sheepish smile and a shrug of his shoulders to erase the entire episode and continue to laze his life away. We had contacted both of his parents numerous times. They were too busy to meet us but over the phone they gave us their verbal commitment that they would work with their son at home. Time and again, these commitments were not fulfilled and the boy continued to owe us tons of homework. We felt great pity that Mengwei was so resistant towards our well-meaning advice and encouragement. By nature, he should not have been underachieving, as he was very bright and was insightful in presenting unique perspectives on issues discussed in class. He was ready to participate actively in class activities but the main problem we were facing was that he was not able to produce any written work that he brought home to complete and this was becoming a huge hurdle to overcome in his preparation for the PSLE. We looked through his school records to find out more about his parents. On record, both were gainfully employed and were reasonably well-educated at the tertiary level. Our other colleagues, who had taught Mengwei in previous years, were surprised to hear of the rapid decline in his attitude towards work but were unable to tell us more about his parents as they were usually elusive during the meet-the-parents sessions. We were baffled by what caused this boy to be in such a predicament. Our questions were shortly answered when the health team from the ministry conducted their annual health check in school.

We were in the staffroom, busy with our marking, when the doctor in-charge summoned all his subject teachers to the library where the health check was conducted. We trooped down, not the least expecting to hear what she had to tell us or to show us. She announced matter-of-factly that she suspected that Mengwei was being physically abused at home and requested that we send him to the hospital for a more thorough examination. We were shocked and lost for words. Never once through our many sessions of scolding, coaxing and counselling had we ever suspected this nor had he uttered a single word that was associated to family violence. The following sight which greeted us was not pleasant; we saw bruises and scars of various shapes and sizes on his upper torso and his upper arms. The locations of the evidence of physical abuse were perfectly hidden under his school uniform and the sleeve of his shirt was of just the right length. We were appalled by what we saw; and when his form teacher asked him about it, he just gave us his usual sheepish smile and shrug of shoulders. It was then that it dawned on me that that was his coping mechanism. It was not that he was being lazy or unmotivated or wasting his talents away; he was helpless in his situation, and a sheepish smile and a shrug was all he could afford to allow life to get by. In the capacity of a parent, I questioned how his parents could inflict such physical and emotional harm on their own child. I was suddenly weighed down by a huge sense of dread, wondering if these were part of the verbal commitments his parents had given us over the phone.

Mengwei did not say much at first. He just mentioned that he was careless and had fallen down at home, thus injuring himself. After being pressed further, he relented and admitted that it was his mother who had used him as a punching bag whenever she had arguments with his father over financial woes. On further clarification, we found out that although his dad was a graduate, his qualifications from China were not recognised by many companies in Singapore. After his father was retrenched from his previous employer, he had not been able to find a stable job and the subsequent rejections resulted in him giving up on himself. His father began to idle away most of his time by playing online computer games at home. To make ends meet, his mother had to hold down two jobs and her pride stopped her from applying for financial assistance from the school. Often Mengwei's parents would fight over financial matters; and to worsen the situation, he was not performing well in school. In moments of frustration, his mother would lash out at him with whatever she was holding in her hands; it could be a ladle or a pair of chopsticks or even a clothes hanger. The case was taken over by the Ministry of Community Development, Youth and Sports (MCYS), and Mengwei was hospitalised for two weeks while an investigation was carried out to evaluate if the home situation was safe for him to return.

Mengwei was eventually allowed to go home after two weeks and the situation at home improved. The teachers worked with him closely to catch up on lost time and he managed to do well enough at the PSLE to be admitted into an elite boys' school. On the surface, it appeared that all's well had ended well, but this incident kept me wondering if we had really done well as his teachers. Have we been so engrossed in our pursuit of our A*s that we were unable to detect Mengwei's unhappiness? Or was Mengwei only willing to show us his indifferent attitude as we had not really tried to understand him as an individual and that our focus had always been on academic performance? What students present to us in school is what they want us to know about them and that is only one façade visible to us. There would be many other sides of them which they may not be willing to reveal, for fear of being judged or for fear of being disapproved. The question is: how can we, as teachers, find out more about our students to fully understand them as individuals to help them learn and grow?

Lesson 3: What should we do with this difficult child?

In the whole of my 10 years of teaching, I have yet to come across any student comparable to him in terms of bad behaviour, poor attitude and emotional burden. Whenever any teacher mentioned the name "Elliot*" in the staffroom, there would be resounding disapprovals muttered, followed by "what did he do again this time?" as the common response given. "Elliot" is also a name feared by many teachers whenever they need to go into his class to relief the subject teacher who is on medical leave. Elliot is in Primary Six this year and unfortunately I have been assigned to be his form teacher and his Science teacher. I really did try to be positive about the whole situation despite being "nominated" for this job, as my Head of Department felt that I was the ideal candidate to help this boy do well in the most important year of his primary school life. I remember, clearly, patting him on his back at the end of the first day of school, saying, "We had a good day today. Let's hope we have another good day tomorrow." On hindsight, perhaps I should not have said that as there were no more good days that followed.

When Elliot joined our school for GEP at Primary Four, rumours had it that teachers from his previous school popped champagne to celebrate his departure. At first, I could not comprehend why, but now I am only looking forward to doing the same when he graduates at the end of this year. There were days that the mere thought of having him in my class revolted me; there were days I had to completely ignore him and treat him as invisible; there were days I had to resort to mean sarcasm to get my message across to him; there were days he spent reading at the back of the class and I let him; there were days I had to make him stand outside the classroom; and there were days I had to use the discipline committee and corporal punishment as a threat. I went through each day with mixed emotions and I did not know whether to be sad or glad that I was not the only one feeling this way. Those are just some of the strategies my colleagues and I have adopted so that lessons could carry on as usual in our classroom.

Reading this account thus far, one would wonder what the child could have done to deserve such uncaring and cold treatment from his teachers. What right do the teachers have to treat this child in such an unfeeling and unfair manner? What effect would such negative demonstrations have on the other students? These were some of the questions which went through my head as I became disillusioned about my role as a teacher in such a class. It is true that a teacher should ensure that her students learn well, that their well-being is taken care of and that sound moral values are instilled and good character is built in her students. However, if helping a child who is unwilling to help himself is at the expense of the rest of the students in the class, is it justifiable to sacrifice him and just focus on the rest of the students? If helping a disruptive child deprives the rest of the students from fair and equal opportunities to learn, is it justifiable to sacrifice him so that the rest of the students are able to maximise their individual learning capacities? I was caught in a dilemma where it was difficult to strike a balance between doing my best for the rest of my students in class and being equally fair with Elliot. At times, I even wondered whether I had been over-indulgent with my emotions in hoping that he would be moved by my sincerity into really wanting to change, or whether I had given him way too much allowance.

I have to admit that it is really difficult to remain neutral and unbiased towards this child. Elliot antagonises on purpose to get a reaction from his teachers and peers on a daily basis. He will purposely be defiant towards teachers in school to challenge their authority. He is disruptive during lessons by shouting and moving around to take his classmates' belongings without permission, with the intent of creating chaos. He turns physical by using his fists on his classmates when they retaliate to his oppression. However, we have also observed that he is capable of selecting his mode of behaviour with different teachers and he would choose to cooperate when he feels that he can benefit from the situation or when he needs a favour from the teachers. He can be manipulative in ways where his parents would at times help to find excuses to defend his misbehaviour. On further communication with his parents, we found out that his main caregivers from young were his grandparents, as his parents were not able to care for two young children at the same time. Elliot and his elder brother were born in the same year and they are about eleven months apart in age. By the time Elliot went home to rejoin his parents and his elder brother, he was already a difficult child to manage. It did not help that his father has been physically punishing him severely from young. We do not know whether it is Elliot's personality or the home situation he is in or a combination of factors, which has resulted in him becoming extremely rebellious from a young age. His high intellect may perhaps have contributed to his complex emotional needs which cannot be fulfilled or understood and it has worked against him to a large extent.

As a parent, I do feel sorry towards Elliot's plight and his possible feelings of abandonment since young but as his teacher I am sorry to say that at times I cannot feel the same way. His parents have attempted to gently remind us that he is just a child and he does not really mean what he says to us in class. We may be older and wiser but we are human after all. The words he said in class to either antagonise us or to show defiance will definitely be hurtful no matter what. It is not easy for us to receive the bulk of his emotional baggage, but we still have to strive to be as fair to him as any other child in our class. As his teachers, we will definitely have to try our best to work with him to manage his bad attitude and his behavioural problems. We even put in place special contracts to reward him whenever he puts in the effort to improve and we addressed the rest of the class to appeal for their patience and understanding in tolerating the disruptions during lessons. The gifted education branch also made provisions for him to receive socio-emotional support from a trained counsellor. The crux of the issue now is: if we invest all our time, effort and resources on improving this single child are we being fair to the rest of our students who need our attention? Is it also fair to his teachers when the emotional hard work we put in reaps little effort on his part to improve? Our emotional labour becomes negative and is drained as we mask and manufacture our emotions to remain unruffled (Hargreaves, 2000) when confronted by his defiance in class. After much emotional struggle and many futile attempts and chances given to Elliot, the teachers collectively decided to focus our energy on the rest of the students as we feel we should not shortchange them any further.

Reflection and Discussion

Recalling my first encounter with Shunren brought back bittersweet memories. It had been a struggle for a relatively new teacher like myself to keep up with the fast pace of the gifted students and my prior teaching experience in the mainstream classroom had not prepared me well. I suffered a culture shock in the beginning with their overwhelming responses, as I had never come across a full class of students who were all ready to speak up at the same time and were striving to out speak each other in their answers or to resort to arguing to prove their point. Not having a good understanding of the traits of the gifted students would result in teachers labelling them as being show-offs, arrogant, talkative or even rude. However, as Hollingworth (cited in Silverman, 1990) explained, gifted children in general have the difficulty of remaining silent when they have an idea they want to express and it is not an easy task for them to hold their tongues. There is also a tendency for them to argue as their need for exactness in all mental performances and their keen love of precise facts result in them not being able to resist the temptation to set someone straight if they perceive the slightest loophole in a statement (Hollingworth cited in Silverman, 1990). That was what made Shunren seem so obnoxious in the beginning when he was being critical in the comments and the arguments he made. However, Hollingworth found that it is possible to teach these gifted children to listen quietly and respectfully to others, to speak according to some order of procedure, and to restrain their disappointment at failure to be heard. Their teacher would play the important role of educating them and, in time, these gifted children would learn self-government in these aspects.

It was also my experience with Shunren which convinced me of the importance of curriculum differentiation in meeting the learning needs of different ability groups to maximise individual potential and to motivate learning. Though some school reformers may proclaim that education for the gifted is nothing more than special privileges securing advantages to an already "advantaged" group (George; Margolin; Sapon-Shevin cited in Silverman, 1997) leading to an unhealthy avenue of encouraging elitism in our schools and our society, I still feel strongly that a gifted education does have its merits. As stated by Tomlinson (2005), "differentiated instruction" is a philosophy of teaching, which purports that students learn best when their teachers effectively address variance in students' readiness levels, interests, and learning profile preferences. She emphasised that the key goal of differentiated instruction is to maximise the learning potential of each student. If we can have learning support programmes and different foundation subject combinations to cater to the learning needs of students who are less academically inclined, it should be justifiable that we have programmes to support the learning needs of high ability students as well.

The second story on Mengwei made me realise that when I am caught in the rut of pursuing academic excellence in our merito-cratic school system, it is so easy to lose sight of my students as indi-viduals. Now, I constantly remind myself that each of my students brings with them different sets of experiences from home and that I should not be too quick to make assumptions or judgments about their behaviour in class. It is also important that teachers work closely together to understand their students' personality, interests and needs to be able to meet their socio-emotional needs and to be sensitive towards any changes in their behaviour or emotions. By understanding our students, teachers can help them to achieve bet-ter understanding and acceptance of their own nature, and antici-pate how to react to circumstances in their lives (Johnson, 2000). I cannot help but feel that, as teachers, we have perhaps failed Mengwei. If we had been able to intervene earlier, he might not have been a victim of repeated physical abuse.

Mengwei's story also reminded me of the harsh reality of the competitive society which we live in. Though many Singaporeans are up in arms to voice out their grievances of how tertiary edu-cated immigrants are causing unnecessary competition with local Singaporeans in the job market, we have neglected a certain group of immigrants who came here thinking that there are greater oppor-tunities for them to provide their families with a better life and to provide their children with a better education, but are left disillu-sioned. Mengwei's father was one of them. He is tertiary educated but unfortunately his qualifications were not fully recognised in Singapore. We do have many students from China, and most of their parents are working either as professors in our local universities or as fellow researchers in our laboratories, and we had assumed Mengwei's father to be one of them. If we had been more sensitive towards Mengwei's home environment, we could have perhaps ren-dered assistance to him and his family earlier. What schools and teachers should be aware of is that there may be a small group of migrant students who are not settling in as well as we assumed them to be and that we would need to pay more attention to this group of students.

The third narrative, in which I have shared about Elliot, constantly keeps me in a moral conflict debating whether I have made the right decision in focusing my efforts on the rest of the other students in my class and abandoning him. In all honesty, though the teachers may have taken certain measures in class which appeared to have disadvantaged him, we did make other necessary provisions to work with him to manage his misbehaviour but our efforts yield minimal efforts on his part to change for the better. From Elliot's perspective, it may seem like the teachers are all against him and he is deemed the victim but from the perspective of the other students in the same class, they are the victims as their learning has been badly compromised due to the numerous disruptions during their lessons. From my personal perspective, perhaps the teachers are the real victims in this situation as we are caught in his emotional turmoil and we have willingly or unwillingly shared his burden while we try to help him resolve his issues. We are also stuck in a moral dilemma where we have to stand by the decision we have made regardless of the outcome. What I realise to be most important in this situation is that we remain clear that the intention behind our actions is for the common good — in the best interest of all the other students whom we are equally responsible for.

Conclusion

Johnson & Golombek stated that "Inquiry into experience enables teachers to act with foresight. It gives them increasing control over their thoughts and actions; grants their experiences enriched, deepened meaning; and enables them to be more thoughtful and mindful for their work" (Johnson & Golombek, 2002, p. 7). This quote resonates with me as when I started inquiring into my own experiences, I realised that much of my understanding of my students may have been built upon assumptions, mostly taken for granted, which I have not been aware of. In the process of writing this chapter, I had to question and reinterpret the ways which I have been thinking about my students, my colleagues and myself. Certain realisations which turn up as ugly truths are not easy to accept, but when I become more aware of my own actions, I can learn to avoid these pitfalls in future.

What I hope to achieve is that in the process of helping my students becoming "gifted achievers", I do not neglect them as "gifted children". I have to look beyond to see that the child in front of me wants to be acknowledged and accepted as a child, not just as a smart kid labelled as "gifted". As Roeper sums it up aptly, "education of the gifted child can only be successful if we include both the gifted Self strand and the talented education strand in our educational structure... we need to clarify our philosophy of education. We need to look at whether we educate for success, or educate for the self-actualisation of the individual child. Do we want the child to achieve and succeed according to our homogenised standards or do we educate for Self-growth and the success within it?" (1996, p. 19). Well, I for one would definitely root for the latter.

* Pseudonym used.

References

Cross, T. L. (2002). Competing with myths about the social and emotional development of gifted students. *Gifted Child Today*, 25 (3), 44–46.

Dai, D. Y. & Renzulli, J. S. (2000). Dissociation and integration of talent development and personal growth: Comments and suggestions. *Gifted Child Quarterly*, 44 (4), 247–251.

Griffin, G. L. (2001). Parenting gifted adolescents. *Gifted Child Today*, 24 (2), 54–58.

Hargreaves, A. (2000). Mixed emotions: Teachers' perceptions of their interactions with students. *Teaching and Teacher Education*, 16, 811–826.

Hoge, R. D. & Renzulli, J. S. (1993). Exploring the link between giftedness and self-concept. *Review of Educational Research*, 63 (4), 449–465.

Johnson, K. E. & Golombek, P. R. (2002). Inquiry into experience: Teachers' personal and professional growth. Teachers' narrative inquiry as professional development, pp. 1–14. Cambridge: Cambridge University Press.

Johnson, K. S. (2000). Affective component in the education of the gifted. *Gifted Child Today*, 23 (4), 36–40.

Morelock, M. J. (1996). On the nature of giftedness and talent: Imposing order on chaos. *Roeper Review*, 19 (1), 4–13.

Roeper, A. (1996). A personal statement of philosophy of George and Annemarie Roeper. *Roeper Review*, 19 (1), 18–19.

Silverman, L. K. (1990). Social and emotional education of the gifted: The discoveries of Leta Hollingworth. *Roeper Review*, 12 (3), 171–178.

Silverman, L. K. (1997). The construct of asynchronous development. *Peabody Journal of Education*, 72 (3&4), 36–58.

Tomlinson, C. A. (2005). Grading and differentiation: Paradox or good practice? *ProQuest Education Journals*, 44 (3), 262–269.

Chapter 4

"Caring Teacher Award" or "Caring Student Award": Teachers' Experiences — Shaping Beliefs*

Sivagouri KALIAMOORTHY

Teachers who Shaped Me...

"What is the role of a teacher?" and "what is teaching?" are two very fundamental questions that we are always forced to ask ourselves as teachers. We often rattle off a long list of answers without realising the weight these questions actually carry. While I am not certain whether I have comprehended their true meanings, what I know is that I am glad that I had my mid-career switch from a tax officer to a teacher. The sense of satisfaction that I have gained and am still gaining has shaped me into the teacher that I am now. Our past experiences with teachers and students, I feel to a certain extent, have shaped us in our perceptions and approach towards teaching, especially in the early years.

*Big thanks to Dr. Tay Lee Yong, Dean ICT/Research, Beacon Primary School and Mrs. Shanthi Suraj Nair, Dean Curriculum, Beacon Primary School.

Experiences — As a Student

Year after year, without failure, I was "labelled" as a "talkative girl" or a "vocal" person. These comments were not only verbalised but also reflected in the most prestigious report cards throughout the 10 years of my school life. I remember the days I was caned for these comments. I can also vividly remember the reason why a Secondary Two Tamil Language teacher had selected me to represent the school for the zonal debate competition. As I recall her words to another teacher, "no need to think, just choose her; since she cannot shut her mouth, let her talk," and their heartless laughter. I was not chosen for being bold to ask questions or for my skill in articulating my thoughts but rather because I was a sickening or irritating child who only liked to talk; an "empty chatterbox" in short. The urge in me to prove them wrong was intensified. I worked very hard on my script and anticipated my opponents' arguments for the motion. When I emerged as the best speaker for that round, all my Tamil Language teacher could offer was, "not bad, at least she did not spoil the school's name and now we have something to report back to the Principal." Interestingly, as I recall those incidents, I wonder if teachers really go beyond the surface to understand the child or simply react to what they see as the obvious. The success of winning a competition — does it merely mean glory for a school or is it a way to realise the hidden talents in pupils waiting to be nurtured?

I came from an era (Asian culture) where asking questions was a taboo. I began to hate "History" for the sole reason that my history teacher was forcing it down my throat. Day in, day out, she would read the chapters word by word from the textbook and would exclaim, "Do you all understand?" And all the "good students" would diligently nod their heads in response and she would be so pleased with them. But then I, the "evil trouble maker" who could not just accept anything she said at face value, would be quizzing her for more information or clarification on the chapter. She would be extremely infuriated and once even exclaimed, "Just memorise the content and the model essays and I guarantee you 100% you will get an 'A1' for the GCE "O"-Level, no need to know more." I had often wondered whether my teacher knew more than what was spelled out in the textbook. "Is History simply a subject for memorising and regurgitating?" "Are we studying a subject merely to score an 'A1'?" What was worse was that my history teacher did not even realise that my questions were derived from the extensive reading I was doing on my own. When the teacher could not fuel my interest in the subject I sensed a slow death in my interest for the subject as well because I simply could not motivate myself to study and memorise a subject just to get a distinction. As I ponder, I cannot help but wonder why a teacher would take so much trouble to teach a subject. Was it to ignite the interest of her students and inspire them to learn more about the subject or to just ensure that the students know what is necessary to get the promised grades?

As I reminisce, it was quite different for Mathematics. My Mathematics teacher used to be big-built, but as time went by, we noticed that he was balding and had lost weight. Something was not right. That was when our form teacher broke the news that my Mathematics teacher was suffering from leukaemia and urged the class to cooperate silently, and I was specifically asked not to give any trouble. I did not know what that illness was all about until one of my classmates told me that this illness can cause death. I was very sad for him. I remember cleaning the blackboard and keeping the classroom clean for his lessons. My entire class cooperated and we all did our homework on time. I became very quiet and controlled myself in clarifying my doubts. Then, one day he called me to the teachers' room and I still could remember his words. "Siva, you have a special talent in communicating and the guts to stand up for what you believe is right, and a soft heart that you often shield with iron. Be yourself and if you need to ask something to clarify and learn better, you must do it." Those words somehow struck a chord with me and without feeling any shame, I was crying to this man whom all had feared but who had understood me very well. No one, not even my family members had said anything so kind and understanding to me. He made me look at him in a different light and respect him for who he was and not for the "Teacher" title he had. I became myself as he clarified my doubts and made me realise

I could do questions that required me to think and analyse. He taught me precision, the importance of being accurate and the power of practice needed to sharpen the saw. I am thankful to him for helping to lay a strong foundation when I did my computer programming course in the undergraduate degree programme. My Mathematics teacher taught me a very valuable lesson of understanding students as individuals with different needs, abilities and learning styles. I began to believe that, as a teacher, winning the hearts and minds of pupils is fundamental in laying a positive foundation in their learning journey.

My most memorable subject was Literature. My Literature teacher was a wonderful, high-spirited woman. Her lessons were lively and stimulating. She went beyond the textbooks and transported us to a new world. We explored the underlying themes and meanings of texts from different angles. The most unforgettable experience was the role I played as Lady Macbeth. I remember her praise and the way she sat down at the back of the hall clapping and cheering loudly after I said my lines. I fell in love with Shakespeare and when I shared this with her, she challenged me to read other texts that were not tested in the GCE "O"-Level. I read *Merchant of Venice, Hamlet* and *Julius Caesar.* They were my most memorable days for I had so much fun chatting and arguing with her trying to make meaning of and exploring those lines. Until this day, whenever I sit down with my older children who are studying literature, I sense a revival of the joy that was always there whenever I revisited those texts that I had once enjoyed with my teacher. I may not have scored a distinction for the subject but what I have gained from those days was precious and close to heart: I learnt about life, the reasons behind failures, human weaknesses and strengths as well as the power of influence. The interest in Literature is still alive in me.

One powerful lesson I have learnt from all my teachers is that "teachers do have the power to make or break a person." I did not realise then that these experiences I had with my teachers had unconsciously shaped my perceptions, beliefs and approaches in my teaching career. It is against the background of my own formative years as a student that I choose the incidents that had helped me to uncover my strengths and weaknesses as a Teacher. The memories had shaped me and ignited a passion that I never knew existed. I guess it is because of my Mathematics teacher and my fierce love for my pupils that this passion got me going despite all the reforms that have been taking place at a roller coaster pace. For the purpose of this chapter, I have changed the names of my students. All names mentioned are pseudonyms. The next part of the chapter will relate my journey as a teacher and how my students have impacted my teaching career.

Experiences — As a Teacher

As I entered the conference room in my ex-school for our usual contact time meeting, I was greeted with congratulations from the middle managers. Puzzled, I turned around and looked at my subject head for an answer and he just gave a smile. My Principal started off the meeting explaining how this teacher had gone the extra mile in motivating the students, guiding them as their moral support. When my name was announced I was caught by surprise. I realised the students were Jane, Sue and Sean. Mixed feelings gushed up within me. I wanted to tell everyone that it was the other way around instead! They had taught me to feel for my students and cherish every moment with them as their guide, friend and mentor.

I first taught Jane in Primary One. She was a sweet and an intelligent girl who was always smiling. When the class was learning Tamil letters and phonics, I found it amazing that she could already write sentences. I sent her first "masterpiece", a short poem dedicated to her mother, to *Tamil Murasu*, the Singapore Tamil newspaper. It was selected and was printed on its Mothers' Day special edition. I still could remember the happiness we felt when we celebrated as a class. I enlarged the original copy, pasted it on the class noticeboard and laminated the original. When I met the class again when they were in Primary Four, all my students had grown taller, prettier, more handsome and more confident. I almost felt the maternal pride. I noticed that everyone was present except for Jane.

When Jane did not come to school the following week, I started asking around. I checked with her form teacher and was upset that she did not make the effort to find out reasons for the girl's absence. Frustrated, I went to the general office and got Jane's telephone number and called her. No one was at home. I tried to call her parents' mobile phones only to find that the lines were no longer in use! Worried, I decided to go down to her house after school that day. I ran into Jane's aunt and inquired her about Jane. I was stunned. The girl had been suffering from a blood disorder and had been going through therapy. I was guilty of not taking much interest in finding out about her illness. All I was concerned about then was that Jane was covered under medical reasons and, as a teacher, I had done my job by finding out about it and recording it in the attendance register. What followed next was a turning point for me. I managed to contact Jane's mom and all I heard were weeps. I managed to gather in between the sobs that the doctors had declared Jane's medical condition to be a special case, one that they were yet to find a cure for. She had to be on heavy medication and be hospitalised most of the time. When her condition worsened, she needed high doses of steroids and painkillers. I asked for her ward number and went to see her after school. When I saw Jane, my heart felt like it was in severe pain. The girl had lost her dense dark hair she had treasured; her beautiful features were hidden beneath her bloated face due to the steroid intake. Despite all the tubes running over her body, the 9-year-old greeted me "vanakam asiriyae" (hello teacher) with a difficult smile. I just did not know what to do and all I managed was a smile in return. That was the day I shed my first tear for a student. The brilliance in Jane's smile has stayed in my mind all these years. When I am trying to pen these down now, I can almost hear Jane's calm and delightful voice trying to reassure me not to worry and that she was managing well. We talked for a while and I shared with her a little of what we had done in school. Sensing that she was in great pain, I stopped the conversation. I asked her if she needed any help from me. Her face lit up and she asked me to pass her homework to her brother who was studying in Primary One so that she could complete them in hospital. I nodded and gave her my phone number assuring her that she could call me whenever she needed me. I am not sure whether I did it on impulse or was overwhelmed by emotions but I felt a little relieved knowing that I could do something for this little girl when she needed my help. I truly admired Jane. Despite the frequent medical leave she had to take every week, she kept to her word and never failed to do her homework. Jane had never compromised on her neat and beautiful handwriting nor did she give me substandard work. She never took her sickness as an excuse to do less than what she believed in. Her perseverance taught me that if one cares enough for something, nothing can stop one from achieving it.

In the second year of my teaching career, I took up a part-time degree programme at the Singapore Institute of Management. There were times when I felt so overwhelmed, juggling family, work and studies, that I stood on the verge of giving up. During those times, I thought of Jane and I saw how insignificant my problems were as compared to hers. Jane's optimism charged me with renewed passion and strength, and I began to look at my students as unique individuals with respect. Teaching Tamil became my way of supporting them and my idea of teaching was no longer focused on the narrow subject content delivery. Once I asked Jane if she was willing to try one of the revision papers I had prepared and she replied with her usual smile, "Asiriyae (Teacher), would you choose to give us something to do if you do not believe it will help us in learning? You have clearly told us why we are doing these and I understand and trust your intentions." I was touched by the girl's faith in me and felt empowered.

As I began to realise that there was a growing number of children who come from non-Tamil speaking environments, I became very careful in ensuring that I did not force the learning of the language down their throats but rather focused on motivating them to learn it with joy. My painful experience in learning History acted as a clear reminder in shaping my approach towards teaching the Tamil language. I might be able to get my pupils to score distinctions perhaps by flooding them with worksheets and drilling them on specific exam components; however, that approach may not be able to kindle the joy in learning the rich Tamil language. Inspired by my Literature teacher and my self-discoveries, I capitalised on the beauty of the Tamil language and exposed my pupils to content beyond textbooks. From my past experiences, I firmly believe that learning should not be confined to textbooks but rather learning should be rigorous, promote pupils' curiosity to explore and learn new things independently. To ensure that pupils are self-directed learners taking charge of their own learning, I feel that as a teacher I have the responsibility to ignite my pupils' interest in learning. In one of the Primary Five lessons, there was a reading passage introducing some of the Indian musical instruments. This lesson sparked a lot of questions for which I did not have the answers. I also discovered that some of my pupils were learning traditional musical instruments and they were very knowledgeable about some of the instruments. This also made me realise that teachers are not the sole-embodiment of knowledge. Having an open mind and facilitating such discussions will unravel pupils' interests, abilities and knowledge that go beyond confined texts. My pupils asked a lot of questions and I had to do a lot of reading on the various forms of Indian music to facilitate the rich discussion that followed. In fact, this was a topic covered extensively in the secondary school syllabus. However, admiring my pupils' curiosity, I challenged my pupils to go and do independent research and share their learning with their classmates. Those were the days where Information and Communication Technology (ICT) was not pervasively used and we had to manually search for information. As a class we collectively drew on one another's knowledge and capitalised on each other's learning. We had rich discussions and, as a class, used the knowledge to compose a song and create a makeshift Indian musical instrument which led to the pupils performing "Villupattu", an Indian folk song, which we dedicated to the school during our school's annual Tamil Competition Day. Those were some of my most memorable lessons and even today, when my students come over to my house for a chat, they would talk about how much fun they had during those lessons. My students were stretched and we were featured in the Contact magazine for this innovative programme. My students had spurred and inspired me to adopt and experiment different strategies. These experiences had taught me that teachers are not the "embodiment of knowledge" and that, if students set their mind to it, they can do miracles and be "teachers" teaching teachers.

Jane's case had also taught me never to take pupils' absence from school lightly. Sue, a Primary One girl from India, joined the school when she was eight years old. In Term 2, she was absent from school for more than one week. As much as I wanted to find out what had really happened to her, I was praying very hard too that she was not suffering from any critical illness. When I called her mom, she said that she did not wish to talk about her daughter and slammed down the phone. I was very disturbed. I tried burying myself in marking and going for a hair-cut so I would feel less stressed. Not seeing the girl for the next two days, I could not contain my anxiety anymore; I went to the equally worried form teacher who shared that Sue had not been answering calls from the school. Before we went for a home visit, I made a last attempt to call her home from my home. Before Sue's mom hung up, I said to her very curtly that if she was not going to provide sound reasons for her daughter's absence, she would have to face severe consequences. The mother relented but merely mentioned that Sue had not been feeling well and would be on medical leave for a few more days. Though I felt slightly relieved, the way she had sounded triggered doubts at the back of my mind. I could not fathom why she had not given us the information earlier. Sue came to school the following week. Her cheery smile was missing from her face. She looked quiet and withdrawn. I wanted to find out what was wrong with the child. I told her mom that I needed to inform her of Sue's outstanding work so I waited for her at the school gate. I sat down with her and showed her the homework. I explained that we would draw a plan for completion. I then shared with her the change I noticed in Sue. Sensing that the mom was uncomfortable,

I insisted on finding out what illness the child had and assured her I had the child's best interest at heart and would support her in ways I could. She broke down upon hearing my words.

Sue's mom had a very good male colleague, a father of two, who was also from their home state. He became a very good family friend and sometimes, when he drank with her husband and got heavily drunk, they would put him up for the night. Sue had an elder teenaged sister and a younger sister in nursery and her mom did night shifts often leaving the girls alone at home with their dad. The teenaged sister had confided with her teachers that the man took advantage of her mom's night shifts and had forced the girl to have sex with him. He even threatened that he would harm the family if she told anyone. The girl had been suffering in silence for three months. When the teenaged sister discovered that Sue was also abused by him, she informed her secondary school counsellor. Sue's parents were notified and actions were taken. During those weeks of absence, all the three girls were sent for medical check-ups and were receiving professional help. On hearing what the mom shared, I could no longer hold my tears and at the same time was very furious with the mother for not monitoring her children's well-being and being so naïve to trust strangers. At that moment, I lacked the skill to either control my emotions or say something to console the mom. All I could manage was to assure her that I would monitor Sue's behaviour and provide all the support I could from my end. Sue was of my daughter's age and both girls were in the same class. To think about what she had gone through was simply devastating. It was a very traumatic case and now I realise that what I had seen in her eyes was pain. There were times that she would casually tell me all the things the man had done to her. It was cruel and heartless and evoked such strong emotions in me that deep in my heart I felt like shooting him dead. I was not sure how to support her, the do's and don'ts. To protect the child's identity, I could not even speak about it to my fellow colleagues, friends or family. I requested to speak to the counsellor so that she could advise me on how to handle the situation and how I could look out for tell-tale signs.

The counsellor and I had countless discussions, and I updated her weekly on the progress. At that time the Internet was not commonly used. I went to the library and borrowed books to read and spoke with my Child Psychology tutor to gather more information. A few months later, when I could see a slight improvement in her behaviour, it gave me immense satisfaction. This had made me a different person and I felt I had grown a little more mature. This incident had taught me valuable lessons. Firstly, being a mother of two girls, I learnt that I had to monitor the children's behaviour and have good communication with them. Secondly, I needed to observe the changes in my students' behaviour and ensure that I have tried my level best to find the root causes of problems, if any. Thirdly, I learnt to trust my instincts. Somehow my gut feelings were right, though I cannot use scientific methods to explain these feelings.

Though it was not a requirement of the syllabus, I used this as a way to connect with my pupils. I started weekly journal writing with my upper primary pupils, encouraging them to reflect and record the most impactful events that had occurred in the week. The entries were like television serials that mirrored the students' innermost thoughts and the type of day-to-day struggles that they faced. Hence, the journal writing had become my mode of communication with every individual student in providing the emotional support and guidance tailored to their needs. After the first few entries, students became more forthcoming and shared their feelings concerning their classroom experiences, how they were coping with the different subjects and teachers, their little desires, family problems, friends' and classmates' reactions to them and so on. I did not realise that journals could be a very powerful tool to learn and understand pupils' innermost feelings and thought processes till it helped me to understand my pupils and the issues that surrounded them. I did not realise that, in the process, I was also building stronger bonds with my pupils. However, with each entry I read, I became intimately involved with the issues and went through emotional conflicts.

One of my Primary Six pupils, Sean, shared that he was disturbed when he was called "gay" by his fellow friends. He wrote that he felt hurt when his fellow classmates made fun of his walking style. In subsequent entries, Sean mentioned that he wanted to do well in his exams but did not know how to go about it. I was aware that he did not walk steadily, but I was not aware that my students could be unkind and hurt one another. To gather more information, I gently probed him to write more in the journal entries. That was when I discovered that he was not having any breakfast. His father had been jailed because of drug addiction. He had two younger siblings and had to help out with all the household chores after school. The school was unable to give him pocket money because the mom was too busy to drop by and sign the necessary forms. I spoke to the form teacher and we both agreed to help provide him with lunch and tea breaks. According to the form teacher, Sean excelled in his languages but was weak in Math and Science. We thought that with extra help he would be able to pass the Primary School Leaving Examination (PSLE) and graduate. Sean was happy to stay back in school but his mother was not. He mentioned in his journal that she was having difficulty in coping with the household chores and wanted Sean to go home to help. In one of the subsequent entries, he mentioned that his mother had already found him a job as a cleaner in a coffee shop for extra income. I was taken aback when I read those entries and I thought I had to do something quickly. I urged him to think about his future and convinced him that he would pass his examination.

It had become a tug of war between Sean and his mother at home. She insisted that it was his duty to work and support her and that he would not make it in the examination but Sean was adamant in doing his utmost for his studies. Sean worked very hard in his studies and his preliminary results showed significant improvement. Sean was motivated and promised that he would strive to do better. His determination impacted us and we knew that we could not give up on him. On Teachers' Day, he wrote in his journal how grateful he was towards us. To me, such an appreciation was the best Teachers' Day gift a student could give. However, during the PSLE oral examination Sean did not show up. I called his home and his mother said that she had overslept and did not wake him up. She said it was perfectly fine for him to miss his examination. I told her that we would be there in 15 minutes and she had to make sure that Sean was ready by then. My school's Operations Manager drove us to pick him up. When he came to school, the form teacher was ready with his breakfast. After breakfast, we had to talk to him to encourage him to do his best in the examination. On the day the PSLE results were released, we were pleasantly surprised when Sean passed with "A"s for both the English and Tamil languages, and obtained a "C" and "D" for the other two subjects. He had exceeded our expectations and qualified to go to the Normal (Academic) stream in a secondary school! I was overjoyed. I realised that our faith in students will help them to achieve their aspirations. Although grades are not everything, seeing the joy of my students, I realised the important affirmation good grades had on their self-esteem.

Experiences —— Shaped Beliefs

The "teacher" in me is very much shaped by the past experiences with my teachers and students. It has an unspoken power of influence in shaping my belief system and has impacted my teaching practices. The early experiences as a student helped me to understand my needs as a student and how I would want my teachers to support me in my learning journey. Even after so many years, I was still able to recollect both the positive and negative impacts my teachers had had on me. I became more conscious in understanding my pupils' needs and the efforts I should put in to nurture them. Though, in my opinion, excelling very well with good grades is not as important as igniting a passion in the subject, I cannot deny the positive affirmation and boost in confidence good grades have on my students. Thus, as a teacher I also need to be mindful of the impact results have on my pupils and help them to achieve their best. My experiences with my students, "my young teachers", have also taught me valuable lessons. I realised that being a teacher is about touching lives forever. My pupils have motivated me to go beyond the basic call of duty of delivering lessons, to nurture and mould the charges under me and guide them to be self-directed learners. As a teacher, it is critical for me to earn my pupils' trust, bond with them and help them to achieve better results. Thus, indeed, my past experiences with my students and teachers have shaped the teacher I am today.

Chapter 5

Confessions of an Accidental Teacher

Bernard Kim San SIT

Growing up at the time when the Singapore economy was rapidly expanding, choosing teaching as a career was viewed as a "safe" option with little prospect of achieving the 5 C's (Cash, Condominium, Car, Country Club and Credit Card) which were coveted by society as a measure of a person's success. Stated simply, the perception of teaching then was that it was an honest job which could provide a decent standard of living. Needlessly to say, choosing teaching as a career did not feature prominently among my peers. However, having performed reasonably well for the General Certificate of Education (GCE)"A"-Level examinations, I was faced with the prospect of being a financial burden to my family should I decide to continue my education at the local university. Not wanting to place unnecessary financial stress on my limited family savings, I reluctantly applied for a government scholarship to finance my university education. Fortunately for me, my application was successful and I was informed that I would be joining the Civil Service as a teacher upon my graduation. While glad that the scholarship would relieve me of my financial worries, it came at a price — the scholarship came with a five-year bond, which meant that I would be teaching for at least five years. I started my university education at the same time the economy was undergoing a financial crisis and was very grateful for the scholarship. It was truly a blessing as the worsening economy would have meant that my family would not have been able to finance my education.

The three years of university education and one year of teacher training gradually convinced me that I could make teaching a career. I also believed that the teacher training course had adequately prepared me to teach my future students. Upon receiving my posting letter, I could barely contain my excitement and looked forward to teaching my students. I eagerly set foot in the neighbourhood school I was posted to and tremendously enjoyed the initial few months teaching the secondary one students. However, my honeymoon period would soon be over and it was not long before I discovered that, as a beginning teacher, I was ill-prepared for the challenges that were to confront me.

That challenge came in the form of NSK, a pleasant and unassuming 13-year-old student from the Normal (Academic) stream. NSK was one of the brightest students in my class and it was a joy teaching him. Although from the Normal (Academic) stream, he was always prompt with his assignments and bothered to clarify his doubts whenever he had trouble understanding the topic being taught. He also took it upon himself to help his classmates understand their schoolwork. It was no surprise that he ended the year as the top student in his class and qualified to be promoted to the Express stream. However, when I congratulated him on his excellent results and promotion to the Express stream, he suddenly turned silent and I could see him fighting to control the tears that were starting to well up in his eyes. I was taken aback by his reaction and had not expected him to react in this manner. Wanting to understand him better, I had a lengthy discussion with him regarding his promotion. One topic led to another and it was not long before NSK shared his fears and anxiety about moving to the Express stream.

NSK shared that despite wearing spectacles, his eyesight had been steadily deteriorating throughout the year and one reason he was able to perform well for the examinations was due to the help from his two best friends, MT and C. They had been studying together throughout the year and had been helping NSK overcome the problems with his deteriorating eyesight by checking his notes and reading to him. MT and C had also performed well for the examinations but did not qualify for promotion to the Express stream. Being promoted to the Express stream would result in NSK leaving his current class and joining another class, and he was fearful that he would not be accepted by his new classmates. He was also apprehensive about switching streams as it was more academically demanding. I explained to NSK that the promotion to the Express stream would provide more educational opportunities and that he would waste one year of his life if he stayed on in the Normal (Academic) stream. As a last resort, I even shared with him that I was confident he would find new friends in his new class and do well in the Express stream, but he would not accept his promotion. I was at a loss and did not know what more I could do to help him. Thankfully for me, MT and C came and together, we managed to convince him to accept his promotion to the Express stream. I was glad that we were eventually able to convince him to accept his promotion to the Express stream, and silently prayed that we had made the right decision — I would not have been able to forgive myself if NSK did not succeed in the Express stream.

The talk with NSK made me realise that the teacher training that was provided was insufficient in equipping me with the knowledge and skills to help him. Up to that point in my life, I had been brought up to respect the decisions of adults and never questioned their decisions. The encounter with NSK was an eye-opener and made me a more reflective person. In addition, the experience also highlighted how little I knew of the various processes that have been put in place to help students. I had all along viewed the annual health checks conducted in schools as a waste of curriculum time. However, the conversation with NSK revealed how important such checks could be as it highlighted his deteriorating eye condition.

Two years passed before I had the opportunity to teach NSK again. He had grown to be a respected senior member of his

Co-Curricular Activity and had maintained the close ties he forged with his best friends. However, his eyesight had deteriorated to such an extent that, even with spectacles, his examination papers had to be enlarged to facilitate his reading. When we spoke, I was amazed at how much he had grown and how mature he had become. He had accepted his deteriorating medical condition and was determined not to let it get in the way of his pursuit for academic excellence. He worked diligently and did well enough at the national examinations to pursue his interest in a polytechnic. Upon receiving his results, he thanked me for initiating the change in his life before joining his friends to celebrate their accomplishments. I was relieved and thankful that I had made a difference to NSK, and viewed the whole experience as an indication of having survived my initial years as a beginning teacher. More importantly, it also made me realise how influential a teacher could be in helping a student realise his potential.

Not long after NSK, I had Hock in one of my Secondary Four classes. He appeared arrogant and displayed a rebellious streak within him. A few teachers shared that he looked like a gangster and were afraid to teach him. It did not help that he had a discipline record that could be mistaken for a marathon route. However, there was something within him that made me take notice of him and I continued teaching him in the same manner as I did with the rest of my students.

One day, several students reported that a huge fight had broken out in the coffee shop outside the school. The fight appeared to be between rival gangs and a few students were involved. Fearing for their safety, I quickly alerted the Discipline Master (DM) and together, we rushed to the coffee shop. Upon reaching the coffee shop, I was greeted with a scene reminiscent of a warzone. Tables had been turned and there were pieces of glass strewn all over the floor. Out of the corner of my eye, I noticed a group of students fussing over someone. Approaching them, I could not help but notice that some of them were in tears and they appeared very anxious. Parting the group, I saw a very agitated but bloodied Hock being restrained by the group. He appeared to be directing his anger at someone. Upon seeing his bloodied head, I instinctively moved in to inspect the extent of his injuries before instructing some nearby students to call for an ambulance. Hock had sustained a huge gash on his head and was bleeding badly. Some students handed me a packet of tissue paper which I used to try and stem the flow of blood. It seemed an eternity before the ambulance arrived and took Hock to the hospital.

I did not see Hock for the rest of the week and learnt from the DM that he received 16 stitches for the wound on his head, and the whole incident was being investigated by the police. It seemed that he had offended a student who was part of a gang and the gang members had waited for Hock at the coffee shop before pouncing on him.

When I met Hock the following week, he had a bandage round his head and we shared a light moment over his new "turban". I seized upon that moment and engaged Hock in a discussion about his feelings towards school and his aspirations. He shared that he had not had many positive experiences throughout his time in school. He felt that the whole world was against him and cited numerous occasions when he felt he had been singled out by both teachers and students. Reflecting on the latest incident, he shared that some boys had been staring at his girlfriend while on their way to school and she felt uncomfortable. Not wanting to confront the boys, they decided to leave the place and take an alternative route to school. However, the boys took offence to their "detour" and decided to wait at the coffee shop to confront him. At the coffee shop, the confrontation soon spiralled out of control and, before he could react, he was hit on the head with billiard sticks. This infuriated him so much that it made him want to get back at the culprit. It was only after seeing me that he realised he had been badly injured. Changing the subject to focus on his aspirations, he shared that he was not afraid of hard work and wanted very much to emulate his father. His father had been the sole breadwinner and it pained him tremendously to see his father struggle every day to earn enough money to support the family. He suddenly turned his face away from me and I could see him struggling to hold back the tears that started welling up in his eyes and shared that he felt he had let his father down. He wanted very much to perform well and make his father proud but was ashamed of the numerous occasions when his father was called to the school as a result of his indiscipline. He felt helpless and I felt then that the drained look on his face was calling out for help.

Reflecting on my discussion with Hock, I realised that he had grown up being misunderstood by his peers and teachers. As a result, the quality of his interactions with his peers and teachers had been poor. The poor interactions coupled with the frustrations of being misunderstood often led to conflicts with his peers, which also explained the numerous occasions when his father was called to school. I shared my opinions of Hock with my DM and we decided to put in place a monitoring system to help him "stay out of trouble". The monitoring system would require Hock to stay back after school until 5 pm everyday to catch up on his school work, have one of the discipline teachers to acknowledge the time he would leave school and, finally, have his parents acknowledge the time he returned home. When I spoke to Hock about the monitoring system, he was apprehensive at first, as he felt that his freedom was being compromised, but relented when he discovered that he could use the sessions for revision and preparation for the upcoming national examinations. For the next few weeks, Hock was a model student and his grades gradually improved.

However, it was not long before Hock had another run-in with the discipline teachers. This time, he was caught sporting long hair and suddenly lost his temper and started hurling vulgarities when confronted by one of the discipline teachers. The teacher was stunned by his sudden outburst and demanded that he be caned for being disrespectful. Hock did not return to class after the outburst and I found him sitting quietly by himself in a vacant classroom. Upon seeing me, he immediately started to recount how the events for the day had unfolded. He shared that the teacher had approached him in a threatening manner and tugged painfully at his hair. Taken by surprise, Hock let out a string of expletives which was noticed by the teacher. This made the teacher pull harder causing considerable discomfort and he instinctively hit the hand pulling his hair, aggravating the incident. He knew he had broken the school rules and was prepared to face the consequences. However, he felt that the teacher was also partly to blame for causing the incident to escalate. If only the teacher had conducted herself in a more civil manner and avoided any physical contact, none of the follow-up actions would be required.

Hock was caned as a result of his outburst. However, instead of his usual feeling of anger at being caned, he willingly accepted his punishment and promised to exercise more self-control in future. Throughout Hock's remaining months in school, there were several more outbursts including one with the Principal. For each incident, I would lead him through a cycle of recollection and reflection to help him realise the need for more self-control and to offer strategies that he could use to prevent a repeat of such incidents. In addition, he would also approach the relevant person to offer his apologies. The time interval between his outbursts gradually increased and I felt encouraged to see the gradual transformation in Hock. This change was also noticed by his parents who took time off their busy schedule to attend his graduation and to express their appreciation to the school.

My interactions with NSK and Hock may have taken place more than 10 years ago, but they are firmly etched in my memory. More importantly, these interactions at such an early stage of my teaching career have helped me uncover the true meaning of being an educator. As I reflect on the interactions with NSK and Hock, I am reminded of The Starfish Story about a young man's attempt at saving starfish as the tide recedes. I feel that as educators, we can and should make a difference to our students in the same way the young man made a difference to the starfish. This can be done through improving the quality of teacher–student interactions and support for teachers.

Both NSK and Hock showed me the importance of developing quality teacher–student interactions. Through developing good interactions with students, teachers can unlock the heavy load some students carry with them every day. This was especially true for Hock, whose successful and dramatic turnaround could be attributed to the quality of student–teacher interaction that had gradually grown to a state where he felt comfortable sharing details of his private life with me. It was only through this interaction that I was made aware of his bad educational experiences, and that set in motion a series of activities to support him in his education.

In addition to developing good teacher–student interaction, teachers need to be aware of the various support structures that have been put in place to support them in educating students. Reflecting on the training I received as a trainee teacher, I noted that it was primarily focused on pedagogy and assessment. While this was essential in planning for the delivery of lessons, it did not prepare me adequately to support student development in the social and affective domains, and this left a void in my knowledge and capability to better support NSK and Hock in their education. The situation today has improved tremendously and most schools are provided with dedicated counsellors to support students in their learning. However, the responsibility lies with the teacher to familiarise themselves with the necessary support structures that have been put in place to support students in their learning.

To conclude, my entry into education was not by choice but the interactions between NSK and Hock have helped me realise that every student is important and, as educators, we should do what we can to support them in their education.

Reference

Loren, E. (). The starfish story. Retrieved from http://muttcats.com/starfish.htm (accessed on 9 November 2012).

Chapter 6

Growing and Learning from Teaching Different Students in the Context of Change

Lawrence LAU

My Little Flame: Holding onto Beliefs

Throughout my career as a teacher, I have had the opportunity to talk to many other teachers on why they had chosen this profession. Very often, it had to do with happy recollections of being inspired by a teacher in their lives — and how they had made a difference. While I also had a few good teachers, my reason for choosing and staying with teaching as a profession was the opposite — I was disappointed and felt cheated by many of my teachers. My teachers usually stressed on coverage — little attention was placed on the meaning of what was taught, and little effort was made to check our understanding.

The first time I remember being angry with my teacher was in Chemistry class. I was a Secondary Three student in a boys' school. I had just received back an assignment on volumetric calculations, and to my surprise, I had apparently gotten one of my answers wrong. Upon closer inspection, I realised that my answer, as well as the calculation, was correct, and my classmates had the same answer. The difference was in the working — I had refused to use the formula my teacher gave, preferring to use step-by-step deductive statements instead. When queried, she dismissed my point, saying that I should have used the formula. How can a teacher ignore good science and insist on a formula? My learning experience was replete with similar teachers — I had a mathematics teacher who spent two years writing lots of worked examples on the board, only to turn around once in a while and ask: "OK? Any questions?", before continuing. Needless to say, I did not do well in mathematics for the whole two years. This was essentially the same in junior college (JC), and even university. I detested that — what was the point of cramming all the formulae, dates and details without understanding? I therefore, became a self-appointed revolutionary — someone to teach things right, teach for understanding, and I hoped to change science education for the better, to make a difference. Little did I know that this journey would be fraught with dark moments that seemed insurmountable — it was my original conviction and perseverance to make a difference that carried me forward, to become a better teacher.

Despair and Hope: The Real World

My first dark moment came very early in my career. I was posted to a far-away secondary school (something the Ministry of Education (MOE) called "principle of equal misery") in the East. It was a neighbourhood secondary school where a police car was parked in the school almost every day. At that point of time, I was all ready to "change the world". I was assigned to teach the entire Secondary Three cohort Physics and Chemistry. My first lesson with the 3N class was memorable. There were about 30 students in that class and only four of them were non-Malay. I was surprised at the few students that were actually present in the class as I entered the classroom — there were only about 15 there. When I asked one of the students where the rest of the class was, he gestured towards the next classroom, which was a storeroom. I quickly realised that the "missing" students left by the back door of the classroom and went hiding there. Knowing that I could not leave my class behind, I had to abandon any thoughts of chasing after these students and went back to the classroom to take attendance.

As soon as I started to make my introductions, the majority of the class that remained started going to the back of the classroom and started their own conversation — only four students were left sitting in front. Sensing my hesitation, one of the students told me that this was the usual order of the day. While my four students were engaged on a task, I took the opportunity to talk to the group at the back — they basically ignored whatever I said and carried on with their own chatting! Knowing that challenging students in the classroom is usually a bad idea, I had no choice but to carry on the lesson with the four students. When my lesson was finally over, I went straight to the staff room and spoke to the senior staff members there. They shook their heads and told me that there was little anyone could do for them. (I learnt later that sometimes they would fight or throw furniture — hence the police car.) I was shocked: how could anyone not prepare for his or her own future? Did they not care?

The next lesson, I prepared the best demonstration that I could for the topic at hand and showed it to the class. That was well received by the four students in front, but made no difference for the rest of the class. A wave of despair came over me, and it stayed with me for years of my teaching career. It was not until seven years later when I participated in a pilot study that I found out that about a third of Normal (Academic) students would rather be working than to stay in school — in fact, we were keeping them there against their will! This alleviated the despair somewhat, but the shadow of it stayed with me.

But there was hope — the best class of the level gave me something to look forward to. This was a place that I could try out my ideas, and the students loved it. I even had groups volunteering to perform a demonstration for the class on my behalf. No one ever slept in my lessons, and that became a strong encouragement for me. The best gift of hope, however, did not come from this class. It came unexpectedly from the class I liked the least — that Normal class.

As it turned out, one of the four students, Ning, stopped coming to school. After some digging via colleagues, I learnt that Ning was actually from a broken family, had run away from home, and now stayed with an older man. She tried to put her life back together by coming to school, and she had actually re-joined the school a few weeks before I was posted there. Apparently, she had stopped coming to school again, and went back to the man. I saw her for the last time as she returned briefly to presumably get some paperwork done, and she passed me a letter, and thanked me. In the letter, she thanked me for trying my best to teach the class, and told me how much that meant to her. I was stunned. I then realised that my effort was not wasted at all — at least it had helped one student, and there was hope. I had managed to hang on with the last bit of my conviction, and made a difference to at least one young person's life.

My Professionalism Questioned

To continue my original goal to make a difference, I applied to a prestigious boys' school, and was accepted as one of the youngest teaching staff. It was there that I confirmed my calling was true. As before, I taught all the Secondary Three classes Physics, and that was a wonderful place to teach — the students were motivated, and the hands-on sessions that I had provided really made a difference. The support staff was fantastic: they built whatever I asked for. What was really special was the culture of the school — I could almost see the word "excellence" everywhere. It was almost like a field you can experience — you just know what is expected of a teacher. I was about to find out, with a large dose of humility, what excellence meant.

The day started like any other, except for one thing — I was asked to meet with my Head of Department (HOD). As I confidently sat in his office, he told me bluntly that I had been guilty of "slipshod marking". As I respectfully asked for clarifications, he showed me four errors I had made while marking a whole level of workbook exercises, and that I had omitted the periods at the end of each option for multiple-choice questions. I was flabbergasted. I thought that I was a good-enough teacher, and I had been conscientiously marking my work. I knew that I had to mark much more carefully, which was difficult — I ended up spending a lot of time after school just to finish the marking. I started doubting myself if I was ever going to satisfy my HOD, but I still felt the fire … I wanted to do this, even if it meant I had to arrive at the school as the sun rose, and watch the sunset from the staffroom as I finished the day's marking! I persevered through the long workdays, and after some time I came to realise why my HOD was critical to such detail. A month or two after being called into his office, I heard that a parent had complained to the school that his son's homework was marked wrongly (fortunately not for my subject), and had made a big fuss over it. I then realised that the culture of the school had a lot to do with the expectations of the parents. This was never a problem back in my first school in the East! My HOD had not been nitpicking — he was ensuring that parents would never find fault with the school over errors in marking. I could see the world of difference in the culture. As a result, till this day, I still try to mark carefully — I had to chew through what my students write, and be very careful as I mark. My ego had been so large for a while that I failed to see that the small important things do matter, and I was never going to let that get in the way again.

Finding my Heart

Up till that point in my career, I was still very much the "emotionless" teacher — I tried not to show personal happiness nor anger, favouritism nor disdain. I just taught the students Physics — an inflexible but nevertheless interesting subject. I never thought that I should have an effect on my students, much less be a role model. My students performed as expected, and I was satisfied with the results. However, I learnt at my next school that, once I let go of the "cold professional" façade, my students could achieve much more than I thought possible.

It was an autonomous secondary school, ironically back in the East. My first year in the school was a breeze — compared to the previous school, my students were almost as motivated, and the culture was less perfectionist in nature. I was freer to reflect and experiment on my teaching, but it was not in the classroom that I influenced one of my students, Hong. He was an average boy from an average class, with an average interest in science, and performed around average in class tests. He did not show a lot of drive nor responsibility — he seemed happy to perform just at that level. At that time, although the school had a basic compulsory Information and Communications Technology (ICT) programme, there was no computer club to cater for students who wanted to expand on their interest in this subject. As my hobby was in Information Technology (IT) and electronics, in my spare time, I started a computer club in the school.

Hong was one of the first students to join the newly formed club. As a small club (all boys), I let down my guard and became more of a friend than a teacher to them. Hong began to respond positively to me — he would tell me his frustrations and hopes. During the long sessions as we prepared for the club's first major competition, we became closer friends. The day we went for the competition, we were somewhat relaxed about it, knowing that our chances were slim as we were up against "big guns", but we knew that we had tried our best. It came as a complete surprise when our entry was named the winner! We defeated all the big independent schools and clinched the first prize. During this period, I saw a change in Hong's classroom behaviour too. He became more alert in class, volunteered answers in my lesson more often than before, and started to perform better also. Hong was never the same — he became much more self-confident, and went on to graduate with honours. He is now an exchange teacher with United Nations in Japan. From Hong, I learnt that when I make positive and personal connections with students, it makes a difference to their attitude. This experience has fundamentally changed my initial direction — I had initially only wanted to be a "clear" teacher, but now I want more — to be able to touch lives, and watch them grow up. In short, I found my heart for teaching.

Holding Onto My Beliefs

My next school was again in the East. It is a typical neighbourhood school with a rich history, and I taught a number of upper secondary classes from different streams. For the pure science class, I focused on getting students to understand the subject and adjusting the pace to match their progress. This meant I finished the entire syllabus way after my other colleagues. Some people doubted my approach of not rushing to finish the syllabus, and not giving out "enough" homework for my students. Despite the scepticism, I held on to my original belief that teaching and learning should focus on understanding rather than on mere worksheets and assignments. The students responded positively and the classes were a joy to teach. I know my approach is correct as my students did very well for the national examinations. Moreover, after I left the school, I received a Teachers' Day card from a group of my ex-Secondary Three students. One of them said,

> *"... I miss you* [sic] *teaching. Physics is a lot more interesting when you are around... And you care whether we understand what you teach or not."*

I wonder if they know that I missed them very much too. I had persevered on to teach well, and this time I knew that I was on the right track.

Ideals Challenged

When I moved to my current school, the challenge was different — I realised that I still have room for improvement in my classroom teaching, and I survived through the self-doubt when a student of mine broke down and cried in class.

My current school is a small secondary school outside of MOE, with small classes of 25 or less. This opens up opportunities for me to try out different ideas; and this time I can monitor what individual students are thinking and doing while the lesson is going on, and I have more time to reflect on what has taken place.

As it turns out, my best learning experience came from a Secondary One girl called Mandy. She came in with a very low T-score and had blossomed throughout the first two years with us, and had just managed to earn a place in the pure science class. However, despite my now-trademark demonstrations, Mandy continued to struggle with Physics. It was then that I became more aware that the mental processes in her were different from that in her classmates. I would do a demonstration to address a common misconception to produce discord, and then explain the correct concept. It usually works with most students. In the case of Mandy, she continued to struggle. It became clear that she was processing the concepts separately, creating and memorising each example as disjointed parts, rather than seeing how they fit together. I then saw the importance of assessment for learning, where I would probe and respond in a more directed manner. Mandy improved somewhat, but still did not make significant gains. Time was running out for her as she entered Secondary Four and, at that time, she was still failing almost every Physics test and exam. One day, Mandy was struggling through my Physics lesson as usual, and as I went around to check on their understanding, I paused behind her. I could see that she was hopelessly stuck at a step when most of her classmates had already moved on. I was a little remorseful, as I knew that question was a little too tough for her to handle, but I thought I had no choice as I had very able students in the same class. I whispered to her "Hang on… don't give up!", and she almost immediately started crying! I was shaken — I have never had a student cry in my class. She sobbed for the remainder of the lesson and I tried to avoid her as much as possible, feeling guilty as if I had said something wrong. I never knew what had happened until Teachers' Day when she gave me a card. Inside she told me how thankful she was for me trying to help as much as possible, and that she was really touched when I encouraged her on that day. How relieved I was!

I wanted to redouble efforts to help her out. I had to force myself to re-examine what I had done wrong or neglected. My thoughts eventually went to concept-mapping. As an early teacher, I had dismissed concept-mapping as a fad, as students already had a good grasp of the ideas already. However, I realised that Mandy's own concept map would be an excellent platform to discuss her problems, and it turned out to be true. Her concept maps lacked critical links and showed unnecessary duplication of concepts. As I worked through her concept maps, she improved greatly by the preliminary examinations, and eventually exceeded her expected score by a grade. My reflection in this episode showed me that I had to always question my assumptions, and this has since remained part of me.

This has also taught me to consider using differentiated instruction to help students like Mandy while catering for confident students who are also present in the same class. This year I will be embarking on my second run of my experiment to achieve differentiation in my class; and for other present and future Mandys, I hope I will eventually be successful.

In the blink of an eye, it has been 17 years in teaching. As I pride myself on what I have achieved, there is also a thorn at my side — a comment made by my wife. As my classmate, my wife eventually stayed in a neighbourhood school for her entire career until she left the service. While I was sharing with her on what I have achieved with my students, she remarked (perhaps fed up with my "gloating") that my achievements were expected, as I have had very able students anyway. I was furious — but retreated to think it through. Have I done enough for my less able students? While reflecting on this, it dawned on me that while my initial convictions changed, I had never been afraid to move on — to keep improving for the sake of my students, and I had come out stronger. That is also one of the reasons why I wanted to get on to differentiated teaching — would I be able to become a more well-rounded teacher, or would it be even possible? I know one thing — even if I fail, I know I would not give up so easily. That is my strength, my little flame which I can count on to keep me going.

Part 2:
Working with Colleagues —
Source of Energy or Wear or Tear?

Overview

Aristotle Motii NANDY

Many, if not all, teachers enter the teaching profession with the ideals of the simplicity and pleasures of working with students in order to make a meaningful difference in their lives. Although working with students has its fair share of challenges given the myriad cultural, social and economic make-up of the students we teach, many a time, teachers who end up leaving the profession, or have at some point contemplated switching careers, do so due to challenging circumstances involving relationships or incidents with their peers and superiors such as a department head or even the Principal. Part 2 brings to light the significant role of collegial support in our work as teachers, and illuminates the strong emotions that are evoked, both positive and negative, in such interactions. This overview, interlaced with excerpts from the narratives presented in this section, draws attention to how the nature of collegial relationships influences teachers attitudes towards work at different stages of their career trajectories, as well as probable underlying factors that influence the nature of such relationships.

Most, if not all, narratives in this section, as well as those in this book, start with Huberman's survival and discovery stage as beginning teachers acquaint themselves with the actual ropes of the profession, a great leap from the theoretical foundations and brief practicum stint offered in pre-service teacher education. During this difficult period in learning to work in a school environment, the nature and level of support they could receive from colleagues, and hence the working and personal relationships they form, play an important role in determining how the early years in teaching are traversed. Many of the teachers, whose stories are shared in this book, emphasised the need of good mentorship to help novice teachers navigate through the chalky waters of the beginning years.

For instance, in Vimi Sambwani's reflection of her professional journey as an educator and school leader, she recounted the vital role her mentor had played in the beginning years of her life as a novice teacher, which formed the rudder of her professional growth as an educator.

> "Over the weeks, I began to realise the importance of a mentor in my teaching. Mdm Zubeidah became a powerful influence in my life. She began sharing the positive and negative aspects of the classroom and I was extremely grateful for her candid ideas ... The truth was that Mdm Zubeidah did not lead herself to believe that she had nothing to learn from a novice teacher. Her humility strengthened our relationship within our small school community. We spoke honestly with each other on paper and we were able to break down the usual solitary isolation felt by a teacher wet behind the ears, and this helped to expand our professional friendship."

The willingness for experienced teachers to wholeheartedly welcome and guide beginning teachers on board the boat of teaching also featured in Song Hwei Fang's "The Accidental Teacher", in which she shared how her colleague's encouragement of her potential and allowing her to take positions of responsibility had helped her develop a thunderous passion in the field of education and eventually transformed her into a school leader.

The working climate created by the waves of interactions of other teachers in our teaching voyage is also essential. The following excerpt from Sheikh's "The Looking Glass Self" illustrates how having a collegial working environment supported a beginning teacher pass the disappointment and struggle in being posted to a department not of his choice or expectations.

> "I was disappointed with my work allocation, as I knew that it meant that I had three classes of English marking. Even before I went through the torture, I had heard of this cruel and unusual punishment, which had led to very high attrition rates amongst English teachers. Surprisingly, this disgruntlement soon turned into a growing sense of wonder and joy at being an English teacher due to the amiable, dynamic nature of the English teachers in the department .... I thoroughly enjoyed the contact that I had with these personalities even though it could be barb-filled standardisation meetings or even the pressure cooker environment of setting an exam paper."

Conversely, the gradual disintegration of the department of his closely-knit colleagues resulted in a complete reversal in the level of enthusiasm and vigour at how he perceived work. While his tasks and daily activities remained the same, the change in the social environment made the same routine unbearable. The reverberations of this sentiment are strongly felt throughout the other narratives presented in this section.

In addition, it can be seen in these teacher narratives (as well as those found in other parts of the book) that teachers' career trajectories are non-linear; for instance, each time a new event occurs in the professional (or even the personal) life of the teacher, he or she may be thrust to the survival stage all over again. This includes accepting a promotion, teaching a different demographic group of students, moving to a new school, and even working with a new supervisor or colleague. A fitting illustration of the recurrence of the survival and discovery is from Fatimah Othman's narrative titled "Leadership: The Hardware vs The Heartware", wherein the transfer of a Vice Principal to a new school made the author feel as if she were starting all over again.

> "I felt that I was revisiting the Survival Phase all over again in terms of overcoming the challenges in the new school context, which included having to adapt to a new school culture, new colleagues,

new job responsibilities as well as to a new Principal, all of which had different expectations of me than the school that I was from. The new learning curve was steep and painful, to say the least, but nothing had prepared me for the bitter experience I learnt about leadership."

Thus, the complexity arising from relationships may arise at any juncture in our career trajectory. Remaining focused or effectively resolving a collegial relationship is not as straightforward as it sounds. The root cause can often be that of power.

Similarly, the fear to express one's disagreement with a superior stems from several factors, one of which is the nature of the appraisal system in schools that affects teachers' performance ranking and hence the size of our rice bowls. It is clear that such power relationships hinder genuine open communication. For instance, in Yee Teng's narrative, "Sunshine after the Rain", a miscommunication with the Reporting Officer (RO) had caused the teacher to decide not to join the department as a subject specialist for fear of the adverse impact of her relationship with her RO on her performance ranking.

> "She did not clarify and was not interested in my explanation. Her emotions had overtaken the willingness to reason and listen … I would imagine she would now think differently of me as she felt betrayed that I did not inform her of my intentions. I also wondered if it would adversely affect my performance and relationship with her as a superior."

It is evident that the notion of clear and honest communication, as well as the ability to separate or clarify the personal and the professional, begs our attention as education professionals. I posit that such an endeavour for clarity and honesty warrants a change in mind-set and being true to our identity as teachers. This includes having a disposition for reflection and introspection and constantly reaffirming or reassessing our fundamental purpose for entering the field of education. Personally, I have realised the importance of exercising patience in the face of adversity, humility notwithstanding our position and prowess, and respect for the feelings of others in all our dealings. This was something that dawned upon me during the process of being part of the editorial team of this book, in my working relationship with one of my fellow team members. Incidentally, this thought has been appropriately and accurately expressed in narrative, "To Stand on My Own Two Feet", where Ting Ting, a Chinese Language teacher, reflected upon the turmoil in her relationship with her department head.

> "… the very first thing that I see emerging so loudly throughout this narrative is, surprisingly, 'I'. I have always been regarded as (and thought so myself too) a respectful and modest person who is always considerate of other people's feelings. Thus it was rather uncomfortable for me as I saw the egoistic notion of the "I" being so prevalent throughout … . it seemed that just because I thought I was doing the 'right thing' in wanting to improve on what I thought was not done correctly in the teaching of CL, I seemed to expect everyone else to accept my ideas readily and to share my enthusiasm; if not, then there would be something wrong with these people."

The predomination of the "egoistic self" in our dealings with others sometimes seems to get the better of us, as if it were some indomitable force. Not only does it propel us in our quest for power or domination, it can also provide the excuse to avoid accepting responsibility for our actions and taking a humble stand. It could compel us to believe that we are, or rather "I am always right" or that "I can do no wrong". Rarely do we consider the position of others whom we interact with; rarely do we pause to empathise with them.

To conclude, the incidents recounted in the narratives presented in Part 2 span the experiences of teachers at different stages of their career trajectories and at varying positions of leadership. These episodes include relationships with mentors, peers, subordinates, as well as with those in superior leadership positions, and reflect both positive and negative encounters. In all cases, the notions of power, communication, and identity pervade in varying degrees throughout each of the narratives. Examining them a notch deeper would reveal the notion of the meaning and purpose of being a teacher and how it influences at a subconscious level our decisions and interactions with others.

Chapter 7

Attributing My Professional Growth to My Mentor and My Students

Vimi D SAMBWANI

There are countless memories that have been etched in my mind. The strongest and clearest ones are those of me as a teacher, spanning a period of 15 years. In many ways, these experiences have moulded me into what I am today, from a potent combination of events borne out of the classroom and the staff room. I would like to share some of these personal anecdotes that have paved my professional journey.

A Novice Teacher and Her Mentor

I began my first day in Bedok Town Primary School, comforted only by the fact that it was a stone's throw from my residence. We may have done our practicum but it was the first day when we were actually viewed as a teacher by our students, armed with all the theoretical knowledge and ready to conquer the world. Needless to say, I looked very confident on the exterior, but was a bundle of nerves inside!

The first day, though, started off rather innocuously; we were led around a tour of the school and introduced to teachers in the staff room. Things moved up a notch, though, when I was first introduced to my Primary 3 class; I immediately sensed that the children were subtly sizing me up, noting flaws and trying to look beyond my strict exterior. After a while, it was announced that I would be joining my class on a school trip with two other Primary 3 classes. I was quite nervous about it, as the children did not really view me as an authority figure yet; so looking after them in an uncontrolled environment would be quite a task. The one consolation I had, though, was that a more experienced teacher, Mdm. Zubeidah, was tasked to keep me company. The school trip now looked less daunting!

When we finally boarded our school bus, the children began to settle down but just 20 minutes down the expressway, it became a different matter. Trying to keep 40 odd children quiet and disciplined in a bus, I quickly discovered, was an extremely challenging affair. But, thankfully, Mdm. Zubeidah showed me a thing or two about instilling discipline when, all of a sudden, she stood up in front and gave a stern do-not-fool-around-with-me-or-else glance, and the rest of the bus ride became a breeze.

Wow! What made her command that kind of respect? I want to be like her, I thought to myself! Walking around in the zoo, I got to chat with Mdm. Zubeidah about the children in my class. Her insight and grasp of the dynamics in the class were very helpful in making me focus on issues like, who was going to be a difficult child to control and who would potentially test my limits!

During the break at the zoo, I felt inclined to play with the children, but I reluctantly maintained my distance, ensuring that I behaved professionally.

The adventure playground consisted of a significantly large wooden climbing frame, complete with slides and climbing walls. Keeping a look-out for 120 children mixing with their peers from another school is an arduous task, especially when they are all running and bustling around. The children were all very excited and getting them back into an orderly fashion was chaotic, especially since I did not know any names to call out!

To say the least, the entire experience was quite significant for me; I felt like a child all over again, watching all the children running around. Trying not to join in was very hard. I also got to experience what being a real adult is like. I was treated with respect and involved in all the gossip between teachers!

Over the weeks, I began to realise the importance of a mentor in my teaching. Mdm. Zubeidah became a powerful influence in my life. She began sharing the positive and negative aspects of the classroom and I was extremely grateful for her candid ideas. As I shared with her the lack of being able to connect with the pupils and getting through to them, she shared that, "As teachers, we cannot be aloof or detached. We cannot withhold personal information and pretend not to have any emotions, or merely feign ignorance about what is happening in these children's lives." Her advice resonated well with me; it was the missing link that, until then, I was unable to discover. I was, up to then, giving so much focus on what I was teaching that I had neglected whom I was teaching.

Mdm. Zubeidah went on to share the benefits of personal journaling. She informed me how she had used the students' personal journals, which they wrote on a weekly basis, to open up about their personal struggles, their aspirations or learning difficulties. These journals were windows into their worlds. It struck me, at that point in time, that her emphasis on personal journaling was fuelled by her realisation as a teacher that relationships between entities are fundamental to learning. We must learn to interact honestly with our students. We must be able to weave our subjects and the fabric of our lives so that we can foster these interconnections between ourselves and the world around us. Finding, and making, time to have constant dialogues with our pupils and showing special interest in their self-development affect these children significantly, albeit positively. As a novice, I began the slow but important journey of understanding that the essence of teaching is really about being people-oriented.

I was excited to try out this new strategy with my class. I kept a personal journal myself and asked Mdm. Zubeidah if she would like to read and help me along this journey. Mdm. Zubeidah had a daughter about my age and I felt that she extended her motherly role to me too. What surprised me was that she was willing to let me read her personal journal too. It was difficult at first to be honest and direct in my journaling and I was hesitant to express my experiences. But, as I moved into writing, it was empowering to feel her support and I reciprocated with her.

The truth was that Mdm. Zubeidah did not lead herself to believe that she had nothing to learn from a novice teacher. Her humility strengthened the relationship within our small school community. We spoke honestly with each other on paper and we were able to break down the usual solitary isolation felt by a teacher wet behind the ears, and this helped to expand our professional friendship.

Students as Powerful Learning Experiences

After the significant impact of a mentor in my teaching career, I went on to realise how much effect my students also had in my daily life as I grew and learnt with them. One student in particular who left an impact on me was in my Primary 6 class, Racheal (not her real name). Racheal was a bright student and was a joy to have. She was every teacher's dream — bubbly and lively in class, and aspiring to get into Raffles Girls' School (RGS) and then to the university. Racheal was a self-motivated student who had a bright future ahead of her.

Gradually, however, I began noticing a change in Racheal's behaviour. Among other things, this included a sharp and dramatic reduction in the quality in her school work. Her good conduct and chirpy demeanour began to disappear. Racheal was often sick while preparing for the Primary School Leaving Examination (PSLE). Everyone thought it was the stress of examination that caused it and I often stayed back after class to counsel her.

Her parents saw me on several occasions to discuss Racheal's dramatic change. After a battery of medical tests, Racheal was shockingly diagnosed with cancer of the throat just three weeks before the PSLE exams. It was Stage 3 by then. She underwent an operation to remove part of her tongue and had to go for physiotherapy every other day. She had to repeat her final year in her school. I visited her very often and her friends were a great source of comfort too. Despite this setback, Racheal was positive about life. She neither complained nor wanted to give up. She began high-dosage chemotherapy infusions.

She was all geared up to get back to school in January the next year but a growth was detected on her neck. The dreaded prognosis revealed that the cancerous cells had spread to her neck and, later on, to her bones. Every day after school, Shu Fang's good friends, who had moved to Secondary One, and I would visit her. By this time, she was bed-ridden and could hardly talk. However, we were able to communicate and, more importantly, understand one another's concern and care. My heart went out to Racheal's mother who took care of her day and night. It was clearly the power of maternal love that spurred her on. She never left Racheal alone unless we were there to relieve her duties.

Racheal, of course, needed strong financial support for her medical treatment. It was during this difficult time that we witnessed many people coming forward to give a helping hand. We were fortunate to get donations from generous people such as her former teachers, classmates and juniors from her school. The school organised a donation drive and collected over S$100,000 to pay for Racheal's treatment. Tragically, Racheal fought a brave battle but eventually lost her life. The money collected for her was then given to the Singapore Cancer Society to provide financial support for youths with cancer.

During her brief sojourn in this world, Racheal taught me a very important lesson about life. It is fragile and we should treasure every moment with our family and friends. When I told Racheal that she had inspired me to become a better teacher, she hoped that I would touch the lives of children who need a listening ear. Today, I always remember what Racheal had endured and I make it a point to reach out to children who are going through difficult times in their lives. Teaching is really more than the curriculum and a formal job — it is about establishing a genuine connection with people, and learning lessons of life.

Racheal's desire to live the last days of her life to the fullest was amazing. In illness, she even went to church on a stretcher. She was in great pain but she persevered. She made us promise that her funeral would be a celebration of her new life in heaven. We were told to put on colourful clothes. I have never seen a more courageous person who could accept death without any regrets. How many of us have this positive attitude towards life? Not many of us. Through my journey with Racheal, I have learnt that every day must be treasured.

Knowing You Can Make a Difference

As a teacher, I always waited in anticipation of the type of students that I will be getting at the start of the year; I would get excited with what I could accomplish together with them. I also expected students to be diligent and meet the demands of the syllabus. From my end, I was prepared to inspire them to enjoy their readings.

Once, we were reading an excerpt from Roald Dahl's book, *Charlie and the Chocolate Factory*, to take a break from the normal textbook. I had just gotten Fathul, a new student in my class, in the third month of the year. When it was his turn to read, I asked him to read a couple of paragraphs. With his head lowered, he mumbled, "I cannot read." I thought I had heard wrongly, so I asked him to read again. To my total dismay, I discovered that the child could not read even the sight words. I did not say much at that point of time in order to avoid embarrassing him further. Towards the end of the day, however, I called for Fathul to stay behind after class. He waited with his head still lowered and I could almost sense his despair as he stood embarrassed and helpless before me. I went up to him and placed my hands on his shoulders. I sat beside him and slowly but surely helped him with the words that he could not pronounce.

Despite his inability to read, I was moved by Fathul's tenacity and zeal in wanting to learn. I was not sure how he was not able to read up to this point as he came from another school. But I did not want to dwell on the past and took it upon myself that I needed to help

Fathul to be able to read. I told Fathul, "If you are willing to put in the effort, we can work together on this." Fathul nodded his head and I could see his eyes fill with joy. We started regular sessions of one hour after school each day and Fathul would diligently wait for me outside the staff room.

I later realised that it was a lack of self-esteem and parental involvement that had caused Fathul to not be able to read for a period of four years in primary school. I taught him how to decode and break words into syllables, the different vowel sounds, etc. I was constantly using phonetics to help him decode words. Then I taught him to recognise basic sight words too. I also enlisted the help of the learning support coordinator to help him in her spare time. After narrating Fathul's situation to her, she agreed generously to render her help. She did so without questioning.

Fathul progressed by leaps and bounds. His mother was so proud of him and continued to thank me profusely. After an eight-month period, Fathul held up his hand to read and read almost like a trooper. I stood in front of the class as he read the text and I felt an overwhelming sense of pride. When he finished, he turned to me with a huge smile and said, "Miss Vimi, I can read, I can read!" "Yes, Fathul, this is the result of your hard work and your efforts," I replied. He left not long after that to move on to secondary school. Till this day I remember him leaving school and giving me the biggest hug and saying, "I will always remember what you have given me."

Till this day, Fathul has been in touch with me. We lost touch for a while as I moved on to another school, but we somehow got in touch with each other again. He is currently training to be a pilot. I am so proud that, as a teacher and a human being, I could make that difference to a child. It is moments like these that make teaching so meaningful in our lives.

Fathul's episode made me realise just how wide the spectrum of students in a school was. Some were more privileged than others and some possessed more advantages over others as they entered the school environments. Whatever their entry points may be, however, as teachers, we play the critical role of levelling this playing field as much as possible. The school environment, and especially teachers, must not neglect the backgrounds that the students come from and we need to fuel their passion for learning. This incident taught me the importance of being aware of the needs and difficulties of my pupils in the class. I am glad I intervened in Fathul's learning for the better. The interesting thing was, without consciously realising it, my activities as a teacher became focused on Fathul's needs in the classroom, as opposed to a standard syllabus.

Reflecting on the Leadership Experience

After serving several years as a teacher and subject head, a new challenge arose as I moved on to the position of Head of Department (HOD) for English. I was gratified that the senior management in my school had confidence in my capabilities as a teacher. I am eternally indebted to the educators in my life who have been great role models for me to emulate.

In the last 10 years, the department was headed by two experienced Heads of Department. The former HOD, Mrs. R (not her real name), was on medical leave for long periods of time and was waiting out her time for retirement. The previous HOD, Mrs. J (not her real name), was in her forties and had stepped down earlier due to family commitments. She was hoping to succeed Mrs. R after she retired, considering that now her children were much older. My Principal, however, had put my name up for appointment due to the fact that I was familiar to the job, and had on several occasions stood in for the previous HOD when she was on medical leave. A lot of my staff did not expect me to be appointed so soon, as I had only 7.5 years of service. Instead, Mrs. J had 20 years of teaching experience. She was an efficient and diligent teacher who showed a positive attitude towards her work. If assigned a task by the Principal, she would get it done almost immediately. She believed in keeping the Principal informed of her achievements. She was also co-operative with the staff and older members in the English department liked her and had hoped for her to be the new HOD. However, her relationship with some other teachers was hardly cordial.

There was little cohesion in the department especially with regard to the programme and activities. The previous HOD had set the programmes and procedures without much consultation with the committee members. A number of us were left to do our jobs or carry out our responsibilities without much supervision from the HOD. The department needed to review some programmes that had been running yearly but without much significant effect on student learning. New strategies had to be developed to manage these problems. In addition, some teachers were not motivated to perform.

I was given the task of initiating a new reading programme for the school. Among other things, it was discovered that the previous HOD had done nothing about the weak readers, some of whom were in Primary 6 and were still unable to read. Being astonished by the results of the survey that I had conducted, I decided that something had to be done to tackle this problem, which, if left unsolved, would only escalate over the years. Hence, I started to source around for appropriate materials for use by the teachers with the help of my language support coordinator. Next, I needed to work out details with my committee members as I thought I should not work everything out on my own but require the input of my members. So I called for a meeting with the 10 committee members. When I posed the idea to them, they responded with mixed and hesitant reactions. I sensed the older teachers being apprehensive and uneasy about the new programme and, perhaps, they felt that they would be in for more work with my taking over the department. The other members of the staff who had been on friendly terms with me prior to my appointment were somewhat cooperative but they too were uneasy about the change.

I persevered and presented the new programme to my committee, along with the survey results and results of the tests done on the weak readers. I explained the rationale to my team members. However, due to the shortage of time, I had to make some decisions on my own with minimal input from my committee. I was, after all, expected to produce results.

To complicate matters, Mrs. J was directly opposed to the programme. She opined that the revamping of the timetable to include reading slots would be disruptive and that the weak readers could be handled by the language support coordinator. She felt that things were working fine under the old leadership and I was merely trying to create more work as this would look good on my year-end report. After showing the statistics, she finally relented, albeit grudgingly, saying that she did not have a choice as eventually I was the Head! Being a new HOD, I was not very sure how to handle the situation. I merely mentioned that perhaps the Principal could explain it further. She turned defensive and accused me of trying to make her look like she was not doing her job. So I told her that the Principal had approved of the programme and felt it should be carried out as it was obvious that something was needed for these weak readers. The other members merely sat quietly throughout the meeting, observing the show and taking silent notes.

The reading programme also entailed the teachers sacrificing some of their tea and lunch breaks to provide support to the weak readers. I underestimated this as a problem and did not anticipate the groundswell. One teacher in the department felt that the school had become a "prison house". However, the other teachers were unwilling to voice out such dissatisfaction.

In the weeks to come, the programme was implemented. Eventually, teachers got infected with the teaching bug and became quite excited about the programme. Some experienced teachers who were initially apprehensive were willing to try. They provided me with valuable feedback that it was working with some children. I was encouraged. Mrs. J's feedback, however, was that it was not working in her class, and she expressed her dissatisfaction to the Principal. I was rather annoyed, but chose to be careful about my reaction.

As the new HOD, I was concerned about several issues — to review the current English programmes and their effectiveness, to inspire the teachers who were monitoring the programmes under their charge to improve their performance and to look into the problems with weak readers. I revamped the timetable in the middle of the year to include reading slots and unsettled the staff with the new changes. I knew what I wanted in the department and, to achieve my current results/objectives, I was uncompromising in my attempt to achieve these objectives. Due to the fact that the time available to complete the task was limited, I chose to use a more directive style. Most of my efforts were focused on task completion and there seemed little recognition of individual or group needs. I failed to realise that, in attempting to achieve results, how things are done is equally important. It was important to initiate structure, but not at the expense of fostering positive relationships.

Many team members who accepted the programme were upset by these changes. Some, like Mrs. J, chose to verbalise it, while others did not. Indeed, there was a lack of flexibility in my leadership style. I made little attempt to analyse the context to realise that some of the staff were set in their ways and were not ready for the immediate changes in the reading programme. I also failed to consider the key impacting factors. Although it seemed my intention was to build teamwork and team approaches, there was little effort initially to build cohesive units. To ask teachers to help with the reading programme meant getting them to sacrifice their personal time — which was unfair to them and led to dissatisfaction. Although the task might have been daunting, it would have been possible to win the long-term commitment and support of the team if I had understood and recognised their individual needs and difficulties.

It was then, as a HOD, that it dawned upon me that power increases the distance between leaders and followers. In retrospect, what was needed was a more cautious and personal approach to change and time should have been taken to get to know the team members and their working style better. In this way, the situation could have been evaluated and the behaviours changed to match the requirements of the situation. A useful insight for me was that without a good relationship and some degree of respect and trust, a leader will have a difficult time getting teachers to comply with a situation, regardless of the power he or she may have. I learnt that a good leader needs to be flexible and understand the capacity of people to cope with ambiguity.

From Educator to Researcher

I remember sitting on the green sofa in the staff lounge with Mdm. Kan, a senior teacher in the school. She wanted my input on an action research project that she had taken up recently. Therein lay the dilemma. I stood there as a newly appointed Vice Principal (VP) to Peiying Primary School. I had never been involved in an action-research project and here I was wondering if there was anything I could offer Mdm. Kan.

Mdm. Kan's proposal made me discover that my role required me to provide the curriculum leadership to teachers that my professional training had not prepared me for. I realised that I needed to be active to set a research agenda, conduct it and take an active part in each stage. At this level of leadership, learning is all about being self-motivated and taking the bull by its horns. Over the weeks, I read about the need for more collaborative research to bridge the gap between educational theory and practice. Mdm. Kan, by engaging in her action research, was providing a classroom teacher's voice for research and the opportunity was allowing her to create new knowledge. I felt new intellectual energy and excitement building up in me.

I seized an opportunity at the next VP's learning circle meeting to moot this idea to the other VPs. I presented before them the importance of providing curriculum leadership to our teachers. I suggested that we may want to form a team of VPs and engage in an action research ourselves so that we were better equipped to guide our teachers. I saw this as a forum for us to pose our queries and demonstrate our support for change. Up till now, we had read about "action research" and schools as "centers of inquiry" and teachers as "reflective practitioners". It was so powerful. Although all the VPs in the cluster were not able to commit their time, the ones who were interested decided to come together. But the question in all our minds was, "How do we begin?"

The VPs, as collaborative researchers, began with what we knew. One of the VPs, Mr. Chua, introduced us to Mr. Hairon, who was with the National Institute of Education (NIE) and at that time completing his doctorate study. We contacted him and he was more than willing to assist the Vice Principals as a group. He led us through the research journey. First we deliberated on our ideas. All of us as a group felt a sense of growing energy, intellectual interest and connection. We worked out our research question, "How to Develop in Our Key Personnel a Better Understanding of Strategic Thinking?" We conducted our literature review and it provided a working background for the research. For the project, we had planned that each supervisor was to identify two key personnel (KP) who would be invited to come on board and present the action research project. We thought that less experienced and/or more junior KP would benefit more and would be more interested in the developmental opportunities that would arise as part of their involvement in the project. We also thought that they would be more open to dialogue with their supervisor on how to improve this particular competency once they understood the difference it could make to their work.

The research method chosen was essentially qualitative and inductive in nature. The primary research tools were question-naires, reflection journals, scenario planning and dialogue session for clarification of the KP's thinking.

Harking back to my days of personal journaling with students, I suggested getting the team to maintain personal journals to docu-ment and share our experiences and express our concerns. The agreement was unanimous! Mr. Hairon was very encouraging throughout this research journey and helped to steer and focus our direction. He encouraged us to find a platform to share our research project. Finally, through his encouragement, we presented our paper at the Educational Research Association (ERAS) conference. I could not believe it! There I was standing before a room of academics presenting research — and this was our research! It was both a new, refreshing yet quite unsettling scenario.

At each stage of the project, I was gaining invaluable skills that I could use in the future. The journaling helped us strengthen our relationship as a research community. More importantly for me, it helped us forge stronger and deeper professional relationships as well. It was nice to know that we could share our frustrations and failures with our colleagues and share this action research journey with them.

This was indeed a beneficial experience for me. The research experience I gained through this work was invaluable because I learnt that I had different and complementary strengths. I learnt to listen and try to understand the different perspectives of my colleagues. I learnt to understand myself better and develop a richer sense of how I can grow personally and professionally. I gained invaluable insight by doing and taking an active part in conducting research. I also learnt the rigours of sifting through data and conducting qualitative research. I was empowered in having a voice that directly affects my belief system. I also understood the strength and support that exist in collaboration. I was better equipped to assist Mdm. Kan now and more convinced of the power of action research.

Conclusion

I started and will, in all probability, end my career as an educator. At the same time, I have also learnt that growing to be effective involves wearing different hats and constantly reflecting on your learning experiences and gleaning lessons from them.

I cannot rank any of my experiences as being any less, or more, instructive. From the day I first walked into a class of curious wide-eyed students — tentative and wet behind the ears — through my engaging experiences of learning, from teachers like Mdm. Zubeidah, fellow VPs, and students like Fathul and Racheal, every such experience has been a nugget to mould me into what I am today. As I continue my educational journey, I realise that if I wish to continue to be relevant to my students' lives as a teacher, I need to be constantly open to new opportunities and learning experiences that exist before me. It is the sum total of these experiences that provides us with new seas on which to sail. At the end of the day, is that not what education is about — not merely arriving at a destination but travelling with a new view?

Chapter 8

"The Looking Glass Self" — Locating My Professional Identity from Interactions with Students and Colleagues

Sheikh Luqmahn Bin AHMAD

Introduction

Politics, as I learnt in my Political Science 101 course back in my university days, exists as long as there are more than two people working together. It is sometimes defined as "social relations involving authority or power". Being a teacher, as I have learnt over the years, involves social relations on various levels and many of these relations involve power — teacher and student, teacher and colleagues, teacher and lecturer, teacher and supervisor etc. This really echoes what a classmate frequently reiterates, "teaching is a people business". I see a distinct thread weaving through most of my experiences and, thereafter, in my reflections. Most of these experiences deal with my relations with people; be they colleagues, lecturers, superiors or students. As I seek to make sense of the stories of my experiences, I found it helpful to use Cooley's "Looking Glass" theory as a guide for my reflections. This, again, is a throwback to my Sociology 101 course. There are three main components of the looking glass self (Yeung *et al.*, 2003).

- We imagine how we must appear to others.
- We imagine the judgement of that appearance.
- We develop our self through the judgements of others.

In many of the relationships I will be sharing through my stories, I realise the relevance of the "looking glass" as I really define myself, sometimes personally and most times professionally, from my interactions with the personalities in the stories mentioned in the following paragraphs. I am very conscious of my actions and how they can be perceived by people, though sometimes I realise I need to disregard popular opinion for fear of forsaking my principles, most important of which is a question which guides my way, "how do the students benefit from this?" I realise also that I can be hyper-aware of my race, language and background, though this can sometimes be a self-defeating mentality to possess. Due to this same hyper-awareness, I am very grateful for the opportunities or praise directed towards me and therein lies my undying loyalty to this source. On the other side of the mirror, our perceptions of people are also key to the quality of those relationships. False or misconceived perceptions can be very damaging and unproductive, and they can be very difficult to repair.

Origins

Similar to many stories I have heard, I did not start out wanting to be a teacher. I realise that this issue may sometimes be considered taboo as there are many in our profession who are in it merely for the money. For me, it was the same. I had always wanted to be a journalist or work with the Foreign Service, but those fields were notoriously difficult to get into; moreover, it was a matter of my livelihood at that point since 2003 was a very bad year for graduates. After hundreds of applications, which included one to the Ministry of Education (MOE), I was still without a proper job and working odd jobs as a door-to-door salesman and an airline customer service officer amongst others. My esteem was hitting rock bottom and I was always wondering why nobody would hire me. Was it my race or the language I spoke? Ever since National Service, I have felt the impact of being part of a minority race. I was never given the opportunity to be an officer, and even as a police officer, I saw many products of obvious race-based policies (again, a very sensitive national issue). But honestly, this perception of self thus forms a large part of who I am; and I still struggle with it, as I know that this chip on my shoulder can be a huge stumbling block in my interactions with people.

Since I had friends who were teachers, I applied for teaching as well as I saw no harm in trying it out. I knew then that MOE would normally let us try out teaching as "contract teachers". My sister was a teacher and would frequently discourage me from signing on, citing the huge marking load and the endless administrative duties. I paid her no heed. I had always been good in my language and was active and interested in sports; hence I thought that being a Physical Education (PE) teacher with English as my second teaching subject could be a good fit. I further thought that being a teacher could be a stepping-stone to something else, as I honestly did not see myself being a teacher forever. I applied three times to be a teacher before I was finally accepted. I enjoyed my six months in School A due to the great colleagues I had and the bubbly, enthusiastic students I had the pleasure of teaching. I was hooked, line and sinker, to the multi-faceted, dynamic nature of the job and, more importantly, to the interaction with the students, and proceeded to sign my soul to the government —— for the next five years, at least. I still did not see myself as a teacher forever, but I knew I could enjoy being a teacher for the next few years.

Comfortable Environment Equals Productivity

Before I applied for teaching, I never actually knew whether I had the affinity for it. When I was posted to School A for my contract teaching stint, I was quite excited since I knew it was an all-boys' school and I thought that I could relate better to boys. My first teaching subject (CS1) was PE followed by my CS2, which was English, and I thus expected plenty of PE classes with maybe one or two English classes. But this expectation was woefully unfulfilled as I was tasked to teach at least three English classes, which meant that I had very few PE classes. However, I eventually found out that this was the norm and it happens in most schools if you were an English teacher (since EL teachers were in such limited supply). It was also at this time that I learnt about the negative perception that other subject teachers normally had of PE teachers. PE teachers were normally envied due to the lower marking loads they had and this sometimes even affected their ranking in certain schools. There was even talk that if you taught only PE, it was a dead-end job, which meant that promotion would be slow and difficult. This would be my first introduction to how perception can sometimes too often, be reality.

Regardless, I was disappointed with my work allocation, as I knew that it meant that I had three classes of English marking. Even before I went through the torture, I had heard of this cruel and unusual punishment, which had led to very high attrition rates amongst English teachers. Surprisingly, this disgruntlement soon turned into a growing sense of wonder and joy at being an English teacher due to the amiable, dynamic nature of the English teachers in the department. The English department then had an Acting Head, Mr. EPL, who had a calm, soothing demeanour as well as a fun-loving Subject Head, Mr. HZ, alongside other bubbly, yet effective personalities like Mdm. TZ, who made life as an English teacher actually enjoyable. They guided, taught and encouraged the young teachers. They made sure that the Scheme of Work was always neatly structured, and even worksheets and the like were prepared at the departmental level, which left us teachers to work on effective deliveries. I had time to prepare interesting, exciting lessons which really engaged the students. I thoroughly enjoyed the contact that I had with these personalities even though there were barb-filled standardisation meetings or even the pressure cooker environment when finalising examination papers. As I compare my experiences then with my experience now, I recognise the power of a comfortable working environment — how such an environment could actually make work fun and prevent it from becoming a chore. In my present school, with ineffective, transient leadership within the English department, English teachers feel overstretched, always pressed for time and even guilty for not being able to give their best to the students. Effective leaders are actually people with great organisational skills and who have excellent interpersonal skills. They make the work environment for their subordinates as comfortable and non-threatening as possible. These experiences taught me very valuable lessons about leadership and the kind of leader that I want to be. With their constant encouragement, support and their pronounced faith in my abilities (their "judgement of me"), I wanted to strive even harder to develop myself and to fulfil their expectations as well as the developing expectations I had for myself.

Ups and Downs of Teacher Training

After my six-month stint teaching in an untrained capacity, I welcomed teacher training in the National Institute of Education (NIE) with bated breath. I realised how ill-equipped I was when I was teaching, and I was excited at the prospect of learning skills, strategies and such in NIE so that I could become a more effective teacher. But I quickly came to realise that many of the modules I would go through were on the whole ineffectual and superfluous.

One of the classes which we had to attend was Educational Psychology, which, though in its essence had its merits, was taught by an academic who had never taught in a classroom before. We had expected to be tutored by either retired or seasoned teachers who had come from the ground and could connect the abstract, sometimes lofty theories presented in the textbooks with concrete examples from their illustrious career. Instead, the examples used by her were strictly those listed in the textbook and separate from the reality on the ground, especially to those of us who had taught in schools before. She exacerbated the situation by reading from the PowerPoint slides she had prepared, which was as far from engaging teaching as it could get. We became quickly disenchanted, uninspired and frequently rose to question assumptions made by the tutor, which little by little made our relationship with her quite acrimonious.

Again, this perception that an academic was useless in the practicalities of everyday teaching overwhelmed our common sense. Maybe it was the brashness and arrogance of youth which made us behave in such a manner, but, in retrospect, the entire situation could have been handled in such a manner so as to be beneficial to both parties concerned. We should not have let our disdain for her background colour our reactions, and we could have instead married what little experience that we had with her expertise in theoretical knowledge. This could have enabled us to work together to bridge this theory–practice divide.

My experiences in NIE, however, were not all negative. Besides the wealth of knowledge I received from my PE lecturers, I was totally blown away by my tutor on English Language teaching. Ms. C was a former Vice Principal who had chosen to veer into academia, and her methods and sheer effectiveness as a tutor were impressive. Her classroom management skills were so effective that it managed to harness the unruly energies of a class of PE teachers into hard, productive work that we even enjoyed. She made everything systematic and engaging, and there was hardly a time when we even had time to doze off, as we were wont to do, due to the physical exertions we normally had in the morning lessons.

Personally, she served as a great pillar of support for me. She had always encouraged me and told me how she had enormous respect for my abilities, and her confidence in me prompted me to develop myself further. She continued to mentor us through the two years we were in NIE and I still do keep in contact with her through email. The last I saw her was when she was in the Curriculum Planning and Development Division (CPDD) in the midst of the 2010 English Syllabus change. Even then, she was sharing with my then Head of Department (HOD) her assessment of my abilities in English, much to my embarrassment. Till today, I continue to use the teaching methods she had taught us and am still trying to match up to her level of effective time management. She serves as an inspiration of what an effective teacher should be.

The Importance of Having a Support Network

I was lucky to be posted to School B with a sizeable number of teachers from a variety of disciplines. I still remember how, when we were first posted in, there were not enough tables for us, which resulted in us sharing the large table in the school workroom. Although inconvenient, we had some very good times there since there was always somebody working at the table when we got back from lessons; and as such, we could always share a joke even when working together. It was interesting to see our insignificant work area become overcrowded with books and those piles of books starting to grow higher as the days wore on. Over the two years, our support network of close colleagues became invaluable despite having gotten our own tables by then, as our work commitments grew and our responsibilities increased exponentially. We would frequently go out for lunch or dinner together which, in retrospect, was essential in keeping us happy and emotionally balanced. But as they say, "good times never last" — the first departure from our happy little group was our "super" scholar who was destined for bigger and better things with his automatic posting to MOE Headquarters. Another colleague who was the heartbeat of the group decided to move on to Northlight School to pursue her interests, which effectively killed the group. Soon after, yet another member of the group started distancing himself from us for some personal reasons.

It was around this time that I started entertaining ideas of being overworked. I had never noticed the amount of work that I had before and, upon self-reflection, I found a connection with the loss of my support network. I realised that after the disintegration of this group, I started becoming less and less excited about going to work. It was not as if I had no other friends in school, but the level of closeness and trust was difficult to replace. "We develop ourselves through the judgements of others" and our bond ensured that no matter what happened, we would have people supporting us, watching our backs, so to speak. We knew that no matter how unpopular some of the initiatives rolled out by us were, we always had people who would support us and even rally that support for us. Thus, working life has never been the same. I can only hope that this kind of relationship can be cultivated once again with another group of friends, but with the kind of competitive environment that Enhanced Performance Management System (EPMS) and ranking have engendered amongst colleagues, this will be an uphill struggle.

Thoughts on Defiant Students

My first bad encounter was with a Secondary Two student in my first month as a trained teacher. I can still remember it like it was yesterday; my tightly clenched fists, my body shivering with anger, my mind working furiously to defuse the situation contending with the indignation I felt at the student's gall. The explosive encounter that I had with this particular student started from something as innocent as me asking the student to tuck his shirt in as he walked past me. The student blatantly ignored me and walked on. I raised my voice and asked him to stop. He turned around and started shouting at me, "I know ah! No need to shout what!"

"I did speak nicely but you ignored me! Come here and stand up straight!" I raised my voice as I realised the defiant manner in which he was standing. He walked straight up to me and stared at me face to face, which made me lose my cool. I pushed him away and he reacted to my push by slapping my hand away as he continued staring at me, in complete defiance. I reacted immediately by shouting even louder, "What are you staring at me for? Who do you think I am? You think you're a gangster? Tuck in your shirt!"

He still stared at me like his life depended on it, "What gangster? Where got gangster? Talk so much!" This provoked me even more and I refused to back down as, by now, a sizeable crowd of students had crowded around us and I knew they were waiting to see how I would react. As a new teacher, I knew that how I handled the situation then would determine how all the students in the school would react to me in future. I could not let the student get the upper hand.

By this time, I was practically screaming at the top of my voice, "You better shut up! Tuck in your shirt and go back to class! The rest of you, I'm giving you one minute to get back to class."

As the boy turned around to walk back to class, I was still brimming with anger and this was compounded by the manner in which he walked, which was in the typical "gangster" fashion. In my mind, he was trying to show the students around that he was not cowed by authority. I went on to shout, "You better hurry up back to class! Don't walk like you own the school!" I waited all the way until he entered his class before reporting his behaviour to the Discipline Master.

Reflecting on my thoughts and emotions during the exchange, Cooley again interjects intermittently — was it my thoughts or my imagination that created a picture of how I appeared to both the student at hand and the surrounding students? And I did, in fact, imagine the "judgement of that appearance"; that I had to put up a strict, no-nonsense front as a new teacher in the school. But was I really wrong in my assessment that a less than firm handling of the episode would be an invitation for more trouble from other students wanting to "test" me?

This particular experience came to mind at a recent Classroom Management seminar I participated in. The speaker, an American and a former teacher who spent many years in the worst schools in the United States, reminded us that students have bad days too. Students are humans and some come from utterly dysfunctional family backgrounds and their bad days can sometimes be unimaginably bad, and this sometimes acts as catalysts to their reactions to teachers' admonishments. They may sometimes explode and he taught us that we should never lose control of our emotions even though we are humans ourselves. He used a surfing analogy of "going under the wave" instead of crashing headlong into the destructive force of the wave. He advised us to keep our voice and tone even and calm but this definitely does not mean that we are giving in or losing our authority in any way. Punishment would still be meted out, but just not there and then. I have no way of knowing how I could have improved the confrontation with this knowledge in hand as I am not sure I could have controlled my anger, but I guess this is a process that all teachers, especially those quick to anger, must go through. I think it goes back to recognising that students have bad days, and that sometimes we just need to give them a break. Perhaps on that day, that particular student was having a bad day, and I had not stopped to give him a break.

I was not surprised, though slightly disappointed, that he was expelled from school a few months down the road for various offences. This disappointment was due to the fact that we had lost yet another student. Sometimes, you ask yourself, "What else could I have done? Could I have done more?" Could I have suppressed my dislike for his attitude and seen through the façade he had put up? Should I have approached him, perhaps during his detention, to speak to him in an entirely different context? Through the years, I did learn that students react differently when alone. They tend to be calmer and introspective, even remorseful, when approached individually — there seems to be a madness (perhaps hormone- and ego-fuelled) which inflicts them when other students are around, which is another affirmation of Cooley's "looking glass". Through many similar incidents, I have learnt the impressive benefits of talking to students, for example, after scolding them in class, or giving them punishment. Somehow, justifying to them personally really helps. Sometimes, you wish that hindsight could be bought in stores. "Would he have been saved if I had made the effort to talk to him?" Now, the question will forever remain unanswered.

Complexities of Power Relationships

When I received my first posting, which was to School B, I came in with an experienced teacher who was recruited to be the Subject Head (SH) of PE. We became firm friends as our age gap was negligible and we had similar interests. We always worked together, organising school events like the school's annual Sports

Day, Cross Country, and the Secondary One Orientation Camp alongside everyday duties like PE lessons and the Fitness Programme. I found him to be a fair, reasonable superior whom I respected because he was able to "walk the talk" and frequently even sought my opinions on various matters besides mentoring me on various aspects of my daily work.

The problem, if I can even call it a problem, would be the dichotomy between the friend and the professional. He was recently made my Reporting Officer (RO), which effectively meant that I had to report to him and that my performance grades, and hence promotion, would largely be dependent on him. I sometimes found the two difficult to reconcile as I found it a very slippery slope to climb — from both sides. It could sometimes be very difficult to criticise a friend outright and I sometimes wonder if he was able to do it. For example, I was unsure as to whether he could immediately point my mistakes out to me or even inform me about the severity of certain mistakes I made in relation to how it affected my performance grading.

This again goes back to the first and second component of Cooley's "looking glass": that "I imagine how I must appear to him, and I imagine his judgement of that appearance". This affected my relationship with him as a friend on a profound level — I feared to let my guard down as I felt that I was constantly being assessed. It was very sensitive as our EPMS and ranking mechanism affects our "bread and butter". As mentioned by a classmate recently, the RO effectively has god-like powers in a ranking exercise. This superior–subordinate divide was the issue at hand here, and I was really undecided as to whether a divide was an inevitable part of life or if a commitment to honesty and candour between both parties could bridge that divide.

Politics at Play

Another interesting anecdote deals with the interpersonal relationships we have with other colleagues in the school. This same friend/ superior was not well-liked in certain quarters because he was labelled as a "glory-hunter". They had the notion that he supposedly grabbed the recognition for the projects that he worked on with other people. My first reaction was that of disbelief as having already known him for many years, I really did not believe that he was such a person. Moreover, having also worked with him for close to four years on many projects, I knew this to be untrue. I wrestled with the idea of informing him about how certain people felt about him and what they were saying about him behind his back as, firstly, I did not want to be a "tattle-tale" and, secondly, and also more importantly, I did not want to create an unhealthy working environment in the school. On the other hand, as a friend, I had this obligation to inform him about whom to trust and whom to be careful about. On top of that, the knowledge could help him tailor how he related to these specific people.

Eventually, I decided to tell him, to his utter surprise. Although he was disappointed with what he heard, I tried to tell him that this knowledge was more to give him an inkling about how he was perceived by people and how, maybe, he could do something to alter this perception. I wanted him to know the reality of people's perceptions and not his imagined one, as "self is developed through the judgements of others". I did not want him to wrongly develop himself thinking that everything was acceptable. I learnt many things from this episode — not least that perception is everything and that, despite our best intentions, we can still be misunderstood. Managing people's expectations is a very delicate matter and it is not something to be taken lightly.

The Power of Negativity

If there was ever a more negative, cynical person, I doubt that person could compare to my ex-colleague whom I shall name X. I first met him when I joined my school and, since we were in the same department, we interacted to a fairly large extent. Initially, I did not really feel that there was anything wrong with him as he was quite friendly to me and frequently told me stories about the history of the school with regards to various members of the staff, the management, etc., and since I was new and knew next to nothing, I quite enjoyed talking to him. However, as the months passed, I realised that most of the stories told by him were of a negative nature: this particular HOD likes to "wayang" (work only in view of authority); this particular Principal was a womanising, biased character; a particular initiative was rubbish and a waste of time; and the like. It was difficult not to get influenced by his opinions as his efforts to "warn" me against certain people would naturally lead me to be more cautious when working with those specific people; in retrospect, I realised this to be rather unproductive.

I began to notice this pattern of negativity when he spoke badly about my SH whom I was close to. It was only then that I realised he had a problem with all forms of authority and that this negativity and cynicism was beginning to affect me in a subtle but unconstructive manner. More and more, I felt quite disturbed by his comments to the extent that I completely stopped talking to him as he was like a constant "wet blanket" who disagreed with everything and was unhappy with almost everybody. The story with X did not end there. Over the years, he became worse and worse to the extent that he passed rude, unnecessary remarks during our departmental meetings, which prompted me to find out the reason for his unpleasant disposition.

He was apparently misunderstood and mistreated by the previous Principal on various occasions. He had also been "stabbed from the back" by a superior whom he was very close to during his years as a beginning teacher. The trauma of those experiences served to mould him on a fundamental level, which resulted in the cynical, negative person that he had become. This again serves to exemplify Cooley's point about the "looking glass". In X's case, an isolated judgement by the Principal on him was the catalyst, which led to his downward spiral to a "me against them" mentality. This, in turn, led to many imagined persecutions by innocent figures of authority. How this relates to me is very simple — I know that it is very easy to be a disillusioned, cynical person and that my past experiences can in fact be fodder for such an eventuality. Working in our particular system of recognition via performance bonuses, performance-linked increments and promotions can lead to many situations where you would feel under-appreciated, victimised even. X is a cautionary tale I use to prevent myself from playing the "victim" as it is a very tempting road to go down.

There have been many reports about the power of positive thinking but I feel sometimes that negativity is like an indomitable virus, which can deteriorate to epidemic-like proportions that positivity simply cannot compete with. It is alarmingly easy to fall into the trap of negativity, as it is very insidious. Its influence is subtle and is almost impossible to detect unless you are especially looking out for it.

My school currently has an alarming negative atmosphere attributable to my Principal who, in his few years in the school, has come up with a slew of unpopular initiatives. There are so many negative remarks flying around that it can be difficult not to join in. As much as I try to remain positive (and here, I seek guidance from some of my supervisors who are able to remain superhumanly positive despite being the most burdened by our Principal), I sometimes get sucked in. This is especially worrying since perception is everything and this negative perception is starting to become a blanket rule when it comes to the teachers, so much so that even when a new initiative which might benefit students is being introduced, there is unhappiness and resistance amongst the teachers. I see this destructive spiral of events and I seem helpless though I know that eventually it would be the students who would suffer as they would be taught by tired, demoralised and uninspired teachers.

The lesson here is, again a simple one. History has proven time and again, that a leader has such an immense responsibility to see beyond the confines of his ego. He cannot allow himself to be surrounded by sycophants who agree to his every word and for a state of criticality to be left uncultivated. Instead, the leaders must allow policies to be challenged. The current system is such that teachers from the ground are afraid to speak out as they may be perceived to be troublemakers and penalised during the ranking exercises. A leader must thus first establish that he values constructive criticism, which is critical for positive change. When it is my time to be a leader, this is what I need to learn, though it is easier said than done.

Of Stagnation and Illumination

After teaching 13- to 17-year-olds in a typical neighbourhood school for some years now, I have found that I have almost imperceptibly, but still significantly, "dumbed" myself down. After years of trying to figure out how these teenagers think, what their likes or dislikes are, and trying to engage them at their level, I sometimes find myself speaking and writing in a different way as compared to when I was in university. I tend to use simpler words, avoid complex or sophisticated ideas and the like. I knew I had to stop the "rot" and it was then that I decided to pursue a Master's degree so as to intellectually stimulate myself. I initially wanted to take up a Master's degree in Political Philosophy, as that was what I read in University, but there were either no available courses which I could apply for or I was not eligible to apply for them, in Singapore at least. I then chanced upon an advertisement for the Physical Education and Sports Science (PDCM) programme by NIE and the rest as they say is history.

After close to two years of taking the course, there have been plenty of ups and downs. There were many instances when I was bogged down by so much work from school and I still had an assignment from some particular module to complete, when I asked myself, "Why am I doing this? Why am I torturing myself?" But the truth of the matter is that I love every minute of the course. I love the intellectual skirmishes, I relish the intense debates that I have in class with a group of like-minded peers and I even savour the last minute completion of essays (not unlike this one) — this is *"mein kampf"* but I am enriched by this struggle in so many ways. Though my purpose in joining this course was largely selfish, I believe that in that self-centred motive lies a selflessness that even I did not realise. I realise now that I have to remain relevant to be of benefit to my students, I have to stay intellectually fresh so as not to be fatigued by the monotony of the everyday work, and I need to have time to myself so that I can be the best that I can be. On top of that, being in the company of like-minded individuals week after week and in the interactions that we have in our group work, discussions (physical or virtual) and the like have enriched me in many intangible ways. I have been updated with various strategic initiatives from MOE past and present and cultivated a network of teachers from all over Singapore. Most of all, the new friends I have made serve to fill up the vacuum in my support network caused by the departure of my close friends from school.

Conclusion

As I read through my somewhat chronological journey as a teacher, I realise that I have learnt many things from many people and, as a result, have grown in so many ways. The social interactions that I have had as a teacher impacted me on many different levels and, relating these back to Cooley, they have made me the individual I am today. I feel like I am a patchwork quilt and the patches consist of these experiences that I have had, good and bad. Though I do not know what the future entails for me, I do know that the quilt is not even half done. I am looking forward to knitting up the rest of the metaphorical quilt.

Chapter 9

Leadership: The Hardware versus the Heartware

Fatimah OTHMAN

My Belief and Philosophy of Leadership

Is this what personal integrity is all about? Are there really no ethics in leadership? Do leaders only work towards achieving their self-interest and personal agenda? These were the questions that constantly played out in my mind during the last two years when I was transferred to another school as a Vice Principal (VP) in December 2009. Although I was not a newly-appointed VP, I experienced the same teething challenges as a beginning teacher in the "Survival Phase". According to Huberman (1992), the first phase in one's teaching trajectory is during the initial three years of entering the teaching profession and it is known as the "Survival and Discovery" phase (p. 126). I felt that I was revisiting the Survival Phase all over again in terms of overcoming the challenges in the new school context which included having to adapt to a new school culture, new colleagues, new job responsibilities as well as to a new Principal, all of whom had rather different expectations of me than the school that I was from. The new learning curve was steep and painful, to say the least, but nothing had prepared me for the bitter experience I was to learn about leadership.

One of my core responsibilities in the new school was to look into the professional growth of the teaching and non-teaching staff, as well as into staff well-being. I enjoy these responsibilities as I am a people-oriented person and I had been told by my previous Principal and Superintendent that my strength lies in working with and managing people. I believe that the time and effort spent in establishing rapport and bonds with a person at a personal level will go a long way and will definitely be of help should difficult situations crop up in the professional context. To me, the heartware definitely takes precedence over the hardware of leadership although I recognise that both are important. The incident that I am about to describe attests to this personal philosophy but, unfortunately, not everyone shares this philosophy of mine.

Mrs. Rahman's story

Mrs. Rahman* was an excellent Mother Tongue (MT) teacher who had taught in the school for the past 30 years. When I was posted to the school in 2010, she was already 59 years of age but her age was not an obstacle to her giving her best. In fact, she was the teacher who reported to school the earliest daily, by 6.20 am. Without fail, she would be in the classroom from 7.00 am till 7.40 am every morning to conduct supplementary MT lessons for the weaker students. In addition, she embraced the school's culture and mission of respecting the dignity of the staff and students and manifested the school's Teachers' Creed in her thoughts, words and deeds. She was also very proud of the ethnic culture and was still active in professional development, both in attending and conducting workshops for the MT department teachers.

To further illustrate the extent of her dedication to teaching and to her students, as well as her great expertise in delivering results, I will relate my personal encounter with Mrs. Rahman even before I was posted to the school. I actually knew of Mrs. Rahman in 2009, a year before I was posted to the school. This is because my daughter, Hanis, had studied in the school and was taught by Mrs. Rahman in Primary Six. Mrs. Rahman took over the class from a less experienced teacher after one term. I was truly grateful to Mrs. Rahman as she was able to motivate Hanis to take an interest in the subject and pulled her grade up from a C in Term 1 to an A at the Primary School Leaving Examination (PSLE) within barely seven months! She did so with her nurturing ways and pep talks, and interested the students in MT by introducing them to classics and poems. She also conducted daily supplementary lessons before school started from 6.50 am till 7.20 am.

Both my Principal and I, who were posted to the school at the same time, thus had a good impression of her from our observations and feedback from the EXCO. We felt that she was extremely kind, diligent and strived to do her best when given any responsibility, and she epitomised what a teacher should be. Hence, we felt secure to leave her to her RO without any additional support from us in terms of addressing underperformance or human relationship issues. Or so we thought…

Based on my detailed records, it happened early one morning on 4 March 2010 at 6.40 am. I received a phone call from a parent of a Primary Six student taking Higher Mother Tongue (HMT). Mr. Nitai* was obviously very upset and his voice boomed into the telephone speaker. This was the gist of our telephone conversation.

Mr. Nitai: "Is that the VP? I want to complain about your MT teacher, Mrs. Rahman, who teaches my daughter in 6 Excellence! How come your school has teachers like that?

Me: "Good morning sir. Yes, this is Mdm. Fatimah, the VP. How may I address you and how can I assist you?"

Mr. Nitai: "I am Mr. Nitai. I won't tell you my daughter's name but I am very angry with Mrs. Rahman. Do you know that my daughter is so terrified of her and does not want to go for her MT lessons? She is so strict, always shouting at the girls. Why is she so rude? Actually, I want to complain to MOE but I thought I speak to you first, and if after that there's still no improvement, I will surely go to MOE!"

Me: "Please calm down Mr. Nitai. I would like to help you. Perhaps you can give me one or two days to verify what you have told me with Mrs. Rahman. I will definitely get back to you after my investigations.

Mr. Nitai: "OK, I leave it to you to handle the matter but if, as I said, there's no improvement, I will go to MOE!"

Me: "Yes Mr. Nitai, I have understood your message. Thank you for your feedback and I will contact you soon when I have completed the investigations. Have a good day ahead."

Mr. Nitai: "OK, thank you. I will wait for your call."

What I had just heard from Mr. Nitai did not match what I knew Mrs. Rahman to be and you can imagine my disbelief. The father had expressed his concern that his daughter was not happy in Mrs. Rahman's MT class as she was very strict and impatient and even shouted at the girls and made remarks that were uncalled for. He also mentioned that the teacher also called the girls a derogatory term meaning "stupid".

My role in Mrs. Rahman's story

As part of the investigation, I had to verify the claims with Mrs. Rahman; and she explained that the comments were taken out of context and she had never used such words, more so since she respects the dignity of the students. She said that she was overly anxious for our students whom she felt were getting more complacent and lacking the drive to try their best and succeed. She also felt that the standard of MT in Singapore was getting from bad to worse and she was doing her best to prevent the situation from going further downhill.

From the interviews conducted with the students, the Reporting Officer (RO) and I realised that Mrs. Rahman was just over-zealous in her duties and in her teaching, and thus she gave a lot of homework to push the girls to do better. It was revealed that she was a little hard of hearing in one ear and that was why she appeared to be raising her voice or sounded very stern when she talked to the students, especially to the younger girls. There was also a generation gap between her and the students, and they were biased against her old-fashioned dressing, way of thinking and naggy ways. We also realised that she was starting to have class management difficulties with the lower primary class as she could not manage the active, chatty and inattentive students.

I spoke to her and advised her to be more patient with the girls and to give them pep talks instead; positive illustrations to encourage them to work hard would be a better solution. It would also make the environment more cordial and pleasant for everyone, more so with high ability students, who would have their own strong opinions about things. She was receptive to the feedback and suggestions for improvement and agreed to be more patient, as well as talk to the students and build a rapport with them.

Mrs. Rahman seemed to take the advice given to heart and all was well between her and the students for the next few weeks. Unfortunately, that was not to be as, within the next month, three more complaints came in from the parents. What really went wrong with Mrs. Rahman that year was really a mystery. In all, from the first complaint on 4 March 2010 till the last complaint on 1 November 2010, there were about eleven from parents and students themselves had come to my office to express their grievances! A few parents also complained to the Full-Time School Counsellor (FTSC) and their children's form teachers about Mrs. Rahman, and they in turn updated me. Their complaints regarding Mrs. Rahman were targeted more at her attitude towards the students rather than on her teaching or marking. A number of parents were also angry that she carried out supplementary lessons every morning as they felt she was depriving their children of more sleep. When I explained that it was not compulsory for their daughters to attend, they demanded that Mrs. Rahman stop conducting the lessons or else their daughters would lose out to those who attended. Such were some of the more demanding and unreasonable parents who really make a teacher's job really tough these days and I was more determined than ever to help Mrs. Rahman in whatever way I could.

Although I was kept very busy managing the upset parents and students, and had to do many rounds of interviews with students to verify their claims and then counsel the teacher, I was not angry with Mrs. Rahman. Having known her to be a warm person and an excellent teacher, I had a soft spot for her and felt more sad for her and wanted to know why she was going through such a rough patch with the students and parents, when this had never happened in all her years of teaching. I was also worried about her self-esteem and well-being too, and I often caught up with her just to check on her status. Although many parents had threatened to complain directly to MOE, I am glad that I was able to mediate and close the cases at my level. I was able to do so by telling them how good and committed a teacher Mrs. Rahman was with my personal testimony about how she had helped Hanis, who still remembers her with fondness. The parents were also appreciative that I did not take their complaints lightly and had done my investigations before updating them of the outcomes and follow-up actions promptly. Although I sometimes had the thought that perhaps I was too biased towards Mrs. Rahman, sheltering and protecting her too much and in fact doing her more harm, I shrugged the thought away in the belief that I was being true to my philosophy of leadership with a heart.

True affirmation of leadership with a heart?

Throughout the whole year of managing Mrs. Rahman, the complaints and the investigations, I always kept in mind my position as a VP and updated my Principal faithfully on the full details of every case and the follow-up actions taken. My Principal seemed pleased with the way I handled the various stakeholders and constantly affirmed my progress, saying that she supported my actions and that she was glad I had managed to stop any parent from complaining to the higher authorities. She was also pleased with the sincere effort and improvements made by Mrs. Rahman. She expressed her gratitude to me for being so diligent and for spending so much extra time managing these cases on top of my other administrative and professional duties. There was not a moment that caused me to suspect that she was not pleased with the way I was doing things.

In fact, she even had the School Staff Developer (SSD), whom she was grooming to be a VP, sit in with me as I did my investigations with Mrs. Rahman and the students and also when I updated the parents thereafter. She felt that managing the stakeholders' expectations was a key responsibility of school leaders and felt that the SSD had much to learn from me in this aspect. Of course, I was very pleased and grateful thinking that I had such an enlightened supervisor who recognised my leadership philosophy and contributions. Hence, I felt affirmed in my leadership philosophy and was happy carrying out the extra duties despite the heavy workload.

Despite the many complaints, Mrs. Rahman still kept up a strong front and was receptive to any feedback given. Based on her RO's observations and my own, as we made our daily rounds, we could see Mrs. Rahman making a big attempt to employ the strategies we recommended. However, whenever I spoke with her privately in my room, she admitted that she felt very demoralised, very upset and disappointed that this should happen near the end of her teaching career. It did not help that she could not understand what was happening and was starting to get paranoid of stepping into the classroom in case she did something wrong again. I spent a lot of time just lending a listening ear and trying my best to reassure her that she was still a good and dedicated teacher. I was very mindful not to let her lose her self-esteem or go into a depression, given the fragile state she was in.

Tensions and cracks: Part 1

However, sometime around the middle of the year, my Principal was getting frustrated with all the complaints about Mrs. Rahman. She called Mrs. Rahman into her office with me and told her that if she did not put a stop to all the complaints, she would be given a warning letter and a "D" grade at ranking that year for not maintaining a good relationship with the stakeholders. She also mentioned some of the things that I had told her during the investigations with Mrs. Rahman and made it sound like I had disapproved of Mrs. Rahman's actions as well. One can only imagine the shock and disbelief when I heard what my Principal had said in the session. In fact, to put it bluntly, I felt betrayed as I had no idea that she had felt that way about Mrs. Rahman or about the situation, and that she had not informed me earlier that she was calling for the session. I really felt so bad for Mrs. Rahman and felt that I had led her on and "betrayed" her trust too, like a two-headed snake.

After the session, Mrs. Rahman asked to talk to me in private where she really broke down. I could not help myself and I cried as well, as I just felt so sorry for her and for being betrayed. She had on many occasions mentioned that she was fortunate and appreciative to have me as her VP and for helping her through the crisis. I tried to console her by telling her that she had made lots of effort to improve, and I also apologised to her and explained that I had known nothing of my Principal's intentions. Mrs. Rahman was understanding and I was grateful that she believed me and did not think any the worse of me. Being one who was respectful of people in authority and who liked things to be in a state of harmony, I did not dare to question my Principal on why she had called for the session without my prior knowledge. On hindsight, I should have been brave and spoken up about how I had felt. There was definitely much tension there but I chose to keep quiet instead. By keeping silent, I showed that I was timid and could be taken advantage of. It also showed that I did not believe in Mrs. Rahman enough to speak up for her. How stupid I was!

Tensions and cracks: Part 2

Well, from then on, things between my Principal and me just were not the same as before. I was now very cautious when talking to her and my suspicions showed. When in the past I used to be more open and friendly with her, I now spoke only when necessary or when she asked me questions. Alas, things only got worse as Mrs. Rahman was still getting complaints; so, at the beginning of August, my Principal instructed me to pen a warning letter to be signed by the both of us and given to Mrs. Rahman. Again, I was too timid to question her motives and speak up for what I felt and believed in. I felt so bad penning the letter and sitting in same room when the letter was handed to Mrs. Rahman. She was sternly reprimanded by the Principal for not showing an improvement and not manifesting the school's Teachers' Creed. She was also told off for not being loving and nurturing towards the students like any teacher should. Again the Principal warned her that she would most likely be given the "D" grade at ranking that year. At that moment, I felt sick to the stomach to hear that from a leader, who was meant to inspire hope, not fear. I also felt disgusted with the system that called for school leaders to assess and rank teachers. Who are we that we are given the authority to do so to others and for others to do likewise to us? This is the part of the hardware of leadership that I still grapple with and have difficulty coming to terms with.

It was a truly demoralising session for Mrs. Rahman, and despite her pleading with the Principal and my affirmation of the improvements she had made, my Principal turned a deaf ear to us. It was yet another "betrayal" incident for me. Once again, this was the decision and action of the Principal without consulting me although I was the one who had been dealing with Mrs. Rahman and the situation all the while. However, being the timid person that I am, I brushed my feelings away and immediately got the RO and FTSC together to think of how we could better support Mrs. Rahman in her even more fragile state now. As mentioned, my teachers' well-being is always more important to me than anything else as their mental state of being will affect the way they teach and interact with the students.

The first thing the FTSC, RO and I did was to have a counselling session with Mrs. Rahman to assess her emotional state and then we talked to her about managing her anger and frustration. We told her that she could not take full responsibility for the students and hold herself accountable for all their misdeeds. Finally, we also advised her to see things from the students' point of view: that they would prefer a warm, nurturing teacher who could joke and laugh with them.

True affirmation of leadership with a heart

Although there were still complaints till the end of the year, we were heartened that Mrs. Rahman had made an effort to put into practice our recommendations and seemed to be a bit more relaxed and cheerful. The three of us made extra effort to meet up with her almost daily to ask about her or offer her advice or a listening ear. Fortunately, as her class results for all the levels she taught were very good and as she was making an effort to improve, she was not given the "D" grade. She took that as an encouragement and recognition, and her self-esteem increased and she was motivated again. There was a positive change in her whole outlook of teaching and towards the students and the parents. I was very happy for her and all the effort spent on helping her when two students and a parent told me that they could see a change for the better in Mrs. Rahman. The two students even mentioned that they were starting to enjoy Mrs. Rahman's lessons! These positive strokes were happily conveyed to Mrs. Rahman who took them as further encouragement to do even better.

The whole episode that year also held many learning points for me as a school leader. We advocate differentiated instruction for students, but what about for teachers? We emphasise student-centredness, but what about teachers? A teacher's well-being is also very important as how she feels will definitely have an impact on her students. It also reaffirmed my belief that we should always spend time and effort to build good interpersonal relationships with the teachers first, so that they will be more receptive to our suggestions and feedback without being defensive when difficult situations arise.

It is precisely because of my strong philosophy as a school leader, in valuing teachers and leading with a heart, that all turned out well for Mrs. Rahman. Unfortunately though, the episode was also a turning point for me and caused me to reassess my priorities.

Where's the ethics in leadership?

I was in for a really rude shock when my Principal conducted the year-end work review session with me sometime in October. She outrightly told me that she had marked me down for not being able to manage Mrs. Rahman's situation well. She said that I was a weak VP who sided with the teacher and did not take the parents' and students' views seriously. She felt that I was also too soft with Mrs. Rahman and that was why the complaints kept on coming in despite me spending so much time counselling her and advising her. She felt that the time spent with Mrs. Rahman and the investigations could have been used more productively in developing the other teachers and on more strategic matters. When I asked her why she had not told me so all this while and had instead reaffirmed my actions, she said that she was hoping that I would be able to realise my "mistake" and "wake up" on my own. She also said that I would not have been able to take her harsh words and carry out my duties if she had told me off from the start. She also admitted that although I did not manage the teacher well, she was glad about the way I managed to appease the parents and students. She also went on to bring up other instances of my "wrongdoings", which she had never mentioned in the past. I knew then that nothing I said would be able to reverse her decision and her perspective of me and of the situation as she was a hard-headed and stern woman. I held back my tears, from feeling betrayed and humiliated, and let her go on although by then I was numb to what she was saying. That sickening feeling I had when we handed Mrs. Rahman the warning letter came gushing back again. Is this how a leader guides and motivates her subordinates? Where is the ethics in leadership? My previous Principals had always emphasised that personal integrity is a value that has to be applied to all aspects of our job in order to gain the respect from others. They also taught me that leaders have to walk the talk, be honest and fair, so as to set a positive tone and culture for the staff and students to emulate.

After the very painful session, I went back to my office and went about the day's duties as per normal although I was breaking inside. It was only when I got home that evening, in the privacy of my bedroom, that I finally broke down and cried my heart out. All the bottled up and pent up feelings of pain, hurt, betrayal and even intense bitterness came out in torrents of tears. Why did she not tell me and guide me when I did not do things right? Was she only using me for her benefit and self-interest? Why did she put up a front and pretend that all was well between us? Again, where was the ethics in her leadership? I realised that both my Principal and I had differing leadership styles and I knew that I would never compromise my philosophy and beliefs. I also realised then that I had lost all respect for her as I felt she did not have any personal integrity and did not value my dignity as a person, which was central to our school's creed. After

I had calmed down and thought through carefully, I felt that it would be best for me to take a break and to re-focus my priorities on my family and my own professional development by applying for professional development leave to pursue my Masters' degree. When I told my Principal about it a few days later, she supported my application and agreed it was best for me to take a year off to reflect, re-charge and renew myself professionally.

My learning: Part 1

On the whole, there were two different directions in which this whole episode panned out and concluded. On one hand, as a supervisor, I found it personally satisfying and fulfilling the way I managed the episode with Mrs. Rahman and all the stakeholders involved and I would not have changed anything. At the end of the year, just before the start of the December vacation, Mrs. Rahman came into my office with a beautifully wrapped Christmas gift to thank me for helping her through the difficult year. She gave me the gift, hugged me and, with tears in her eyes, whispered, "If not for you and your kind understanding and assistance, I would have suffered a mental breakdown." Mrs. Rahman's RO and the FTSC had also affirmed my actions when they told me that they had learnt a lot from me in terms of managing people in a humane and compassionate way. The parents who had made the complaints were also appreciative of the way I had managed their feedback, done the investigations and resolved the issues between Mrs. Rahman and their daughters. These affirmed my belief and philosophy of leadership and convinced me that the heartware was definitely more important in leadership.

I am also truly heartened that MOE has come out in strong support of our teachers. In the 2012 MOE Workplan Seminar opening Address by Minister Heng Swee Keat, he said that in order to have "teachers who care, we must care for our teachers. Not just school leaders, but parents and our community at large must support our teachers" (MOE, 2012).

It is a good reminder that, at the end of the day, we are dealing with people and not just processes or products. It also re-affirmed my belief that a core responsibility of school leaders is to look after the well-being of the staff and that it should not be overlooked in the pursuit of achieving excellent results or to achieve one's personal agenda. According to Hargreaves (2001), school leaders need to provide emotional leadership in terms of encouraging and supporting their teachers' professional initiatives as teaching involves a lot of emotional work and human relationships.

My learning: Part 2

On the other hand, although I did not gain favour with my Principal as a supervisee, the bitter and painful episode held many invaluable learning points for me. Having had the year off to do this Masters' course has given me the opportunity to reflect on my beliefs and practices as a school leader as well. A few modules on this course, including writing this narrative, have made me realise that I may not have seen things from my Principal's perspective objectively. I had seen the whole episode from my perspective as a diligent VP who had done her best for her teacher and yet was unfairly judged. On hindsight, I now realise that what she had said makes sense and that I had been very defensive when she had correctly pointed out my weaknesses. The humiliation of being told off, coupled with my pride and self-pity, had immediately erected a barrier between us.

I now realise, too, that I may have been too soft with Mrs. Rahman, sheltering and protecting her by speaking up for her and deflecting all blame away from her even when the students were able to provide the evidence. Perhaps I had also indulged in her self-pity and seen things only from her point of view and not from the parents' or students' perspectives. Was I too biased towards her only because of my intense gratitude for what she had done for Hanis? Did I actually do her more harm by doing so and thus slow her rate of learning and improving with each complaint? I also agree with my Principal that I had "wasted" time with Mrs. Rahman when I could have used it more productively to develop the other teachers and for more strategic matters. By focusing all my energy on only one teacher, I had neglected developing the others who would have benefitted from my guidance as well. As a leader, I had to have a heart for all within the school, not just for one particular person.

Being able to come to terms now with what had happened then and to see things from my Principal's perspectives have helped to ease the bitterness and pain that I have been carrying with me the past year. In a sense, too, this narrative has definitely created a mediational space through which I have been able to self-reflect and recognise the contradiction in my beliefs and practices as a school leader and that of my Principal's, much like what Golombek and Johnson (2004) posited.

Perhaps I would have been more receptive to my Principal's comments and feedback if she had told me these things over the course of our daily interactions. The manner in which it was put across was also very harsh and definitely did nothing to respect my dignity. This is a good learning point for me too because, as school leaders, what we say and do and how we put things across have many implications. We must learn to do so without crushing another's self-esteem, self-confidence and, most of all, self-worth. To me, school leaders play a critical role in setting the tone and culture of the school and we must always walk the talk in order to gain the respect of the staff.

Although leading with a heart, to value the teachers for their worth and as humans beings, will still be my priority, I will keep in mind the wider context and be more aware of the implications of my actions. I must say that, despite all that has happened, I am at peace with myself and that is what matters most, and that I am able to respect myself in all that I do in both my personal and professional capacities.

*Pseudonym used.

References

Golombek, P. R. & Johnson, K. E. (2004). Narrative inquiry as a mediational space: Examining emotional and cognitive dissonance. *Teachers and Teaching: Theory and Practice*, 10 (3), 301–327.

Hargreaves, A., Earl, L., Moore, B. & Manning, S. (eds.) (2001). *Learning to Change: Teaching Beyond Subjects and Standards*. San Fancisco: Jossey-Bass Inc.

Huberman, M. (1992). Teacher development and instructional mastery. In A. Hargreaves and M. G. Fullan (eds.). *Understanding Teacher Development*. New York: Teachers College Press.

Ministry of Education (2012). Opening address by Mr. Heng Swee Keat, Minister for Education, at the Ministry of Education (MOE) work plan seminar, 12 September 2012. Retrieved from http://www.moe.gov.sg/media/speeches/2012/09/12/keynote-address-by-mr-heng-swee-keat-at-wps-2012.php.

Chapter 10

Sunshine after the Rain — A Reflection on My Teaching Career

*Melanie**

January 2008 was a memorable month for me, as I had become a teacher then. It took me tremendous courage to switch careers. Prior to teaching, I held a job as a mechanical design engineer in two local shipbuilding firms. I had selected mechanical engineering in University as there was a strong demand for engineers then. The career was deemed as highly respectable, with good future prospects and commanding quite a reasonable starting pay. Attracted by these perks, I entered Engineering without giving much thought to whether I would be interested in the job. Working in the marine industry was extremely tough. I had to juggle various demands and learn on the job quickly as I was thrown into various projects immediately after joining the company. The learning curve was undeniably steep. However, I learnt the ropes quickly and undertook a number of large projects. Being an engineer requires both analytical and negotiation skills, as we have to be involved in systems design, site inspections and meetings with both vendors and customers simultaneously. I also honed my skills in multi-tasking as time went by. With such a hectic lifestyle, long hours at work and constant pressure to deliver the product on time, I started asking myself if this was what I envisioned in a long term career. I did not see myself in this career for life as it was far too stressful, I had little time for my family and I found myself unable to spend time on my interests and hobbies. I was suffering from a mid-career crisis. It was after four years in Engineering that the thought of a career switch fleeted across my mind.

When I was younger, I had seriously considered taking up teaching as a career. I found teaching very meaningful and enjoyable, and I also liked the fact that teaching would allow me to interact with people. I enjoyed the interaction with youths and wanted to help them develop as better persons in their journey towards adulthood and independence. I did not have relatives who were able to give me valuable advice on my career choices. I had the naïve impression that teaching involved mainly interaction with students with little focus on administrative tasks. I also thought that there would be lesser politicking and meetings with bosses as the main bulk of time spent would be on lesson preparations and teaching in the classroom. I wanted a career switch and teaching seemed like the next best thing.

I discussed with my mother on this matter. She strongly opposed the idea of me being a teacher as she had the impression that teachers had a heavy workload and lacked work-life balance. She must have talked to her friends whose children were teachers and that led her to come to this conclusion. However, I was very insistent that I wanted to seek new opportunities in my career and went ahead to apply for a teaching position. My mother was disappointed at my decision and would pass snide remarks, and she even predicted that I would eventually regret my decision. She persuaded me that it was a rash decision to give up on a high paying job. She knew very little about the stress that I was facing at work and could not come to terms with the fact that I would rather forgo being an engineer. The tensions that I faced during that period were intense. I tried to avoid my mother so that I would not argue with her on this matter. Despite the opposition, I decided I really wanted to teach and went ahead with the interview without my mother's support. I succeeded in the first interview. I was rather surprised with my persistence in my career switch as I had always been rather obedient and agreed readily to her wishes. It was a refreshing change for a start as it was a first step to recognising what I really wanted for myself instead of following blindly what most people deemed was the right thing to do. The short stint of teacher training in the National Institute of Education (NIE) gave me the opportunity to induct myself to the pedagogies in teaching. I felt I was ready and confident to be a classroom teacher. My mother, upon seeing my dedication, also decided to give me her blessings and secretly hoped that her fears would not come true.

I was assigned to a Special Assistance Plan (SAP) school in the eastern part of Singapore, with subject specialisation in Physics and Mathematics. Throughout the four years in teaching, I was fortunate to have great Head of Departments (HODs), Reporting Officers (ROs) and colleagues who rendered help to me in whichever way possible. I liked the warm and cooperative atmosphere in school and looked forward to working with the students and colleagues daily, or so I thought. During the first three years of teaching, I was assigned to teach both Physics and Mathematics due to manpower considerations. I devoted a huge amount of time to improving my pedagogies. My main focus was on classroom teaching and I was extremely concentrated on lesson delivery. With my background as a mechanical engineer, I admitted that I had greater fascinations with teaching Physics compared to Mathematics. It was partly due to my ability to relate many relevant applications of physics to real life. I was eager to share how the knowledge of weight and centre of gravity in Physics is critical as it determines the stability and propulsion system of ship design. My Physics lessons consisted of trigger activities such as demonstrations, videos to illustrate physics concepts and computer simulations. I was obviously excited to share with my students the interesting facts and expose them to such applications beyond the classroom. On the contrary, I found myself inadequate when it came to teaching Mathematics. I would feel frustrated with myself at delivering a "boring" Mathematics lesson, with more emphasis on the skill sets and techniques instead. Interestingly, students tend to find Mathematics more manageable compared to

Physics. They tend to derive greater satisfaction in the subject as they tend to score better. Physics is seen as a more abstract and difficult subject to grasp. Thus, even though I preferred Physics, it was practically more challenging to gain students' interest in the subject.

Though I was teaching both subjects, the school had assigned Mdm. T, the Mathematics HOD, to be my RO. Mdm. T entered the school in the same year as me and assumed HOD position then. I would consider Mdm. T to be a rather dynamic, driven and assertive lady. The Mathematics department consisted of mainly younger, inexperienced teachers. Upon assuming her role, Mdm. T considered it one of her main responsibilities to level up the teaching expertise of her staff quickly. To this end, she set high expectations and requested staff to adhere to certain standards and routines when teaching Mathematics. Other initiatives that she implemented included the sharing of resources, frequent sharing sessions and encouraging all staff to attend courses related to pedagogy. Her leadership philosophy was firmly grounded on the fact that when her staff performed well, it was a strong affirmation of her leadership abilities. Such beliefs were strongly affirmed during my yearly work reviews where she would constantly stress the importance of young officers being more "visible" and proactive in their undertakings. Her reasoning was that people in the organisation would notice the officer's contributions, which would be an extremely useful criterion for one to rise up the ranks.

I had just joined the teaching fraternity not too long ago and my main concern was to polish my teaching and learning so as to assist my students in gaining valuable knowledge. I was not very concerned about promotions, as long as my yearly bonuses were reasonable and reflected my contributions to the organisation. On the other hand, Mdm. T's priority was focused on enhancing her job holders' (JH) performances and contributions. She was greatly involved with the happenings of her staff and would expect to be notified if there were any concerns or issues pertaining to student matters that would invariably implicate staff. I was unable to reconcile with her way of thought as I thought she was too rigid in her way of thought. Nevertheless, I followed her instructions respectfully without questioning. Even though I had been working in the private industry for several years prior to teaching and I was used to voicing out my opinions, I did not put forth my views on this matter during our meetings. I supposed it was due to her assertive nature whereas I was not so confrontational in my approach. Moreover, I had this impression that unlike the private sector, where office politics can be rather intense, there would be very little politicking in the teaching organisation and that as long as I perform my teaching duties well, I would be able to achieve my due recognition. In my opinion, Mdm. T seemed to be overly concerned with fame and recognition, and I found that it was not necessary to announce one's contributions so visibly. If a job was well done, it would be recognised anyway.

Despite my disagreements on some matters, Mdm. T was an extremely supportive RO and gave me many opportunities as a beginning teacher to experiment and coordinate various projects. Under her charge, she provided many opportunities for me to develop my leadership potential, such as recommending me to be the overall in charge of the sponsorship committee for our school anniversary dinner. I was grateful to her for giving me such chances. Our relationship was cordial, and sometimes I felt that my personality, being the adaptable person I am, allowed me to follow her working style more easily.

Interestingly, I never thought that I would encounter a significant event in my teaching career involving a conflict with Mdm. T. It all began in November 2011, and I clearly remember that it was this period of time when our school decided to undergo major renovations. One of the first tasks undertaken by the contractors involved the construction of a single staffroom in the school blocks. As our school has a long history, the staffroom consisted of five different rooms at various locations. To enhance communication, it was timely to build a common staffroom. During the renovation period, a makeshift staffroom was constructed for the Physics department. The makeshift staffroom was able to accommodate roughly 10 Physics teachers during the interim period. Even though it was small, we found the temporary staffroom to be a nice and cosy area. The Physics department consisted mostly of male teachers, who were also formerly from the engineering industry, and it was headed by our Section Head, Mdm. S. I enjoyed the rapport with my Physics department colleagues as they were jovial and easy-going. The atmosphere in the staffroom was relaxed and we enjoyed the luxury of talking and joking without disturbing the rest. The Section Head of Physics, Mdm. S, was also seated in the staffroom then. Mdm. S used to be an engineer as well. She was a spontaneous, straightforward and humorous lady. She communicated with us easily and had no airs about her. Her style was more relaxed and, though she may not have been as assertive as Mdm. T, she was able to gather the support of her colleagues to get the job done. I found Mdm. S more approachable compared to Mdm. T and felt less tense during her presence. I also treated her more like a colleague instead of a superior.

What triggered the unexpected event was the discussion on subject specialisation. Two of my female colleagues, who were straddling both Mathematics and Physics, requested to specialise in Mathematics and it was approved. As they were both Mathematics major students during University days, it was more manageable for them to teach Mathematics. With this arrangement, they would be full-fledged Mathematics teachers beginning 2011. Though the Physics department would have fewer teachers, Mdm. S understood their inclinations and was agreeable to the arrangement. I had given little thought to the idea of subject specialisation due to several reasons. Firstly, most of the Science and Mathematics teachers in the school tended to straddle both subjects in their early years of teaching. Secondly, I never found it a big deal to specialise, partly because I was happy teaching both subjects. Though I was able to relate to the real life applications in Physics better, I found that most students found greater satisfaction solving Mathematics problems and it was a breeze to teach Mathematics. Besides, most of the students did very well in Mathematics and the results were an affirmation that I was teaching them well. With such considerations, I was comfortable teaching both subjects. Lastly, I was happy having Mdm. T as my RO and I did not want to rock the boat since my RO was supportive. In the event that I had to specialise, Mdm. T might no longer be my RO and I would have to start building up a relationship with my new RO, which would take time and lots of communication.

I remember there was a casual discussion with Mdm. S and a few colleagues about subject specialisation in the staffroom. During the discussion, I did mention that the benefits of subject specialisation would be lesser subject preparation and lesser meetings to attend. I blurted out casually that, if given a choice, I would not mind specialising in Physics. I was able to answer this question very frankly because I personally felt more at ease teaching Physics. My choice was purely based on my greater interests and confidence in the subject area. Not a thought arose with regard to the department dynamics and relationship with my superior. Besides, it was a hypothetical question which I naively thought would have no implications, as I had assumed it was an informal conversation. Little would I expect that such a statement would be the start of a string of troubles that would cause me sleepless nights in the weeks to come.

I had totally forgotten that this discussion had taken place until a week later when Mdm. T came to me during flag raising ceremony. She requested to see me in a discussion room immediately after that. She seemed rather upset and disturbed. It did not occur to me that anything was wrong. When we were seated, she started firing off and questioned why I wanted to specialise in Physics but had not told her directly even though she was my RO. She was upset that she had to learn of my plans from someone else, and she felt that I was not frank about my feelings with her on this issue. I was taken aback by the sudden turn of events; in fact I was shocked! The confrontation took place so abruptly that it took me a while to understand the situation. After I had gathered my thoughts and clarified with the relevant parties involved, I then realised this was the sensitive period of manpower deployment and that Mdm. S had talked to the HOD (Science) about my interest in specialising in Physics! Due to manpower considerations, the HOD (Science) was more than eager to take me into the department as a full-fledged Physics teacher. I sorted out the situation, which had arisen due to a misunderstanding resulting from miscommunication from both parties. I tried explaining to Mdm. T the entire situation. Apparently she was annoyed that

I had approached the Subject Head privately to request for specialisation, which was definitely not the case. During our conversation, she discussed at length that it was her responsibility to ensure that her JH were well taken care of under her charge and that meant giving them opportunities to excel at various platforms. However, if I decided to specialise eventually, it would be a wasted effort on her part as she would no longer be my RO after that. I was stunned when she said that she would release me to the Science department since it was something I wanted, and she saw no point in grooming me in Mathematics if the decision was for me to specialise in Physics in the near future. She gave me several days to think it over and requested that I give her my reply.

My first instinct upon hearing it was that of disbelief. I was definitely not ready for such an abrupt turn of events and my mind was bursting from the complications that had resulted from the mindless remarks I had made. I was devastated as I had never anticipated something like that coming from her. During the next few days, I cried and thought hard about this incident. Firstly, I was upset, and felt that Mdm. T was very harsh in her actions and had not tried to understand how I felt. She did not clarify and was not interested in my explanation. Her emotions had overtaken the willingness to reason and listen. Besides, I was not ready to specialise as I had spent time on improving my Mathematics pedagogies during these past years, and there were plans for me to undertake a financial literacy project for the Secondary One students next year. I was full of anticipation for the upcoming projects. All my efforts and previous contributions to the department would have gone to waste if I were to be suddenly deployed in the Science department. Besides, I was also upset that Mdm. S did not clarify with me on my intentions and had made the assumption that I would be ready to fully teach Physics the following year. I felt totally helpless and victimised in this whole incident involving power play between two departments. I felt like a chess piece being manipulated and thrown around. Though Mdm. T asked me to think through and give her a reply, I could not imagine myself staying on in the Mathematics department after such a misunderstanding, which many people had come to know of soon after.

I imagined she would now think differently of me as she felt betrayed that I did not inform her of my intentions. I also wondered if it would adversely affect my performance and relationship with her as a superior. I felt truly helpless and abandoned by the Mathematics department. I was fortunate to have the support of my family members who comforted and gave me valuable advice that enabled me to tide over the difficult period.

I had also tried to clarify with Mdm. S about this incident. She was apologetic about the turn of events. She consoled and welcomed me with open arms to the department. I became a full-fledged Physics teacher in January 2011. Interestingly, I did not reflect much about how Mdm. S had played a significant part in causing the conflict and remained cordial with her after that, probably because I was in need of emotional support and she was there as a colleague for me. Upon reflection, I was sure she played a part in triggering this event but it would not have been possible without my support in this case. There were definitely misunderstandings and misinterpretations of my actual intention during the communication between Mdm. T and the Science HOD. As a teacher, I felt sandwiched, emotionally drained and helpless, as I was unable to fend for myself amidst the confusion.

The unexpected turn of events meant that I was quickly removed from all Mathematics department communications, which meant that I no longer needed to attend the year-end department meeting since I was no longer part of the team. I also had to answer many questions from curious colleagues who noticed that abrupt change in department deployment. Unfortunately, I also noticed that some colleagues in the Mathematics department, whom I was friendly with initially, had started avoiding me. They started to view me differently. It was as if I had betrayed the department by choosing to abandon them at this stage in time. After trying to explain to some colleagues about what had actually happened on several occasions, I reckoned that it was pointless to discuss this incident any further as there were different viewpoints on this matter. I was also disturbed by the unnecessary gossip and mindless comments from colleagues who were not involved in the issue. I felt embarrassed when I thought about how naïve I had been during my casual conversation which resulted in my being embroiled in this situation. I had no wish to further discuss and clarify the details of the event with anyone. I wanted to move on in my career.

This incident left an indelible impression on me. As I revisited this incident again, I had to confront my feelings. I reflected that I should have been more careful with my words and that communications under different situations would lead to unintended consequences. On second thought, I reflected that there could be better ways to handle the situation. Ever since I began my career, I had not encountered direct conflicts with colleagues and bosses. In reality, I prefer a non-confrontational approach to resolving issues. As a young engineer fresh out of school, my relationships with my bosses had been more of the deferent style and it had worked well for me over the years. I had not crawled out of my cocoon to be upfront with regards to my stand and opinion on certain issues. That had resulted in my lack of experience in handling difficult and tricky situations.

In the instance with Mdm. T, I could have been more honest with my feelings about teaching both Physics and Mathematics during my work reviews. I did secretly prefer teaching Physics to Mathematics, and admitted to putting in significantly more effort in my lesson planning in Physics. Instead of just griping about it, I could have made more effort in developing stronger pedagogies in Mathematics by attending more courses. I could have been more open and honest during such discussions, and also worked on a more appropriate approach to resolve the internal conflicts that I was experiencing. By conveniently brushing this matter aside, I gave Mdm. T the impression that I was happy with my current career projections and my deployment in both departments. Through this incident, I have realised that effective communication in an organisation is critical. It is not wise to wait for things to happen before I speak up my mind. Also, it is important to be clear in my communication with my co-workers. A thoughtless phrase could have very different implications for another and it is a necessity to be mindful of forthright speaking and to use the appropriate channels to speak up in an organisation.

The incident has definitely opened up my eyes to the bureaucracy inherent in an organisation. In the previous organisations that I was at, there clearly was politics beneath the surface, and we saw it most clearly during the weekly meetings where departments come together to make decisions. I was rather naïve to assume that a school or institution would operate differently from a business organisation since the school revolves around the needs of the learner in contrast to commercial considerations. I have a greater appreciation of the manpower issues, deployment and power struggles in organisations. School leaders, HODs and even teachers struggle to resolve these constraints. In my case, the incident invariably created a good opportunity for a power struggle, and I had also incidentally become a victim of it.

Two years on, I am now a key appointment holder (KP) in the same institution. Being in this position enables me to appreciate the operations, issues and constraints surrounding the institution. I have begun to understand how Mdm. T felt when she heard from others about my request. I have also pondered on how I would have handled the situation differently if I had been in her shoes. I would also appreciate that my fellow workers trust me and approach me directly when they are encountering difficulties at work. I have learnt to be more careful in my everyday conversations with others, as well as my communications with my committee members. As I look at the more vocal and newer colleagues who have joined the institution, I constantly remind myself to be more vigilant in my speech and actions and to conduct myself in a responsible manner. Whenever there are opportunities, I also encourage the younger colleagues to be more positive in their actions and thoughts. Even if there are disagreements, they should seek appropriate platforms to constructively voice out their opinions instead of grousing with one another.

Nevertheless, I do think that the event was a blessing in disguise. One and a half years on after the incident, I now have better clarity in my work scope and also enjoy having the flexibility and time to prepare my Physics lessons and improve on my pedagogies in my area of interest. I focus on building positive relationships with my fellow colleagues and we work together as a team to level up our expertise in our subject area. I have also learnt to let go of the unhappiness that I harboured towards Mdm. T as I realised that this incident is a learning point in my career and it is childish to bear grudges as professionals. Our relationship gradually improved over the years through gradual contact in our job areas; we were both able to let go of the incident and share with each other our experiences at work. In reality, I would not be where I am now if not for the support and opportunities that she had given me. I was glad we were both mature and able to look at the matter objectively and to reconcile whatever grievances we used to have. No doubt the incident created troubles and tensions in my teaching career, but I have gained serenity and a sense of closure. The wisdom gained from the incident truly benefited my development as a teacher and will continue to do so in the years ahead.

*Pseudonym used.

Chapter 11

To Stand on My Own Two Feet

Ting Ting LEE

Looking back at my entire trajectory starting from 1994 till now, it is certainly nothing short of a never-ending string of changes and progressions. Along the way, the journey is of course interwoven with its fair share of ups and downs, tears and laughter, success and failure, just like everyone else's. For this chapter, I have anchored my narrative inquiry on one period of my career that was really etched in my memory. It is with this inquiry that I have finally uncovered the real lessons that this extraordinarily trying period is meant to teach me — about the impact of my egoistic self in framing the whole context of much of my sufferings then, as well as the shock of how a significant part of my personal beliefs has been proven to be wrong and irrelevant in reality.

In 2002, I returned to the education service after a short stint outside; and having missed teaching for the past two years, I was all ready to plunge right into the work of teaching and working with the students.

The new environment seemed decent enough. The Principal, Mrs. A, was a strict and no-nonsense person who had high expectations of all teachers to produce results, including the Chinese Language (CL) teachers. The Head of Department (HOD), Ms. B, in her late fifties, was a very traditional Nantah-graduated CL teacher with strong beliefs and pride about the value and traditions of CL. As the HOD, she "ruled" the department with an iron-fist, and often was explicit in highlighting the importance of the CL teachers' compliance to her leadership and high expectations at work. However, she pushed herself hard as well and treated everyone fairly well, and the department functioned and got along as normal as it could.

As the newcomer and the youngest CL teacher there, I seemed to have started well too. Having been brought up in a traditional Chinese home, I had learnt to treat all figures of authority with respect and obedience, and was often praised as the "good girl" whom many elders were especially fond of. With this attitude and mannerism, I assimilated into the department's culture quite easily, and, not unexpectedly, seemed to have won Ms. B's approval quickly; I was all ready to do my best in this new school.

However, despite my respect for the school's HOD and CL teachers, I could not help but find that the way CL was taught was generally rigid and mundane. The Scheme of Work (SOW) followed the textbook activities closely with an emphasis on rote-learning of basic language skills so as to enhance the very weak language foundations of most students. As a result, CL was commonly perceived to be a very boring and difficult subject that many students disliked, which I could empathise with fully. Based on my teaching experience in other schools, I believed that to put things right, I would first have to work on connecting with the students as well as making the lessons more interesting. And so I did. I tried hard to work around the stipulated plans outlined in the SOWs, and exercised flexibility in creating spaces for a variety of language activities to be included in my lessons. Within a few months, the atmosphere in my classes perked up gradually, and I was quite happy with the progress made in my students' learning.

Simultaneously, while all this was going on, I was also very eager to share my ideas and strategies with the HOD and other CL teachers, but their responses were lukewarm, which I did not really mind. The fact that the HOD did not once voice any concern about my sharing (even though there was no explicit approval as well), plus the compliments from many teachers of other subjects (who had noticed the positive changes in my students), assured me that I was really doing the right thing the right way. Or so I thought.

Then, slowly and subtly, things started to change. Gradually, there was less and less space for me to share my ideas during meetings, and the suggestions that I proposed to add on or improve the department's programme were always met with much questioning from the HOD before they were eventually vetoed. I was getting very puzzled and frustrated, as it got more and more difficult for me to get things moving the way I saw that it should, and I could not see what the problem was as I was just earnestly trying to do my best for the department's work. I was not stepping on anyone's toes, and really only wanted to do good for the department. Furthermore, as I continued to treat the HOD as respectfully as before, she was actually getting more and more guarded and politely distant with me, and I was really baffled. I did not get much support from other CL teachers as well, as they did not seem too keen to get too close to me either. Neither was I to them, actually, as I already had a strong network of friends beyond the department to make up for my deprivation of friendly relations within the department.

In fact, I was really grateful to the circle of friends for rallying around me, especially more so when it was getting quite obvious that I was being isolated in the department. These friends were teachers from other departments, and were already in a closely knitted clique when I joined the school. Somehow there was this sense of affinity among us, and they readily accepted me into the clique. Apart from the fun and companionship, they were also helpful in providing all kinds of insiders' information and stories necessary to orientate me in this new workplace right from the start, especially those concerning my HOD. Oh yes, all about her and what she really was like — a "dowager"-like high-handed manager who could be harsh to anyone who dared to question or challenge her authority; a defensive and insecure porcupine who would readily offer her sharp spikes to anyone who got in her way. All these were shared with me with the good intention to prepare and caution me in my dealings with my HOD, and I was grateful for that. Talking to them about my problems with the HOD really helped, as they were always quick to point out some subtle messages or implications in the HOD's words or actions (which I shared with them) that I very often had failed to see, and this in turn helped me to interpret and decide on how best to manage the situations as they were. Many heads were certainly better than just mine. Life was hard, but I kept my head above water.

Then one day, it happened. We were planning for a CL day camp for the Secondary Four students, and the HOD wanted me to be in-charge of a vocabulary quiz. Seeing that many students could find this boring, I then suggested, as tactfully as I could, to replace the item with a songs appreciation session. Rather to my surprise, this time Ms. B agreed readily! And so, I set to work as hard as possible, determined to do it well so as to convince Ms. B about what to stimulate students' learning interest for CL with, and how.

On the day of the CL camp, Ms. B announced to the teachers that she had reshuffled the day's programme, and my song appreciation had been rescheduled to be the last item at 4.15 pm, so as to give me more space in case I overrun the time. I was really grateful and just so glad that I was finally making some progress with her. Then at around 4.10 pm, I started to get quite anxious as there seemed to be no sign of the second last item ending. Finally when it ended at 4.20 pm, Ms. B went up to the front of the activity room and spoke to the students about the importance of CL and also thanked the teachers for their hard work in organising the CL camp. Twenty minutes later, Ms. B told the students that because they had been good, she would release them earlier at 4.45 pm instead of the stipulated 5 pm. The students cheered loudly at this pleasant surprise, and all were dismissed… without ever knowing that there was a songs appreciation session waiting for them.

I was completely stunned into silence, and could only helplessly watch the students filing out of the room. Ms. B, on the other hand, just told the teachers to clean up the room and left without a second glance at me. Nobody came up to speak to me, even though I could feel some sympathetic glances here and there. I just could not believe what had just happened.

It was when I shared this with my friends that I really broke down and had a good cry over wasted effort and this sense of being played out by Ms. B. My friends were as indignant and angry, and all felt that Ms. B had really gone overboard this time round, and that if I continued to be submissive and did not stand up to her for my rights, sooner or later worse things would come.

And so, extremely unhappy and hurt, I decided that I would learn to stand up to protect myself. And the first thing I did was to email the principal Mrs. A about my situation, and subsequently was asked to see her almost immediately after. Mrs. A assured me that my good work with the students had been noticed and that I should continue with it. However, she also urged me to be patient with Ms. B, as she belonged to the old school of thought, and would find it difficult to accept new ideas and changes. Mrs. A then told me that it would be best if I could leave the matter to her, and I should just carry on with my work and wait for things to get better. Though reassured, I was somewhat not too satisfied or convinced by what Mrs. A said, as from the horror stories told to me by my friends, I knew how nasty and vicious Ms. B was capable of being, especially so when Ms. B had become more and more aggressive by sending a very clear message about her unhappiness with me after the CL camp. Department meetings became tense sessions wherein it was always between Ms. B and me, where she openly criticised some supposed wrongdoing of mine, and I tried to counter and defend myself. Then, loud and sarcastic comments from Ms. B about how "some people" are really so full of themselves started to find their way to me even in the staffroom. Life was really getting very hard indeed. I was fighting very hard for survival, at the same time very cautious that I should not be caught doing anything wrong. Whenever I found it too much to take, I would always turn to my friends to find solace in their unwavering support in my fight against Ms. B.

Then one day during a meeting, when Ms. B was accusing me of botching up a job that was actually another teacher's responsibility,

I could not take it anymore and quarrelled with her, with everyone else stunned at this showdown. Then, in the heat of the quarrel, I actually blurted out a dare for Ms. B to go with me to see Mrs. A so as to "thrash things out". At this, Ms. B suddenly became silent, and her face paled from the initial redness of anger. Then, she refused, saying that such incidents are "family matters" that should not be brought up to the Principal's level, and ended the meeting abruptly. It was then that I remembered that Ms. B had always seemed so quiet and rather mousey when Mrs. A, the non CL-speaker, was around. I suspected she was probably afraid to face Mrs. A as she was definitely in the wrong.

As usual, my friends were all angry with Ms. B's behaviour, and everyone agreed that this was really the last straw, and that I should do something about it to settle the matter once and for all. With my friends' backing, I thought it was only right to let Mrs. A know how bad the situation had become. So, the next day, I went to Mrs. A's office and poured everything out to her. Knowing that she was a fair and just person whom I had come to admire over time, I was expecting her to be on my side since I had done nothing wrong to justify Ms. B's behaviour towards me. However, this time round, I noticed Mrs. A's expression getting graver as I went on and on. Finally, she held up her hand to stop me half-way, and asked, "What did I tell you to do the last time you came in?" Taken aback, I stammered and was dumbfounded. Then Mrs. A continued, "You did not listen to my advice at all ... I know you have many friends around you but you must really have a mind of your own. You'd better stand on your own two feet or you'll find yourself in really big trouble soon! Now stop all this nonsense, get out and think hard about what you should do now!"

I could not remember how I got out of the office. But for the first time, I did not go crying to my friends. All day long, and even in my dreams that night, this phrase of "stand on your own two feet" kept ringing in my ears. What did Mrs. A mean by this? As I pondered over it, I gradually realised that I could have been too reliant on what my friends said, and in a way had allowed myself to be manipulated by external voices and the opinions of others who did not have a direct stake in my situation. Even though people may have been genuine in wanting to help me, their opinions or suggestions were only offered to me, and I was not in any way forced to take them. For example, though they may have been in a more objective position to help to second-guess Ms. B's words and actions against me, they would not have known the actual situation as well as I myself did, and I should have had enough sense to "stand on my own two feet" to know what should and should not be taken from what was offered to me. By choosing to listen more to my friends instead of taking Mrs. A's advice more seriously, I could have unwittingly created much more trouble for myself.

And so, with this realisation, I sheepishly went to see Mrs. A the next morning, apologised to her and shared my thoughts with her. She then gave me a good scolding, but in the end told me that she was glad that I was willing to admit my mistake; and she reassured me that the school would be fair to both Ms. B and me, and that it was important for me to cooperate in working to resolve the matter. Later that day, Ms. B was seen leaving Mrs. A's office angrily, but she was tight-lipped about what had happened inside. Not long after, Ms. B announced that her application for early retirement based on health reasons had been approved, and she was to retire at the end of the year. And no, she did not tone down much during her last few months in school, but the thought of nearing the end of my sufferings was what pulled me through.

When Ms. B finally left on an extremely bitter note at the end of 2002, my friends congratulated me on winning the fight. However, apart from the sense of relief from having to endure all the fault-finding and omnipresent sarcastic remarks, I was not elated at all. I was too exhausted to want to think more about it, and was just glad that everything was over. And no, I did not feel that I had emerged as the winner. In fact, even though I would like to think that I have gotten over it and moved on, this matter has remained as a nagging presence at the back of my mind that just does not go away.

Now, almost 12 years down the road, and having for the first time put this period down on paper, I can still feel the strong emotions as I felt then. And just as what Golombek & Johnson (2004) said, through this piece of writing, I am now enabled to look at that period from an "other" perspective, what is more an "other" who has 12 more years of experience with life and teaching. So, what would this "other" person see now?

Well, the very first thing that I see emerging so loudly throughout this narrative is, surprisingly, "I". I have always been regarded (and thought so myself too) as a respectful and modest person who is always considerate of other people's feelings. Thus, it was rather uncomfortable for me as I saw this egoistic notion of the "I" being so prevalent throughout.

To start with, it seemed that just because I thought I was doing the "right thing" in wanting to improve on what I thought was not done correctly in the teaching of CL, I seemed to expect everyone else to accept my ideas readily and to share my enthusiasm; if not, then there would be something wrong with these people. For example, when I spoke about the CL teachers' reactions to my ideas and proposals as being "lukewarm", I did not bother to ask for their reasons for the lack of enthusiasm to my ideas, and had instead only taken my own teaching experience, the HOD's opinion and other people's affirmation to be the indicators of the validity and credibility of my ideas. Even with Ms. B's opinion, I had selectively chosen to look at what she did *not* say (about possible issues about my ideas) for necessary justification for myself. Apparently, I did not seem to think that there could possibly be any problem with the ideas that I have proposed to start with. And I shudder now to see how I had actually been so self-assuming and had so easily bypassed the valuable feedback of those who knew best about and were more experienced in the teaching of CL in that particular school context, and instead had turned to "outsiders" for advice. How wise could I have been then?

Furthermore, looking at how I have described my "plight" at having less and less space to promote my ideas in the department, as well as how Ms. B's "questioning" about these ideas, I have also realised that I did not seem for once to think that what Ms. B had asked could actually have been real professional questions about some loopholes in my ideas. Instead, I had chosen to take all those questionings as a personal attack right from the beginning, even though I might not have realised it then. As I thought about how my friends had been helpful in cautioning me in sharing the entire "insider's" information about Ms. B, I suppose then I had unconsciously taken their lens and was prejudiced against Ms. B from the very start of my interactions with her. Even though I thought I was respectful to her, my mannerisms were probably tainted with my impression of Ms. B as a small-minded "dowager" capable of malicious acts; and Ms. B could have picked up the subtle messages and, understandably, did not like it. In other words, contrary to my belief that I had started right, I had instead started totally on the wrong foot without giving the CL teacher, Ms. B, and myself, a fair chance to begin with. What is more, looking at how "I" had behaved then, I am starting to see this person who, despite all her passion in teaching students, had behaved in a conceited and brash manner that reflected such an egoistic and self-righteous person that I myself would loathe as a colleague. That is to say that while I was busy pointing fingers at Ms. B and the other CL teachers for not giving me the necessary support and acceptance, I was probably none the better, and had not really behaved well towards them. As the saying goes, "it takes two hands to clap"; the CL teachers and I sure had clapped loud and clear, but regrettably in the wrongest possible way.

Consequently, I had also pointed at my friends as being the influencing force in my behaviour towards Ms. B. However, apart from being weak-minded and allowing myself to be manipulated by those external voices and opinions, I could have chosen to take on their side to feed on my ego that was obviously not fulfilled in my work in the department. I was happy that these teachers recognised my ability to stimulate my students' interest in learning CL, and was glad to have their sympathy and shared outrage at Ms. B to help nurse my bruised ego at not being accepted in the department, as well as to justify my unfortunate life then. Ultimately, it was still the problem of me, myself and I much of the time. Here, what Mrs. A said about the importance of being able to "stand on my own two feet" would then take on another layer of meaning. Apart from pertaining to my ability to have a stronger mind against external voices and opinions, it could also refer to my ability to stand up to and not let that big ego of mine dominate my actions and judgements so prevalently.

Conversely, my accumulated experiences of being in the managerial positions as a Subject Head and then as a HOD over the past years have now allowed me to look at Ms. B and the CL teachers very differently. Even though, in all fairness, no one was totally faultless in the whole episode, I suppose things could have been very different if I had been more mindful of my CL colleagues' backgrounds and personalities, and, as what Mrs. A had advised, been more "patient" with Ms. B and the other CL teachers.

To start with, I do not think I was too conscious about the state of the situation that Ms. B and the CL teachers could have been in while adapting to the fast changing context and relative expectations of CL teachers as a result of significant changes in the linguistic landscape in Singapore. At the point in time when I was posted to the school, the proportion of Chinese Singaporean students coming from an English-speaking home background was already increasing very quickly over the years. Many such students did not like CL, and always complained that it was a boring and irrelevant subject as an explanation for their negative attitude towards it. CL teachers, being in the front line of CL education, became the key group to bear the brunt of all this, as they were often blamed to have made CL boring and unattractive to the students through mundane rote-learning based methods, thereby "contributing" directly to the generally low level of motivation and achievement for the learning of CL. As a result, CL teachers were generally not regarded highly by school leaders, colleagues and even students. And in this so-called traditional "English" school, the situation was even more so.

Looking back now, I can see how demoralised and helpless many of those CL teachers could have felt then. Not that I was unaware of it back then, but being blissfully effectively bilingual and gamefully experimenting in my teaching of CL had allowed me to relate very well with the English Language (EL)-speaking school leaders, colleagues and students. Thus, I guess I did not empathise fully with most of my CL colleagues who were struggling with using English to effectively communicate with others beyond the department, especially more so in such a predominantly EL environment. In fact, I myself could have unconsciously been regarding them as lesser beings and that might explain why I somehow just did not think of valuing or even getting their opinions about my ideas seriously. From the whole narration above, it is so clear that I had never really taken notice of their presence, as their faces, words and actions were so significantly absent all through. Oh my goodness…

And so, what about Ms. B then? Come to think of it, if the CL teachers were not coping with the school context well, then Ms. B being the typical older Chinese-educated CL teacher who was also not too proficient in EL, was probably also having a difficult time trying to come to terms with all the drastic changes in the CL policies and curriculum that were often contradictory to her strong sense of pride for CL. In addition, since Mrs. A was posted to the school, she had emphasised on a high standard of teaching and learning with the introduction of many significant changes, including the implementations of some advanced pedagogies on a school-wide basis — in English of course. As the HOD now, I could imagine the kind of stress that Ms. B must have been facing then, and it did not help that she had always struggled to communicate effectively with Mrs. A. Putting myself in her shoes now, I could see how, in addition to all these contextual stresses, the presence of someone (me) who seemed to be everything that she was not — especially in the part of being able to communicate effectively with the others (including the Principal) and in fitting well into the English-dominant work environment — could have elicited much more resistance and hostility from her as compared to under normal circumstances. And now, learning about how the notion of Self is really highly contextualised, distributive, interpretive and constructive (Bruner, 1990), I have also started to wonder if the horrendous Ms. B was really who I had seen, or if it was an alternate self of hers that was unfortunately formed and distorted by the immense pressure resulting from work reality. She could have been a nice person under that insecure and porcupine-like surface — a nice "aunty" who perhaps would have liked me better if we had not met under such circumstances …

Incidentally, this brings me to ponder upon an imminent question that my tutor and classmates asked repeatedly — why of all people did I choose her for my NI? What I finally realised, after reading and thinking through what was written so far, is that apart from all the intense suffering described, perhaps what hit me the hardest was the fact that my interaction with Ms. B totally jeopardised and denied the legitimacy of my strong beliefs about the virtues and merits of being respectful and obedient to elders. As the first "elder" who was not appreciative of my "goodness" and who had hated me instead, Ms. B had shocked me into the cold reality wherein being a "good girl" is just not enough for one to survive. Nope, it takes much more than what my sheltered and cushioned little world had equipped me with before my posting to that school, and it is rather painful for me to realise that what I had always believed in is after all not so "correct" anymore. Together with all other complications such as that arising from my interactions with my friends and other colleagues, I have learnt that the world is really not that simple after all, and that I should say the long-overdue goodbye to the naïve period of my life, and really learn to stand on my own two feet if I am to survive well in this world. Ah yes, I guess it is this "goodbye" to the never-to-return innocence and simplicity of my life that I still cannot let go of after all...

References

Bruner, J. (1990). *Acts of Meaning*. Cambridge: Havard University Press.

Golombek, P. R. & Johnson, K. E. (2004). Narrative inquiry as a meditational space: Examining emotional and cognitive dissonance in second-language teachers' development. *Teachers and Teaching: Theory and Practice*, 10 (3), 307–326.

Chapter 12
The Accidental Leader

Hwei Fang SONG

Life is like a box of chocolates. You never know what you're gonna get.

**Forrest Gump, a movie based on the 1986 novel
of the same name by Winston Groom.**

In every box of assorted chocolates, there are some wrapped in gold foil, their contents unclear; only by removing the foil would you see what lies within. Others are not wrapped; their contents quite clear with the inner fillings delicately decorated on the outside. There are also others; plain-looking and without any hints of what may be inside. Life is like that too, isn't it? No one can really say for sure what the next moment might bring — a sweet milk chocolate or a bitter dark one.

As I trace back to the origins of my career trajectories, the onset seems to result from a series of happenings starting from 1997. Life prior to 1997 was a luxurious gold-wrapped piece of seemingly delectable chocolate; a happy family; a lovable first boy-friend; more-than-presentable "O"-Level results. The future was bright. Life was as good as it got. Within a span of two years, all of these disappeared — a bite of that piece of chocolate now turned bitter.

In 1997, my father passed away without any forewarnings. My two younger sisters and I watched him turn blue right before our eyes, helplessly. In the same year, I left home, with my sisters, to live with my aunt's family upon finding out that my mother's boyfriend had moved into our house one afternoon, within weeks of my father's demise, and that they were already together before his death. At the end of 1998, I was amongst one of the lowest scoring "A"-Level students in one of the leading junior colleges. Shortly after, I broke up with my then-boyfriend, my first love. I was at the lowest point of my life.

After the "A"-Levels, with no money and no decent qualifications, I tried my luck at a local polytechnic, with the hope that I would be decently employable at the end of another two years. To pay for tuition, I worked most afternoons, sometimes till late, at a nearby café, hoping to earn a little more overtime pay to cover my expenses, tuition fees and have some left for my sisters' pocket money. It was tough having to work and study at the same time but surprisingly I did well, considering the little time I had to revise and do my work properly.

Thinking back, it was probably during this period of time that I developed a certain degree of tenacity. A diploma was my only way out at that time. With only an "A"-Level certificate, notwithstanding the poor results, I would not have a decent future. I could not and would not give up doing well.

There is a Chinese saying, "苦尽甘来" (*ku jing gan lai*) — difficulty will pass and things will look up thereafter. Life certainly started to look up a little upon my admission to polytechnic. I met Dennis there. He is two years older than I am. Thus, I looked up to him as a big brother I never had. He was my pillar of strength; someone I could rely on in times of need. He is a man of few words; never frivolous, never intrusive but who dispenses good advice when approached. Thus, sometimes when I had no clue what was going on, I relied on him to make decisions for me, even important ones. Till this day, he remains one of my best and trusted friends.

"Eh, we are graduating soon. What plans do you have?" Dennis asked me during lunchtime one day.

"Don't know leh. Haven't thought about it. Maybe look for vacancies in tour agencies?" I tried answering after some moments of silence; my inclinations were naturally towards the tourism industry since that was my specialisation in my final year.

"I am applying to become a teacher. I want be a Chinese teacher," Dennis continued.

We did not continue this conversation further as my thoughts brought me further and further away from the canteen where we were, as I pondered over what Dennis had brought up. I vividly remember Dennis looking at me, perplexed. "What can I do? What do I want to do?" I had no plans at all. During my two years of studies in this polytechnic, all I knew was to work and study, study and work. I neither had the time nor the courage to think of the future.

"Hwei Fang, you want to apply to this with me?" Dennis handed me an application form a couple of days later. It was an application to be a teacher.

"Come, let me help you fill it out," Dennis, who probably knew I did not have any plans, pulled the form away from my hand and started filling it out without even waiting for my answer. For the past two years, I had relied on him much. I certainly did not mind him making the decision for me this time round too.

"Do I want to be a teacher? What does a teacher do? Do I even like children to begin with? What do I want to do exactly?" I recalled a conversation with my ex-boyfriend after the "O"-Levels, regarding our future. He wanted to be a professional soldier. I told him I wanted to be an interior designer. But that was then, when the future was bright. Now, I was not that sure. The future was not as bright as I wanted it to be. I looked at Dennis furiously filling out our forms. How could he be so sure of what he wanted to do?

A few months down the road, a week before graduation, one of my lecturers asked me if I wanted to work for her friend who was in the Exhibitions industry.

"It will be a good stepping stone to the Exhibitions industry," persuaded my lecturer.

Without any concrete plans, I agreed and I was the new Administrative Assistant in an association for the Conventions and Exhibitions industry. A few months into planning Golf Networking sessions for the umpteenth time, while standing before the lifeless fax machine, faxing invitation card after invitation card to the 100-odd members of the association, a certain feeling overwhelmed me. Is this what I was going to be doing for the rest of my life? I could not bear that thought. There I was, armed with only a diploma, an educational qualification that was neither here nor there. I suppose, subconsciously, I knew I could do much better than that but how I was going to achieve that, I really had no idea. And to achieve what? I was still clueless.

A few days later, I received a letter. It was from the Ministry of Education (MOE), requesting for an interview for the position of a Primary School teacher. At that point in time, that letter presented a window of opportunity for me to escape from the mundane work at the association. I argued: If I liked the job enough, I could have a professional diploma; and if I did well enough, I could carry on with the degree programme with financial backing. If I found myself unsuitable at any time, it would be just a month's notice away from freedom. It seemed like a win–win.

Unlike the many applicants I met outside the interview room at MOE Headquarters, I was not among those who had a calling, who wanted to make a difference in someone else's life; I only wanted to make a difference to my own life. This was just a handy escape for me at that moment in time. It was most ironic that I got through the interview. Dennis, on the other hand, who was so passionate about being a Chinese teacher, was rejected. He was despondent, of course, but nevertheless happy for me and that, between the two of us, at least one of us got through the interview. He even volunteered to be my guarantor when I decided to pursue my diploma in education, knowing that I had no one else.

One can never tell what life would bring the next moment. A different choice. A different encounter. A different timing. Any change in any variable of life would completely change one's course of life. The same bitter chocolate is no longer that unpalatable; it now exudes a slight hint of sweetness when held long enough in the mouth. Isn't this like life? When one holds out the bitterness long enough, one might just be pleasantly surprised at how positive the experience might turn out to be at the end.

Although sending in the application was not of my own volition, I made the choice to try this job out. And I was pleasantly surprised. During my 10-month Contract Teaching period, it was through my Co-Curricular Activity (CCA), the Brass Band, that I discovered the joy of interacting with and influencing young minds; but most importantly, I did not have to drag myself up from bed every morning to yet another dull day of work in front of lifeless machines. Besides CCA, other aspects of school were equally dynamic. There was always something interesting to do with the many festivities and diverse activities. With so many different pupils, there would always be many interesting exchanges. So, with this most plausible and painless option available, I took this chance life offered me and got myself into the National Institute of Education (NIE) for a diploma in education. Two years down the road, in one of my happiest moments, I did well enough to "cross-over" — to continue on with a two-year degree programme in English and Literature, a door that had shut in my face five years earlier.

Those few years of physical toil and emotional turmoil added a new dimension to who I have now come to be — how sweet the after taste is of a bitter chocolate! To pave a way out for myself, I took up the best option I had in furthering my education in a local polytechnic. Then again, when opportunity presented itself to escape from my then mundane job, I took it up and enjoyed the working experience that teaching provided me at that clueless but critical deciding period of my life.

University education treated me well. Not only did it help to rebuild my confidence, it also expanded my horizons to the immense amount of knowledge that goes into teaching, allowing me to appreciate the craft — just like how chocolate connoisseurs appreciate their fine chocolate through smell, sight, sound, touch and taste. During my time at NIE, I also discovered my appreciation for planning lessons. And it is this inclination that would lead me to consider taking up the leadership role that I currently play as the Subject Head for Citizenship Education and Social Studies.

My first and current posting was to my alma mater, where I spent my formative years in the happiest and most carefree manner. Till today, I cannot help but feel how intriguing it was the way things were panning out for me. Going to work now had a different meaning for me. I recall the many happy moments I spent dreaming about the future at the different corners of the school. It was the most wondrous feeling, like picking out the sweetest milk chocolate piece from my box of chocolates, holding it out under the sun, admiring it but not bearing to put it into my mouth, for fear that I would finish up the chocolates all too quickly.

The various people I met in the course of my life played pivotal roles in presenting opportunities and shape how I have come to be who I am today. One of them is Dennis. The other is WC, a current colleague and good friend.

If I compare Dennis to chocolates, he would be a regular-shaped milk chocolate covered with smooth, silky milk cream — always understated but dependable. WC would be a funky irregular-shaped milk chocolate with a nutty filling — zealous but steadfast.

He was the first person to introduce himself to me when I stepped into the school for the first time. The following year, when I was transferred to the Pupil Development Department where he was the Subject Head for Character Development, he provided much needed help to push me from a "behind-the-scene" kind of role in the English Department into being in the "limelight", addressing both pupils and teachers in the hall on a regular basis. Being in front of a crowd was never my forte. Thus it was a rather steep learning curve for me. If I had any choice at all, I would never offer any answers in class; I would never be a group leader; I would never volunteer to be a presenter. But life springs its surprises at you sometimes; I was presented with a platform to perform all that I avoided my entire life: to offer solutions, to be a team leader and to hold large-scale presentations.

It was also because of WC that I was roped into the Students' Council as a Teacher Advisor, and subsequently into the Prefectorial

Board, stretching pupils' leadership potential while simultaneously honing my own leadership capability. At the onset, I joined many of these activities simply because they seemed like genuine fun. However, over the years, WC's zeal for his role as an educator really rubbed off on me in a positive way; and I, slowly but surely, started to see the importance of all these activities and how these really impacted change and development in the young lives we handle day in and day out. From a clueless and fearful girl, I was maturing fast into a firm and confident woman, not just in my body language, but also mentally, deliberating about the role I play or could get to play in the education system. Teaching is really a meaningful career, no matter how clichéd this line seems to be.

Towards the end of my second year in the school, my ex-Principal took notice of a very small project I did with WC and subsequently invited me to be on the management team on a number of occasions. While I was flattered, I did not agree immediately. I was not sure that I would be able to do the job well. WC told me that I was lucky to have my efforts noticed by the so-called "right" people in such a short span of time. I did not disagree. In fact, I concurred. I was just lucky.

In the same year, WC needed help developing a character curriculum and persuaded me to help him. After much persuasion, I came under his wing to become the Character Development Coordinator. With the help of the previous coordinator, I developed and introduced a six-year character curriculum based on our school core values. I made use of the basic teaching idea of Habits of Mind to re-create a weekly assembly package. This package not only reinforced my penchant towards curriculum planning, but also strengthened my belief that I was somewhat capable in what I was doing. Garnering the year's Outstanding Contribution Award further concreted that belief.

Subsequently, I got to participate in various school-based projects with various knowledgeable others even though I was just a very young officer. I was invited to the cluster young leaders' tea session. I was handpicked to revamp the school core values with a team of very experienced Subject Heads and Heads of Departments. I co-led a team of teachers and pupils on our school's first service-learning trip with the ex-President of the Service-Learning Club in NIE. I was also roped in by the School Staff Developer to plan our first fund-raising event, a learning carnival, together with the Admin Vice-Principal and the Physical Education (PE) Head of Department. In 2011, I was appointed the internal Subject Head of Citizenship Education and Social Studies, alongside WC, to champion Character and Citizenship Education in the school. I went for the interview and was officially appointed this year.

Many a time, as I think back about WC's comment, I wonder if Lady Luck was really taking pity on me, taking a special turn on her wheel to favour me in compensation of my previous years of misfortune. A recent conversation with my current Principal uncovered a revelation. According to her, I have a certain air of doggedness in my approach to work. Even when things are tough, I persist on and complete the work in the best possible way. She said that it is a quality that leaders must have. It then dawned on me that I might not be merely "lucky". The decisions I made and attitudes I took to coping with the various events following my father's death formed the basis to who I am and how I approach work. *I could not and would not give up doing well.* It is exactly this quality that has brought me to where I am today.

These couple of years of participating in various committees and initiatives allowed me to see education as a bigger picture, as compared to teaching a class of pupils. It allowed me to experience how the leadership path can allow me to expand positive influence on the many lives that pass through my hands. When I was roped in to revamp the school core values, I visited a number of schools whose expertise lie in their quality character education programmes. This experience opened my eyes to an additional prospect of being a change agent. In contrast to my bitter teens, I was swayed along by circumstances and could only make the best choices I had within my means. I was not a change agent. I was a victim of the changes that happened to me.

For once in my life, I seriously contemplated taking a stance, and not to sit on the fence waiting to be swayed by circumstances. Heading higher up the leadership track is a likely possibility. Only as a leader can I exert enough influence to initiate changes in curriculum decisions aligned to my beliefs, one school at a time.

In parallel, my private life also took a turn for the better these few years. I am financially independent and do not need to worry about money issues; I reconnected with my first love, my best friend, we got married and I gained a pair of caring in-laws; I treat my aunt's family as my own as they treated me and my sisters as their own; the relationship between my mother and I never got back to where it was before but it is at least cordial; many fast and genuine colleague-friends were made during the course of my work. Once again, life is good.

Life is like a box of chocolates. You never know what you're gonna get. Sometimes you get a bitter chocolate with a sweet lingering aftertaste. Then it surprises you with a wonderful interior that continues to astound you long after you have finished savouring it. Other times, you might pick up another whose taste you would never be sick of — always predictable, always dependable. Once in while, you chance upon a funky one — a catalyst ready to excite and inspire your taste buds. But most importantly, when boxes of chocolates come your way, do not be too quick to reject them even if they are not compatible with your usual tastes, for you never know when you would be surprised by what they hold within.

Part 3:
What Shapes a Teacher?

Overview

Huey Min SUN

The forming of teacher identity is a complex yet vital issue in the educational development of the nation since "[t]eachers' perceptions of their own professional identity affect their efficacy and professional development as well as their willingness to cope with educational change and to implement innovations in their own teaching practice" (Beijaard *et al.*, 2000, p. 750). Important as it is, teacher identity is formed through a dynamic process — it is neither fixed nor imposed from outside, but rather, as Sachs (2005) pointed out, "negotiated through experience and the sense that is made of that experience" (p. 15). The teacher narratives included in Part 3 of this book exactly demonstrate this dynamic process as part of their personal and professional growth, that is both emotional (Rodgers & Scott, 2008; Zembylas, 2003) and bound by the shaping factors that are context specific and sensitive to external environments, such as the social, cultural and political situations (Bruner, 1990). Examining these factors and the shaping processes of teacher identity are essential in understanding its formation and the implications for supporting the meaning making of teacher personal and professional lives.

Teachers whose narratives are featured in Part 3 wrote about such factors as family background (Goh Li Meng, Anu Radha, Siti Aisha Said), their beliefs in certain pedagogy or assessment (Goh Li Meng and Rachel Ong), the kind of work assigned to them (Annie Seng), the teachers' relationships with and their perceptions of their supervisors and fellow colleagues (Goh Li Meng, Jackie Ang and Siti Aisha Said). Central to teachers' work is the interaction with their students that most writers of the narratives in this book wrote about — both good and bad experiences.

The Teachers' Backgrounds

The teachers' backgrounds include their personal experiences like education received, a former teacher as a relevant model (Beijaard *et al.*, 2000, p. 754), and critical events in earlier days (Kagan, 1992; Beijaard, 1995). The early success in learning the Maths 12 times-table indeed gave Li Meng the sense of achievement in Mathematics. For Anu, she was grateful for the help given by her teacher, Ms. Ann, who transformed her from someone who felt inferior because of her grades in the Primary School Leaving Examination (PSLE) into a confident person, so much so that she herself decided to extend help to her own students. As Ms. Ann had helped her to become a better student, Anu, in turn, wanted to pass on her help to her student, Lionel, for him to grow out of his family problems. Siti Aisha recalled the characteristics of the teachers who had taught her and made her determined to emulate them in being: "strict but caring, respectful and respected, kind and nurturing and last but not least, patient!" Her remark, "[p]ast experiences as a student played a major role in determining the characteristic of a good teacher," reflects the feelings of many and it is a reminder to all teachers and teacher educators on the pivotal role of teachers.

Pedagogy

While the choice of subject discipline may affect teacher identity, as "disciplines may tend to have particular teaching cultures of their own" (Barty, 2004; Pennington, 2002; Varghese *et al.*, 2005, in Beauchamp & Thomas, 2009, p. 184), pedagogy which concerns how teachers engage students certainly may also affect the formation of teacher identity. Beijaard and De Vries (1997) found that between the didactical and subject matter sides and the pedagogical side, many teachers found that the pedagogical side was more important than the didactical and subject matter sides. Rachel's belief in Problem-based Learning (PBL) is certainly one good example, as she saw the new approach to learning as a way of achieving the purpose of learning and not teaching to the test. Her identity was shaped and reshaped by the process on learning how to use PBL to facilitate student learning. This learning process is vividly described in the following paragraph:

> *I felt schizophrenic at times, as on one hand, I accepted logically the ideas about constructivism and centering the learning on the student. On the other hand, enacting it was to fight the 'teacher' in me. I finally came to appreciate the struggle in my students and recognised the process of building a 'learning character' when I persisted in my efforts not to just transfer knowledge. It was like a butterfly coming out of its cocoon. It had to struggle to build the strength in its wings before it could really fly. If it were released too early without a fight, the butterfly would not form as it should and cannot fly.*

Work Assigned

"[T]eachers derive their professional identity from (mostly combinations of) the ways they see themselves as subject matter experts, pedagogical experts, and didactical experts" (Beijaard *et al.*, 2000, p. 751). In the Singapore education context, teachers' expertise (as required) extends beyond academic subjects, as its education system is unique in that non-academic areas like Co-curricular Activities (CCAs) are given significant weight alongside academic subjects. This expansion in the teacher's expertise can have a significant impact on his or her professional life. Annie was one of the teachers who was affected by being assigned to be in-charge of a CCA — Netball, a game that she hated. Annie's dislike for her CCA also affected her motivation to lead in the CCA and even her sense of professionalism. This case made clear how the right match could bring out the potentials of the teacher to serve his/her students, the school and the wider society well, while the mismatch could cause tension, self-doubt and even sense of loss of professionalism and shame to him/her. How Annie felt towards the CCAs assigned to her has a wider implication, as the allocation of CCAs to the teacher could impact the students more than the teacher himself/herself.

Relationship with and Perception of Supervisors and Colleagues

The teachers' relationships with and their perceptions of their supervisors and fellow colleagues whom they interact with closely shape teacher identity, as in the case of Jackie and Li Meng in Part 3 of this book. Jackie was particularly affected by the management style of one of her supervisors that it had not only affected her health but also her desire to continue with teaching — "my passion for teaching would extinguish if I stayed on." On the other hand, she felt that her fifth Principal's beliefs resonated with hers and that helped her to grow as a teacher and a middle manager. To Li Meng, how her colleagues handled the assessment in a differential way provoked her sense of fairness and professionalism. In addition, in Chapter 7 of Part 2, Vimi was struck by the humility of her mentor who was willing to learn from a novice teacher like her. The guidance given by her mentor and their close relationship helped her grow professionally.

Responses from and Relationship with Students

Relationship with students is central to define teacher professional identity (Beijaard *et al.*, 1995; Hargreaves, 2000). Teachers who are committed to engaging students for effective learning would inevitably be affected by the lives and responses of their students. In this collection of narratives, Li Meng's inexperience in setting exam papers resulted in the underperformance of her students in comparison with students of other schools. She saw the situation as "competition" and lamented that "[t]hat competition caused me to feel frustrated and unfulfilled in my work."

When one of Anu's students, Lionel, had problems which affected his behaviour and school work, she questioned her role as a teacher and her capacity to be effective. However, when Lionel made it to the polytechnic course of his choice and thanked her personally, she felt "[t]hat moment was all the recognition, praise and validation I would ever need to reaffirm that teaching is what I was meant to do."

In fact Vimi's NI in Part 2 also displayed how the students can affect the teachers. Vimi recalled that her student Racheal, who battled cancer courageously, inspired her to be a better teacher. Her success in helping another student, Fathul, to read also brought her satisfaction as a teacher and reaffirmed her calling to be a teacher, as she narrated, "I am so proud that as a teacher and a human being, I could make that difference to a child. It is moments like these that make teaching so meaningful in your life."

Identity Formation is an On-Going Process

The shaping process, regardless of the factors causing it, is a continuous process. For Li Meng, her being tested in different schools and interacting with different people continued to shape her — from a teacher who believed in academic ability to doubting if assessment was able to accurately measure a person's true ability; from believing that studying hard and doing well was the route to higher career prospects to putting more emphasis on character and integrity. The belief in PBL for Rachel was a journey in itself as indicated in the title of her narrative. Siti Aisha also discovered her strength as she moved to different posts.

It is inevitable that identity would change with time, as it is an ongoing process and not a fixed entity (Sachs, 2005) and involves many differing contexts and relationships. Indeed, "historical, sociological, psychological, and cultural factors may all influence the teacher's sense of self as a teacher" (Chong & Low, 2009, p. 60). All these factors also interweave the social and the individual, relating "to the discourses and the community that we work within" (Clarke, 2009, p. 187). The formation of teacher identity begins even before they begin their initial teacher preparation programmes. Sutherland *et al.* (2010) opined that "An individual's prior knowledge and beliefs act as a filter for interpretation of his/her experience" (p. 456). The teacher training programmes aid students to construct a "collective self or a professional self during the process of learning to teach" (Danielewicz, 2001, in Chong & Low, 2009, p. 60), and thus can make a difference in the forming of their identity. Such an impact is reflected in quite a few narratives in this book, including Sheikh's in which he felt the positive influence of one of his National Institute of Education (NIE) lecturers even after his training days and continued to use the pedagogy taught by this lecturer. While recognising the shortfall of another lecturer and felt disenchanted, fortunately he did not allow himself to be negative but reflected on how he could react better.

Indeed, how teacher identities are formed at the initial stage and how they change over time, what caused the change and what could be suggested to help teachers continue to resonate with the calling of the profession would have serious implications not only on teacher education but, on a broader scale, the effectiveness of education as a whole.

References

Beauchamp C., & Thomas L. (2009). Understanding teacher identity: An overview of issues in the literature and implication for teacher education. *Cambridge Journal of Education*, 39 (2), 175–189.

Beauchamp C., & Thomas L. (2011). New teachers' identity shifts at the boundary of teacher education and initial practice. *International Journal of Educational Research*, 50, 6–13.

Beijaard, D. (1995). Teachers' prior experiences and actual perceptions of professional identity. *Teachers and Teaching: Theory and Practice*, 1, 281–294.

Beijaard, D., & De Vries, Y. (1997). Building expertise: A process perspective on the development or change of teachers' beliefs. *European Journal of Teacher Education*, 20, 243–255.

Beijaard, D., Verloop, N., & Vermunt Jan, D. (2000). Teachers' perceptions of professional identity: An exploratory study from a personal knowledge perspective. *Teaching and Teacher Education*, 16, 749–764.

Bruner, J. (1990). *Acts of meaning*. Cambridge: Harvard University Press.

Chong, S., (2011). Development of teachers' professional identities: From pre-service to their first year as novice teachers. *KEDI Journal of Educational Policy, KJEP*, 8 (2), 219–233.

Chong, S., & Low, E. L. (2009). Why I want to teach and how I feel about teaching — Formation of teacher identity from pre-service to the beginning teacher phase. *Educational Research Policy and Practice*, 8, 59–72.

Chong, S., Low, E. L., & Goh, C. K. (2011). Developing student teachers' professional identities — An exploratory study. *International Education Studies*, 4 (1), 30–38.

Clarke, M. (2009). The ethico-politics of teacher identity. *Educational Philosophy and Theory*, 41 (2).

Danielewicz, J. (2001). *Teaching selves: Identity, pedagogy, and teacher education*. Albany: State University of New York Press.

Flores, M. A., & Day, C. (2006). Contexts which shape and reshape new teachers' identities: A multi-perspective study. *Teaching and Teacher Education*, 22, 219–232.

Hargreaves, A. (2000). Mixed emotions: Teachers' perceptions of their interactions with students. *Teaching and Teacher Education*, 16, 811–826.

Kagan, D. M. (1992). Professional growth among pre-service and beginning teachers. *Review of Educational Research*, 62, 129–169.

Pepper, R. C. (2009). The impact of motivation to lead on college students' cocurricular involvement (doctoral dissertation). Retrieved from http://search.proquest.com.libproxy.nie.edu.sg/docview/305136600.

Rodgers, C., & Scott, K. (2008). The development of the personal self and professional identity in learning to teach. In M. Cochran-Smith, S. Feiman-Nemser, D. J. McIntyre and K. E. Demers (eds.), *Handbook of Research on Teacher Education: Enduring Questions and Changing Contexts*, pp. 732–755. New York: Routledge.

Sachs, J. (2005). Teacher education and the development of professional identity: Learning to be a teacher. In P. Denicolo and M. Kompf (eds.), *Connecting Policy and Practice: Challenges for Teaching and Learning in Schools and Universities*, pp. 5–21. Oxford: Routledge.

Sutherland, L., Howard S., & Marauskaite, L. (2010). Professional identity creation: Examining the development of beginning pre-service teachers' understanding of their work as teachers. *Teaching and Teacher Education,* 26, 455–465.

Van Veen, K., & Sleegers, P. (2006). How does it feel? Teachers' emotions in a context of change. *Journal of Curriculum Studies,* 38 (1), 85–111.

Zembylas, M. (2003). Caring for teacher emotion: Reflections on teacher self-development. *Studies in Philosophy and Education,* 22, 103–125.

Chapter 13
Being Tested

Li Meng GOH

My earliest recollection of being formally assessed was by my mother for my 12 times tables as she prepared dinner. I was about 5 or 6 and would sit on the kitchen floor memorising the times table while she cooked. My mother would then test me. I usually got every question right and would be rewarded with a smile and praise. Before the end of primary 1, I had mastered the 12 times table completely and always led my class in Mathematics tests and examinations and this continued up the levels. It gave me a sense of achievement and control which motivated me to strive to always excel in Mathematics. My parents' and teachers' approval, classmates' admiration and a sense of superiority whenever my classmates asked for help also played a part in stimulating and motivating my interest in Mathematics.

The adrenaline rush I felt just before an examination was similar to the rush just before running a 100-metre race. I was not afraid of examinations and tests throughout my student life and proceeded to major in Mathematics in university and trained to become a Mathematics teacher. I did not realise then that I had a competitive streak in me as I was a first born and had always topped my class without much struggle. However, this record of successes did not prepare me for any kind of failure later in life. Influenced by a family value and a culture which places academic excellence as key to the individual's achievement, I subconsciously perceive a person's worth in terms of his/her scholastic successes.

Tested as a Beginning Teacher — My Assumptions of Students' Learning Attitudes

I started teaching in a junior college (senior high school) right in the middle of the students' mid-year examinations. I was deployed to help in marking the papers for the classes that I would be assigned to teach subsequently. This became my introduction to examination marking! I was careful and consulted with the more experienced colleagues on all doubts before adding up the marks.

The following week's lessons involved my having to return the scripts and to check marks with the students, all of whom I was meeting for the first time. I remember going to my only Arts class to return the papers. Most of them had failed as they had been taught by various relief teachers since they started Junior College 1, or JC 1. While checking their marks, one boy, Adam, came up to me and said that there was a mistake in his marks. His cover page showed 1 mark for question 9 but the mark on his script indicated 6. He had failed by 4 marks. If the mistake could be adjusted, he would have passed the examination. This was the first time that I had met a well-mannered, soft spoken boy. I checked his solution. It was wrong and deserved only 1 mark! He had not changed his solution but just the mark next to it with a red pen which had a slightly different colour from my pen. What was I supposed to do? I tried to collect my thoughts while staring at his solution and finally promised to take it back to check with the Head of Department (HOD). Adam asked me to change his mark on the spot. I realised then that he had assumed that I was just another relief teacher and could be pressured to do what he wished. I really did not want to confront him on my own. I refused and took the paper with me when I left the class. I wondered what he had expected. Surely he should know that he could not get away with it! After conferring with the HOD, the case was brought up to the Principal. Adam's parents were called in. When confronted, he admitted to his dishonesty. He was asked to leave the school as he was already a repeat student with a record of other misdeeds since the previous year. I was surprised by his parents' lack of protest and the calmness with which they received the news as they almost seemed prepared to take him out of school. Compared with them, I was very much disturbed and far from feeling calm. I also felt that there was no closure as I had no chance to talk to him again.

My HOD told me not to worry about it but I was quite upset. Why did he cheat? Was it worth losing his integrity just to pass the examination? The value of passing the examination was apparently greater than the value of his character. After having failed the year before, was the fear of failing yet again so great? What messages had parents, teachers, schools and society imparted to students about the value of their academic achievement? Did my parents and friends value me because I excelled in my studies? Was winning their affirmation the reason for me to work hard to achieve good results? Or did I really enjoy learning and believe in the value of resilience and perseverance? Perhaps I had always believed that studying hard and doing well is the route to more options and better career prospects later in life rather than to personal growth and development. After all, this is a meritocratic society which accepts excellence in examinations as a requirement to success in life. In the process, have we equated a student's worth with his or her academic results or worse, perceived his or her achievement as of more worth than his or her total identity? As a teacher, what kind of message should I be sending to students about their worth and their examination results? There is a *need* to re-emphasise the importance of integrity and taking responsibility for our decisions. Taking examinations had never been as straightforward as I thought. Thinking a little deeper, it was hard for me to empathise with Adam.

Three months into teaching, I was observed by two officers from the Ministry of Education (MOE) Gifted Education Unit conducting a lesson. I was then asked to join the gifted education programme (GEP), teaching secondary school Mathematics. I was excited. However by then I was rather attached to my students and really wished to see them complete their "A"-Levels (senior high school leaving examinations). Hence, I asked for a one-year deferment and it was granted.

It was comforting in the first one and a half years of my teaching to have three other new teachers with whom to share our struggles, which included the sometimes tragic and sometimes hilarious mistakes we made. Assuming that students had mastered the "O"-Level Mathematics content simply because they had passed the "O"-Levels was my greatest mistake. I realised I had been totally misguided. Many of them had forgotten what they had learnt in secondary school. They had merely crammed for the high stakes examination and had not really fully understood what they were taught. However, as I observed their lifestyle and work schedule in the JC, I realised that they would probably repeat their learning process, as there never seemed to be enough time for thinking and reflection for each individual subject.

Teachers, myself included, seemed perpetually to be rushing so as to complete the syllabus within the stipulated time, even though we were not happy with how we were teaching. Things had not changed since I was a student. There was always a fear on the teachers' part that they had covered less than teachers in another college. The competition was not just among students. It was among teachers and schools as well.

During this time, my pedagogy was not based on any theory I learnt in teacher education but more on how my own teachers used to teach me. I basically asked the students to model after my way of thinking, learning, taking examinations without really caring about whether they had really understood what they learnt. I felt like a coach of a running team whose only way of coaching was to run with the runners and asking them to run like me.

Despite the stress from the examinations, I forged close ties with many of my students. It was an exciting time of discovering so much diversity among my students. I never knew that students can have so many different perceptions about the purpose of studying and so many different ways of studying, e.g. studying for their parents, studying so as not to be left behind, studying for a better future, studying for want of better things to do, studying to compete with siblings, etc. Few actually believed in studying for personal development.

Tested as an Examination Setter — My Assumptions as a Teacher and About Teachers

After one and half years in JC, I joined an independent school to teach Additional Mathematics for both GEP and express classes. The first time I had to set part of the first common test paper for the gifted classes made me really nervous.

First, I considered my students who had very mixed abilities. Two were highly gifted. One could write beautiful poems and stories but every piece of Mathematics assignment seemed like torture to him. Between these two extremes there were a spectrum of diverse interests and abilities. I was truly challenged. The materials provided by the GEP unit were investigative in nature; treating the students like true Mathematicians. I loved the materials as they were so refreshing and different from the textbooks I had used as a student. It was like coaching a team of athletes in a state-of-the-art gymnasium to train them with high-class equipment. But the students thought differently. They struggled with the new equipment and even fell down at times.

I realised now that I had made wrong assumptions about their abilities as they were labelled "gifted" and so had not been taught enough basic knowledge. I also did not know how to scaffold the materials nor differentiate the content or process for the mixed ability classes. I just assumed that they would love it once they got used to it, just like me. I had not gone down to a micro-level to understand their true struggles. My misinterpretation of their "giftedness" became my stumbling block in teaching them.

The first common test was co-set by three Additional Mathematics teachers, one from each of the three schools then offering the gifted programme. With my students in mind, the questions I set were mostly application ones, requiring little evaluation or synthesis. When I met with the other two older and more experienced teachers, Rose and Henry, to discuss the full paper, I thought "My kids can't possibly pass this paper!" Rose and Henry had been teaching Secondary Three Additional Mathematics for three years and were well-acquainted with each other. They did not object to my questions but I requested for them to simplify some of theirs. "These are GEPers (students in the GEP). They need challenging questions. We have to keep these," so they claimed. This practice was repeated for the rest of the tests and examination that year. As I had no idea what and how they taught their students and was afraid to ask for fear of showing ignorance, I usually could not gauge the kind of questions they would set. My students fared badly. It is as if they had trained really hard in the new gym and instead, had to run a long distance race for which they were not prepared. Most gave up half way or even stumbled and injured themselves.

I really felt like a failure who had let my students down. Rose and Henry were happy with their students' results but offered no advice to me. I thought teachers were supposed to help each other? I felt judged and assessed even as my students were assessed. There was much frustration for myself and my students. Yet I was hugely relieved that neither my HOD nor my Inspector questioned my teaching. On hindsight, I should have shared my problems with them and asked for help and advice but I was afraid of showing my weakness which might compromise their evaluation of me.

The whole episode caused me to question who had the power and authority to set test and examination papers, within schools and at the national level. And who did the examination or their results serve most — the country, the schools, the teachers or the students? It also brought home to me that even for the best and brightest, examinations could be painful and the students were at the mercy of the setters who might or might not care about their learning and development. The alignment or gap between what was learnt and what was tested determined to a large extent the results of the test. I also began to recognise that assessments could be highly political and competitive not just for the students, but also for the teachers.

That competition caused me to feel frustrated and unfulfilled in my work. I lost confidence in my teaching and also felt left out from the apparent comradeship and friendship between Rose and Henry. Instead of staying on to improve my teaching and my understanding of the students, I reacted by asking for a transfer back to a JC. Acknowledging that my love for learning was not as great as my fear of losing in the teaching competition *was* painful. Perhaps I should have taken the initiative to dialogue with Rose and Henry in greater depth to try to understand their perspectives and practices in teaching and assessment instead of just getting upset with them.

Since then I had also realised that Secondary Three was the most stressful year for a student. Many students would start to assume leadership positions in their activities or services. The transition from practical applied Mathematics in lower secondary to the mostly pure and abstract Additional Mathematics in Secondary Three was difficult and painful for many students. The different pedagogical approach and emphasis by the new Mathematics teacher did not help. If I had known all these then, things might have been different. But the lack of support and sharing in that culture caused me much anxiety. Friendship and cooperation among teachers were not as I had imagined.

Tested as an Examination Driven Teacher — My Approach of Teaching to the Tests

I was transferred to a neighbourhood JC with only three years of history. I felt welcomed by the Head of Department and colleagues. In time I found that the department was united in wanting to help the students understand what they learn, be able to apply and so succeed at the "A"-Levels and subsequently improve the ranking of the school.

There was sharing of resources and teaching experiences and with my department's influence, I started to seriously teach for the examinations. I studied the "A"-Level syllabus, the 10-year series, discussed examiner's report with my colleagues to prepare my lectures and tutorials. My lessons became highly structured, focused and aligned to the examination requirements and included advice on time management, problem solving skills, memory skills and ways to avoid mistakes. Interactions with students focused on how they can improve or on remediation for the failing students. Class tests and school examinations were set to be as similar to "A"-Levels as possible and just a little harder in terms of interpretation and application. It was like conducting circuit training to prepare athletes for the national fitness test. The almost identical training and testing conditions ensure high achievement provided the athletes trained hard.

The first time I had to set targets in terms of percentage of passes and quality grades increased my awareness of the competitive nature of examination. I had established a rationale for my teaching, to help my students do as well as they possibly could in the "A"-Levels to facilitate their pathway to further studies. My students responded by doing increasingly well. I felt justified by their results. I had also established a rhythm and pattern in my classes and gained acceptance in the staffroom community by our mutual belief that "we can achieve". The "A"-Levels became truly our instructional and learning goals.

Tested as a Stay-Home Mum — My Role as a Mother

During these eight years, I also became a mother to three children, Nicholas, Joyce and Jonathan. Balancing school work and family was really challenging at times especially when the children fell ill. I constantly struggled with the guilt of not being able to be with my children when they were sick and not being able to spend as much time with my students after school as before. By the time Nicholas started primary school and began to struggle with Mathematics, I made the difficult decision to resign from teaching. I had been doing well in school. I had been approached to be HOD and to go for interviews in the curriculum branch and examinations branch all of which I turned down as I was quite sure that I wanted to be on the ground teaching students. My parents and colleagues all questioned my "insensible" decision. There would also be a loss of income but most importantly, I had to stop doing something that I enjoyed. On the other hand, was I really ready to be a home-maker and housewife? Moreover, Nicholas disliked school and was unhappy and anxious every Sunday evening. He could not cope with the adjustment of a big class of 40 after a small personal kin-dergarten class. He endured bullying in school by other boys as he did not dare to either make a stand or report to the teacher. Both his health and mine suffered. Afraid that he would drop out of the system, or that in the future he would attribute his failure to a lack of my attention, I resigned from teaching. After I actually resigned, a few colleagues quietly told me that they wished they could resign to take care of their own children as well! In this day, it seems taken for granted that educated women are judged to be successful only if they can have both a career and a family. Giving up your job to stay home with the children implies a failure in the social and eco-nomic sense. Coping with my mother's disappointment in my per-ceived loss in status was the most difficult for me. But I had experienced raising children and having a career at the same time, when I had felt like a failure as a mother.

One particular colleague, Soi Kheng's sharing stood out. He was an experienced Mathematics teacher with two undergraduate children who majored in history and English language, respectively, and they did not particularly like or excel in Mathematics. His advice to me was to relax and encourage the children to develop in what they can excel in and not expect them to love Mathematics like me. I found it hard to accept it at that time but realised the wisdom of his words much later.

The four years that I stayed at home observing my children learn helped me understand how children learn and understand in primary school and it subsequently helped me relate to my students better. Seeing Nicholas' struggle with his studies also brought home the fact that I had often projected my own studying experi-ences onto my students instead of trying to understand their learn-ing difficulties. During this period I was like a personal trainer to my children.

When Nicholas completed the Primary School Leaving Examination (PSLE), I thought I had fulfilled part of my responsibility as a mum. I thought Nicholas would become more independent and confident in secondary school and I could return to what I loved to do. I decided to apply for a part-time teaching post in the independent school where my ex-HOD had become the Principal.

Tested as a Retrained Teacher — My Understanding of Teaching

Joining the new school signalled a new beginning for me with new discoveries. It was the year after the "Teach Less, Learn More" call from Prime Minister Lee, and MOE had developed the PETALS framework which was a student-centred curriculum to engage student learning. The whole school training for differentiated instruction and ongoing assessment for learning was refreshing and exciting for me and I experimented with new pedagogical approaches (pair and group discussion, presentations, Information and Communication Technology (ICT) and assessment formats (peer assessment, self-reflection, exit questions, comments marking, alternative assessments). I felt like I had been given a new well-stocked tool box and began to explore the tools within. Students were like athletes who had to undergo holistic cross training which contributes to overall fitness and not just prepare for a race or competition.

After teaching two "O"-Level track Secondary Three classes for two terms, I was surprised and agitated by a change in school policy. The Mathematics department, with approval from the management, had decided to implement banding in Secondary Three classes. How could they do this? All the girls in the school had obtained either A or A* for Mathematics in the PSLE (Primary School Leaving Examination) and I could not imagine how negative the impact on their self-concept, engagement and motivation would be on the students in Band 3. Already, with the integrated programme (IP) track and the "O"-Level track, a handful of students in the "O"-Level track felt that they were perceived to be lower class students and lacked confidence in themselves. To now further divide the students into three bands based on the mid-year examination results seemed unfair, even harsh, as they were not aware that their results would be used for such a purpose. Although I did raise some issues and doubts, I was shown some research which supported banding with long term improvement in students' achievement despite initial student distress or demotivation. I realised then that apart from intuition, I lacked professional knowledge about educational issues or policies. I had to deal with it somehow.

I had no peace of mind even as I accepted the new deployment of a Band 2 "O"-Level class and a Band 3 IP class. I already knew all the students in the "O"-Level class so there was minimal adjustment there. However, on the first day of Term 3, I approached the IP class with some trepidation and a well-rehearsed motivational speech with forced cheerfulness. I was greeted by a subdued class. Some looked resigned, some looked frustrated and there were a few sullen stares. I did not blame them as even I felt bad for them.

One girl, Pei Yin, in particular, seemed more unreceptive than the rest. She was a highly articulate girl with critical perspectives because of her extensive reading on philosophy but she struggled with Mathematics. She often questioned what was taken for granted, "Why must we study pure Mathematics?" Most students just accepted that it was an important subject. When I started the topic on calculus by introducing differentiation from first principles a few weeks later, Pei Yin struggled with the work for a few minutes and then exclaimed "This is pointless. I'm not going to do it." She complained about the fruitlessness of the whole exercise while other students with the same sentiments just grit their teeth and carried on. What could I do with her? I searched desperately for some alternative resources and shared my problem with a colleague. I was delighted when I found that he had a book on real life applications of calculus which was meant for non-mathematicians in business, science or even media. It contained an excellent range of calculus applications and interpretations in different contexts but with very algorithmic descriptions of the Mathematical formulae and no proofs at all! I intuitively knew that it would appeal to Pei Yin. Instead of forcing her to work on the proofs and exercises with her classmates, I lent her the book to read and make notes for herself. This was the first time that I had allowed a student to deviate so much from the norm. I wondered what would happen.

After a week, we had a discussion about what she had read and she said "I can't understand everything but it's *definitely* more interesting than your notes and the textbook." I was right that she would like the book! She grudgingly struggled to catch up with the class and once we reached the applications, she could contribute to both group and class discussions. Interaction and dialogue with her improved my pedagogy and enriched her class participation as she was not afraid of asking questions and giving answers that revealed her misconceptions, unlike other students. I welcomed Pei Yin's ideas and critique which helped the class to open up and gradually other students were willing to risk making mistakes in class discussions. She always gave me something to think about when I left the class. I rather enjoyed it actually as I felt that I was learning while thinking about them.

Pei Yin was my teacher in a very real sense as she had shown me that students might fail or dislike Mathematics due to their inability to relate to the content meaningfully. They may be learners who need to appreciate the essence or purpose of the content first before they are ready to engage to work at the small incremental steps necessary to build the big picture. I was forced to question what I had to teach and why I teach in order to have meaningful discussions with her. I started to look at the various topics more critically in terms of their connections with each other, with other disciplines and with the real world and required my students to do so too. Modelling self-reflection to students, I became much more aware of why certain instructional approaches worked with some students but not others. The conception that students need to be active participants in their own learning and assessment was shaped during this time. I had become co-learners with my colleagues and students as we engaged with Mathematics learning in a more open manner, exploring learning possibilities through reflection and imagination.

The openness of the colleagues here and especially the sharing of some Secondary Two Mathematics teachers really helped me understand my Secondary Three students much better. Their attitude was totally different from when I first taught in a secondary school so many years ago. Although the first year was very stressful for me again, sharing with another colleague who joined the school at the same time from a JC helped both of us understand that we were not alone in our struggle to change our pedagogies and cope with the increased marking load requiring our formative comments.

Tested as a Critical Learner — My Beliefs about Teaching, Learning and Testing

Three years ago I stopped teaching again to support Nicholas as he prepared for his "O"- and "A"-Levels. I could sense that he was trying hard in his Mathematics so as not to let me down, as he felt that as the son of a Mathematics teacher, he had to do well at Mathematics. He also requested me to stop work. I did not want to let him down either although I was not as anxious about his results as before. The three years in the previous school using a student-centred approach — which emphasised assessment for learning alongside summative assessments — helped me to recognise that he cannot be judged by his results alone. However, he was by now really entrenched in the examination-centred system and often felt stressed and anxious. After his examinations, in order to show my children that one can still study no matter what age, as well as to address my ignorance of current educational policies and research, I enrolled for the Master in Education part-time course.

I found myself invigorated and refreshed and challenged in so many ways. I had to question my own assumptions and beliefs about teaching and learning. In the course, concepts of meritocracy, streaming and banding were questioned, various critical perspectives of equity and equality were presented. The emphasis was on the lower ability of the marginalised, lower socioeconomic status (SES) students and their lack of opportunities or exposure. Even as I questioned my own concept of equality, I observed that there was an assumption that students in the elite schools were privileged with extensive opportunities and enjoyed an unfair advantage. Having taught in two independent IP schools, I found that there were still students who would be considered marginal and whose stories were not always heard. Some faced consequences if their results slid, almost every batch would see a student suffering depression caused by not being able to cope with the stress of perceived failure and perceived parental disapproval over results or performances. My heart really went out to them.

Talks on consequences of cheating were given before every examination to help them resist the temptation that can be so real to some of these top students, due to their fear of failure. Yet, there were still cheating incidents. Many decisions were made apparently with the students' best interest in mind, which may not have included consideration for their fear or insecurity. Other students on scholarships (students with merit recruited from around the region), admired and envied by many, struggled with pressures — from fear of not meeting expectations, from lack of allowances that would prevent them from going out with other, more affluent classmates, or even being ostracised because of their accents. Many of their issues seemed small and insignificant compared to students from neighbourhood schools and yet, from their perspectives, their fears about failing in the system in one way or another were very real. These students may require teaching and guidance just as much as students in neighbourhood schools. Or perhaps I am just trying to justify myself. In these schools, I definitely would not face some of the outright discipline cases and defiant or rude students that some of my friends had encountered in the neighbourhood schools.

Looking back, I had started as a young, enthusiastic, idealistic teacher believing in my ability as a good student passing all examinations with flying colours. Through Adam, I saw that my apparent love of learning might mask a need to win approval and the need to be valued for my achievements. Working with Rose and Henry showed me the political side to teaching and brought out of me a fear of losing in the teachers' competitive environment, leading to my subsequent focus on examination-driven pedagogy. It brought out my need for others' recognition and approval based on my achievements. I interpreted my students' success at the "A"-Levels as my success. After seeing various students failing the system and suffering consequences, my first resignation was prompted by my fear that the same would happen in the case of Nicholas, if I made no change, and that he would blame me for it subsequently. My fear of being judged a bad mother if Nicholas failed might not be so different from my mother's fear of how others would judge both of us when I resigned from teaching. Gaining assurance from his PSLE score which admitted him to the Express stream, I returned to teaching with greater empathy for my new students even as my practices with new pedagogical methods transformed my beliefs about learning and assessment. Talking with Soi Kheng helped me recognise that subconsciously, I had expected my own children to outperform me in studies and careers as had my own family. Neither of my parents was a university graduate, yet my three brothers and I all had honours degrees or a master's degree. Work and income wise we also exceeded my father's level. But it was unrealistic to expect that the children will always surpass the parents in every way though that would be most parents' wishes.

Teaching and learning with Pei Yin increased my capacity to be more accepting of diverse learning styles and surprisingly, I became less trusting of assessment results as a measure of ability. During that period, my frequent self-reflection on my teaching, sharing with my colleagues and my students' responses to me helped me assess my own work better. I gained confidence that what I taught them could help them to continue learning in the long run and was not just focused on the examination criteria. After so many years, I felt liberated from being judged by my students' and my children's results. Although examination results are still highly regarded, especially in Singapore, helping the students to learn to self-evaluate and self-regulate is so much more essential for them to recognise who they are and who they can possibly become. At each of the turning points in my life, my emotional trauma or dissonance was the start of self-reflection leading to decisions that changed my course of action. I have gained much insight into myself as a teacher, as a mother, as a person in school and at home, which has been achieved through the interactions with my parents, children, colleagues, students and my own internal dialogue. What my parents taught me and what they expected of me had a profound influence on my decisions in my work and how I relate to my own children. It was really hard to change certain perspectives even when I wanted to. My perceptions in turn had an impact on my children and their perspectives of learning and examinations.

Although I stopped teaching again when Nicholas was preparing for his "O"-Levels, this time, it was definitely more than to reassure him my reason for doing so was my fear for his failure. Whatever the outcome of his examination, as his mother, I was assured of his integrity as a person, and of his strength in and his love for music and language. This realisation came about through sharing among colleagues in my last school both at personal and professional levels. The writing of this narrative also offered me a mediational space where I gained more insight into my actions and thoughts.

I find in myself a sense of latent excitement even as I contemplate returning to teach next year in school and as my children face new challenges. Nicholas will be taking his Associated Board of the Royal Schools of Music (ABRSM) piano diploma examination for performance and enlisting in the Police Force to serve National Service very soon. I know my unseen motivations and beliefs will continue to be tested through my interactions with my children, colleagues, new students and new pedagogies in a new school, regardless of which school it will be. The sharing space afforded by the community of teachers would afford a space for me to uncover and learn more about myself and improve my professional skills.

Chapter 14
My Germination Process

Annie SENG

If I may turn back the clock, I would like to relive my happy past. Unfortunately, life is such that there are always ups and downs. I view myself as a seed planted in various fields waiting to germinate. When nurtured it would grow, mature and flower. Naturally, when ignored it would be stunted, would not sprout, would shrivel and remain lifeless.

In my teaching career, I have taken charge of three different Co-Curricular Activities (CCAs). In this story, I would like to share some of the challenging experiences I faced for each of the CCAs under my charge.

My First Struggle — As a Dead Seed

This happened in the third school which I was posted to near the end of the 1980s. I was summoned by the Principal to her office one afternoon. That was the first and only time I sat facing her directly, a close encounter with her. She was twice my age and had that Empress Dowager stature, the symbol of a powerful iron widow who ruled China, as she sat on an oversized armchair. She had demonstrated her self-centredness. She was the typical

Principal — authoritative and domineering. That was how Principals were looked upon those days.

Without advance notice, she told me as a matter of fact that she would have me in charge of the CCA — Netball. I replied that I had no experience and would not do a good job. In a cold tone, she retorted she would send me for training and she passed me an application form. I asked an innocent question, "How long would I be in this CCA?" Her response, "Nobody knows, today you see me here tomorrow you may not." I was dumbfounded by the tone in her voice. There was no give and take; no negotiation. No chance to protest. I wished I were consulted first. I knew that was the end of our conversation. The meeting was brief but final.

I felt lost and disillusioned. I was already facing difficulty adjusting to the afternoon session. For the past few years, I was accustomed to teaching in the morning. I wished the Principal could have asked me about my new adjustments. This would be more comforting. She did not. She lacked the personal touch. Timing was important. Things could have been different if there was an induction programme and option offered for my preferred CCAs like what we have now. There must have been other teachers who faced the same challenge like I did and it drove them to make a difference for the system to be improved. As for me, I chose to be stuck by the high-handed system and to suffer in silence. I succumbed to the authoritative style.

On deeper thoughts, I wondered why she had a dual complex. At Monday Assembly she would be the charismatic, seemingly caring Principal who spoke to the entire school about how students should behave and show respect for the teachers. She could have adopted a consultative approach where there was mutual respect for differing views. She had thrown me onto the netball field without nurturing me. The only nourishment given was sending me for the training. After the death sentence she imposed on me, she had never bothered to find out how I was coping and whether the students were learning from me. Is it not fundamental for all Principals to know their staff ability and capability well including the non-academic domains such as CCAs?

Certainly, it was crucial for the school to match teachers to the right choice, if CCA was integral to provide students a holistic well-rounded education. I was like the seed strewn in a vacant hole. CCA was compulsory and hence there must be a teacher in-charge. At that point in time, I was not mentally prepared to nurture students in qualities such as resilience, tenacity, confidence and perseverance through Netball. I needed more hand-holding in a new environment. Surely the Principal at the pedestal knew much better.

CCAs were totally different from the discipline I had been trained to teach. I viewed myself as a teacher to fill the vacuum to meet the needs of the school and not that of the students. This was not right. Are we not meant to serve our students to the best of our ability? I knew I would do injustice to the students. The interview had marked the beginning of my misery as the teacher in-charge of Netball, playing dual roles of coach and administrator. Me, as the coach? Not even in my next life. I have no sports inclination. I was not meant for sports. No matter how much training was injected in me, nothing was going to change. I simply had no flair in playing the game or being the coach. I blamed no one, not even Mother Nature who has not endowed me this special quality. I still accepted my fate, though unwillingly.

Training was on weekday evenings. For three months, every Tuesday, after school at 6.45 pm, I plodded to the National Stadium to attend the theory session. Vaguely, I remember the class but I could not recall a single participant. I was like a robot entering and leaving class because the button was switched on and off. Naturally, as a teacher I passed the theory test effortlessly. I was not meant for the practical, not to mention how to coach the sport. This could not be part of my professional development.

Every Thursday evening, I would be at Petain Road to have my practical. There were the others — fit, athletic with the perfect make-up of a Netball player. I could not remember where I was except that the court where we practised at was next to the red light district. Fortunately, I met another teacher and I found solace in knowing her. I was glad to have met another similar person. She was more senior and taught in a primary school. She, too, was compelled to join the training. Our commonality was that we were "hopeless" for the sport. I had been told never to use this term on students and yet I was applying it to myself. In life, things are often ironical. Together with my teacher friend, I often stood by the side of the court engaged in small talk. Could we have made a difference if we had spoken up? We did not try. It was not a usual thing to do. Instead, we had chosen a more timid path — to be silently bullied by the system. I wondered how many more of our kind were left unnoticed.

At the Netball court, I was lost. For the others, their movements were swift, efficient and professional; they knew exactly how to move the minute the whistle was blown. I was clumsy — I could not run, pass, jump, shoot or handle the alien ball. I was the stray seed left to be stampeded. It was frustrating. I would rather be given remedial classes as I could do a better job helping the weaker students in their Geography. Handling the ball was totally different from handling students which I already had been doing for 10 years. Netball was not my forte. There was no sense of belonging. I was attending the training and not being the student.

The best consolation was my boyfriend then who would diligently come to give me a lift home. I was grateful to him as he never failed to show up at the right moment. He was supportive.

I met the Netball students twice a week. They were bubbly, self-directed, and they were my "teacher" instead. I was at a loss. I felt I had betrayed them; every single one of them. They had no idea about the mental stress their teacher was facing. They knew of my incompetence, my inadequacies. They never complained. They were lovely girls. I could not help them much, I was only physically present. They persevered and tried their very best to perfect the skills. I could not help to bridge the gap nor give them the new horizons to improve and perform better. I was quick to spot a leader, Mei Jia, among the group. She was the student-coach leading the team in warm-up and other practice skills during the training sessions. Student leaders are often a teacher's best friend. I had to count on this tall superior being, Mei Jia, to train the team. I gave her full power to manage the field activities. Having learnt the lesson from the Principal, I made sure Mei Jia would pre-consult her practice plans with me before she activated the team. Thankfully Mei Jia had great people sense and the team members respected her.

The agonising days worsened when it was close to the competition dates. Participating schools had to provide an umpire. Most schools sent their teacher in-charge. I was desperate. I could not umpire. I would not know when to blow the whistle, not even when training with the students. It was a game, a competition that must be professionally handled. I had to look for and keep on trying to get an umpire. A week before the tournament, I frantically searched the telephone guide and my finger never stopped to dial. I braved myself and became thick-skinned enough to ask for help. I called the Netball Association — for three years I had kept making the calls but they had never sent anyone, and I never got to reach anyone. Finally, I managed to get a Mrs. Mah from a polytechnic. I gladly parted with my S$10 for her service. I heaved a great sigh of relief when the team lost. What an irony to feel happy when my girls had lost! The girls looked demoralised and dejected. What kind of a coach was I! I was a traitor! What I cared for was that the burden to look for an umpire had ended!

I grew more and more disillusioned. There was no hope for a change of CCA. Teaching life was mechanical and stressful during CCA days. I was brought up to be a survivor and had tons of patience, being able to adapt and be happy in any awkward situation. Now, I started to have self-doubt. I decided to be true to myself. It was tough facing the girls. I knew I would never add value to them. My conscience was telling me that I should not continue to "cheat" them or the system. I was miserable from the start. Within the first year, I attempted for a transfer, which failed. I struggled and survived three years in this suffocating environment! Today I envy my colleagues. Their timing is right as they are supported by a coach who is specially paid to train and equip students with the necessary skills. This should be the way to run the system.

Even though the experience here had brought unpleasant memories, on hindsight, I felt I could have moved out of my comfort zone. It was my personal mental block that told me Netball was not doable. In those days, there was no mentor to guide you. I was left to swim on my own, otherwise, things could have been different. I had forgotten how I was able to shoot, guided by the patient lecturer during teacher training basketball practices. I was delighted and exhilarated then when I was able to score when guided by the right technique. Nevertheless, being a coach was a totally different matter. You need to have the right skills and techniques to perfect others. I happily left the school as an ordinary teacher.

My Second Struggle — As a Wild Seed

The dead seed had landed on a new field in the next school in the early 1990s. Even though I play no musical instrument and have no musical background, I was put in charge of the school band. I became the wild seed because I found myself playing multiple roles as the teacher in-charge of this CCA even though training was carried out by the instructor. My role was to administer the affairs of the Band, which could be varied, more diverse than that of the Netball teacher. The germination process for my personal growth was slow and dull as I was always following instructions given by the instructor.

I remember that I was advised by the instructor to buy a large collection of musical instruments which amounted to a huge sum of money. It was not easy to convince the Principal that the money was well-spent as she was particularly meticulous about financial matters. I found myself in a dilemma stuck in between the Principal and the instructor.

There were other things I dreaded doing. For instance, I had to stock-keep the instruments regularly for safe-guarding for the auditors. Stock-checking was a tedious and massive job with a whole range of musical instruments to track. When instruments were spoilt or needed servicing, I had to call in the repairman. These were usual disruptions that were added a burden to my teaching load. Should a teacher not be spending more time in the classroom rather than doing such annoying tasks? I felt these odd jobs should be the work of support staff. I have colleagues who were disillusioned by these extra CCAs, which drove them to resign from the system.

Another challenge with heading the Band was recruitment, which was an annual headache as it was not a popular CCA. The CCA Open House was an air of festivity; but competition was stiff; each CCA group would attempt different marketing strategies to recruit new Secondary Ones. My CCA had the advantage as my members could easily make the loudest noise with their musical instruments to draw the crowd. Nevertheless, I had to literally grab the Secondary Ones and convince them that Band would be their wisest choice as it could promise them a good CCA grade at the end of their four/five years of commitment.

For the next nine years, I witnessed the change of three instructors and nine batches of band members. Strangely, I found myself becoming a recruitment officer instead of a teacher. When an instructor decided to leave, it was my responsibility to look for a replacement. This was another example of the extra duty that a teacher had to do. Extra Co-curricular Activities (ECA) rather than CCA would be more apt. Incidentally, the old name for CCAs was ECAs. The name has been changed to better reflect its role; one of which is to provide students a holistic education.

In Band, I was often at the mercy of the instructors and students. The instructor would plan activities for the students and as teacher in-charge I had to follow-up. In addition to the long hours of training, there were two inevitable activities in band. Attending camp was a common activity for the members. Obviously, the teacher in-charge had to be present as well. Public performances were also regular. These could be indoor or outdoor performances.

Let me focus on camp, which usually lasts three days and happens during the June or December holidays. At the whim of the instructor, camp would often be held in another school where he would gather all the other schools he coached together on the pretext that each school could learn from one another. I would chaperon my students and land myself on unfamiliar ground in a different school. Being fearful of the dark, you could imagine how torturing it was for me to sleep in an unfamiliar staff room for two whole nights. I felt totally alone. The students would usually be sleeping in the school hall. For me, the entire camp was meaningless and time-wasting as I could not connect with music.

I remember an indoor performance in the school hall — "Band in Concert 2". As the teacher in-charge this was a new challenge for me. I had a long to-do list. These included the invitation of special guests, publicity about the performance, sale of tickets, booking of venue and other logistics preparations. Together with the instructor and the senior members, we racked our brains to think of ideas which would make the concert a spectacular one. The performance also meant longer practice hours and days. I found myself heavily involved in pushing the sale of tickets. Despite the effort put in I felt detached at the end of the performance.

On deeper reflection, I could have congratulated the members or called for a celebration at the end of the performance. I could have written "thank you" cards to the seniors. I did not do any of these. Being an introvert, I felt it was not necessary to do so. I was more anxious to get home. My behaviour was a reflection of my previous Principal. I too, lacked the personal touch.

Outdoor performances were regular as well. I dreaded the performances at the Botanic Gardens or the Pavilion at Harbour Front. These performances were often held on weekend evenings, which meant less time spent with my family. This time, I was the gatekeeper — I had to collect the school keys in advance on Friday and on either Saturday or Sunday open the school gate, disarm the alarm system and wait patiently for the instruments to be loaded onto the lorry before the musical pieces were ferried to the performance venue and back to school after the performance. The return trip was often an agony. I was eager to end the evening fast. However, students would be taking their own time to clear the school ground — they would be excited and taking photographs in the band room. I would be waiting impatiently in the canteen.

If I could relive the moment, I would join the students in their excitement after a performance. I never did. Perhaps by doing this, I would have bonded with them better. My rapport with the band students was superficial. They bonded better with the instructor. I was often envious of the instructor. I had no one to blame except myself, I was over-reliant on the instructor. During their practice,

I had chosen to stay in the staff room marking and preparing lessons. If only music had more meaning for me, the situation could have been different. If only I had been more thoughtful and concerned about their progress, I would have connected with them better and be happier. Anyway, I left Band without any regrets.

Today, I have totally divorced myself from all forms of Band activities. The multiple roles I played like an octopus with eight tentacles had made me wild and fluid. From this experience, I never introduced camping activities in my next CCA. Band has taught me that the way to win the hearts of the students is to bond with them; doing practically everything with and for them.

Experimentation and Self-Discovery — As a Growing Seed

My breakthrough came in 2000 and my germination process was steady in the initial years and grew rapidly in recent years. This time, I was approached by the Principal who confirmed I would helm a new CCA. The sad news was that the Green Club was initiated to accommodate students without CCA — if I may use the term, "dropouts" from other CCAs. I found myself relearning and taking on new roles.

I recall meeting officers from the Sungei Buloh Wetland Reserve (SBWR) to discuss our Adopt-A-Park collaboration, which was conducting guided walks along the Mangrove Boardwalk, by the Green Club Ambassadors. The challenge I faced then was to inspire students who lacked the aptitude, to master the content and develop the ability to speak confidently in front of an audience. These were necessary attributes of a guide. I learnt from my Netball days that "when there is a will there will always be a way". The official adoption of the programme was a few months later. I needed the student guides to take the visitors along the boardwalk. True enough, I discovered and managed to inspire 10 potential guides from my Geography class to come on board the programme. There was no doubt that there was a great difference in the learning calibre and attitude between the "dropouts" and the new-found 10 students. Passion had driven the group to be committed to the cause.

For the next three months, the students had their intensive training by officers from SBWR. They had to travel three times a week to SBWR on their own on public transport. The journey there was tedious and long with the switch between bus and the Mass Rapid Transit (MRT) train followed by a 20-minute walk into the wetlands. I was happy for the students when they finally mastered the art of guiding at SBWR. I witnessed the first sweet success of my students' efforts and they were ready to lead the Guest-of-Honour during the official adoption. Today, I have put in place a senior–junior mentorship programme to ensure the sustainability of our Ambassador Programme at SBWR. This was my first green project, which has turned unique for my school.

Our guiding programme at SBWR kicked off well. The learning journey was an important initiative which served two key purposes. It allowed the Secondary Ones to appreciate nature. At the same time, the Green Club students had the opportunity to develop their confidence when they carried out guiding. Today, all students in my school have visited SBWR at least once. The programme has given life to the wetlands, and more importantly, greater returns for my Green Club students in terms of social skills. To date, I have raised interest in more than 10,000 visitors, including both schools and organisations. Through hard work and patience, I have trained more than 100 student guides since we started. Our initial programme with SBWR was supposed to last for five years. However, to this day we are still strong partners.

Over the years, I have made numerous trips to SBWR — I have totally lost count of the number. I have left indelible footprints there. Each trip was a new learning experience with each batch of Secondary Ones. There was always something new to see or learn. They were either spotted by me or excitedly pointed out to me by my students or the visitors we brought. I have finally found joy in Mother Nature. I hope to share the joy I have experienced with more visitors and welcome schools who are willing to engage in the service of my student guides.

When I first started, "green" was not the "in" thing. Green was not popular. Today it is totally different with so much news about climate change and other environmental issues. In the early years, I had the liberty to experiment and make new discoveries. The first discovery was my personal strength in the area of green. This was significant for now I find myself watering my own seed and allowing it to grow through discovery and experimentation. On my own accord, I was willing to learn and adopt new ideas from attending workshops and exhibitions regularly. Becoming an Environment Education Advisor (EEA) of the National Environment Agency (NEA) in 2004 was a turning point for my commitment to the club. I learnt and was inspired by how other schools and organisations carried out their green activities. I picked up ideas and turned them into my own to benefit my club members. My efforts paid off.

What prompted my interest and spurred me on was the very first trophy that my students won in an Environmental Quiz. I often look at the trophy with pride. It was my maiden achievement and I realised how important it was for teachers to go the extra mile to coach and provide a platform for students to excel. The extra hours that I put in for the students were worthwhile. In Green Club, I had the power, the wisdom to make careful selection of activities that benefitted the students. I was totally the captain. I was tired of following directions given by the instructor while in Band.

My second discovery was via the Principal who gave me the space to improve and spread the wings of the club. I recall how she verbally told me one evening at the parade square that she would turn "green" into the niche for the school. I was sceptical then. Now, I can look back and easily chart the milestones of my green achievements and I have finally found my soul in this CCA.

Things between 2006 and 2009 moved very fast. Progress moved in tandem with our shift to the current school site. Various green spaces were adopted and many green partnerships were forged during this period. I was responsible for every progress, every development — the school's status for Environmental Education was well-established and recognised in the national arena. The recognition and affirmation of our green programmes came through various accolades the school received. In all these successes, I played a significant role working closely with students and various green partners. I was kept busy, but derived great satisfaction from it.

The seed had grown steadily and was growing progressively taller and fuller. My career took a new turn when I was promoted to senior position for Environmental Education in 2008. That year, I was recognised for my green efforts by NEA and was honoured the Eco-Friend Award. As I look back, all these happened because of a simple act in the late 1990s when I invited a recycling vendor to set up a recycling corner in the school to remove the waste generated from students' test papers. Instead of seeing the papers being burnt or thrown away, I felt I had to do something. Little did I realise that through that small simple act, I would be rewarded 10 years later. It became a turning point for my professional career.

Challenges Faced

Being in the senior position has its challenges. I was not afraid of work. We were constantly invited to share our ideas with other schools. Sharing at different platforms was frequent as we had many visitors who were keen to learn about our green programmes. My mentor Principal took it upon herself to guide me through without wavering. She took a personal effort to listen, to work through my delivery patiently several times to boost my confidence. This reminded me of my natural instinct to hide under the table when I was in primary school when questioned by teachers. This weakness is hard to eradicate. I may falter, however, I am glad because I am appreciated, my confidence has grown and I now have developed a new view of myself. My mentor Principal is the kind of person we want in the education service.

More Green Seeds Planted

My third discovery was the commitment of the Green Club members. Without the hard work and the support of the students, it would have been impossible for Green Club to have reached its current status in the school. Over the years, I witnessed the pride and commitment the students put in for every activity they were engaged in. For example, I noticed how Edward, one of the Green Club members, overcame his fear of water at SBWR when we were involved in the Dragonfly project. He was able to brave his fears and wade in the pond to take shots of close-up views of the dragonflies.

I enjoyed watching how Green Club members effectively displayed their public speaking skills at various platforms such as during the Ministry of Education (MOE) Excel Festival and during Clean and Green Carnival exhibitions. They would be eager to share with various visitors at the booth about their project involvement. They never failed to live up to expectations. Together we learnt and enjoyed all the activities we did — whether it was area clean-up or research projects. I also made it a point to reward deserving members by recommending them for the Eagles Award or Eco Award for their contributions to the club.

I admire the green values in them as they were never embarrassed about the activities they carried out, be they beach cleaning or litter picking. In the early days, the club was often shunned by many students because they felt they would be involved in menial tasks. Today, it is a prestigious CCA in the school and students have to be auditioned before being admitted to the club. I no longer have to accept "dropouts". This is a great turning point for the hard work I put in all these years.

The senior Green Club members also benefitted from the work attachment programmes as they had opportunities to work in an authentic working environment with different organisations we collaborated with. It was great watching students learn and take initiative. I am glad I have many such students in the club. From a humble beginning, the club has grown in status as well as in numbers. Even though things may seem to have stabilised, I am constantly looking for new collaborations and directions to develop my students further and to ensure sustainability in our programmes. The plant has not stopped growing. In fact, it has flowered and seeds are produced as seen in my students. Many of them too have germinated along the process as they became more committed to the club. I remember John, Linda, Kah Meng and many more. They have excelled in the club and have carried the green values on to the next stage of their tertiary education.

Conclusion

We may be the architect of our own career cycle. We may choose to take centre stage or the back seat to shape our professional career. However, as demonstrated, it is essential for schools to match teachers, in this case, with the right choice of CCA. A mismatch could be detrimental for both teachers and students as demonstrated in my story. The seed could remain a seed and eventually die or the seed could take root, sprout and grow not into one beautiful plant but into many kinds of beautiful offspring.

Chapter 15

Leaders that Make or Break Your Career

Jackie Chye Chen ANG

Now, sitting in front of my computer, I cannot help but think of these two school leaders, so vastly different in their support for their staff. As I think about these events, I cannot help but realise that the support system for new managers at that time was really lacking and how this had actually affected my work–life balance.

I had always thought only women are capable of being two-faced, but Mr. Tong proved me wrong. This new Principal, an old man, who was about to be retired, had his own tricks up his sleeves. I was even naïve enough to think that he would just go with the flow and be happy with his big lump sum of pension money when he came to our school.

On one hand, he came up with many radical changes which really garnered much support from the staff. One of them was to stop parents and maids from entering the school freely, in the name of waiting for their child. We were more than pleased to see our school canteen transformed from a maid agency centre to a serene eating place. For this, he deserved my respect. On the other hand, he became the oppressor in the Executive Committee (EXCO) meeting room. There was no freedom for objections. It was simply a boring one-man show. Among the management team, we came up with the slogan "Mr. Tong knows best". In his eyes, his decision was still the best. He must have split personality or perhaps he should be getting the Oscar for Best Actor.

I wonder if I was too sensitive then. I noticed I was being tasked to start many new programmes. My Head of Department (HOD) would always enter my staff cubicle and say, "Boss asked me to give you this." I was given many extra assignments, on top of my current duties, all in the name of developing my potential. I looked among the subject and level heads. No one had as many assignments as I did. I never had any problem with the Enhanced Performance Management System (EPMS). I just had to think of using more papers. "Developing, developing and developing" seemed to be the shackles on me. I could hardly breathe. Was I so incompetent that I had to be developed in so many areas? How long would this development even last? I talked to my colleague John about my unfair workload but he ended up teasing me that I must be the "hot" favourite of the year for getting so much attention from the boss. I was the only one picked to be sent to Chicago for my cluster US study trip on innovative practices. I could only roll my eyes. Well, I was leading the Innovation and Enterprise (I&E) team after all. I really did not think he picked me out of favouritism. Anyway, he did not pay more attention to this project as this was just another task from the Superintendent. I vividly remember that I was talking to him on the bottom-up approach and he did not seem to be convinced about it. However, I must have been in hot water then as I could feel the intense heat. He seemed to be scrutinising what I had been doing and did not seem to be satisfied with it.

I remember that finally I had the courage for a "showdown" with my boss. I did not want to talk to my HOD as I knew he was powerless and defenceless over my plight. I showed him my EPMS and talked in detail about the fact that I was getting married that year and I could no longer cope. I was pleading for a favour, humbly, so that I could still survive. I was thinking that he would empathise with me and let me off.

He then spoke to me softly, yet firmly, "Jackie, you are doing fine. You know, in my previous school, whenever I was testing out my management team, I would allocate tasks to individuals. If anyone survives, I would add more to his load. I would continue doing so to test his breaking point. I believe I have not overloaded you yet." His words were like shards of glass. I felt numb from my wounds as he later rattled off about the Orchid hybridisation programme that I was in-charge. I seemed to have lost my sense of hearing for the rest of the time. I could not even remember what he had said about the programme. In his eyes, I was still not given enough to prove my worth. This man did not care if I was sinking. I was simply a pawn in his eyes to achieve his target.

I must have been desperate or too brave to speak up and I simply gave it to him, "What if I snap?" He stared at me but I could not be bothered. I needed to walk out with some advantage. He finally gave in and took away one of my CCAs, Brownies, but he also broke another bad news, in exchange for this. "You know, Mike is going away for MLS[1] in February and later on, he has an important reservice[2]," he smiled sheepishly. I felt as if my boiling point had gone beyond 100°C. This sly fox had planned this while he sent me away to Chicago for a study trip. My tone was cold and I had to excuse myself quickly from his room, knowing there was no point continuing the discussion.

I felt betrayed and confronted my HOD for not telling me his plan. As usual, he defended it by saying that it was the boss' idea. I knew there were the preparations of new Science rooms and eco-pond, department work and examination matters for me to take over during his absence. It was not much of a deal in exchange for one CCA. I had to concede defeat to my old boss. He had the last laugh after all and I just had to push on.

Before I knew it, my health was failing me. I was losing five kilograms in a month even though I was taking at least four meals a day. My colleagues thought I was on diet to prepare for my wedding. How could I have the mood to even think about that? I was drowning in the sea of pills. Sometimes, I even thought I could not make it.

---

[1] Management and Leadership Studies: a three-month training program for middle managers at NIE.

[2] A regular period of training for reservists in the Singapore military.

Every day, I had to drag my frail body to work on the programmes and the logistics work. It was as if trouble never ends. There were problems with my wedding preparation as well, especially when my other colleague was having her wedding on the same day at a nearby venue. I must have been utterly down in my luck. Besides settling issues for my new workload, I had to settle my list of guests. My husband Ken said that both of us must have visited the same geomancer who pulled a trick on us. "Burn-out" as pointed by Evans (1996), must be the state I was in, as I did not feel "rewarded and the task is endless" (p. 95).

By late June, my HOD was finally back. I thought my knight was here to save me from all this work but I was absolutely wrong. It did not take long before his promotion to be a Vice Principal (VP) spread to my ears. Apparently, he had gone to the Superintendent straight and asked for the interview. Obviously, my Principal was not very pleased either as he skipped one level to get his promotion. How unethical he was! I had been on my feet since I was in this position and very often, he was out of the school. There was not much mentoring from him to talk about. Something is really wrong with the system. And I naively thought that there would be an opportunity for me to learn the ropes slowly. I really did not know the job scope well enough to take over. I guess he was also quite eager to climb up the ladder and my struggles were no concern of his. With the sly leader around, he had taken things into his own hands as he had been told by the Principal that he was not in line for promotion. This must have pushed him to do something more drastic. I have no stomach for all this office politics.

Yet, he still had the cheek to comfort me that my efforts had finally paid off and that I would be the next-in-line to take over his position as a HOD. On the contrary, my world seemed to collapse before my eyes at that moment. I was not ready for this position. I wanted to have a breather, not a promotion. What is the point of being a HOD when you do not have the opportunity to even enjoy your life? These people did not seem to see my agony. This knight had turned into a killer, stabbing me for the second time. I did not talk to him for one week even though his cubicle was only opposite mine.

It was only when my best friend cum colleague fell sick that I realised that I had to throw in the towel. She had an auto-immune disease and her kidneys were affected. I broke down in tears upon hearing this news. What if the same fate should befall me? My memory of witnessing my university classmate die on the last day of our final examinations came haunting me. She, too, worked too hard and as a result, one of her brain arteries burst. I had to ask myself if it was worthwhile to slog to death. All these promotions over the years were too fast for me to adapt to. I had not even stood firm at one level before being pushed up another. On the other hand, my colleagues were wonderful and I felt reluctant to leave, but there was always a greener pasture for me to graze on. I told my hubby about my worries. All that he asked was if I was happy to stay on.

It dawned on me that my passion for teaching would be extinguished if I stayed on. The common practice of the school is to pick teachers who are strong in teaching to be in the management team because the pre-requisite of the management team is to have good repertoire of pedagogy. I guess, in the past and even now, the poor middle managers are supposed to manage both the school programmes and be instructional leaders as well. This is really draining as I look back at my role as a new middle manager. I was thrown to a new field when the Ministry of Education (MOE) had just started to expand the middle management team for each school and there was no clear job scope or proper mentoring system for new middle manager in the past. I was supposed to learn on the job and at the same time, provide my professional knowledge to help my other Science subject teachers in their teaching skills. However, in reality, there was not much time for me to really adjust as I was given too many new assignments as MOE, at that time, was really throwing in many initiatives. I still remember that I was not even taught how to manage financial matters for the department or even how to work out department plans when my HOD was away. I was supposed to read from the documents he left. I was really hoping for someone to guide me to perform all this administrative work before throwing me into the deep sea.

I remembered my little *kung fu* disciples in class 6-3, whom I enjoyed playing with using all the car tyres and a steering wheel.

My experienced teacher, Mr. Singh next door, even thought me silly to "borrow" so many things from the garage. I also remember my gang of fatsos in class 6-8 who stood under the hot sun with me to see how I caught the caterpillar and lizard. They would squat down with me despite their big size, when I picked up the lizard's tail, trying to show them its body parts. But it was more than fun. I should be staying with my kids, instead of staying in the cubicle doing all the paper work. I felt like such a misfit. At that point of time, I knew I had to ask for a transfer. I needed to get in touch with more kids. Perhaps my struggles and my grievances had arisen from the fact that I prefer the teaching track to the leadership track.

I think I had to count my blessings then. Mr. Tong did not block my application. He simply told me sarcastically that he would not keep someone who did not have the heart to stay on and that no one was indispensable. I was disheartened to hear such remarks for all the efforts I had put in for the past few years. Despite this setback, Lady Luck had laid her eyes on me for once. My health picked up and my gang of great colleagues, my true knights, came over and helped me out in most of the wedding details. Finally, I was able to be a happy bride.

I still remember that Mr. Tong, my HOD and even my VP did not turn up for my wedding dinner. Perhaps they had found me to be a quitter, or perhaps they did not want to offend either brides for attending one of the weddings or maybe they were not as ingenious as my other guests, who planned to go for both weddings. They had even rotated among themselves in deciding which half of the session to attend so that the tables did not look too empty. After all, the venues were only separated by one lift. Whatever the reason might be, I was not disappointed at all as I knew though I might have lost my prospect as a HOD but in exchange, I had gained two more new roles — a happy ordinary teacher and a blissful wife. A lot of times we think we have lost some, but in actual fact, we will find ourselves gaining more. I enjoyed my new roles for many years until I met Ms. Sum.

Ms. Sum, on the other hand, was an entirely different school leader from all my other Principals. In fact, she was my fifth

Principal. I remember that she told us that nothing is more important than the pupils' results because that is our core business and we had a big crowd of parents hawking or even spying on us. I still remember that we had to walk discreetly along the corridor of block C because there would be a resident who would video-tape us from her unit for any "wrongdoings" and send it straight to Ms. Sum's email. I felt disgusted at this act and felt that my privacy had been invaded.

Nevertheless, Ms. Sum always had her way. There was once that this resident claimed that our pupils would suffer from piles as our teachers took 10 minutes to dismiss the pupils during recess from the parade square. She shot back at this chap with strong evidence that there was no medical proof and even cited that the Ministry of Defence took a longer time for their cadets. It really shut the fellow up. She always gave these nosy-pokers nicknames like "No Home Four" (in Hokkien, it means "no manners") and stressed that these people were simply literate but not educated. We always laughed at her jokes and found that she was forthcoming and daring to dismiss the parents' complaints. How I wish that we can have more such school leaders!

I remember during my first year with her, I had a problem with one of my pupils, Hank. He showed signs of depression and became quiet. I discovered that the problem lay in his family. His mother was obsessed with certain religious practices and he was highly disturbed by it. I tried to help him on many occasions and spoke to him. Even the counsellor was at her wits' end as she had no authority to get the family to go for counselling. As things got worse, he started self-mutilating and behaved weirdly. I informed Ms. Sum about him and we arranged a meeting with the parents and Hank.

I thought she would side Hank and convince his mother to go for counselling. However, I was wrong. She turned the table over and made Hank see his mother's point and both parties' mistakes in handling this sensitive matters. Both sides gave in. I could still remember how his father broke down and hugged Hank tightly and his mother wept.

My baffled look must have given me away. After the meeting, she asked me calmly, "Think about what you want out of this meeting." Then, she explained to me that rebuking his mother's action would only make their relationship worse. She needed Hank to understand how much his mother loves him though she might have used the wrong method and how important the family was to everyone. It struck upon me that I could have been too eager in trying to protect Hank and forgot that he still had to return to his family and that mending their relationship was the top priority. In my eyes, she was objective and far-sighted. I was glad I was not in her shoes to handle this matter, or else I would have messed up the whole matter and put his mother on defensive mode. It would have been a lose–lose situation for both. From this incident, my admiration for her in handling parents grew.

A year later, my Vice Principal came over and approached me to offer me the leadership track. I almost yelled, "What a déjà vu!" I had rejected my previous school's offer due to my traumatic experience with Mr. Tong. I was reluctant to accept it again and I frowned despite his eagerness to push me for it. However, being diplomatic, I told him that I would think over it first.

I think I must have been very poor in my acting. Before I could come up with excuses to reject this offer, Ms. Sum approached me and had a long talk with me. She was candid about the fact that the school was short-handed in particular for the management team and that my HOD was very new and young on the job. Moreover, the school was expanding the upper primary classes from a mere two classes to 10 classes. After all, I was the most experienced Science teacher. I had been helping my HOD to vet papers and organise school-wide programmes. My organisation skills and Science knowledge must have captured her attention. Obviously, I was then on her list of choices. Still, I did not accept the job immediately as I could not get over my previous encounter as a Level Head.

I talked to one of my colleagues, Ms. Ang, whom I respected a lot. She was a retired HOD and was very knowledgeable. In fact, she was one of the authors who wrote my Primary Science textbooks. She advised me that it was not a great idea to reject the offer as I was still young. In fact, opportunity will not strike again, not to mention for the fourth time. My husband, likewise, was supportive of the idea. He was very enthusiastic about me getting busy so that I would not be too pre-occupied with my little angel. "Go and keep yourself busy so that you will not become schizophrenic one day," he teased me. What was wrong with paying attention to our only child? I did not want to miss being with her during her childhood and spending time nurturing her. Who would take care of her and my family chores? Could I really keep a work–life balance?

Yet, I had to admit that Ms. Sum was a nice person to work with. She did not put up any airs and had always kept her door open for anyone. She even went down to do the ground work with the teachers whenever there was a big event. You could hardly differentiate her from others if she did not introduce herself as a Principal. The school was cosy and like a family, though like family members, we had our little bickerings at times.

There, I realised that what I was seeking was the intrinsic motivation to take up the role. Very often, leaders think that having extrinsic rewards like more performance bonus works well. They do not understand that this "carrot" of theirs no longer serves as a catalyst for good performance but instead for people like me, it serves as nothing but stress. I do not want more grey hair over my job. Financially, I think I can settle for what I am having now. Having three meals on the table for my family is more than enough for me. Yet, to see me as a person, to recognise my potential and to develop it at my own pace, are really important to me. And I could see that Ms. Sum was able to do that.

The mentoring system from MOE was also kicking in at that time, though I did not think my Senior Teacher was clear about how to mentor new middle management. She simply created documents for my HOD, VP and myself to sign and left us to negotiate the job-scope. However, I had the privilege of having a young VP and HOD so everyone was really new on the job. We discussed clearly on many occasions what my job scope was and I was understudying my HOD with other HODs showing me the ropes. Though I cannot claim that I was knowledgeable about the work, it was clearer when they coached me, showing me how they would do the planning for the department. My persistence in questioning everything before I got into the job paid off.

Anyway, I accepted it at the end. The interview was a breeze. I remember that she teased me on how the Superintendent kept on smiling and joking with me while all the other interviewees did not make it that day. I shrugged my shoulders and I thought that perhaps I was honest and I did not prepare for the interview. Destiny must have decided that it was time for me to take up the job. I was sent for a few middle management courses which was again new initiatives from MOE. I think they must have heard our grievances as the turnover rate for middle managers was quite high. In fact, Ms. Sum told us that they needed at least another 2,000 middle managers to fill in the vacancies at that time. Nevertheless, those courses were beneficial as there were many administrative skills which I think my VP would not have been able to share clearly with me. I even noticed middle managers who were in the job for more than 10 years attending the course. It really shows how lacking the support was in the past for middle managers.

True enough, I did not regret my decision. Ms. Sum was more than a superior to me. She was motherly and made sure that we, young mothers, had time with our kids. She allowed us to bring our children to school for some major events like Mid-Autumn festival and Vesak Day celebration. She even offered to babysit our EXCO group of children, while we were busy with the events. It was true that she had her way with young kids. The children were kept busy by her and we could feel at ease to carry out our duties. She even reminded my VPs not to exceed the time for meetings as she knew we had to fetch our children in the evening. "Don't let their children be clamped up by child-care centre. The fine is hefty!" were the words she always used on my VPs who were either single or workaholics themselves.

Even with my new roles, she did not push for more tasks though my HOD for Pupil Management wanted me to take over the School Staff Developer (SSD) job. She knew I was not comfortable with it. Instead, I was able to go deeper into my teaching pedagogy and pass on the knowledge to others at more workshops and peer mentoring.

I worked with my HOD on new teaching resources and we were bold enough to replace some of the books that the students used with our little new inventions. We were both young and were learning the ropes so there was much consultation with each other and I could learn well what she was doing. I was also able to monitor our graduating classes for the next three years. All these were done within my comfort zone though it was a new area for me to work on.

When I had my second child, Ms. Sum was worried over the tainted milk incident in China. She reminded me, "Jackie, keep to breast milk. Nowadays, the milk powder is so unsafe." She made sure that all nursing mothers had a maternity room as all of the sudden, we had a baby boom for those two years. More than 10 teachers gave birth during this period. I think our Prime Minister must be very happy to hear how we tried to increase the low birth rate.

All these little reminders were touching. They showed that she really cared for the people around her. It was not the age or experience she had that infected me, but the genuine concern she had for the people who worked for her. She was like a wise old owl who can provide advice when needed and a mother hen who can shield the children from harm. An "emotional leader", as stated by Hargreaves (2002, p. 178), her encouragements and participations in many events showed her persistence to build a culture of care and growth. Conversely, Mr. Tong, who was so indifferent, somehow, had caused us to "retreat into our shells and withdraw from engaging with change" (Hargreaves, 2002, p. 179).

Sometimes, I really wonder if the ministry should conduct workshops for principals to teach them emotional leadership. They should even be tested on their aptitude and attitude. Now that I put Mr. Tong and Ms. Sum on the weighing scale, it is like putting Hitler and Buddha together. They have the same number of years of service in teaching field and both are near retirement. Yet, the impact they had on is so different. We are not in the corporate sector concerned only with results. Every day, we face and interact with people, be it our pupils, our parents or even our colleagues. The human touch and understanding is so crucial and yet so complicated. How can one leader differ so much from another?

Many a time, I think of my career. How I convince myself to go on or to step back from the leadership path really depends on the path my principals lay for me. It is like a child learning how to walk. I think it is important not only to have clear hand-over process for people who are new on the job but also the opportunity to understudy their mentors and be shown the ropes. I, for one, will stretch out my hands to others, for I do not want them to follow my footsteps. As the ministry comes up with so many new job titles, there is a real need for someone who is familiar with human resource to sort out all the support systems required for this massive expansion of middle managers.

However, ironically, there should be enough support and time given for young and inexperienced middle managers to get the hang of the job before they are thrown into the deep end. Time is always a factor that our system fails to see the need for. This vicious cycle can only be stopped if there is an insightful school leader who can see this. How do we strike a balance? I do not know.

On one hand, I am part of the workforce but on the other hand, it is also important for the bosses to recognise that we do not live for just our work. We, too, have our families who give us our motivation to work. Our profession is so unique that I think no other profession can be compared with it. It is our passion for and belief in our next generation that push us on, for I believe that if I really care for others' children, someone else will care for mine on their journey to life-long learning.

But, all these thoughts perhaps are just my wishful thinking. Probably what the ministry wants are leaders who can push people to work hard.

(*Note*: *Names of the characters are fictitious.*)

References

Evans, R. (2001). *The human side of school change: Reform, resistance, and the real-life problems of innovation.* San Francisco, CA: Jossey-Bass

Hargreaves, A., Earl, L., Moore, S., & Manning, S. (2002) *Learning to change: Teaching beyond subjects and standards.* San Francisco, CA: Jossey-Bass

Chapter 16
Chapters of My Teaching Career

Siti Aisha SAID

Prologue

An astounding educator is like a great inspiring book. The moment you hold on to the book and flip through pages after pages of it, you begin to fall in love with it because of the impact of the storyline. The book is so good that you do not mind reading and reading it again, taking it along with you to cruise your journey of life and making events of the stories an analogy of your life experiences. It is difficult to find that great inspiring book. And I always believe that it is just as difficult to find a great inspiring educator. As such, my vision is always to be an educator who inspires and my mission is to always find ways to achieve my vision.

Chapter One: I Got the Book

"If you are looking at careers after your studies, do NOT be a teacher," Mr. Lee said while the whole class stared at him, puzzled. He took out a pack of his medication from his shirt pocket, flicked it in mid-air and continued his speech. "See, where does my money go? Everything is spent on my heart medication and all the other doctors' appointments. Haiya ... don't waste your time. Join other professionals," he said before leaving our class.

Reading the above might make you ponder if my class gave him hell then. Well, you are wrong. We did not. Really! Mr. Lee was my accounts teacher when I was in Secondary Four. He was not the first teacher who gave unfavourable comments about becoming a teacher. In fact, there were a few other secondary school teachers who told us to carefully consider if teaching was a profession we were keen on. After hearing that from them and looking at how stressful life was for some of them, I almost swore never to be a teacher. Hah! But that was then... three years down the road, my journey hit a T-junction. Destiny prevailed over my original plans. Instead of turning right, I made a left turn.

I went into the teaching academy after my "A"-Levels. No, not because I wanted to be a teacher, but because I had to be one. I could not afford to pay for the university fees even if I were to be accepted and I did not want to throw myself into the working jungle yet. I became the sole breadwinner for my family at the age of 19. I had to support three younger siblings who were still schooling at that time. I wanted to continue to study very much and going to the National Institute of Education (NIE) was the only option of furthering my educational journey while getting paid, enabling me to support my family as well.

I stared at my hands. The book is in my hands now. Whether the book is a bestseller really depends on how well my story turns out to be.

Chapter Two: The Journey

One would never have guessed that I would end up in teaching. Being meek, shy and quiet, people would only wonder if I would be teaching in a school for the blind, deaf or mute. I, myself, am still amazed by my bold step to enter a world where your voice will have to be heard and your intelligence will be constantly challenged. Nevertheless, the road to the path less travelled (then) was undertaken. I cruised slowly to find that love in the journey that I was reluctant to embark on.

It was a journey full of anxiety for me. I never liked to speak in public. Catching me talking to a group of people was a rare occurrence. Teaching is a really uphill task for me. I started off this almost impossible task by asking myself what kind of teacher I want to be. How would I want to be seen by the students? What are my strengths and weaknesses? How could I overcome my weaknesses and work on my strengths?

I began to look for my model teachers, teachers that I would look up to. I scrolled down the list of teachers in my mind. From my primary school to my college teachers ... and I found a few. They possessed the characteristics that I felt were important as a teacher — strict but caring, respectful and respected, kind and nurturing and last but not least, patient!

Only very few teachers came to mind who possessed these qualities. One of them was my Chemistry teacher who was also a discipline mistress in school. Students feared her but she was a wonderful classroom teacher. I like strict teachers. Firstly, students will not fool around with you. Secondly, lessons can be delivered smoothly. Thirdly, there will be fewer problems created in class. And so, it was a strict teacher I would be.

The next important characteristic is patience. To be a patient teacher is crucial. I can be quite a slow learner at times so I really adore teachers who patiently taught me until I understood the lessons. I also believe that the teaching world is not as beautiful as portrayed in the TV adverts by the Ministry of Education (MOE) — "If you got what it takes, teach". Well, they should well put it as "If you REALLY got EVERYTHING it takes to teach, then TEACH". I remember seeing the advertisement showing students in the laboratory smiling and enjoying themselves, while the teacher laughed along, portraying a contented look on her face. However, what was playing in my mind while looking at those adverts were my classmates fooling around in the lab and eventually breaking a few test tubes. My Science teacher screamed at them for being careless and reckless. Breathe in, breathe out ... yes, I believe there are a lot of challenges in the profession and realistically, you really need to have an abundance of patience to be a teacher.

Past experiences as a student played a major role in determining the characteristic of a good teacher. Fully armed, I walked into the primary school that I was posted to with dignity. Every day, I would put up the persona of a lion waiting to pounce on any victims at bay. I was very strict with the students and my voice was loud enough to be heard across the block of classrooms. Well, even the Primary Fives were more scared of me than their form teacher who was a discipline teacher. My colleagues looked at me in amazement, often wondering how this soft-spoken woman could strike that level of fear from the students.

One particular thing that I would do after I entered my classroom was to check the students' homework. Normally, the first five minutes of the period would be dedicated to silent reading of a Malay storybook. While they were reading, I would go round and check their homework. Even if they had failed to do one of ten questions, I would question them. My interrogation would have put off my pupils then. Afraid of being questioned, they would do their work diligently.

Nonetheless, when I teach, I would ensure that my pupils understand what was taught. The weaker ones would be called up after school hours. That is when I would help them slowly until they could manage the basic skills needed in the particular topic.

I needed to balance myself. As much as I liked to be strict, I must also be patient to my pupils' needs. This was especially so as the school that I was posted to was a relatively notorious primary school and the socio-economic status was one of the lowest. Hence, to discipline the pupils, I had to be strict, but to empathise with their plight and help them succeed in life, I had to be patient.

Chapter Three: The Conflict

Like a great book in hand, I began to flip through the pages of my teaching life. Year after year, I began to fall in love with teaching. Teaching taught me a lot about learning. As I taught, I learnt to be more empathetic. As I taught, I learnt to be more human than the human that I already was. I began to see learning beyond what is written in textbooks. It went far beyond examinations too. I began to question the need to have examinations when it created more disengaged learning than a more engaging one. I could not stand it when a good teacher was being associated with someone who gave a lot of worksheets to the students and drilled them to get excellent results. Worksheets and drilling do not equate to learning for the test of life. My contestations to such regimented and traditional ways of teaching affected my pedagogical choice in teaching and learning. Why did I need to follow the school's learning culture if I could have a choice to change it for the benefit of the students? Why should the number of worksheets and the amount of drilling for the students be a measurable tool of teacher success? What if I could teach them just as much without giving them the pile of work other teachers gave? Does it mean I am a bad teacher if I do not follow the norm? Could I reject this "proven pedagogy of drill and practice"? It was a tough challenge for me as a beginning teacher because I needed to prove myself to the HODs that my method of teaching was feasible. I also needed to prove that students could learn just as much from me as from very senior and experienced teachers. And the exasperating part of it was when my capability was questioned because apparently one of the teachers' child was in my class. So, as a mother, she was "very concerned" if my teaching would affect the Primary School Leaving Examination (PSLE) results of the class. Well, my left hand column was telling me her concern was more for her child. That was my first encounter with a "difficult" parent!

I began to feel the heat of teaching. The assessment had started. And I was the one being assessed. I maintained my composure. Be patient and persevere on was my mantra. That was a very trying period. Conflicting ideologies on education and keeping to my "ideal teacher character" was pretty tough. I was new and I knew that I needed to learn. And I needed to learn fast because I was given a graduating class with only six months of teaching experience. However, I could not convince the other teachers because I was still an infant in the teaching fraternity. So I told myself, actions speak louder than words. If I could not convince others with what I said, I could try to show them what I could do.

Months built on and my first PSLE results were out. I could not sleep the day before, thinking of the possibilities of a major disappointment if my class was unable to produce quality results. That morning was my judgment day. My journey on the bus felt exceptionally slow. It was one of the longest bus rides I had ever taken. Upon reaching school, I almost thought I was going to suffer a heart attack. My heart was beating fast. I tried telling myself, if I was going to drop dead before I entered the school gate without knowing how terrible the results of my class were, that would be the most blessed death ever. I chuckled at my silly thoughts. Sigh ... again.

As I stepped into the school, I saw my Subject Head. The moment of truth would be out soon. "Come and see your students' results," said Mdm. Hasnah smiling at me. As I entered the staffroom, I realised the rest of the teachers teaching the level were already there busily looking at their class results. There was no time to feel guilty because I was late, or should I say, the last to arrive. I began to glance through the results of all the PSLE students, picking out my pupils taking Mother Tongue EM2. I heaved a sigh of relief. Apparently there were only 12 students who had gotten distinctions in Malay Language (ML). Out of the 12, 10 of them were my students. With the exception of two students, the rest of my class had received an A grade! That was quite an achievement for me. I really thanked God for the exceptional results. That somehow put paid to the other teachers' perception that belittled the capabilities of new and young teachers. That moment of happiness is etched in my mind. It reaffirmed my belief that education is more than just exams and worksheets. I believe students need to enjoy learning so as to reap the true goodness of education. And that reaffirmation created a new confidence in me to hold on to my belief and do whatever that would benefit the students most. Ultimately, the results would follow suit. The survival phase concluded on a positive note.

The following six years in the school were filled with interesting experiences. Teaching and learning were something that I was beginning to be confident in. My meek, shy and quiet personalities dissolved and I transformed into a new persona of a firm, sarcastic but funny classroom teacher. I tried to balance my strictness with a large dose of my comical nature. It was funny to see my students with this look of confusion whenever I cracked a joke with them. I guessed they were not sure whether to laugh or to just keep quiet. In the end, they would close their mouth desperate not to let go of a chuckle. Oh, poor fellas! From then on, I told myself that I needed to let loose too. I had a fun ride teaching. I grew to love the profession even more. Like a beautiful novel, the story became more interesting as I flipped the pages.

Chapter Four: Twisted Tale

After seven years of teaching in the school, I decided to further my studies in Nanyang Technological University(NTU)/NIE doing my degree in Malay Language and Literature. I studied full time for two years and totally enjoyed the experience of going back to school and studying all over again. After the final year exam of my graduating year in NTU/NIE, I went for an interview at the MOE Headquarters (HQ). Little had I known that I would successfully be selected to join Curriculum Planning Development Division (CPDD) in HQ, a job that I had planned to do as part of my professional development but never thought would come that soon.

Being in HQ, my professional development experienced a very steep learning curve. It was almost a drowning experience for me but I managed to keep myself afloat in the sea of uncertainties and manic projects thrown to us as and when policies were being rolled out. I picked up a lot of confidence and knowledge in my short stint in HQ.

I remember my ex-boss mentioning this to me, "You are here to contribute, not to learn." At that point, I knew the learning curve would be very steep. One of the most challenging tasks that I had was being involved in a secretariat in a taskforce on teachers' review. Never had I dreamt of working with the Director of CPDD and the many Assistant Directors. I learnt a lot from this experience. One of the "ridiculous" jobs, to me, was when I had to craft emails to the Dean of a university for my boss. I was not the head but I had to think like one to craft such emails to my head's counterpart, who was so much more senior in position than me. But I guess the experience paid off. I did give my two cents' worth to my boss about certain issues and I began to see that leaders are also just as human as I. They might not see certain things that we see and they can make mistakes like anyone else.

As I went through the two and a half years of my stint in the "ivory tower", I began to see and question things that were happening then. I began to ask what is a true leader? What kind of a leader do I want to be? Could a leader be the key motivator and a source of inspiration to his/her subordinate? Well, there are many leaders I have worked with. Many of whom I felt were authoritarian and some still held on to their feudalistic leadership style. Very few showed leadership characteristics that engaged subordinates into decision-making, or supported and motivated them. Neither did they pick them up when they fell or celebrate with them when they soared. There were a few exceptions who taught me about true leadership which provided me with useful advice and guidance.

The next phase after my stint in MOE HQ was something that I never thought would happen. My career trajectory became an interesting experimentation instead of a stabilised one. Going back to a primary school was not what I intended to do. After acquiring a degree in ML and Literature and working in HQ, I was looking forward to teach in a secondary school more than anything else. I yearned for new challenges in teaching and believed teaching in a secondary school would be a good change after seven years in a primary school environment. Hence, when the posting was out and I realised I was posted to a primary school, I was prepared to enter Huberman's stabilisation and serenity phase.

But, I was wrong. When I was posted to a primary school in the West, I was made to head the ML department. As a Subject Head to a group of six experienced teachers, it was a challenge to change their perspectives. It took me a year to buy their trust and support. Nevertheless, the wait was fruitful. Slowly, things started to change. The department became more alive and the efforts of teachers in the department were being recognised.

Another challenge awaited me the following year. I was tasked to be the advisor to the Staff Well-being Champions (SWC) team. My team comprised teachers from different departments. I was tasked to lead the team to look after the welfare of the school staff. Tall order? Well, if the previous leader could do it, so can I! I never let anything get to my positive spirit. Just as what I did to my ML department, I observed the people in my team. I took efforts to blend in with them and speak their language. At the end of that year, we managed to pull off a fantastic Year-End Dinner event that really showed the collegiality of the team. We were ecstatic.

Looking at the changes that unfolded in front of me, I began to see strengths in me that I did not realise before. I relate well to people, including difficult people (teachers!). On the downside, I was often put to work with difficult people because no one else wanted to work with him/her! Sigh...

At this point of my career, I brought in the guidance and counselling skills that I had acquired years ago. I also applied the art of nuances in emails and letters that I gathered while working at the MOE HQ. (Well, crafting of emails for my ex-boss paid off!) I applied the skills of people management which I acquired while conducting training sessions in HQ too. I began to see how I had used all my knowledge to create a positive impact on the teachers I worked with in school. From this point forward, I began to do another soul-searching to reassess my career trajectory.

Epilogue

My role as a teacher shifted greatly ever since I joined HQ. As I looked back on my journey of exploring my strengths and weaknesses as a teacher, and how I stood by my belief to be a teacher who would educate students to love learning more than just their results, I began to apply the belief to my current work of developing the teachers in my department/team to help nurture students holistically. I hope they would share the same purpose and belief in educating the students instead of just moulding them to become academic-driven puppets.

Clandinin *et al.* (2010), mentioned about temporality in looking at one's narrative. As I reflected on my journey, I could see how my past has carved a mark on the hardcover of the inspiring book that I was holding. My challenging years as a beginning teacher taught me a lot about perseverance and holding on to our beliefs. My interjectory period in HQ, taught me about leadership. My next cruise to experiment leadership back in school taught me about my capacity to lead. I brought along each experience as a tool to mediate my next move in my career trajectories; I realise how much I have learnt during those experiences which make me think the way I think right now.

My journey does not end here. The book may not have come to its end. I may not have inspiring stories but I am more than happy if I have students who have inspiring stories. A successful teacher will have many successful students. Success should not be defined as merely possessing a high paper qualification or being rich and prosperous. A successful person should be one leading a happy life, and being able to contribute back to the society. As teachers, we lead students to their aspirations.

(*All names in the narrative are purely fictitious.*)

References

Clandinin, D. J., Murphy, M. S., Huber, J., & Orr, A. M. (2010). Negotiating narrative inquiries: Living in a tension-filled midst. *The Journal of Educational Research*, 103, 81–90.

Golombek, P. R., & Johnson, K. E. (2004). Narrative inquiry as a mediational space: Examining emotional and cognitive dissonance in second-language teachers' development. *Teachers and Teaching: Theory and Practice*, 10 (3).

Greenleaf, R. K. (1970). What is servant leadership? Retrieved from http://www.greenleaf.org/whatissl/ (accessed on 12 November 2012).

Huberman, M. (1992). Teacher development and instructional mastery. In A. Hargreaves and M. G. Fullan (eds.), *Understanding Teacher Development*, pp. 122–142. New York: Teachers College Press.

Chapter 17

I Teach Because I was Taught — A Teacher's Story

*Anu RADHA**

The end of this year would mark the end of five great years in service for me as a teacher. In all of these five years, one thing has never changed and that is my personal belief and conviction that teaching is a calling, a calling for me.

The title of this chapter resonates at a very deep level for me. I chose teaching as my profession because I have a deep-rooted sense of wanting to give back all that I have received from a few great teachers in my life. As the narrative unfolds, the constant tension, almost a moral obligation, of having to be the best teacher, for all my students, frequently surfaces. Through narrative inquiry, as I weave through my past and current experiences, it becomes clear that being a teacher is more than just a job for me. It defines me.

I entered teaching, my lifelong aspiration, in 2008, fresh out of University. It is my first career and as I reflect on all the positive experiences that I have had and learnt from, I truly believe that it would be my only career. I had a pretty good beginning with numerous successes in my graduating classes, Co-Curricular Activity (CCA)

229

and others roles and responsibilities. I have to admit that in these five years, my learning curve was very steep, as I moved through the ranks of Beginning Teacher to now Subject Head and Year Head. I believe what made my quick transition that much more palatable was my constant reminder to myself that ultimately, it is always and all about the students. I always tell others that whatever it is, as long as the students enjoyed themselves and learnt something, be it academic or non-academic, then it was all worth it. Though challenging at times, my passion for teaching allows me to see each day as a new opportunity to make a difference in someone's life.

In examining my career trajectory with Huberman's (1992) schematic model of the teacher career cycle, it can be noted that it has been an accelerated ride, to say the least. At the stage of career entry, I transitioned from the role of student to the role of teacher. I have to admit that though I had no prior experience in teaching, I did not have to deal with the "reality shock". As my narrative unfolds, my past life experiences will validate the many lessons that I have learnt about teaching and being a good teacher. Hence, it was almost second nature for me to be able to relate to my students.

I quickly moved into the stabilisation phase. Huberman (1992) explained that during this stage of development a teacher gains confidence in her abilities. I became more comfortable in my role as a teacher and had a sense of independence. The stabilisation stage also means an affiliation to an occupational community, freedom from direct supervision and greater instructional mastery and comfort. However, Huberman (1992) noted that teachers may also experience some insecurities and frustrations during this phase. It was in this phase that I reassessed the meaning of being a good teacher and grappled with the tensions I encountered.

Looking for a turning point, a defining moment in my relatively short career, I thought about the numerous teams I had worked in, with colleagues of differing personalities. I thought about my CCA and involvement in Committees. I thought about my professional relationships with my Reporting Officers, other Heads of Departments and School Leaders. Interestingly, I could not identify a significant defining moment. Personally, if I were to think of a defining moment, a turning point in my career, it would certainly be because of the very core of what I do, my students.

A significant incident did take place. I was to be tested in 2009, only in my second year of teaching. It was a situation where I felt that one of my students was going to drop out of this race of life and that I was helpless. I questioned myself. I questioned my role as a teacher and my capacity to be effective. In him I saw so much of myself and my friends when we were at that age. It was a period of time when I constantly re-lived my past through this student and it was a period of time when I had great difficulty in defining what made a great teacher. I had always felt indebted to the few amazing teachers who made me what I am today. During this difficult period, I was afraid I could be disappointing them by not living up to their standards.

I was the form teacher of a very challenging class, 5N3 (a class in the Normal (Academic) Stream with most students being prepared for post-secondary vocational-technical education). To almost all of their subject teachers, 5N3 was a class to dread. It was a class made up of an interesting mix of students. There were smokers, frequent late-comers, fire-alarm activators, vandals and the list goes on. Never did a day go by without their subject teachers coming over to complain to me about some of the students' behaviour.

However, to me, they were nothing but a lovely bunch of kids, as I had built good rapport with them the previous year. Their lives mirrored my life, as I will elaborate below. It was easy for me to relate to them. However, one particular student stood out. Lionel* was a quiet boy when he was in 4N. He was one of those students who was pretty much "out of the radar". Teachers usually paid little attention to him.

However, I realised that as the year passed, he became more emotional and moody. He would always just make it to the Parade Square in the mornings for the daily assembly, drenched in sweat after running from the nearby bus stop. At times, he would look tired and unkempt. He would be very withdrawn in class, slouched over his table, hugging his school bag. Though he always tried to make an effort during my Science (Physics) lessons, he would spend the rest of the day daydreaming. I tried to reach out to him after hearing feedback from other teachers about the obvious change in him but he had built walls around him. My questions would always be greeted with a quick and soft, "nothing".

I knew that something was wrong and I felt a sense of urgency. Lionel was in Secondary Five now, just months away from the General Certificate of Education (GCE) "O"-Level Examinations. I had to find out what was wrong and how I could help him. Efforts to engage his parents were futile as both parents worked during odd hours of the day and to make matters worse, they were not comfortable English-speakers. Most of the time, my conversation with them would end with them being shocked at their child's behaviour in school. Sometimes, through their broken English, I could almost sense a quiet desperation and immense sadness.

When I spoke to the other students in my class, I realised that he was going through a lot at home. It seemed that his parents were trying to make ends meet. His classmates showed me his Facebook page where his regular status updates were worrying. He would always lament about how other children were luckier than he and how he thought that his life was too difficult. I was very worried as throughout this period it looked as though Lionel was keeping everything to himself, bottling up his true feelings and emotions. I was worried that he would snap one day, resulting in dire consequences. I was worried because I remembered being just like him nine years ago.

Furthermore he was becoming very disruptive and defiant in class, even threatening to throw a punch at his Chinese Language teacher. He also started being late for school. At this point, in my helpless state, I tried consoling myself by believing that all hope was not lost since at least, he was still coming to school every day. But that consolation was short-lived. He reached a new low when he did not turn up for his mid-year examinations (Preliminary 1 examinations). When I called his home, no one there knew where he had gone as he had told his parents he was going to school. When he eventually answered his parents' frantic phone calls to him, Lionel would just tell them that he did not want to go home, not the home that it had become. He returned home after a week and turned up in school a few days later. I had to call his parents down to see the Principal.

In the Principal's office, I met his dad for the first time. I learnt that Lionel's father worked in the construction line and his mother worked part-time as a dish washer in a nearby food court. Throughout our conversation, Lionel looked at the floor, tears streaming down his cheeks. At that point he looked so defeated. He was hunched over, with what seemed like the weight of the world over his shoulders. I could not help but feel sorry for him. I know that he should not have run away from home but I also was not convinced that his parents had created a good home for him to come home to. As he was looking so helpless, I actually felt angry that this child had to be exposed to the harsh reality of life at such a young age. His father was screaming at him in Mandarin. Later I learnt from my Principal that Lionel's father was asking him what more he could do or should do for the family. His father was so disappointed and exasperated over Lionel's behaviour. It was a sad situation. I realised that his parents were not even talking to each other. I knew that no one would truly know what was happening with the family and their family dynamics. They would need to sort out their problems first but time was running out for Lionel. He needed stability and security at this moment. He needed peace and calm.

As his parents were leaving the Principal's office, his father, in broken English, asked me to help, almost pleadingly. I remember that day clearly because I remember going back to the staff room and staring into space. I usually pen down my thoughts in my journal every other day. And on that day, I just could not start writing. I just felt very sad that Lionel, in all of his 17 years, had experienced many more problems than I had ever encountered in my 25 years of existence. I know that it may seem naive and idealistic but why must a young boy go through so much? At that point I just could not rationalise, maybe I did not want to. I refused to acknowledge that this situation was normal, even okay.

That day, I knew that if I did not do something, if I was not there for Lionel, he would fall through the cracks. At this stage, so close to the "O"-level examination, he needed normalcy. He needed to be

able to stay focused in school. I had to be for him what Ms. Ann*
had been for me.

I recalled how my life was changed by Ms. Ann, a teacher who
bothered — bothered enough to ask and to care. You see, being a
teacher has always been a guiding direction in my life. For as long as
I can remember, I have wanted to be a teacher. When I was a child and
anyone asked me what I wanted to do when I grew up, my answer
would quickly, and surely be, a teacher. Perhaps all that I have encountered as a student has shaped, influenced and fuelled me to be the
best teacher I can be.

Of all my experiences as a student, those that I had in secondary
school were instrumental in shaping my character and my very
being. With my Primary School Leaving Examination (PSLE)
results, I went on to a typical "neighbourhood" school. My self-confidence took a beating. I had a fantastic support system in my family
but perhaps that made me feel even more defeated as I did not do
well for my PSLE. The turbulent teenage years began. There were
challenges and I became quite the introvert, worried about what my
peers thought of me and if I would fit in. Peer pressure was everywhere and at times I succumbed to it. My results were inconsistent
and though I was not getting into serious trouble, I was certainly not
applying myself fully in my studies.

One day, my Secondary Two English teacher, Ms. Ann, asked my
class to write a narrative about ourselves. I must have been feeling
very down that day as I removed all pretences and poured my heart
and soul into my writing. I wrote about my low self-esteem and my
fears. I did not think much of the writing after I had submitted it.

A week passed and Ms. Ann met me along the corridor one day.
She paused.

"How are you my dear? I have something for you to do from
today onwards," she said, in her perfect, crisp accent.

I thought I was done for! Little did I know that what she was
about to ask of me was going to set the wheels in motion to change
who I was and would become.

Ms. Ann suggested that I lead the school for morning assemblies
each day. My responsibilities would include getting the school to

stand in attention, recite the pledge and read announcements if necessary.

As she was speaking, I felt the blood drain from my face. To say that I was horrified would be an understatement. At that time, public speaking, actually any form of speaking in front of a group of more than 10 people, was something I would never even try. I was not even a Prefect. Would people not think it is weird that plain old me was helming the morning assemblies? I started to regret ever writing that narrative. It was the root of all problems!

The next morning, I contemplated feigning a stomach ache and hiding in the safety of a toilet cubicle. As I was fretting in the restroom, I caught my reflection on the mirror. As I stared at myself, I realised that there was no running away. I had to do it. Ms. Ann would certainly not let me off.

However, the first day on duty turned out to be a horrid experience. I did not know that the microphone was not turned on. I continued talking into it, much to the amusement of the students below. I felt my face become red hot with embarrassment. Teachers came up to me to tell me that I was too soft and that no one could hear the announcements at the back of the Parade Square. I was so crestfallen. Why did Ms. Ann put me through this? I was hurt and angry all at the same time. Ms. Ann told me to meet her after school at the staff room that day. She told me that everyone, including her, at some point in their lives, makes a complete fool of themselves. She said it was normal and she even congratulated me for having lived through one such moment in my life. She told me that it was not how you failed that matters but how you get up from your fall and move forward.

From then on, I was on duty every day for 10 weeks, alternating with one of the school's prefects. I started to gain more confidence. All of a sudden, I developed courage, even after the "horrid" situation of technical difficulties with the audio-visual (AV) system. It no longer was a chore and I actually enjoyed doing it. Though it may seem to be very trivial, at that point in my life, I needed validation and I needed to feel that I could overcome my fears. The feeling was great. My self-confidence multiplied. I felt myself walking taller as I went through school.

However, there was yet another surprise for me. Ms. Ann told me that I was requested to be the student emcee for the Annual Speech and Prize-Giving Day that year. This time around, there was no hesitation. I knew I could do a good job and I gladly accepted the responsibility. For the next one month, I worked closely with Ms. Ann as we rehearsed for the big day. On one such rehearsal, Ms. Ann explained to me why she had done what she did.

She explained that she felt that she had to do something after reading my essay. She said that she knew I could be a confident speaker and a confident person, so she gave me the opportunities to develop my self-esteem and confidence. But what she told me next resonates in me till today, and I believe will forever.

"I merely gave you an opportunity, Anu. You could have remained in the toilet that day and made excuses to get out of this responsibility. Yes, I saw you running to the toilet! You could have been so overcome by fear of failure that you got paralysed by it, unable to ever face and overcome it. But you didn't. You took the first step, that leap of faith. So remember, in life, nothing is so helpless that it is impossible. Do not underestimate yourself because when you fear failure, that is exactly what you are doing, failing," Ms Ann explained.

I ended my Secondary Two year a different person from when I entered that year. In Secondary Three, I was appointed Patrol Leader in my school's Girl Guides Company. My increased confidence and self-esteem also spurred me to excel academically. I got into the best Express class and did better than expected for my "O"-Level examinations. I went on to a junior college and later to the National University of Singapore to pursue my other love, Physics.

Probably what has an even more significant meaning to me is that some of my fellow schoolmates in my secondary school did not have a "Ms. Ann" to help them. I was lucky because together with a very supportive family, I also had a wonderful teacher when I needed her the most. Some of my friends were not as lucky. They were almost written-off by their teachers. They were the ones who desperately needed a supportive adult in their lives. I had friends in my secondary school who came from broken homes as well as abusive homes. I had friends who would get locked out of their homes at night, quarrelling with their parents. I even had friends who ran away from home because they could not take the quarrelling between their parents in their homes.

I saw first-hand the viciousness of the horrible cycle my friends were in. They had to get out. It was completely understandable that education and studies were not the utmost priority of some of my friends. But their teachers did not understand that. They wrote-off my friends. They did not care. Those teachers were merely trying to teach the subject. They had forgotten that their job and responsibility were far greater than that. They were there only to teach the subject, forgetting that they were supposed to teach the child instead.

This is one of the many memories I recall where I have learnt the power of being a good teacher and the change a teacher can effect in a child's life.

As I recollected my personal experience, I was brought back to reality. I knew I had to do something for Lionel.

The next day, I went to school earlier than usual. I saw Lionel in the school cafeteria. I went up to him and told him that we needed to get a game plan and put it into action. I told him that his new day began that day and that we could only move forward. I did not let Lionel even think, afraid that he would turn a cold shoulder and reject whatever I said. I told him to see me after school every day, where I would review his timetable and help him with Science (Physics). I ensured that the stronger students in the class would sit around him so that if at all he needed help, it was nearby. Interestingly, this also brought the whole class closer together.

I refused to remind him about that meeting with his parents and would always remind him that I would be there to help him. I reminded him that only through having a proper education would he be able to lead a better life in future and make his parents proud. I looked for every opportunity to allow him to experience success, no matter how small it might be. I would constantly praise him for his efforts, regardless of the outcome. I also worked together with all subject teachers of the class so that we would all speak with one voice and be consistent.

Lionel changed himself slowly, but surely. He started to stay back in school and study together with his classmates. His attendance improved and he started to look happy.

The GCE "O"-Level examinations came and I must admit I was nervous. As he saw me waiting outside the school hall watching my students go in for their examinations, he came running to me to show me that he had placed the pen and highlighter that I had bought for each and every one in class in his pencil case. He told me that it was going to bring him luck. As I smiled at the seemingly carefree boy in front of me, I did not know if his efforts were a little too late. I had to wait for January 2010 to find out.

The day of the release of results arrived and I was at my wits' end, worried for my class. I could not believe my ears and eyes when I found out that 5N3 had done better in Mathematics and Science than an Express class. Most of them would be able to go to a polytechnic! Lionel thanked me personally. He was so happy, a far cry from the once quiet, withdrawn boy. That moment was all the recognition, praise and validation I would ever need to reaffirm that teaching is what I was meant to do.

That day, I went home a very happy person. All I had to wait for next was to find out if my students got into the polytechnic courses that they had applied for. Most of them, including Lionel, made it!

This moment was particularly significant for me because when I expressed my interest in becoming a teacher, my dad told me something that resonated with me and will continue to do so.

"Anu, remember, a good teacher can change lives but a bad teacher will certainly destroy lives."

He always told me that what could be a mistake or a comment made without much thinking can actually impact and be imprinted on a young person's mind, enough to destroy his self-belief and confidence. A teacher's action is steeped in great responsibility and power.

Students like Lionel are in our education system. His circumstances and family background almost robbed him of the capital that is so necessary for him to succeed. Being someone who was educated in a typical "neighbourhood" school, I know and have come to fully understand the inequalities that exist in a seemingly meritocratic education system. Students like Lionel need the support, guidance and exposure that they may lack. There certainly exists a correlation between class inequality, socialisation and opportunity for students. Children from families of a higher socio-economic status tend to be advantaged as their more affluent parents can afford "hot-housing", with a multitude of enrichment and tuition sessions for their children. At least their family circumstances would be better in the sense that there is no struggle to make ends meet. These parents are better able to prepare their children for the education system be it due to being better educated themselves or having the resources to ensure that their child's basic physiological needs are taken care of even if they are not physically with their children all the time.

Hence, I have always felt that teachers in "neighbourhood" schools often take on the role of being surrogate parents, looking out for the well-being of a child and being there to understand the child's needs and help the child. Through my life experiences, I have come to an understanding of what it means to be a good teacher. My experiences taught me to see students with new lenses. I understood first-hand the importance of acknowledging and understanding the backgrounds of the various students I encounter.

The incident with Lionel taught me a lot about the power and responsibility of teachers. My passion and conviction were reaffirmed. It was a critical point in my career that has since fuelled me to be the best teacher I could ever be.

*****

Narrative inquiry provided a mediational space for me. When teachers engage in narrative inquiry, they are thinking and writing about the lived experiences and they thoughtfully reflect on their actions and reactions by configuring a narrative to structure and make sense of those experiences (Golombeck & Johnson, 2004). Reflecting through writing my narrative was therapeutic for me. As

I wrote my narrative, I worked through and made better sense of the tense period in my life. My narrative inquiry allowed for this to happen as an important principal dynamic in narrative inquiry is discourse (Leggo, 2008). As Leggo (2008) explained, discourse is all about how we tell the story. Discourse refers to the rhetoric of storytelling, the art and science of shaping and constructing a story for communicating to others.

Hence I learnt that while I attended to the experiences that comprised my narrative, and while I sought to understand the interpretive significance of my narrative, I needed to attend to the discourse of narration. As Leggo (2008) described it beautifully, through narrative inquiry, the conception of narration exists not as a fixed, solid noun but as a verb, narrating, always in process, full of generative action. Through discourse, I gained reaffirmation and a realisation of my conviction and passion for teaching. Facing the existing tension and reflecting on it has fuelled me to continue on my crusade to be a great teacher to my students.

Huberman (1992) reflected on life cycle literature and suggested that teachers will eventually move into a phase of disengagement. However, I refuse to believe that one day I will become disengaged. I believe my passion for teaching, and the force that will ultimately drive me through this career is the opportunities that I have to touch the hearts of those who have come under my wings. To those whose hearts I have touched, it is with great pride and satisfaction to know that they have developed into good citizens and this continues to fuel my calling to be a teacher. These former students, like Lionel, who have far surpassed the expectations that those around them have had of them, make a difference. As they share their stories with me and I witness the contributions that each of these people are making, I am humbled to be a part of the learning experience that shaped their lives. Seeing these former students excel and reach their greatest potential is my greatest reward and validates my decision that I am very blessed because I am a teacher.

And so my journey through my career trajectory continues…

* Pseudonym used.

References

Golombek, P. R., & Johnson, K. E. (2004). Narrative inquiry as a mediational space: Examining emotional and cognitive dissonance in second-language teachers' development. *Teachers & Teaching*, 10 (3), 307–327.

Huberman, M. (1992). Teacher development and instructional mastery. In A. Hargreaves and M. G. Fullan (eds.), *Understanding Teacher Development*. New York: Teachers College Press.

Leggo, C. (2008). Narrative inquiry: Attending to the art of discourse. *Language & Literacy: A Canadian Educational E-Journal*, 10 (1), 1–21.

References

Chapter 18

A Journey to Designing Student-Centred Learning in a Problem-Based Learning Environment

Rachel ONG

The Novice

It seemed grand, is it not? To graduate from teacher training, and finally joining the teaching fraternity. Moreover, I was posted to a junior college (senior high school), where I would be delivering lectures and tutorials, and I would be able to share with my students the knowledge that I had gained in my economics courses in the university. I felt that I would be a good teacher because I was up to date on many of the issues in the field.

Beginning with just tutorial classes (they only gave the lectures to more senior staff then), I prepared for my classes by planning how I would help the students answer the more difficult questions and essay questions in the tutorial worksheet. I had always been conscientious as a student and applied the same fervour to logically sort out the arguments surrounding the economics concepts. In class, when students had questions, I would take the time to explain it to them and watch their faces to see if they understood. It was a nice feeling when I see their eyes brighten up with understanding. However, there were the times too, when a student did not understand despite my efforts to present the ideas this way or another. I felt frustrated. I thought that my explanations were perfectly logical and systematic, how is it then that the student is unable to comprehend?

It was time for me to have a go at presenting a lecture. I was called in to see the HOD some weeks before and she very firmly told me that I was not to use any of the existing lecture material developed by my senior colleagues. She wanted me to read and develop them on my own.

As a beginning teacher, I felt apprehensive with that instruction. The culture was not about sharing, and taking someone else's notes and transparencies was akin to daylight robbery. I tried to see her actions from another light. She wanted me to learn, although in a hard way, to present a topic to my students. Left with no recourse, I set about it, reading the textbook references, and putting the lecture together. The process required me to compile the ideas from various textbooks, sequence the concepts and ideas, and present the topic in a logical and reasoned manner such that students will grasp the key ideas of the topic. I took care to build the concepts, especially the areas which I felt was usually difficult for students to understand. I wanted to make sure that my students did not lose out in the lecture that I prepared and that I included as much as possible from the various resources used. In a way, I realised later that I was forced to be independent in my own learning as a teacher, to construct my own understanding of the subject, although from a pedagogical content knowledge perspective. To do this, I tried to put myself into the students' minds and to imagine how they would be learning the concepts. Little did I know that this was the beginning of being student-centred in my attempts at writing curriculum.

From another perspective, I saw myself as the subject expert. I sorted out the information for my students, so that they would need less time to access the ideas. That is, they did not have to read so many textbooks to learn the topic. When the students had a question, I usually answered it for them. It felt good to know and to be able to teach it to them. This was my role as "teacher — the sage on stage".

I had students returning to see me after they had graduated. What surprised me was that they had remembered little of what I had taught them in the economics classes. I was disappointed because I had put in so much energy and effort to teach them, spending time after school hours with them in remedial work, so that they will pass their exams. At the same time I was also puzzled, but left it as it was and did not think much of it then as I had both work and family priorities to grapple with.

Family commitments forced me to leave the teaching job. However, the boredom of facing the children at home led me to pursue my Masters degree in Economics. This, I felt then, would put me in a better position as an economics teacher when I was ready to return to the teaching service, because I would be better able to handle even the more advanced "Special" paper.

A Chance to Reflect on My Practice

One day, I bumped into an old friend who mentioned that my economics lecturer from my teacher training days was looking for an experienced teacher, to help her out in the pre-service teacher education course for economics. I went to see Mrs. N about it and she took me on as a co-lecturer on the course.

Planning the lessons and workshops on the pedagogical aspects of teaching economics made me look behind the "stage" of my own teaching experiences. One of such lessons was to help my trainee teachers to understand Robert Marzano's framework of Dimensions of Learning. It was a framework to enable teachers to plan their curriculum and instruction in a way that considered Marzano's five aspects of learning. I did not know Marzano's work to begin with. I had to read, find out and understand. It was not a lesson on Marzano's ideas alone, but to demonstrate how his model can enable the planning of an economics lesson. I struggled with my own prior experiences to make meaning of the various Dimensions of Learning and to share examples with my trainees in the lessons. On reflecting after the lesson, I was not sure if my trainees learnt, but I can say that I have definitely learnt — about my craft and about myself as a teacher and a learner. I learnt because I was actively engaged with reading the literature on education and learning, and making sense of it with my own teaching experiences. Moreover, the support that I received from Mrs. N helped me to think critically about my teaching. It was the first few instances when I realised that there was more to teaching than delivering the perfect lecture. It was also my first few engagements with being critically reflective about my work as a teacher. It is funny when you think back about it, that there was never the opportunity or guidance to reflect on my practice as a teacher; I was so caught up with the daily routines and preparing students for the high stakes national exams that ironically, student learning was seldom the focus, despite my efforts. This experience further gave me the confidence to know that I have the capacity to learn how to write a lesson or a curriculum through reading, thinking and working collaboratively with colleagues.

When my trainee teachers went out to the schools on their practicum posting, I served as a practicum supervisor. I had pre- and post-lessons discussions with the trainee teachers where I encouraged them to evaluate and reflect on the lesson that I had just observed. My role as a practicum supervisor sharpened my awareness of a teacher's actions in class and how it affected the students. Being on the other side of the stage helped me to recognise the very same flaws that I would have made as a beginning teacher, only that I was not aware of them then. As I went through the paces of the post lesson discussions with the trainee teachers, I could not help but drew parallels in my own mind about my practice too.

Opening Up New Doors

When I planned to return to full time work, I had the choice of returning to the junior college or to join a brand new polytechnic, which had very boldly declared that they would be engaging with

Problem-Based Learning (PBL) as a core pedagogical approach. I chose in the end to venture into an adventure of PBL, instead of falling back into the more traditional system of preparing students for the "A"-Levels, a high stakes national examination for university entrance. The global economic trends were placing greater emphasis on knowledge based competencies and locally, the Ministry of Education had new initiatives such as the Thinking Schools Learning Nation, which was an attempt to address the knowledge economy's needs. I saw the new approach to learning as a refreshing way to reclaim the ideals of education and learning, and not just to merely teach to the test. What excited me was the prospect of the innovation in adopting such a pedagogical approach, and the promise of "riding the rapids" in a journey with the team. I had an inkling that I would not be bored on such a journey, although I could recognise then that the implementation would be challenging.

I eventually became a staff member in the staff development unit of the fledging new polytechnic, unsure of what to expect and how I was going to do what I suggested. My boss was not entirely reassuring when he said, though in a tongue-in-cheek manner, that if we had any questions, we had to go find the answers ourselves, because he also had no solutions. However, he gave us the reassurance that he would work with us to solve the problems that came along. This set the tone for my learning experience with PBL and my journey into staff development. On reflection, this unique working relationship perhaps furthered my development in understanding constructivist pedagogy.

Engaging With and Confronting Problems

The thought of writing a new module from scratch was daunting and intimidating. What made it more challenging was that it was to be written for a different pedagogical approach. Nothing in my teaching career so far had prepared me for something like this. Well, on thinking back, perhaps developing lessons on Marzano's ideas to trainee teachers was a precursor to this experience. My colleagues were no better than me. We were clueless as to where to start; what we want to achieve or teach; how we were going to go about working the things that we wanted to teach into problems for our students to dwell on. Well, we began by coming up with ideas about the sorts of skills that we wanted our students to attain in our cognitive skills and problem solving modules. We should teach them to analyse, make decisions, evaluate, categorise and make sense of things — all of which sounded like a list of skills from Bloom's taxonomy.

We started by identifying the learning objectives of the various lessons. This came from my training as a teacher in the traditional way of writing curriculum. At that time it made good sense to me as I felt it helped us to be systematic in approaching the issue, drawing logical links through the various thinking skills and topics, as would the textbook.

One day, my colleagues and I decided to break for lunch at the nearby mall, and on driving back to the campus, it started to rain. Suddenly, someone exclaimed, "Look over there at the airplane! What if something was dropped from the airplane and we needed to go get it? How would we go about doing that?" Looking at the wipers sweeping at the windscreen, another colleague asked, "Will you get wetter if you ran in the rain or just simply walked?" As we continued the journey back to our campus, we subsequently suggested ways to try to locate the parcel and what possible information we would need to do that. We suggested testing it out and planned methods to collect the data and verify the outcome.

It was one thing to read about the philosophy of PBL, and literature that examined how people learnt and about student centred learning, and another thing to implement it. Ideas and philosophy had to be made concrete and practical. What was coming clear to me too at that point was that we had to create scenarios which allowed a very natural process of inquiry to explore the issues. Our students can then learn the problem solving process by working through it. I realised that our enthusiasm in proposing ways to solve the problem came about because the problems were organic in a way and related to us naturally. I could see the power of the learning that would come from this. This incident brought out the tension between the traditional textbook conceptions of topics arranged in a sequence, and a rather haphazard way of enabling students to encounter the various learning outcomes that we envisage for them. I can see the lines between the chapters and the sections in the textbooks beginning to blur.

Problem crafting progressed along. We brainstormed scenarios, picked out the learning issues and selected those that would make up the course. If there were no natural inquiry pathways and thinking skills that came out of the cognitive dissonance in the scenario, we rejected the problem. In this manner, we compiled our problems for the module, with its associated thinking skills, and checked if it met the objectives of the cognitive skills programme.

I eventually took on duties overseeing academic matters and had to oversee the running of the module. I had to review and evaluate the problems that were crafted. There was no guidebook to follow. The institution had a unique one day one problem set up which meant that I could not fall back on problems from other PBL institutions as a resource. I learnt to ask certain questions in the review sessions. What kind of inquiry paths did this problem take the students through? I had to ensure that the exploration was natural, that there were sufficient signposts in the problem statement to drive the questions and the inquiry. Problem crafters had to demonstrate that students were able to move from one conceptual jump to another, with clues in the problem, with the resources given and other supporting learning materials. Will the students engage with this scenario or puzzle? What is in it for them to want to even ask the questions to solve the problem? Will they be motivated to learn?

I had become very "tuned-in" to the learning of the students. I have definitely moved on from my days of delivering lectures and being the "sage" in my subject area. My student's motivations, emotional engagement with the context of the problem and the way they moved through, cognitively, with the learning materials was always at the forefront of my mind. This was a far cry from the days when

I put together slides and material for a lecture, and my immediate concern in my own mind was how it made logical sense — to me, as the teacher.

Going to Class and Facilitating Learning

The classroom in a PBL environment was expected to be different from the traditional classroom. The PBL literature tells us that students need to be given the opportunities to construct their own meaning of the knowledge and information that they encounter in the problems. I realised that there was a lot written about the philosophy, but little on the mechanics of "how to" run such a lesson or class.

I would go to class in the mornings, eager to connect with the students and to make them feel comfortable around me. At 8.30 am, I started the class by introducing the problem statement to my class. The students, well trained, in the PBL processes, began to take apart the problem statement and sort out what they knew, what they did not know, and what they needed to go and find out in the course of the day. I moved around the teams checking on their progress, asking questions: "Why did you want to find that out? What relevance does knowing it have on helping you to solve the problem?" I could see my students struggle to make meaning out of the problem statements. They started by asking superficial questions and sought definitions of terms. Through my prodding and probing, they evaluated their questions and determined their direction of inquiry for the day's work and focus.

I would leave them on their own for an hour to work together to find resources, and to understand the relevant resources. I would check in with them again just before lunch. I found this next stage of the process very meaningful. The students returned to class in varied stages of progress on the problem. Going around the teams to ask them individually what they had learnt, they shared how the new information could help them understand certain ideas and concepts. Inevitably someone would ask me how to answer something, and I always gave the hated reply in one form or another: "What do you think? How would you begin to find an answer? What difficulties did you encounter?" This threw the responsibility of finding the answers back to the students. Occasionally, I recognised that they genuinely had difficulties with their understanding and I would give a hint or point them to relevant resources to help them overcome their learning obstacles. I held the premise that my students were not 100% ignorant about the answer, and they had an inkling of how it should be, but needed affirmation from the teacher. I did the "facilitator side-step" move here so that they would build confidence and develop strategies to go about looking for an answer. I often joked with my fellow facilitators that we could write a book on a thousand and one ways to ask the question — "What do you think"? This ability to "side-step" students' queries and to manage their learning obstacles did not come naturally. Telling them the answer and where to look for it was something that seemed more efficient and made sense. It was something that we expected out of our teachers when we were growing up, and if I did not give that back to my students, I felt that I was not doing my job well. It was what I was "trained" to do in my traditional role as a teacher. I felt schizophrenic at times, as on one hand, I accepted logically the ideas about constructivism and centring the learning on the student; on the other hand, enacting it was to fight the "teacher" in me. I finally came to appreciate the struggle in my students and recognised the process of building a "learning character" when I persisted in my efforts not to just transfer knowledge. It was like a butterfly coming out of its cocoon. It had to struggle to build the strength in its wings before it could really fly. If it were released too early without a fight, the butterfly would not form as it should and cannot fly.

One thing that puzzled me was, to what extent did you need to be a subject expert to facilitate a PBL class? It seemed that one can get through a lesson by simply asking the generic questions such as: What do you know? What did you find out? How does what you discovered relate to the problem statement? Did your findings correspond to the other information that your team mates read? And the list goes on … It certainly threatened the faculty members in other disciplines, such as those in science and engineering and the people from the IT faculties. In the initial months in the PBL environment, these colleagues demonstrated resistance to constructivism and PBL. They contended that the students needed lectures to supplement the problem solving, and that they had to be pumped with the "necessary" content before they can apply it to the problem. This belief ran counter to the ideals of PBL and constructivism. In a bid to quell the rumbles, one senior Director thought of a plan to address the concerns over subject expertise. He wanted to prove that you do not need to be an expert to be a facilitator.

My role in this plan was to facilitate an engineering problem to a group of engineering colleagues. I was to use generic facilitation and questioning skills to help them build their learning and to make the conceptual jumps as we proceeded along. Talk about being like a fish out of water. I had to facilitate an engineering problem on electromagnetic fields. I was nervous. Part of my anxiety came from being watched, being put on "facilitation display"; part due to my lack of confidence over the concepts in the problem. I felt paralysed as I did not know what questions to ask, could not determine if the answers that were given were logical, made engineering sense, and could not figure out whether the "learners" were making any conceptual errors, or if they were having difficulties grappling with a concept. As I reflected on this experience, I felt that there was some value in knowing the subject discipline. From the eyes of a teacher, it would enable me to unpack the concepts into pedagogical content knowledge (Shulman, 1987) to better understand how the learners are making meaning out of the problem context. I also realised an interesting point. Because I was not a subject expert, I was able to push the discussion into various inquiry paths and not to funnel the discussion into what an engineer would normally expect. I could not impose my ideas and understanding on the learners. I realised too that I listened more to my learners and tried to make the connections and built from what each one was saying into something coherent. I learnt then that there was a need to strike a balance between being a subject expert and empathising with my students, challenging their thinking and being at the "edge" of their inquiry process.

The Certification Process

Experience brought with it additional responsibilities. In order to ensure quality in teaching and learning in the classroom, the institution introduced a certification process for facilitation. I became one of the guinea pigs to test out this process. I had to write a teaching philosophy statement, analyse and reflect upon my student feedback and grades, and evaluate my students' learning reflections. I had to have a whole day's class videotaped and attend an interview with the certification panel. The panel picked segments of my class and I had to explain why I said this or did that, and what decisions I made at that particular moment in the video segment. Drawing on Schon's (1983) ideas, it was like a "live" reflection-on-action that I was playing out in the interview sessions. The panel was thorough. I had to articulate my teaching philosophy, what I meant when I said that learning is socially constructed. Effective learning takes place best in an environment that is rich with associations to the real world, and through interactions with people. That way, the learner could build upon their prior knowledge and result in a better understanding of their surroundings. Learning is cumulative. At that point in time, I felt strongly that problem based learning is a pedagogy that was able to address this.

Becoming a Staff Developer

Being a staff developer was a whole new role for me. While some may see the roles as akin to a master teacher — a kind of "sage" in teaching, I choose however to disagree. In fact, I feel that my most valuable experience that I could bring into this role was that of a learner. My struggles with learning how to teach, grappling with issues in education, and with learning to develop curriculum for an unfamiliar pedagogy gave me the confidence to face the uncertainty in my new role. I would bring these insights of my own reflection and learning as a teacher into the professional development workshops that I developed and conducted in the course of my work. There was no course that my colleagues and I, as PBL staff developers, could attend and then transfer the training to our colleagues, just like the way we attend an undergraduate programme in economics and then teach economics. We were against merely putting together practices and strategies drawn from "commonsensical" knowledge and practices of the day-to-day classroom.

Who would believe us? How could we make our workshops and ideas credible? I read extensively from the literature on education and on PBL to learn from the research done in various countries to help me conceptualise my workshops. In developing a lesson to help staff build critical thinking and facilitate learning, I drew on ideas from Dewey (1938, 1997) about reflection and learning from experience, Vygotsky's (1978) zone of proximal development, various critical thinking frameworks and writers on Socratic questioning techniques to help staff understand the philosophical underpinnings of their actions on learning and to equip them with the strategies to carry them out in their own lessons. I also read up on adult learning theories to better understand how I could reach out to my adult learners. I found my classroom strategies not very different from the PBL facilitation processes, and realised that I had kept the learner at the centre of the teaching and learning relationship. The only difference was that in the adult classes, the learners had richer experiences to share and to build upon in their learning. Again, there was the question that arose: Who was the learner here, me or them? I think the reason why I enjoyed running the workshop sessions so much was that in the process of reading, developing, and teaching the course, I was growing in my understanding of teaching and of being a teacher. I humbly submit myself as a learner in the sessions, sharing our experiences together and building our understanding together. The sage can take a back seat.

My Journey Thus Far

My views of what a teacher is, and what a teacher knows, or should know, have changed over the years through the various experiences that I have encountered. My role as a teacher in the learning environment is to create a rich environment for my students to explore new ideas. It also gives students a chance to interact and build social skills to function in a real world situation. I want students to take responsibility for their own learning, to have strategies to solve a problem, that is, to be able to think for themselves.

My role as a staff developer is to share with fellow colleagues the pleasure of enabling students to learn. In the process of sharing, I would like them to also appreciate and understand the way people learn, to create suitable environments to learn, and to be able to take a step back to enable them to learn.

In the teaching and learning dichotomy, I have moved from teaching as a focus to the view that learning is actually at the heart of all teaching. Drawing from Dewey's (1902, 1990) view of the child being the centre of learning, learning must be approached from the learner's perspective. Learners learn best when constructing their own understanding of knowledge. I have moved away from the view that the teacher is the sage on stage to the teacher as one who learns with her learners. I believe that in order to teach, we must understand learning, and that teaching at times entails learning together with students. The teacher should adopt a certain curiosity to learn and this way he will motivate his students to learn.

References

Dewey, J. (1902, 1990). *The school and society and the child and the curriculum.* Chicago: University of Chicago Press.

Dewey, J. (1938, 1997). *Experience and education.* New York: Simon and Schuster.

Schon, D. (1983). *The reflective practitioner: How professionals think in action.* New York: Basic Books.

Shulman, L. S. (1987). Knowledge and teaching: Foundations of the new reform. *Harvard Educational Review,* 57 (1), 1–21.

Vygotsky, L. (1978). *Mind in society: The development of higher psychological processes.* Cambridge: Harvard University Press.

Part 4:
What Shapes a Leader?

Overview

Say Pin TAN and Sonia KHAN

Roles and practices are constructed socially (Goffman, 1959; Bourdieu, 1972/2002). One hallmark of *a leader* is the ability to collaborate with others. In a school setting, leadership ability grows as leaders learn and mature in their response to and execution of the roles and tasks and it also changes with interaction with teachers, staff and local communities (Gergen, 1971).

The narratives in this section reveal a journey of school leaders and key personnel towards a collaborative effort through a route of dissatisfaction, reflection and maturation, a journey that shapes them as leaders. Leading becomes an emotional practice as leaders immerse themselves in a cycle of action-reaction-reflection (Hargreaves, 1998).

Three of the contributors have made apt use of metaphors to represent their reflective responses to their circumstances. Say Pin, Thiam Chuan and Siew Khim chose the passing of a day, an adventure and an onion, respectively, as iconic representations of their understanding of the experience of their realities in terms of the other (Docherty, 2004).

The three phases of a passing of day — fresh morning, hot afternoon and cool evening marked the experiences of Say Pin, a six-month old beginning teacher, who became internally appointed as a Head of Department (HOD). With the blessings of two experienced

HODs as mentors, the fledging HOD soon found himself in a state of growing confusion, dissatisfaction and dissonance. Both mentors demonstrated fully the how of leading (i.e. maintaining the *status quo*), but did little to explain the why of doing so. It was not until many years later that he was able to revisit and relayer the experience in terms of the three-dimensional narrative inquiry of temporality, sociality and place (Clandinin *et al.*, 2010). The second phase began with a heated altercation with a colleague whom Say Pin had tried, but failed to reach out to. With patience running thin and pride running high, the "barrage of criticism" was returned with fire "from her own arsenal." As loudly contested as it began, it ended in an eerie deafening silence. Say Pin came to the realisation that people are emotional beings, "How well we manage their feelings will affect how receptive or resistant they are to us." It was this realisation that made all the difference. Finally, the third phase offered reprise as Say Pin found meaning again through a positive experience. This echoes Bruner's (1990) concept of "meaning in praxis" (p. 117) where one is situated and distributed in action, project and practice.

Thiam Chuan's journey, in locating his self, started as a teacher and continued to develop for many years until the point of writing his narrative, as a Vice Principal. His journey began as a beginning teacher with great satisfaction. Three years later, he was beset by monotony and there loomed unhappiness as academic achievements were the only focus and nothing beyond that. Dissatisfied, he searched for meaningful challenges and found one such opportunity when he was asked to lead a school expedition to Laos. The experience led to a deeper understanding of his role as a teacher that involves learning from his students and understanding them, and later on, of his role as a Vice Principal. Through it all, his notion of self was not located in the "fastness of immediate private consciousness, but in a cultural-historical situation" (Bruner, 1990, p. 105). Self was well-situated in a collaborative whole.

This notion is reinforced in the narrative of Aristotle's journey. As much as a school leader possesses a good deal of power and freedom to act, they must come to terms with the notion that they are part of something bigger. Painful as it is, the restrictions, formal and informal, do limit a Principal's freedom of action (Sarason, 1982). Aristotle's journey commenced as a "rookie teacher" with no "relevant credentials in terms of paper qualifications or experience." Sensing his "willingness to learn" and his "earnest drive to excel", he was involved by his mentor, one of the owners of the school, "in the responsibility of school administration and management," thus giving him ample opportunities to learn and grow. He was so involved in his role and responsibilities that he ended up "working at the school beyond the one year which I (he) had initially planned." This involvement earned him the position of Principal in a new branch of the school which he ran with considerable success. But interference by higher ups in the implementation of a school-based change initiative went against his student-centric philosophy, which led him to resign after seriously reflecting upon his personal values and evaluating his goals as an educator.

Thus, leaders not only delve deep into their experiences but also more consciously into themselves within those experiences. As they grow in their respective work realities, they grow alongside as individuals. For instance, Sabariah's narrative highlights how she grew both personally and professionally when faced with classroom and school situations and how she negotiated her racial identity. A student challenged her authenticity as a teacher of English only because she was Malay. An open "contestation of ideas" to "elicit students' understanding and assumptions of race, ethnicity, stereotypes and prejudices" only "concretised" Sabariah's "beliefs as a teacher and classroom practices for years to come." Her journey from a teacher to a supervisor, from "her experiences as a beginning teacher, the feelings of insecurity" to "organising small group discussions on pedagogical and assessment matters" tells the story of an individual teacher, as opposed to a clinical chronology of a teacher's career. Sabariah's values and disposition exemplify Bruner's (1990) concept of the self as a guardian of permanence. As she faces contest along the racial lines, she becomes a barometer of the "local cultural weather" (p. 110), reacting and responding to changing and challenging situations enfolding in her professional life. Her report card came seven years later, when she developed National Education programmes based on the axiom that critical understanding supports curriculum of cultural exposure.

Huey Min's story evolves around events relating to a particular stage in her career when she was concurrently leading two schools. When the management plan ("MOE's decision") took a sudden change, she was left to manage consequences, unexpected and unforeseen that came fast and furious. Inevitably, she was drawn into a web of emotional upheavals and complexities of relationships. In an almost candid way, Huey Min weaves seamlessly between her public and private selves as she manages her own emotions in the midst of fulfilling her professional role as a school leader. As Bruner (1990) puts it, the self is a product of situations involving 'swarms of its participations' (p. 109). Her admission of doubt and heart-ache reveals an earnest and deep search for answers that challenge her values and dispositions. Huey Min draws upon her past and newly-acquired knowledge to represent her new and emerging self. From her Chinese and English education background to insights linked to the Esplanade and a fountain, Huey Min's story is constantly shaped and re-shaped by the sense-making journey of her inner conversations and reflections.

While Huey Min's story centres around a single snapshot of her life, Siew Khim's story spans across her teaching career from a beginning teacher to a leadership position in her current school. The breath of Siew Khim's story provides insights into the life journey of a reflective practitioner. With its fair share of highs and lows, readers are drawn into her personal recounts and accounts of key episodes that influence her leadership style. Her growth as a teacher and a leader comes from her acumen to engage in dialogic processes (Golombek & Johnson, 2004), to mediate and make sense of her impact on others and that of others on her. From her primary school Principal to her family members, it is clear that she as much influences as she is influenced by others. As a concluding remark, Siew Khim celebrates the human spirit as the ultimate source of motivation for her. Indeed, behind every story is the spirit that gives life to the protagonists and sense-making.

Reading through the narratives in this section, one finds that the emotional side of a leader is intertwined with a moral stance that he or she takes. This aspect of moral compass dominates Thiam Chuan's story as the primary shaping influence in his personal story. Of interest is the framing of his narrative in tropes, an unconscious nod to Joseph Campbell's concept of identity via literary tropes, as proposed in his book *The Hero of a Thousand Faces*. This resonates with the narratives of other teacher leaders in the section, where the realisation of being comes when they came to terms with their emotions.

References

Bourdieu, P. (1972/2002). *Outline of a theory of practice.* Cambridge: Cambridge University Press.

Bruner, J. (1990). *Acts of meaning.* Cambridge: Harvard University Press.

Clandinin, D. J., Murphy, M. S., Huber, J., & Murray Orr, A. (2010). Negotiating narrative inquiries: Living in a tension-filled midst. *The Journal of Educational Research*, 103, 81–90.

Docherty, J. S. (2004). Narratives, metaphors and negotiations. *Marquette Law Review*, 87, 846–851.

Goffman, E. (1959). *The presentation of self in everyday life.* Garden City: Anchor Books.

Golombek, P. R., & Johnson, K. E. (2004). Narrative inquiry as a mediational space: Examining emotional and cognitive dissonance in second-language teachers' development. *Teachers and Teaching: Theory and Practice*, 10 (3), 307–327.

Gergen, K. J. (19971). *The concept of self.* New York: Holt, Rinehart and Wonston, Inc.

Hargreaves, A. (1998). The emotional practice of teaching. *Teaching and Teacher Education*, 14 (8), 835–854.

Sarason, S. B. (1982). *Culture of the school and the problem of change*, 2nd edition. Boston: Allyn & Bacon.

Chapter 19

A Tale of Two Schools: Leadership, Perceptions, Perspectives

Huey Min SUN

Synopsis

I was the Principal of two schools (B & C). School B was anticipating moving to nice new premises when a sudden announcement by the Ministry of Education (MOE) crashed the plan. Ironically, the new premises were given to School C which I also helmed. I was faced with the disappointment of School B which saw its dreams shattered.

Later, School C also came to experience the impact of their peculiar perception about the landscaping of the campus. Happily, an innovative change was made to the spot which triggered so much emotional discomfort to the staff, with the creation of a beautiful waterfall and a fish pond below, aptly named our "Fountain of Hope". The process of writing the narrative inquiry (NI) enables me to reflect deeper into the actions I took to resolve the critical issues and the connectedness between the two seemingly unrelated incidents, which both brought up the importance of leadership, positive perceptions and perspectives.

Standing at the edge of our proud new icon, our 'Fountain of Hope', the school choir members raised their voices in joyous singing, while the nine golden kois were released into the pond by the then Minister without Portfolio, Mr. Lim Boon Heng. Loud applause from all the guests sounded just as the choir finished its last note and the kois started to swim swiftly in their new found home. This was the day of the official opening of the new building of my second school, an autonomous school.

I was the Principal of a school in the east before I was appointed Principal of two schools in the west concurrently, one of them being this autonomous school. As these two schools were concurrently under my leadership, should I call the autonomous school my second school? Why should not I call it my third school, or just my school? In my mind, I did not want the naming order to indicate *any* favouritism towards this school relative to the other school I helmed concurrently.

This beautiful school (let us call it School C), was built on a sprawling hilly terrain. The architecture was innovative and took advantage of the hilly site. It even had a lift as there were technically more than four floors because of the multi-level terrain. Only schools with more than four floors are built with a lift, even up till today.

Amongst the guests, I saw the present Principal of School B who was full of smiles and had congratulated me earlier. What would he be thinking? Could the newly-built school on this beautiful site be his?

This beautiful new campus was, however, intended for School B and at this point had been given to School C. To compound the issue, I had been the Principal of both schools.

When I was Principal of School B, it was then a brand new school which was taking in its first batch of students — 507 Secondary One students with 24 teachers in the first year. The intake quality of School B was lower than School C which was an established full-fledged school, about three times the size of School B. Schools B and C were sharing the same premises but functioned in different sessions. The MOE had decided to house both schools in the same premises as a temporary measure while School B's new campus was being constructed and to appoint one single Principal over both schools. School B was therefore waiting for its new building to be completed in two years' time on a beautiful site nearby.

The plan was for a new Principal to be appointed to head School B when its new building was ready and for me to remain as Principal of School C.

The Primary School Leaving Examination (PSLE) guide for students and their parents on choosing their secondary schools indicated that School B was at the new address while School C remained at the old site. School B's parents, students and teachers were naturally eagerly looking forward to their new building.

However, towards the end of the first year of School B, MOE did the unexpected by making a sudden announcement that School B was to remain at their temporary site and School C was to move to the new site instead. This caused utter confusion, disappointment and even consternation among teachers, parents and students of School B.

I was told just one day before the announcement and was taken totally by surprise. There was no prior consultation or communication between MOE and me on this issue. I was merely informed one day earlier than the other people. How would I explain to the parents, teachers and students of School B, which was also my school? Would I be seen as the hand behind it all? The only reason given to me for the change was that School C was now an autonomous school and MOE felt that the new premises was more suitable for School C. Did they consider the feelings of the people of the two schools, especially School B, and mine? Day & Leitch (2001) described the tension in the teachers' lives. The experience of Peter about the distant role of his agency (Day & Leitch 2001, p. 408–409) was like what I experienced with MOE; and the experience of Paddy on his fear of being misinterpreted (Day and Leitch, 2001, pp. 410–411) was similar to my fear of being distrusted.

School C was awarded the autonomous school status by MOE not long before this surprise announcement and I was interviewed by the press on my vision and plans for the school. I stressed that character building was my priority alongside academic pursuits. I was expressing my determination to mould the students into individuals equipped with academic excellence together with good character which would be the hallmark of the school.

I knew I would eventually be the Principal of one school — School C, but as Principal of both schools then, I was also mindful of my responsibility towards School B and that I had to treat the two schools equally and fairly, albeit catering to different needs. I often questioned myself over my treatment of the two schools. Had I not provided resources to both fairly? Had I not always called for the cooperation of the staff and students of the two schools? Had I not asked them to respect each other? Had I not asked the students of School C to help the academically weaker ones in School B? I went out of my way to help School B. When working with School B to formulate the school motto, vision and mission, I managed to enlist the help of the Art teacher of School C, who has contributed much to the art programme of School C to design School B's crest. I went further to tap on a talented music teacher who is also a former student of mine to help write the school song for School B.

When I looked at School B's motto, Beyond Self, I was really not sure then if the staff or students suspected that I had persuaded MOE to give the new building to School C for selfish reasons. It would have been truly ironical if I had plotted for the new building contrary to the School's motto of "Beyond Self". The staff and students could then have questioned my integrity and commitment to the school motto. It wrenched my heart (and it still does) at the thought that someone could have suspected that I had betrayed School B.

I had been treating School B as my younger child and trying my best to nurture and protect her. However, I thought, not many in School B noticed the efforts I put in. Even if some did, these initiatives were forgotten when the big issue of the nice new building being taken away from them became the focus. Students as well as their teachers felt let down and badly treated.

To them, it was not just the building that was unfairly taken away from them. It also impacted on their school image as a second class entity whose interest was second to School C which was an autonomous school with proven track record.

My heart ached. I quickly approached my supervisor, conveying to him what I thought was most important — the building was not the issue, but MOE's decision to let School C use the new building was, as it had a serious and demoralising impact on School B. The last thing I wanted was for School B to feel inferior to School C.

However, I was told that the decision had been made and announced, and that no U-turn was possible. Some options were discussed to pacify the parents, as the initial information given to the parents on school's site was changed in the new announcement. I thought it was fair that as location was an important consideration for students who had opted and were eligible for School B in choosing schools, the new students as well as students already in School B could now be admitted to School C, if they so wished. Even though the intake qualities were not quite the same, with PSLE T-score of School B much lower than School C, I would do my best to help them. This option was taken.

Wasting no time, I gathered the staff of both schools and explained to them the situation and the rationale for MOE's decision. Allowing staff to voice their feelings and concerns, what I anticipated surfaced. They asked:

- Why did MOE make such a decision?
- Why did MOE inform us so late?
- When did you know about this?
- Had the decision makers not considered the repercussions?
- How are we going to answer to the parents and the students?
- Are we treated as second class?
- What is MOE's plan for us — building, staff and students?
- With the option given, how would School B's student number be affected?

I had staff of both the schools come together as I wanted transparency and especially for School C, to listen to and empathise with the sentiments of School B. Although School C benefitted from MOE's decision, I did not want School C to hear from a secondary source about School B's queries and views at the meeting as it could create more misunderstandings and confusion. At the meeting,

School C's staff voiced that they would lend School B support in any way they could. I was pleased with the support from them.

On the rationale of MOE's decision, I could only repeat what MOE had told me. As a civil servant, I could not criticise the organisation, but in my heart, I could not agree with how the matter was managed, especially with the sudden announcement of the plan. There was no lead time, no consultation at all. Even up to today I am still puzzled. I was torn, but as I also did not want my staff to criticise me behind my back, I refrained from criticising MOE's decision. I appealed to the staff to trust me, and urged them to see what had been done for both schools which showed that I had the interests of both schools at heart and was fair to both schools. The staff seemed satisfied with the answers, although I could sense that they were still unhappy with MOE's decision. Was I not too? On the other hand, had I not shown care and concern for the staff and built a good relationship with them for that past year, I would not have been able to gain their trust that I was not behind the swap. I impressed on the staff that the most important thing to do was to calm the sentiments of the parents and students and I appealed to the staff to work with me and to speak with one voice to the parents and media, which I anticipated would come soon. I told them it was important to stand together to overcome adversities, otherwise the problems would become even more complex.

The next day, the news was flashed over the media. There were endless calls from the press, the parents and even the curious residents around the area. As School B functioned in the afternoon, the first thing I did was to call for an assembly of the students and staff of School B at the start of school.

In my mind, I did not want to see School B demoralised nor divided. I did not want them to feel inferior. I wanted them to stay strong in the face of adversity. I wanted them to see that material things such as school buildings were not as important as the school spirit. However, this was not easy to be accepted by the young minds. Along with the same concept, I asked them to observe the physical environment around them. Buildings could be torn down easily and rebuilt, just as what they had seen in their estates, but not the spirit of their neighbourhood, nor friendship forged. I urged the students to consider themselves as the pioneers of the school. They would be the very first batch that laid the foundation of the school. I wanted to instil their school spirit in them, to help them to see the big picture, and to spur them to work harder. In time to come, their performances, in academic and non-academic areas, would speak for the school. Perhaps I had tried to persuade them, but truly I thought it would be better for them to stay on. I believe in the Confucius thinking of teaching students in accordance with their aptitudes and abilities, as it would enable the teacher to design suitable methods to help them learn effectively. There was a wide gap in intake scores of the pupils between Schools B and C, and the teachers in School C would not be able to guide the pupils effectively if most pupils were to join School C. More so, I dreaded to see School B disintegrate or confidence in the school collapse. That would really have been terrible. School B students could opt to go to School C, which to some students was a fantastic offer, as they admired the School C students who donned a different uniform and had a better image. But I told them I was their Principal and I had their interest at heart when I advised them to stay on. I assured them that School C would welcome them with open arms but my advice to them was to think through the issue and then decide. I spoke with emotion and sincerity as this was something I firmly believed in. A building is only hard concrete but it is the spirit that will move mountains. A building projects an image, but our perception of it can change as a result of a change in its use. I hold this belief up to today. As I write this narrative, the image of the Esplanade is floating in my mind. To some it is just a building with a durian shape; to others it is a symbol of art. It has become an icon of the arts now as it is showcasing major Arts events. What if it is turned into a casino? The building will still be the same, the name can remain, but its image and our perception of it would change. I recalled when I studied Shakespeare, I was impressed with the expression: 'What's in a name?'. The phrase reflects my belief that the substance is more important than the appearance. I realise now that the manner I conduct myself and the advice I give also reflect my Chinese cultural upbringing and education. I have been influenced by the many stories I read, like *Liaozhai Huapi* (聊斋《画皮》, a story about people seemingly human on the outside but a devil on the inside), and sayings like *jin yu qi wai, bai xu qi zhong* ('金玉其外, 败絮其中', meaning the external beauty hides the rotten inner decay) (明·刘基《卖柑者言》) which both emphasise on substance. I have also been taught about the power of the human spirit in overcoming adversities. Reading and speaking about Adversity Quotient (AQ) has been my favourite topic. I am encouraged by handicapped but able people like Lena Maria who was born without arms, and stories like the "foolish" old man who removed the mountains (愚公移山). My own struggle to adjust to the loss of my father when I was 10 also taught me that those who cannot be defeated by adversities will only emerge stronger. My beliefs and convictions guided me in my advice to my students.

I also believe that had I not built a relationship with the students and cared for them, they might not have been receptive to my message. This relationship was built partly through regular informal chitchats with the students along the corridors and at the canteen. I remember there was this young prefect of School B who came up to me and said: "Principal, I trust you. I will stay on and ask my friends to stay too." I was very touched. These three simple words "I trust you' warmed my heart. Touching lives has been my commitment and his trust added to my mission and sense of responsibility for my students.

I also met the parents. I believe my sincerity and the options I gave to them and their children won them over. I also must pay tribute to my teachers for their dedication and loyalty to the school and for their commitment in following up with the parents.

The media could smell news that would sell and they put their own spin to sensationalise the story. Some reporters called and necessary information was given to them. Reporters were not allowed to enter the school without permission, but there was one reporter who showed no respect for the school even though there were clear signs that all visitors must report to the office first. She just barged into the premises and openly interviewed my students. I was not prepared for rude reporters like her, but fortunately, as the students understood the situation after the assembly talk, the report she wrote was still positive. Had the grounds not been well prepared, I cannot imagine what negative sentiments could have been stirred up. They would write from the public interest angle, but if public interest has been taken care of, then the issue would be diffused. I learnt a lesson — always be prepared for the media especially in crisis management. Better still, one should learn to turn tables on them and use them as your mouthpiece.

I did a simple survey to gauge the inclination of the current students of School B on their school option. I told them that it was just a survey, and their choice would not be binding. They could change their minds until such time that final decision had to be called for. Out of the 507 students, about 10% or 50 students wanted to join School C. Although it was meant just to gauge the responses and for some planning purposes, it served another purpose for the parents and students to think seriously about their choices. Sometimes one has to make a choice where one would seriously have to consider the pros and cons. In my decision-making process, further to constantly referring to the main purpose and objectives, I tend to regularly check on two main factors, namely, the unfolding of events and the likely consequences which may follow.

In the meantime, keeping my doors open to parents, teachers and students about the issue also helped in building trust and allaying fears. In fact, quite a number of parents came to see me with their children, and there were frequent conversations with the teachers of both schools. School C had been seen as a prestigious school with high academic standards. Hence although her doors were opened to receive School B students, parents and students of School B still were not sure if it was good for them to cross over, coming from a lesser school. My meetings with the parents made me more aware of the parents' concern for their children. They were looking to me for directions and advice. I did my best to advise them. I thought I understood their apprehensions, but did I really understand? I asked myself: how would I react if I were in their shoes?

Changing of perceptions and perspectives could only take place over time.

The number of students opting for School C further dropped dramatically. Out of the 507 students and the potential new comers from the second cohort, only 39 opted to join School C. And out of these 39, only 30 finally joined. I believe it was a good thing that after thinking seriously about their options, the students and their parents were clear about what they wanted.

I kept my promise to the students opting for School C and their parents to help them in their studies and their integration into the culture of the school. I was happy that staff of School C shared with me the same mission to see these students succeed in School C and that they were also willing to give extra coaching to these students so that they could quickly become part of the school community. In fact at first there was some apprehension from the teaching staff of School C that the calibre of School B students would bring down the performance of their school. However, the majority empathised with the students of School B and believed, as I did, that though School C might not be able to handle a big group of students from School B, it is possible, with motivation and special coaching, for 30 pupils to achieve good results. I tracked their performance at the end of 4/5 years and was satisfied that they had been well-looked after.

School C moved into the new premises as announced.

Ironically, not all staff from School C were happy to move to the new building which was originally meant for School B. There were rumours that the site was originally a graveyard and as if to highlight it, there was a Chinese tomb-like mini slope in between the classroom blocks, next to the general office. The slope was from the ground floor next to the general office sloping upwards in between the classroom blocks. There was a tree right in the centre of the slope, and I suppose the architect was an environmentalist, so the tree was not chopped down and the spot was preserved. There were a lot of murmurs in the staff room about this spot. A number of staff rather took a longer route to their destinations than walking near it. Was this not another perception that one has to put right? People can be prisoners of their own cultural beliefs or habits (Connelly & Clandinin, 1994, p. 151).

Isn't a change of perception similar to change of perspective? "Change of perspective can change your life", I hear it over the radio many times by FM93.8 DJ Eugene Low these days. Subsequent events proved me right.

Reactions of these staff members to this site could mushroom into bigger events as negative emotions can affect their own morale and spread contagiously to other staff, even students. Quality of teaching could be affected and staff might also request for transfer. I decided to do something. Why can't the "grave" be turned into a fountain of hope? The hilly slope could make a tiered structure incorporating a pond, I thought. A landscape artist was invited to turn my concept into reality. The tree was preserved and its branches were used to hang different species of orchids. Sprawling green ferns added to the freshness of the place. Water was streaming down the sloping wall into a pond at the foot of the structure where the kois would happily inhabit.

After the 'Fountain of Hope' was constructed, staff no longer avoided the spot. Rather, they would go near it to admire the plants and the orchids. A naming competition was organised. The best suggestion came from a girl originally from School B — she named it 'Fountain of Hope'. It became an icon of the school.

Years later, I met her again. She is now a teacher, moulding the future of our nation. I believe that the incident about the school change and her experience in School C, in how the teachers coached her and her winning the naming contest for the "Fountain of Hope", had an impact on her life.

I felt I did the right thing in building up the school spirit in School B. From the "Fountain of Hope", I see the importance of seeing things from multiple perspectives, especially as a leader. I believe the power of perceptions and perspectives can sometimes overshadow the true facts and hence it is important to have the right perceptions and perspectives.

The process of writing the NI enables me to reflect deeper into the actions I took to resolve the critical issues and the connectedness between the two seemingly unrelated incidents, which both relate to the importance of leadership, perceptions and perspectives.

I am experiencing the experience (康纳利、许世静, 2008) as I am recounting the episode. The writing and rewriting of this NI piece made me relive the days that I lived through with the two schools, especially during those critical months. I realise now that although those were difficult times, they were also meaningful times. At the beginning of his novel *A Tale of Two Cities*, Charles Dickens wrote: "It was the best of times, it was the worst of times, it was the age of wisdom, it was the age of foolishness, it was the epoch of belief, it was the epoch of incredulity, it was the season of Light, it was the season of Darkness, it was the spring of hope, it was the winter of despair...". To me, Charles Dickens constantly put the negative experience after the positive, as if the negative was the eventual consequence. The school change episode for Schools B and C spoke of the opposite order to Charles Dickens' first part of the sentence and became "It was the worst of times, it was the best of times". In this episode, the order to occurrence was reversed with the negative outcome preceding the positive, which turned out to be a favourable outcome. Where there is storm and rain, or even a hurricane, there will also be a rainbow after. There is always hope after darkness.

I have been anxious with the impact of this incident on the school community of School B, and have been constantly watching any news about the school even after I left. I am delighted that the school is progressing very well. I am also happy that the school, in its 10th Anniversary Commemorative Magazine, acknowledged what I did as their pioneer Principal. In the magazine, the pioneering staff also wrote about their positive experience during those two years. The reflective process helped me to find peace with myself and see a lot of hope for School B.

My cultural upbringing and education led me to believe that the inner substance is more important than the outer appearance, that the building is but just hard concrete, and that it is the spirit that would move mountains.

As I searched myself I came to realise that my background and experiences have a profound influence on myself. Similarly as an educator, I am able to make an impact on the lives of my students. This on-going process of lives impacting lives is about 'cultivation' as explained by Connelly & Clandinin (1994): "Cultivation is what we often hear spoken of as education, that is, when someone acts intentionally upon someone else in order to change them, to prepare them for something.... We also understand the process of education as occurring when an individual, as institution or a culture acts upon a person." (p. 154).

On the other hand, I am also alerted by Connelly & Clandinin (1994, p. 151) that our experience can also be our "prison". I am aware that I should not be bound by my own perceptions and be unable to see others' perspectives. My experience should be a "source of freedom" which opens up minds instead (Connelly & Clandinin 1994, p. 151).

My action to resolve the critical incident at School B was intuitive, but upon reflection I realise that it was about knowing the power of changing perception and perspectives. Through narrative inquiry, I was awakened to the fact that I believe deeply in the power of mental models (Senge, 2006), which include perceptions and perspectives. I was in fact "awakened" by "... new ways of 'seeing' our world, to different ways of seeing ourselves in relation to each other and to the world. We begin to tell our stories with new insights, in new ways." (Connelly & Clandinin, 1994, p. 155).

I thought the episode was over and I would not be able to further "transform" my life "with changed actions" (Connelly & Clandinin, 1994, p. 155), when I read this phrase. However, the restorying process, writing and re-writing, reading and re-reading with own reflections and inputs from others, have proven me wrong of my original thinking. "Transformation is the *process* of living out these new ways of seeing in our stories" (Connelly & Clandinin, 1994, p. 155) has a new meaning to me now. I realised that transformation is a continuous process in my professional as well as personal life.

Surely lives impact lives. Not only have I impacted other's lives, theirs have also impacted mine, as "... we are a character in our own stories; others become characters in our stories; … we are characters in others' stories". (Connelly & Clandinin, 1994, p. 149).

This reminds me of a Chinese poem, Fragment (《断章》) by Bian Zhilin (卞之琳), translated by Yang Xianyi and Gladys Margaret Tayler:

> *When you watch the scenery from the bridge,*
> *The sightseer watches you from the balcony.*
> *The bright moon adorns your window,*
> *While you adorn another's dream.*
> (你在桥上看风景，
> 看风景的人在楼上看你。
> 明月装饰了你的窗子，
> 你装饰了别人的梦。
>
> -卞之琳 《断章》)

In this scenery, there are people (you and I) and the environment (bridge, houses, window, moon). All are parts of a serene and beautiful picture, and all are important parts of a whole picture. However, depending on who you are and where you are, different perspectives are formed, and all can be correct.

Educators' perspectives and perceptions shape behaviour, which then shape character. Is not the main purpose of education to shape every child into a good person and a useful citizen? To achieve our task of moulding our next generation, we need to involve all other stakeholders so as to embrace a multifaceted perception of our task. In so doing, we should be able to raise a more balanced citizenry living more meaningful lives.

References

Bian, Zhilin 卞之琳 (1935). Fragment《断章》. Translated by Yang Xianyi 杨宪益 and Gladys Margaret Tayler 戴乃迭. Retrieved Mar 26, 2014 from http://www.en84.com/article-2582-1.html

Bruner, J. (1990). *Acts of meaning*. Cambridge: Harvard University Press. Chapters 2 (pp. 43–65) and 4 (pp. 99–141).

Clandinin, D. J., Murphy M. S., Huber J., & Orr, A. M. (2010). Negotiating narrative inquiries: Living in a tension-filled midst. *The Journal of Educational Researcher*, 103, 81–90.

Connelly, F. M., & Clandinin, D. J. (1990). Stories of experience and narrative inquiry. *Educational Researcher*, 19 (5), 2–14.

Connelly, F. M., & Clandinin, D. J. (1994). Telling teaching stories. *Teacher Education Quarterly*, 21 (1), 145–158.

Connelly, F. M., & Shijing Xu 康纳利, 许世静 (2008), "Xushu Tanjiu — Xiangguan gainian yu fangfa" [Narrative inquiry — Related concepts and methods]《叙述探究 — 相关概念与方法》, translated by Feng Lingqin 冯凌琴译. In Chen Xiangming 陈向明 Zhixing yanjiu, Fanxi yu pinglun. 质性研究: 反思与评论 Chongqing University Press 重庆大学出版社.

Day, C., & Leitch, R. (2001). Teachers' and teacher educators' lives: The role of emotion. *Teacher and Teacher Education*, 17 (2), 4, 403–415.

Golombek, P. R., & Johnson, K. E. (2004). Narrative inquiry as a mediational space: Examining emotional and cognitive dissonance in second-language teachers' development. *Teachers and Teaching: Theory and Practice*, 10 (3), pp. 307–327.

Huberman, M. (1992). Teacher development and instructional mastery. In A. Hargreaves and M. G. Fullan (eds.), *Understanding Teacher Development* (p. 122–142). New York, Teachers College Press.

Senge, P. M. (2006). *The fifth discipline: The art & practice of the learning organization*. Random House Business Books.

Zhilin, B. 卞之琳 (1935). *Fragment* 《断章》. Translated by Yang Xianyi 杨宪益 and Gladys Margaret Tayler 戴乃迭. Retrieved from http://www.en84.com/article-2582-1.html (accessed on 26 March 2014).

Chapter 20

Journey of Growth to be a Teacher and School Leader

Siew Khim TEO

My Aspirations in Their Infancy

A free-spirited person I am. Going into 42 years of earthly existence, I continue to detest rules, protocol and utilitarian policies.
To me, all these are an insult to my whole being as a human who
has the capacity to think and act accordingly. Others would argue
that they are necessary evil as they bring order to the society. I agree
that it has its value but to a limited extent. I guess who I am today
is very much attributed to my upbringing. Born in the late 1960s
where the new nation was working zealously to build its economy,
school buildings were mushrooming at a rapid rate to ensure that
every child of school-going age was provided a place and teachers'
recruitment went in tandem. Reeling back to the good old days as
a student then in a primary school, it was all fun learning and sweating out in the hot sun with bare facilities that define a typical single-
storey school building. Parents then struggled with the hard times
trying to make a living and left the children very much to their own
devices after school. Thus, much of my time was dedicated to imaginative role play as a teacher as there were no enrichment classes or

tuition for me to attend after school. Play-time with siblings would include making toy guns out of wooden planks and pellets made from soft mud. We were just a bunch of "kampong kids" with no burdens or worries hanging over our little minds then and were given lots of imaginative and creative space. There was no strict regime to follow. The frequent absence of my parents due to their business undertakings took them away from home most of the time. I was left under the care of my grandmother, one of a total of 10 grandchildren. She definitely had her hands full with a bunch of rambunctious kids. But there was one single person who had left an indelible mark on my moral map. He is none other than my primary school Principal who always stood stoic and stern. In his long-sleeved, crisp light blue shirt and dark polyester pants, he was indeed a sight to behold.

One day, he gave us a lecture on honesty whilst the school population sat quietly on the cemented floor under the hot morning sun. In an even tone, he said, "A lie is like a fire. You can never ever possibly use paper to wrap the fire, can you? It will eventually burn your hands and fingers. One lie will lead to another. Eventually, you will find that many people who love you will be hurt by your lies. You must learn to be courageous. Admit when you are in the wrong. Don't hide like a coward. You will not be respected...." For some reasons, I was quietly inspired by this gentleman and took in every single word he said. For want of inspirational heroes or heroines perhaps, this impressionable girl was completely sucked into his moral discourse. Decidedly, I was determined to become an educator and everyone would also listen to me one day. This has also shaped in part of who I am as a person, friend, mother as well as an educator. Constantly reminding my students and teachers that they must always uphold honesty and integrity or subject oneself to unnecessary peril became my central teaching and leadership philosophy. Most importantly, they have to confront their fears and muster the courage to own up to their mistakes. Not an easy feat even for a grown adult which brings to mind of a particular incident that occurred in the beginning part of my leadership journey as a Vice Principal (VP).

Just a month into my role as a VP in a new school environment, I was particularly upset by a single incident. I had received a complaint from a parent alleging that one of my teachers had called his son names such as 'fatty' and 'fat boy' during Physical Education (PE) lessons. As with any complaints, I would have to conduct an investigation. I called the teacher into my office and related to him about the allegation made by the parent. I asked him almost point-blank, "Did you call the child by any derogatory terms such as 'fatty' and 'fat boy' at all?" He replied almost immediately, "No". I called up the irate parent and he refused to listen to my explanation and accused me of shielding my teacher and insisted that his child did not lie. He insisted that he wanted a meeting with the teacher concerned. A meeting was set up. I prepared the teacher for the ugly confrontation. In my mind, I felt that there was nothing to fear for my teacher had done no wrong and very soon we will uncover the truth but it was a truth that I had not expected. The parent explained that the child came home very distraught one day and upon further probing, he revealed that the PE teacher had called him names and the rest of the classmates continued to taunt him with name-calling. It was indeed emotionally stressful for the child. My teacher defended himself that he was merely trying to encourage the child to do the exercises in a bid to help him lose weight. The parent's patience was waning and he asked my teacher in a rather stern voice, "Did you call him 'fatty' or 'fatty boy' or not?" My teacher paused for a short while with his eyes lowered, he muttered, "Yes". I felt as if the whole world had just collapsed upon me. I was crushed. He lied to me! How could he? To salvage the whole situation, I had personally apologised to the parent for my teacher's actions and advised my teacher to use other means to help the child lose weight. Case was closed but the aftermath of this incident left me defeated.

I closed my office door and sat there for a long while in silence. I was brought to the lowest level of disgust by my teacher's lack of integrity whilst I stupidly defended him against a torrent of ranting sweeping across my face by this vexed parent who accused him of degrading his son because of his obesity. How could he do that? How could a teacher tell a lie when integrity forms the foundation of the education service? What kind of role model would he be as an educator? What kind of values and belief systems does he hold? This incident has left me aghast and confounded. One can never be able to fathom the level of degradation in the education service if we allow anyone to erode the values we hold in highest regard. I cannot wear a blindfold and turn away when these values are blatantly ignored. Thinking back, I wished I had dealt with this matter differently. I would have sat the officer down and talked through this whole issue with him and make him realise the severity of his actions. I was truly a greenhorn as a school leader then. Over the years, my reputation as a school leader who does not stand for officers who compromise their professionalism and integrity has been well-established in the school. This is really a two-edged sword. For those who could not wait to tell-tale on their colleagues, they come storming into my office armed with their venomous stories and wait in hope that I will mete out the necessary punishment whilst others stood by their friends in the name of comradeship. It is a delicate balance that I need to work harder on constantly. Decision-making has become a staple in my professional life and can result in positive or negative outcomes depending whose self-interest matters more. I pray that my growing wisdom will guide me better in my decision-making and management of thorny issues like this.

Journey of Survival and Discovery: A Beginner Teacher

As the first batch of graduates from the Diploma in Education Programme in 1992, expectations hailed high at the school level because we had been brandished as highly trained teachers armed with the latest innovative pedagogical skills and content knowledge from the National Institute of Education (NIE). In this phase of my career entry, the theme of survival and discovery resonated well. This theme dealt largely with reality shock of having to confront the complexities of pedagogical issues and the initial enthusiasm of being entrusted with my very first class. However, the 13 new beginner teachers were assigned reluctant mentors whose body language was clearly evident that they would like very much to be left alone and with a single message "I survived without a mentor, so can you!" We smiled warmly while they greeted us with disinterested coldness. The heavy timetable and towering marking load did not help to alleviate the painful initiation process into the teaching service. The lack of support from mentors led to a forged alliance amongst the beginning teachers. As they trudged ahead to transform classroom instruction with advanced pedagogical practices, they earned respect and recognition from fellow peers who were eager to learn from them.

Due to the tight time-table, sometimes we could hardly find time to go down to the canteen to buy food. At that point of time, the canteen was also serving food reminiscent of food consumed during National Service days, which was not exactly very palatable. Thus, some of us would take turns to cook something from home or buy something from nearby food centres near our homes. We would also keep each other updated on our teaching progress and share our teaching resources. We celebrated birthdays together and on one occasion, we brought a bottle of champagne to school. We went to the meeting room and popped the champagne. "Gosh, a bunch of teachers gone wild!" one teacher remarked in jest when the cork from the champagne bottle shot up into the ceiling and the champagne spewed all over the room and the ceiling. It had also left a stain on the ceiling board. Each time we entered the room for meetings, we would always chuckle to ourselves when we looked up at the ceiling. It is almost like a mark of our friendship. Time was too precious. Any form of help then to help us cope with the crazy workload was very much appreciated. The negativity continued to cloud us and one mentor even remarked "Do not spoil market!" but that did not discourage us because we knew deep in our hearts that we owe it to our students to do what is right for them. In retrospection, I think it is the passion within us that helped us to surmount the initial challenges that confronted us every bit of the way and kept us going. The peer support for one another as we uplifted each other's spirits helped to a very large extent to relieve some of the unnecessary stress and burden as well. The values and philosophy that we held so dearly helped us to make the right decision in this case.

Journey of Transformation: Head of Department

Recalling the years in the teaching service flooded my mind with memorable and frustrating events. I was appointed the Head of Department for Information Technology (IT) in my third year of service in 1994 and held this appointment for the next three years. I decided that I was not making any progress for the school, neither was there any growth within me, before I decided to relinquish the position to another junior officer. This swelling sense of discontent and self-doubt forced me to take stock of who I am, what I am doing and where I should go next. Perhaps, this was my mid-career crisis. Without further hesitation, I embarked on a journey of learning to enrich and rejuvenate my stale career.

I applied for the Ministry of Education Regional Language Centre (MOE RELC) Scholarship for the Diploma in Applied Linguistics and at the same time took up part time courses at Singapore Polytechnic in Multimedia Development. The latter made me realise that I was truly not cut out for IT-related learning or work. However, the genesis of my intense interest in education, an interest which has evolved into a pursuit for a career in the field, happened during my half year full-time Diploma study in Applied Linguistics. The Diploma programme changed my understanding of education and together with it, the course of my life. It was an international mix of lecturers and students characterised by youth, vigour and intelligence. In particular, I was fascinated by the existing diverse views instead of the politically correct discourse frequently faced in similar work environments. I came to realise that education should be dominated by advanced concepts, assisted by effective pedagogical practices, both of which are crucial in bringing out the greater social role from education. Education represents an area of life where I can achieve satisfying personal and professional development. Nevertheless, as I delved deeper into my work, I became increasingly aware that the *status quo* of English education has room for further improvements. Teaching of English or any subject should not be seen as a means to its ends to attain academic achievement but sharpening of one's minds to engage meaningfully at an intellectual level.

Upon my return to school, I spent the next two years being a "rebel" because I could not fit myself into the rigidity of the school system and found faults with many of the school's laid out operations and policies. The use of Work Improvement Team Scheme (WITS) tools was the latest fad then. My VP roped in the rebellious me and some other teachers to look into this project entitled 'How to have engaging Contact Time?' I thought to myself, "Gosh! What is this? This must be some kind of joke or a cunning scheme! They must be out of their mind or they must have discovered that I had left the school instead of attending Contact Time. Oh gosh! How lame is this?" Nonetheless, I grabbed the opportunity to air my concerns and suggested ways to improve the situation. Guess what? There was no follow up after that. I guessed WITS was merely a means to find out from us what caused the level of disengagement amongst teachers. However, the school was in need of a Discipline Mistress and I was their next best choice due to my past experience as a Head of Department. Thoughts raced through my mind on other possible reasons why I was the chosen one. They probably thought that this would be the best way to handle a "rebel". Of course, I thought to myself it could be the reputation that I had built up for myself as a stern and firm disciplinarian especially having been given the most challenging classes for the whole of my teaching career. I plucked up the courage to take on this undesirable and daunting task for I am one who loves challenges. Instead of griping about unhappiness and allowing it to turn into a vicious cycle, I decided to be proactive and make the positive changes that I would like to see. Another major decision that I made that helped to change the course of my professional and personal growth.

With such a heavy burden weighing on my shoulders, I was back to my task-oriented self again after two years of redundancy and rebellion. I drew up comprehensive plans and goals and achieved what I had set out. The second year was relatively tougher. I was charging ahead of my fellow teammates in my committee but they were not buying into my new plans. They perceived me as a true-blue task master and avoided me as far as possible. Whenever I had the opportunity to meet any of my members, I never failed to get any updates from them with regards to the jobs assigned to them and I would go on like "Hey XXX, have you looked into this yet?" or "XXX, this needs to be done by this Thursday but I have not heard from you yet. What's happening?" However, I never once did ask them about their well-being and neither was I sensitive to their needs. When they could not deliver, I ended up doing most of the work by myself but I enjoyed every single minute of it. The shocking revelation came about when I received my personal report for 360 degree evaluation. I was given high scores and compliments from my supervisors, but not my committee members.

I spent my year-end holidays reflecting on my leadership style and management. I realised that I was not a leader for I had no followers. I was working in isolation and making decisions by myself. At the same time, I was also working on a proposal for my principal to change the organisational structure and mooted the idea that we do not need a Discipline committee to look into discipline matters as it should be seen as a concerted effort of all school personnel. The idea was discussed further and it gave rise to the development of the Level Dean structure. I was deployed as a Level Dean for Primary One and I spent the whole of my year-end holidays planning ways to bond the new team members and to set directions together with them. All the time spent on reflection and strategic thinking had placed me in a better position for a brand new year. Gleaning the finer points from my Principal (mentor) by observing how she dealt with staff had given me deeper insights about empowerment and belief in the human enterprise. She took the time to sit with her staff and listened intently to each and every one of them. She was willing to bend the rules if the circumstances demanded it. I remember how she was willing to offload a teacher who was experiencing difficulties with her pregnancy even though she was a key personnel holding responsibilities. Although, many were not happy by that decision, she stood by it. I was also very upset when she gave me additional teaching load when another HOD could not teach Primary Three Science and redeployed her to handle administrative matters. I realised that she was seeing how best to deploy us according to our best abilities and talents.

She was also patient. When I was tasked to spearhead the Pupil Development Department, I was equally upset because I already had laid out plans for the department that I was leading. All of a sudden, I was thrust into a world of unknown and I was not prepared. I told her that I did not know where to start. I cancelled meetings and told my members, "I am still figuring out what to do. Values education is not an easy area. I will need time. So, that's all for today's meeting." One term went by with inaction from my department. Little did they know that I was seeking answers through reading and research. I struggled so much because I kept asking myself how one builds up one's values system. What are the influential factors? What are our roles as educators? What are the competing tensions? There were so many issues and few answers. Finally, I came up with a skeletal framework. I approached my principal with my grand plans. She looked at me and smiled so warmly and encouragingly. She said, "I trusted that you would come up with something. You did it. Go ahead with your plans." Wow! I was speechless! I was fired up at the same time! I felt so empowered by the faith and trust that she had in me. I realised that the dogmatic style of management would not work in the current reality and the change had to start with me. I realised that my mentor adopted a consultative approach but without compromising her standards and expectations. At the same time, she was willing to embrace new ideas.

I took on a humbling journey and decided that I would try her leadership style. I conducted a meeting that was peppered with critical questions to set the context and to elicit my team members' personal responses, aspirations and dreams. It started with a simple question, "How can we help the Primary One students fit into our school?" That started a torrent of questions, concerns, solutions etc. The experienced Primary One teachers voiced their concerns about the pupils' heavy bags and that the students do not know how to pack their bags according to the timetable. The list went on. We also decided to have the students learn all these important skills through fun and play. Together we also shared a common philosophy, that building character is far more important than completing the syllabus. I was truly in awe by what was happening around me. They wanted to participate. They wanted to be agents of change. Most importantly for myself, instead of delegating the work, I asked for volunteers. They were given a choice. I guessed that made all the difference. It was a fruitful meeting no doubt and in that one year we brought greater innovation to curriculum design and every single member was given a stake in all that we did, which helped to move us at an amazing speed. I became a far more humane leader, learning to see each member of my team as an individual with personal needs, concerns and aspirations. Their lives do not circle around their professional work only. What happens at home will also affect them in their professional work. Although we were awarded the Most Outstanding Contributions Award and conducted two cluster presentations, what I truly valued at the end of the day was the deep friendship bonds forged.

Journey of Reality Check: School Leader

During the Diploma in Departmental Management (DDM) course in 2004, we were tasked to find out from our closest friends about some of the unique qualities that we may possess and be ignorant of. It was kind of embarrassing to ask but nevertheless, I used the pretext of having to do my assignment to probe into my friends' thoughts about me.

Mrs. Yap, a senior teacher in my school, has always been a faithful and nurturing mentor in my long years of service in education. We have grown so close and shared many special moments. Passion, true commitment, enthusiasm are some of my qualities she claimed. However, she also said that I tend to be rather single-minded in my thoughts and action at times and have not taken into consideration the feelings of others. That may have caused unnecessary unhappiness among staff members that I worked with. Some of them secretly admired my tireless commitment to the school and gave me the nick-name "taskmaster". Definitely not a compliment I would say!

Nevertheless, she said that I have changed over the past few months. I am gaining more acceptance and popularity among the staff since I changed my management style that year. She also found me to be very friendly, approachable and understanding with many unfulfilled dreams for education. She likened it to me driving on the highway at 180 km/h with a roadster while others are still abiding the traffic rule by driving at 90 km/h. Gosh! Another stab at my bruised ego! I have often seen myself as a rational and systematic person when carrying out any tasks although I can be quite whimsical at times. She quickly explained that I had misunderstood her. I was simply filled with so many dreams and goals for the school that many of them in the school were finding difficult to catch up because they were still bounded by the mundane routines and procedures in the school. Phew! A smile of relief painted my face. I thanked her for her honesty and forthrightness with me. I learnt that I can make decisions very quickly and sometimes with very little deliberation whilst I also learnt that it may also serve me well to pause and consider all perspectives.

On the other hand, my fellow peer Linda, who is currently teaching in the Hong Kong International School, felt that I am overly unrealistic in my views of education as a whole. I do not blame her for being so cynical for my experiences differ greatly from hers. What she had experienced and learnt in her life had inadvertently cast some shadows in her belief systems. I hold very strong convictions about the role of teachers and how our actions on our students can have such great impact upon our future. But that was not her immediate concern. She suffered some injustice under two Principals and felt that her abilities and work were not appreciated. In her quest for efficiency in her work, she has left out one important aspect: self-reflection. If she had spent more time doing that, she would definitely be an asset to the education field. As shared by Palmer (1998, p. 24),

"The self-knowledge that comes from these reflections is crucial to my teaching, for it reveals a complexity within me that is within my students as well."

Although the session was not about her, I looked at her and I have learnt something more about her and for myself as well. I strongly attest to this as I agree with Palmer (1998, p. 20),

"… the salvation of this human world lies nowhere else than in the human heart, in the human power to reflect, in human meekness and in human responsibility."

We are so caught up with material wants and subscribe blindly to the commercialised world that we fail to appreciate simple things in life. I thanked God for giving me friends that will always stand by me in good and bad times. Going through the vicissitudes of one's life all by oneself can be lonely, painful and miserable.

Many of us entered the teaching profession without ever envisioning ourselves to become school leaders one day. I had similar thoughts as well. In fact, my good friends were shocked to see how I had moved up the ladder to become a VP in 2007. They could not envision me being a school leader. One remarked with disbelief, "Aiyo, you sure or not? Vice Principal? You don't like rules!" How true. Now that I am appointed as a school leader, I feel the chains of entrapment dragging me down further. Passion, Purpose and Perseverance were slowly replaced by Performance, Accountability and Competition. My immediate supervisor often buzzed in my ears when she wanted me to spearhead certain projects, "You are already a SEO 1A1, expectations are higher … Thus, I would expect you to look into several projects this year to justify your performance grade." Or "I would like you to help the school achieve the following awards….etc." The list goes on endlessly. One can easily get lost in the web especially while trying to juggle so many demands all at one go. Not only do I have to juggle the strategic tasks piled up on my plate by my supervisor, I also have to deal with day-to-day issues like discipline cases, teachers' and parents' complaints. At the end of my first year as a VP, I suffered from an illness that jolted me to the reality that I was suffering from tremendous stress and my body was breaking down when I had to go to the emergency unit one evening. The probability of contracting thyroid cancer dawned on me but I took all these in my stride and systematically planned for the necessary measures should I depart from this earthly existence. I was very calm and the notion of suffering from a terminal illness did not faze me a bit. I guess when people have placed their faith in God, they are far more prepared to meet their Maker. The only regret that I may have had was not spending enough time with my family because of my work. Perhaps, this is one of God's many ways to tell me to stop and review.

In my second year as VP, I spent most of my time in the hospital after work tending to my grandmother who suffered a series of heart attacks and stroke. My grandmother was the only person in the world who truly understood me. The other important person in my life whom I adored was my dad, blessed with a heart of gold. His generosity made him vulnerable and adorable at the same time. I wished things were different then. I wished I had done more for them instead of my inner drive to excel in my professional career. The only solace I have is that they are both united in heaven with God. Two special angels in my life who suffered greatly on earth are now enjoying heavenly bliss for eternity. Why do I want to pen this down? I want to remember how special they are to me and always will be.

My illness plus the passing of my grandmother forced me to take a long reflective pause. I realised that much of my energy was channelled to my profession, so much so that I had neglected my family and health. Was it worthwhile? Till now, the question cannot be answered but I had to take stock and review my priorities in life taking cognisance of my personal philosophy and belief systems. The postgraduate course in 2011 came in time for me to rejuvenate and look within myself in seeking a new purpose in life for my next lap. I do not know where it will lead me to next. The joy and sense of fulfilment from helping others in need continue to revive my faith in the human spirit. What remains now for me is to fulfil my dream to be a missionary one day and relieve myself from the shackles of professional burden. I feel like an onion. Dry and brown on the exterior as if drained out of all energy by the external pressures and demands. Inside me remain layers and layers of moist flesh to be peeled off one at a time as I continue to uncover each chapter of my life. I know inside the deep core lies a young shoot ready to sprout and spring into a new life again. The free-spirit lies dormant for now. What would that new life be? I guess it remains to be unveiled.

Reference

Palmer, P. J. (1998). *The courage to teach*. San Franciso: Jossey-Bass.

Chapter 21

New Beginnings:
An Educator's Journey through
the Door of Mentorship

Aristotle Motii NANDY

I was brought down to earth by what I heard. It was clear that Mr. Harinam was in charge as he insisted that the Secondary Two class in the new accelerated programme comprise 24 students, and not 14 students as recommended by my team. After all, he was the owner and Director of the school and I, although the Principal, an employee. Although I had based my proposal on comprehensive assessments of student academic ability conducted by my team of teachers, it was evident that the financial viability, nay profitability, of the programme took precedence. We were at opposite ends of the meeting room and I could feel the tension in my veins as well as the now evident rift in our relationship, a bond which I once had felt was so durable and robust that it would stand the test of time. He had been my mentor and friend for close to four years now, and though we had disagreed, albeit amicably, on many an issue, this time it stirred a sense of bitterness inside me. As our eyes remained locked in an intense gaze, a barrage of thoughts flooded my mind as

I contemplated the path our relationship had taken as well as my incredulous journey in the school thus far.

We had had a great relationship, both personal and professional. Mr. Harinam was the director of a group of schools that catered to the educational needs of mostly upper-middle class Chinese Indonesians, and was then the Principal of the flagship campus where I had begun my career as a rookie teacher late 2001. Though I was not a teacher with relevant credentials in terms of paper qualifications or experience, Mr. Harinam sensed my keen willingness to learn and my earnest drive to excel, and so he took me under his wing as he shared with me the responsibility of school administration and management. He involved me in the day-to-day operations of the school — from planning the assemblies to timetabling as well as writing up the standard procedures for different areas of the school's operations and also teacher recruitment — and even shared with me the concerns and issues he had to address at the top management level, from recruitment policy to budgeting and school expansion. As Mr. Harinam had included me in his meetings with parents, as well as with prospective education partners and businessmen who wanted to be part of the school, I had gained tremendously from his insights as well as foresight.

It was a steep learning curve for me to be thrust into the heart of the running of the school as I conversed about issues and dilemmas usually discussed by senior administrators. At every juncture, I would consult and discuss with Mr. Harinam before implementing any programme or initiative in the school. He would usually ask me to come up with the details of a plan or proposal for a particular initiative or programme and we would problematise the inherent issues that might surface from the proposals made. Our meetings not only took place during school hours but also went on in the evenings (when only the security guards on the night shift remained in the campus grounds) and would extend into the quietude of the night. What was important to me was that he disliked sycophantic behaviour, and instead encouraged discussion and even welcomed disagreement on areas where we differed in our opinions. But even when I felt defeated by his arguments, I relished the growth it afforded me as he helped me see things from a different angle, from a different lens; clearly, he was a master at having multiple perspectives and I his attentive student. More importantly, I felt that Mr. Harinam had a big heart. Although he was simultaneously a businessman and an educator, I felt that he believed in the essence of education, that the students had to be given the best education possible. To him, even if a student were unable to pay his or her school fees due to unforeseen circumstances, he was prepared to reduce or absorb the fees for that student. I was aware and had even borne witness to several such incidents.

And as the school grew from a fledgling educational outfit of about 40 students to a much sought-after institution of an ascending reputation for quality education, so did my role and responsibilities in the school. Life was all about work for me, revolving around the school day in and day out, every single day of the week including weekends and public holidays. And although occasionally I asked myself why I was sacrificing even my personal life for the sake of the school, every time I met Mr. Harinam for our discussions all those thoughts seem to just fizzle out. It dawned on me that I had continued working at the school beyond the one year which I had initially planned simply due to the mentor I had in Mr. Harinam. He was my anchor to the school. In fact, I realised that it was his unassuming personality and unwavering commitment to education, as I viewed it, that impelled me to stay on beyond the one year that I had initially planned. Perhaps, I also felt a strong sense of purpose and that my contributions were genuinely valued by Mr. Harinam. More importantly, Mr. Harinam was my friend, and I was here to help him in his mission in the field of education. However, notwithstanding the closeness that we had, at no time did I allow the proximity of our relationship and the trust that he had invested in me to cloud the fact that he was my superior; I had always conducted myself in the decorum of a subordinate, and was mindful of the adage that "familiarity breeds contempt".

But ever since Mr. Harinam appointed me Principal of the new campus in an upscale neighbourhood in the suburbs of North Jakarta in July 2004, things seemed different. I sensed that we started to grow further apart. We stopped playing badminton or soccer together in the evenings after school as we had so often done before, and the sharing sessions we used to have were no more. The only occasions we did meet were when I decided to dismiss an expatriate teacher (whom Mr. Harinam had hired and had highly recommended) and when we had our first Parent–Teacher Association meeting, which I believe were two significant events in terms of the administration of the fledgling school. Although I had not realised it before, I now feel that a major contributing factor to the dissonance between us was perhaps the physical distance of our work. Prior to moving to the new campus, we worked in the same building and our offices were adjacent to each other; now, we worked in separate campuses some 15 km apart, which consequentially rendered meetings in persons more difficult. Although I had taken it upon myself to write him weekly reports about the events in the school at the end of each week to keep him abreast of the school operations as well as the decisions we were making, the absence of face-to-face personal communication was telling, and it did affect me.

I felt a vacuum and I did confide in my Vice Principal that I missed those times when the personal connection between the two of us was strong and clearly perceived every day. I felt, and perhaps even feared, that I was losing that connection with Mr. Harinam. In fact, whenever there were policy announcements or policy implementations that were applicable across all campuses, I could sense my growing frustration at what appeared to me to be decisions made without consultation, that my input had not been sought. Perhaps the school had grown too big — from 40 students when I first joined to close to 2,000 students in three campuses — that the intimacy in the relationship Mr. Harinam and I shared was now replaced by an impersonal hierarchical edifice. It also appeared to me that Mr. Harinam was making decisions in consultation with the Principal of the flagship campus, and that I was removed from the inner circle. Perhaps I was so used to being involved in the decision-making process that I now felt left out. On hindsight, I wonder if it is due to my insecurity of being left alone to run my own ship, so to speak, or whether it is because I relished the sense of team, the togetherness in building something together, of bouncing ideas and setting goals. Perhaps, it is because Mr. Harinam and I were not as close as we had been before. Although the distance in our relationship was unsettling, I spent little time deliberating on these matters then as I had a mammoth of a task at hand to build the culture of the new school and to ensure it was at least on par with the flagship campus. I had never expected nor desired to be at the helm of the school, but now since I was thrust into the position, I was determined to make my school a success, perhaps even to outdo the flagship campus.

Gradually, I began to rely less and less on Mr. Harinam, and I began to relish the autonomy to build the school culture at my campus, and institute what I believed was important for the education of the students as well as for the climate in which teachers work. I was determined to avoid the mistakes we had made in the flagship campus, and my experience there guided me in my decisions as Principal of the new campus. I was beginning to find my own voice as a school leader. Now, in my new role, I felt responsible and ultimately accountable for the education of the students studying in my campus, not Mr. Harinam. Now, it was I who was directly responsible and answerable to their parents, not Mr. Harinam. Now, teachers came to me to address their needs and challenges in the classroom and in other areas of the school work, and even in their personal lives, and not to Mr. Harinam. Therefore, I felt compelled to make it work according to my understanding and perspective of what made a great school. In a sense, I was living my dream of setting up my own school as I had envisaged before I started working for Mr. Harinam.

And the truth was that I was blessed with considerable success. Within 10 months into our maiden school year, the school culture was blooming and the community was abuzz with the diversity and richness of the programmes that we had. Even students from the neighbouring "competitor" schools next door had decided to enrol in our school. We also had a vibrant parent community that enthusiastically took part in all the school activities as well as actively promoted the school to prospective parents. In fact, Mr. Harinam was very pleased with our progress and, during the few times that we met, he spoke about replicating our school culture-building model at the would two campuses.

Notwithstanding our success, I was very cautious of any new policy or programme implementation at my campus, as I was protective of our budding school culture that we were trying to nurture. In a way, the school was in the survival phase of its growth and introducing something new without thoroughly considering the ramifications would, in my opinion, be detrimental to its health. On the other hand, I sought stabilisation of the programmes we had started, that we needed to consolidate our practices before introducing new ones. Yet, at the same time, I understood the need for the accelerated programme and believed that it would benefit our higher-ability students. However, I felt that to include students who were not able to cope with the compacted curriculum of the accelerated programme was not only educationally unjustified, but would also severely rock the boat of stability. I was also concerned about teacher workload given that the new programme would require intensive curriculum development by the teachers themselves. Thus, by further thrusting upon them the burden to get weaker students within the programme up to speed would be unfair to them. In fact, I tried to alleviate their workload on several occasions by taking upon myself the task of teaching weaker students, or students enrolled midway through the school year until such time they were able to follow the regular lessons without much difficulty. Somehow, I had considered that further adding to their workload in such a manner might prove adversarial to the sustenance of the cohesive and caring culture that we were trying to create. Intrinsically, I understood the strain that teachers would feel, perhaps because I had undergone the rigour of being in a school in its early years, where, as a teacher, I was responsible for several subjects across multiple levels.

I had made it clear to Mr. Harinam that I shared the importance he felt about how the accelerated programme would benefit our academically more able students, as thus far our schools had mostly focused on only helping students who were struggling in their academic subjects. In fact, when he had first informed me of his plan to introduce the accelerated programme I had immediately gathered a team of teachers and quickly got down to sketching out a blueprint of our proposal of how the accelerated programme would be implemented, including the selection criteria for students to be admitted into the programme. It was only after careful deliberation that we came up with a list of students who would qualify for the programme.

However, it was clear that, despite having discussed this issue, Mr. Harinam maintained that there was no option but to increase the number of students in the programme to a full class of 24. His decision was final, and the whole exchange we had kept playing repeatedly in my mind. I nodded, excused myself and left the meeting room. As Principal, I was supposed to convince parents of the merits of the programme for their children. Though they had the option to choose to be part of the programme, I would not be at peace with myself if I had to promote it to parents of the students who I felt would suffer from being part of a programme that was beyond the upper boundary of their zone of proximal development. Reaching my office, I slumped into my chair behind my cluttered desk. What was I to do? As a school leader, I had a key role in either promoting or blocking the educational change (Fullan, 2003). Given my disagreement with Mr. Harinam, I had two options: to stand my ground and resist or cope with the change. Hall (1998) describes those who fight as either "leader-resistors or leader-managers" (p. 136). While leader-resistors challenge the educational initiative and attempt to block it, the latter adopt the change to serve immediate needs of the students. But what was I to tell my team of teachers who had come up with the shortlist of students? How should I explain to them the decision to include students who had not made the initial cut? I felt trapped, trapped between my role as educator, a custodian of my teachers and students and as an administrator, paid to carry out the operations of the school as desired by the owners and directors.

I recalled the many discussions Mr. Harinam and I had on education-related matters along with the fair share of agreements and disagreements, but this particular issue had touched a sensitive part within me. I did not know what it was exactly. I could have gone along with it but found myself unable to. A strange feeling overcame me, a feeling which I am unable to describe in words. It was as if I had a deeper responsibility to the students, for their development, rather than just to the organisation. I was an educator, not an employee of the school, and I felt alone. There was no one else whom I could talk to regarding this. Had I discussed this with my Vice Principal or the teachers, I would have been guilty of stirring discord amongst them. It was my own battle, and I would have to face it on my own.

The next few days were turbulent for me. Just when I thought that things were somewhat stabilising in my new role as a school leader, with a school culture that was vibrant and with a cohesive team of teachers and students, I was given a reality shock. The school after all, as postulated by Hoban (2002), is a web of relationships and structures, and I was but a small part of the ecology. I realised that I was foolish all the while for having a false notion of autonomy. The fact remained that I was dependent on Mr. Harinam and the board of directors in more ways than I had realised, and more importantly, it dawned upon me that I was in no way indispensable. I began to question myself as to what were the compelling reasons for continuing my service at the school. I had no real reason to stay on, except for the students whom I was teaching. The anchor had been fully lifted and I was drifting away. I comforted myself with knowledge from scripture that explained the transient nature of things in the material world. That which comes into existence will eventually cease to exist, that happiness and distress arise from attachment, and to be calm and equipoised one has to be detached from the field of activity. But here I was right in the ocean of material existence, like a boat being swept away by waves caused by the winds of time.

After much deliberation and struggle within, I resolved to tender my resignation. It was heart-breaking but I had to reassess my priorities, and it seemed that I was disenchanted by the whole episode. What does it mean to be an educator? What was I in the field of education for — for position and money or for upholding the ideals that were important to me? However, the fact that I was clearly attached to what we had built over the years, especially the past year, made the decision even more painful. I had practically invested four full years of my life in the school; it was literally a place I could call "home". But somehow I felt a sense of indignation, a feeling that I was standing up for a cause, an ideal. I wondered if I would have felt that way if I had not been in a position of leadership, where I would have merely implemented the plan to introduce the programme as I had done numerous times during my service at the flagship campus under the stewardship of Mr. Harinam. Was it different this time round because I felt responsible for each student under my care, as well as answerable to their parents who trusted my professional judgement? All I knew was that I could not implement the accelerated programme by including students whom I felt were not ready for a compacted curriculum, and that I would not be able to promote it to their parents. I also felt obligated to the teachers as I believed that teaching is an emotional labour and that school leaders should be sensitive to the needs of teachers in and out of the classroom (Hargreaves, 1998). From the educational standpoint, I felt that the demands of a compacted curriculum would require students to be relatively homogenous in their academic capacities, lest they and their teachers face significant challenges in their daily interactions. I finally managed to convince myself that I was making the right decision.

A couple of days later, I met Mr. Harinam again and told him exactly how I felt: that I was unable to bring myself to promote the programme, and that he would have to do it on his own or get someone else to do so. At the same time, I handed in my resignation letter and offered my services until such time he found a replacement. I also assured him that I would leave only eight months later, after the Secondary Four students whom I was teaching had completed their final examinations, the Cambridge International General Certificate of Secondary Education (IGCSE) examinations. I could see it in his eyes that he was taken aback by my decision, but being gracious as he had always been, he told me that he hoped I would change my mind, all the while speaking in a mellowed tone.

Outwardly, he appeared unflustered as he had always been in the numerous situations whenever he faced a setback. However, this time I sensed his sadness, as if he had been hurt, perhaps in the sense that I had betrayed our friendship, the trust he had in me, the time and energy he had invested in me throughout the years.

For me, it was a decision made with a heavy heart; till today, it remains fresh in my mind. I am not sure whether our relationship took a turn for the worse because of the lack of close communication and interactions when I moved to the new campus, or whether it was because of the different sense of professional, and even personal, identity that I had as a school leader. Sometimes, I think I had been impulsive, rash and not level-headed in coming to my decision. Did I not consider the issue from Mr. Harinam's perspective: that the financial health of the school as a private enterprise directly depended on the level of its enrolment and class size? However, at other times, deep inside I feel that there was the hand of Providence in whatever had taken place. Perhaps I would have been too entrenched in my role as a school leader and in the system, and that my growth as an educator would not have been as rich as it has been now.

During the months after having tendered my resignation, most of my dealings were not with Mr. Harinam but with another director of the school. I did meet Mr. Harinam several times, and though we did not speak about the programme after that day, I ensured that the teachers involved in the programme had the necessary support they required. I also noticed that he was making an attempt to mend our relationship. In fact, during the teacher induction programme in July 2005, where teachers were assigned rooms in pairs, he opted to share the room with me. However, the schedule of the induction programme was so packed that we hardly had any time to communicate. Meanwhile, the remaining six months passed by in a flash and I had gradually entrusted the various areas of school operations to different members of the school executive committee, a team which we had carefully built. I was at peace with myself, and with the decision that I had made, as if I were in a state of serenity as described by Huberman (1992). None of the parents, students or other teachers, except for my Vice Principal — whom I had known for years — had any clue of my imminent departure until my penultimate month at the school in December 2005.

On the last day of school, we had a Christmas concert. Just after the finale, I was called onto the stage, and so was Mr. Harinam. The microphone was handed to him and, just as he began to speak, suddenly I could feel my heart thump uncontrollably. He began to speak of my contributions and reminisced the day when we first met in Singapore, where he had interviewed me, as well as the times we had shared over the years. While listening to him, I was transported back into time, and the memories of the years flashed across my mind. We were so much in synch, our educational beliefs, our interests, even the way we worked as a team. I felt a tug at my heartstrings, but I resisted — at least outwardly, I did. Inside, I was overwhelmed by emotion. What was I doing? Why was I giving all this up, all these years of friendship, a great team of teachers and students, a whole career ahead of me and a legacy to build at the current campus? What was I doing? When Mr. Harinam completed his tribute of me, he presented me with a gift, which the staff had prepared for me, after which I spoke a little something in bits and starts. All I could remember was that at the end I was swarmed by students, parents and teachers, some wishing me well, some in disbelief, others in tears. Somehow, I myself could not believe that it was real. But it was. It was time for me to go, time for me to leave all this behind after five years of my life, and start anew.

Since leaving Mr. Harinam's schools, I have had the privilege of working with a wonderful world-renowned motivational speaker and person, top schools in Jakarta, and even with a non-profit organisation in starting a kindergarten and primary school. I have attributed my performance in these organisations to the experiences I had at Mr. Harinam's school, for which I remain always grateful. He provided me with the opportunities that laid the foundation and built my self-belief as an educator. Meeting Mr. Harinam was a key event in my career trajectory as an educator, as he had helped me realise my potential and calling. He afforded me the opportunity, which I believe I would not have had elsewhere, as

I did not possess formal teaching qualifications nor the experience needed for the roles thrust upon me. It is this principle that I have taken with me, that is, to be always willing to give others a chance notwithstanding their formal qualification, just as Mr. Harinam had done with me.

Reflecting more deeply upon the events surrounding this critical turning point in my career trajectory has particularly made me aware of the cause of the underlying tensions in the relationship that I had with Mr. Harinam. I have realised that the issue surrounding the accelerated programme merely served as a catalyst that surfaced the real problem, that of open and constant communication. I have realised that whenever we are in conflict with someone, our attitude can make a difference between damaging that relationship and deepening it. While distance was an issue in my particular situation with Mr. Harinam, I should have made the attempt to bridge that gap. However, I was more focused on achieving success in my new role in the stewardship of the new campus and had ignored the signs of our waning relationship due to a dearth in communication.

I have also realised that relationships play an important part in my life, particularly in my work environment. They give me a sense of belonging, a sense of togetherness, a sense of team that provides the impetus to give my best in the discharge of my duties. Although I had subconsciously enacted the value of this principle in my role as a school leader, this narrative inquiry voyage has brought it to the fore. It has also cemented my belief that for schools to effectively nurture the spirit of education, they should be small in size, where there are strong connections between members at all levels. The bonds that are formed in such schools provide the foundation for growth of not only the students, but also of all members of staff.

I have also realised the enormity of the effect of words uttered by a leader, in particular, an overwhelming sense of empowerment that fuelled my drive and self-belief to succeed when Mr. Harinam told me he "trusted" me and therefore had entrusted the leadership of the new campus to me and not to someone else who was more qualified than I was. Ironically, it was also the finality of his words *vis-à-vis* his decision on the number of students for the accelerated programme that numbed me of my sense of worth and autonomy, although I believe it was not his intention to do so. Sadly, I have yet to be able to apply this truth in practice as I am often overcome by the dictates of my ego. Yet, I am confident that with the passage of time, along with experience and by being more introspective, I will be able to uplift the spirits of those whom I come in contact with.

It was a couple of years after leaving the school that I met Mr. Harinam again, this time while I was doing some consulting work for another school. Time had healed the wounds of our relationship as we had communicated via email several times before. And, over the next few years, our relationship improved steadily; we reflected upon and shared fond memories of the beginning years, while burying our past differences. Mr. Harinam called me to help out at his schools a couple of times towards the end of 2011 and, during our most recent meeting, he asked me to promise him that should I decide to relocate to Jakarta, I would re-join him at his school. Specifically, he uttered the following words that, to me, made the world of a difference: that "the door is always open".

References

Fullan, M. (2003). *The moral imperative of school leadership*. California: Corwin Press.

Hall, V. (1998). Strategic leadership in education: Becoming, being, doing. In D. Middlewood and J. Lumby (eds.), *Strategic management in schools and colleges* (pp. 133–147). London: Paul Chapman Publishing.

Hargreaves, A. (1998). The emotional practice of teaching. *Teaching and Teacher Education*, 14 (8), 835–854.

Hoban, G. F. (2002). *Teacher learning for educational change: A systems thinking approach*. Buckingham: Open University Press.

Huberman, M. (1992). Teacher development and instructional mastery. In A. Hargreaves, & M. G. Fullan (eds.), *Understanding teacher development* (pp. 122–142). New York: Teachers College Press.

Chapter 22

Managing Stereotypes in a Diverse Educational Landscape — A Teacher's Journey towards Self-discovery

Nur SABARIAH Mohamed Ibrahim

To awaken to history was to cease to live instinctively. It was to begin to see oneself and one's group the way the outside world saw one.

— **V. S. Naipaul**

Introduction

"To awaken to (one's) history" is not always an easy task to attempt. Whilst historical narratives are seen as collectively significant in preserving the memory of family or social and institutional units, it is challenging to tease out individual narratives that are often embedded within the larger discourse. Against the socio-political backdrop of collective interests over individual interests, individual discourses or contestation of ideas are often drowned. After some 10 years as an educator in the same organisation, my sense of self diminished in relation to my growing role in the organisation.

I have been in the same school for close to a decade. I have grown from a Beginning Teacher to a leader of various school projects, to Subject Head and to Head of Department. My growth as an educator was negotiated within that space of school context and time. My values on education have been formed prior to joining the education service. Most times, there is harmony or in corporate jargon "alignment" to organisational values. However, there were numerous other instances when there were tensions. In highlighting these instances in my history my sense of self as an educator was clarified.

Do Not Let Him Walk All Over You: A Beginning Teacher's Sense of Self as an Educator

One of the first instances when a student challenged my sense of self happened early on. As a young teacher, I was looking forward to meeting my new classes. I had spent a lot of time planning and preparing my introductory tasks and lesson plans. As I walked into class brimming with excitement, a male student (KW) at the back of the classroom raised his hand and asked, "Are you our English teacher?" Below is a short vignette of the ensuing exchange:

Me: Yes, I am your General Paper tutor.

KW: But you are Malay! You are not qualified to teach us English. What more General Paper! It is a very difficult paper dealing with current affairs and politics.

Me: What do you mean?

KW: The Malays I know are lazy and not clever.

Me: Well, why don't you see the Principal now to request for a change of class?

KW: Maybe but I will wait and see how good you are. I give you two weeks. I'll watch and observe and then only decide. (He sat back and folded his arms at that decision.)

All the while, the other students were silent. Some looked surprised at his open proclamation and a few were eagerly awaiting my response. I was stunned by what I perceived as his audacity. In response, I retreated into my lesson plan and let slip a teachable moment.

On an emotional level, I was nervous and trying to mask it. All I could muster in response was to allow the student the choice to see the Principal. Looking further back into my life history as a student in school, my ethnic identity as a minority never seemed to be an issue except for one instance in Junior College (Senior High School). During an Economics lecture, a group of us were pointed out by the lecturer as Malays and used as an explanation for our supposed weak performance in a recent Economics test. I spoke up to inform the lecturer that some of us did very well in that test. Though I was said to be disrespectful and was punished, college mates of all ethnic groups showed their solidarity when they expressed their commitment to multiculturalism. Buoyed by youthful foolhardiness of questioning the teacher, this incident did not dent my spirit. However, fast-forward six or seven years later, as a qualified adult authority whose credibility is challenged and reduced to ethnic identity, the incident caught me off-guard and I was shaken. In response, I went through the lesson plan perfunctorily and informed the Principal that a student might ask for a change of class. He listened sympathetically and gave me the freedom to decide how best to handle the matter. The empowerment was a trust in my professionalism and that encouraged me to be open about the incident. Feeling secure, I discussed the incident with a few colleagues to seek their opinions. I also questioned my own assumptions about my identity formulation as an educator.

After exploring my options, I decided to allow for a contestation of ideas. I developed a lesson plan. I went to class with a stubbornness and refusal to bow down to the stereotype. But of course, it was easier to be confident after a few days! My subsequent two-hour period was to elicit students' understanding and assumptions of race, ethnicity, stereotypes and prejudices. I facilitated the discussion objectively. I envisioned my classroom to be democratic and at the same time respectful. At the end of the lesson, the class came to a consensus and understood that sometimes, the moral underpinnings of an issue weigh more heavily. That open challenge from a student and its subsequent course of action concretised some of my teacher beliefs and classroom practices for years to come, namely:

Listen to my students and not adhere to my lesson plans strictly

In retrospect, the open challenges are always a rich context for learning, far beyond any lesson plan I can possibly conceptualise. In fact, I often take a provocative stance in class to allow students to speak their minds.

Allow my students to explore, discover and mature

After 10 years, I still grapple with the temptation of silencing their raw thoughts. To allow for contestation of ideas is the ideal that I try to strive for in my classroom.

Be the facilitator during this process

Being open as a teacher means that students trust you. I have come to discover that when there is rapport between the students and me, the classroom environment becomes safe and conducive for teaching and learning.

This particular incident generalised and deepened my teacher beliefs and classroom management practices. In terms of my development, this incident and a few other similar incidents in my later teaching years informed my understanding of multiculturalism and its negotiated place in our education system. For every student like KW who voiced his thoughts, there are many others who will not. For every student who voices his thoughts and silenced by teachers as politically incorrect, the culture of silence will "nurture" apathetic students. I wondered if the National Education discourse at that point allowed pre-university students sufficient space for open and critical discourse.

When given the opportunity to develop the National Education programme in my seventh year of teaching, I decided to go a step beyond enacting the basic curriculum of exposure to other cultures. I problematised that cultural exposure is only skin-deep and thus insufficient, if it is not supported by critical understanding that arises out of engagement. It was, however, challenging to conceptualise and implement a mass programme that aimed at teasing out the common threads of humanity that run through all ethnic groups. While I may have been clear about my sense of self as an educator in the classroom, I have not entirely evolved my sense of self that is situated within the domain of curriculum design at the school level, especially when there are overriding institutional concerns and constraints. Sometimes, aims, intentions and aspirations have to be negotiated within larger socio-political contexts. This remains a developmental stage for me.

Relating and Interacting with Fellow Colleagues: On an Even Footing?

Leading teams can prove challenging when commitment levels differ amongst team members. There is constant negotiation to involve all members and create a sense of purpose. In general, most teams that I have led have been positive and members, regardless of age and years of experience work, collaboratively at fostering good working relations. I have worked under a collegial environment for a few years and was not mentally or emotionally prepared when confronted by a "resistant" team member. Ann* is an experienced teacher with almost 20 years at the school. She enjoys good standing with the school leaders and colleagues for being dependable. I was co-assigned projects and competitions that were traditionally her projects. With success at competitions and school-wide projects being attributed to the partnership with a younger teacher, I was increasingly perceived as encroaching her space. While I was aware of the lukewarm interactions between us, I did not openly address it. On the one hand, I was aware and appreciated that I was tapping her tacit knowledge and institutional memory to implement programmes efficiently. On the other hand, I was resentful that my youth was constantly being raised as an issue during our group meetings.

In retrospect, perhaps, I did not listen carefully to her underlying concerns when she talked about my youth. The build-up of tension culminated with Ann confiding in my Head of Department that I may be an energetic young teacher but insensitive to fellow colleagues' needs. In the mediated session with the Head of Department, it was mentioned that I was a source of stress to Ann. My most immediate emotional response was disbelief, a sense of betrayal that my helpful gestures to a fellow colleague were met with scepticism. I was upset that my intentions were misinterpreted. I was also indignant that student priorities and learning were relegated to a single teacher's needs. I was asked to scale back on student programmes to ensure that Ann does not feel overwhelmed. I could not reconcile that the learning of many was subsumed by the needs of one.

In perhaps what is youthful impetuousness, I repositioned the student programme and its target audience to ensure that the programme survived. The decision I made was based on student and fellow peers' feedback on the effectiveness of the programme. Being a relatively young teacher, the decision I made was not easy, given the political nature of the issue at hand. It was a time when I felt alone. Out of respect for her seniority, I did not attempt to rally support from other colleagues for the programme and decided to do it on my own quietly. It was some years later that I received an acknowledgement from Ann on the programme. Instead of feeling gratified, I was disappointed in myself that I did not try harder to win her over at the onset.

When I left the school, we had reached a truce and maintained cordial relations but I did not attempt to rationalise Ann's and my emotional responses. I had always been content not to bother about it by believing that professionalism has to take precedence and student interests must always be upheld over other competing interests. It is only during my graduate course and recent readings such as Huberman's milestones in a teacher's career trajectory that I begin to grasp the rationality of what I perceived as emotional episodes. My somewhat unilateral conclusions on this matter are being challenged. What I simplistically reduced to an inability to cope and manage personal expectations was really far more complex — a divide between two teachers on different stages of a teacher's life cycle. We were ready for different things and thus the ensuing tensions and struggle to assert our identities. Relating this discovery and realisation to V.S. Naipaul's quote, being awakened to this aspect of my history is "to cease to live instinctively." I have come to accept this chapter of my growth as a necessary maturation process, though the closure came five years later.

Bridging the Gap between an Administrator and a Beginning Teacher: If I were in Your Shoes...

After a certain period on the job, I have reached a comfortable level of familiarity with the system, its people and students. Though taking on a leadership position has its challenges, the work culture made it easy to transit into this role. In my early years as a teacher, led by a trusting Principal who empowered teachers, I always tried to fashion my own leadership style as one that is based on trust in fellow colleagues' professionalism and fairness as a supervisor. In my sharing of this third story, I reveal how easy it is sometimes to lose sight of the individual teachers that I lead in the team. Again, the notion of what constitutes "professionalism" is questioned in this instance and how it can be at odds with wanting to be a fair supervisor.

Recently, while I was working in my office, a Beginning Teacher, Mei, came into my room, unceremoniously closed the door after her, dragged a chair next to me and sat down. The following vignette is a short highlight from the dialogue:

Mei: (in an angry tone) I reject the appointment as the subject tutor.
Me: Why?
Mei: The school cannot make me do what I do not want to do.
Me: Why do you not want to try when the school has faith in your ability?
Mei: It's a new subject. I just do not want to do it. The school must be fair. You must be fair. (At this point, Mei started crying.)

While she was crying, I was gathering my wits and wondering how best to handle the situation as my somewhat probing stance was questioning her professionalism as a teacher. I drew a blank from the recently-attended workshop on how to deal with a difficult situation. A more mature person after failing to win over Ann (second story), I knew that if I won Mei over, I would have the support of the tightly knit cohort of Beginning Teachers to take on this unpopular teaching subject with enthusiasm rather than apathy. Almost instinctively, I decided not to preempt Mei and question what I perceive to be a professional sense of duty. Instead, I tried to remember what it was like for me when I started out as a Beginning Teacher, and respond with empathy. I remember my glaring gaps in knowledge and practice. I remember the feelings of insecurity. I remember failed lessons. I remember the enthusiasm and passion. I remember nurturing mentors. I remember successful lessons. In fact, even as an experienced teacher, I sometimes have flat lessons. With this recollection, all I managed to do at the end of the one-hour dialogue was to convince her to take on the subject as part of her professional development as a teacher.

The dialogue jolted me out of my comfort zone. I begin to question how I had supported the learning of my team of teachers. Had I done enough? Upon reflection, the key members in the team identified that we have been more concerned with the transmission of technical skills to facilitate the teaching of the interdisciplinary subject. Our emphasis has been on "technicising the content knowledge" (Goodson, 2003) and the human aspect of teaching and learning has been overshadowed. What we identified instinctively then, I now understand it through Goodson's lenses. As a result, we reviewed our structured mentoring programme and acknowledged that a beginning teacher needs security and affirmation to acquire the confidence to develop and grow. We set about to build a culture of trust and open sharing by organising small group discussions on pedagogical and assessment matters. During these sessions, we attempted to alleviate teacher anxieties and insecurities by foregrounding them and acknowledging them in the public space instead of leaving anxieties and insecurities in the private and individual spaces. We were however careful not to over-normalise these insecurities as it would trivialise teachers' personal experiences and their efforts to grow professionally. At the end of that teaching year, I wrote Mei a card and attributed the improved mentoring programme to her. Her desire to do something about her situation led to her professional learning and consequently changed the professional development trajectory for her peers as well.

Conclusion

The only reason I chose to highlight these three stories would be that I still remember them vividly and these incidents in different ways forced me to play my cards. In storying these events, I realised a common theme that runs through all three events — listening. In the three stories, I moved from a hesitation to listen, to failure to listen, to a realisation that I need to listen rather than talk. In my various other interactions, I have come to see the value of listening and to connect with colleagues as people with personal, social, and cultural identities beyond their professional selves. As a result of their personal selves and lives that they negotiate within their professional contexts daily, people will have different aspirations. I have come to make a distinction between capacity and aspirations. Instead of expecting uniform standards of commitment and capacity, I appreciate that a system usually comprises people of different aspirations and needs as they chart their own growth in the different phases of their professional lives. The question that remains in my own journey of self-discovery is how to bring about a sense of purpose and commitment in a team of people at different stages of their professional life cycle.

*Pseudonym used.

References

Clandinin, D. J., & Connelly, F. M. (1996). Teachers' professional knowledge landscapes: Teacher stories. Stories of teachers. School stories. Stories of schools. *Educational Researcher*, 25 (3), 24–30.

Conle, C. (2000). Narrative inquiry: Research tool and medium for professional development. *European Journal of Teacher Education*, 23 (1), 49–63.

Goodson, I. F. (2003). *Professional knowledge, professional lives: Studies in education and change.* Philadelphia: Open University Press.

Groundwater-Smith, S., & Dadds, M. (2004). Critical practitioner inquiry: Towards responsible professional communities of practice. In C. Day & J. Sachs (eds.), *International handbook on the continuing professional development of teachers* (pp. 238–263). England: Open University Press.

LaBoskey, V. K. (2005). Speak for yourselves: Capturing the complexity of critical reflection. In C. Mitchell, S. Weber and K. O'Reilly-Scanlon (eds.), *Just who do we think we are: Methodologies for autobiography and self-study in teaching*, pp. 132–141. New York: Routledge Falmer.

Phillion, J. (2002). Becoming a narrative inquirer in a multicultural landscape. *Journal of Curriculum Studies*, 34 (5), 535–556.

Chapter 23
The Passing of a Day

Say Pin TAN

As I look back at my career history from the beginning to the present, be it in terms of history or trajectory, my career story is best summed up as the passing of a day and all that transpires in between.

A day begins with morning, followed by afternoon and ends off with evening. The unchanging three phases that mark the passing of a day can also describe my teaching career. After some 13 years, I am still teaching in the same secondary school that I started off at, as a trainee teacher.

While my career history reflects an almost bland interpretation of the passing of a day, it all changes when I reflect upon my career trajectory. It has all the surprises that a day in our tropical weather can bring. One moment, one is drenched in perspiration under the searing afternoon heat. In the next, one is running for cover from the incessant rain, courtesy of the afternoon showers that frequently come unannounced. As unexpectedly as it begins, the rain comes to an abrupt end. Just as a falling curtain draws a show to a close, a rainbow draping across the dusk-filled sky signals the end of this symphony of changes.

Such theatrics are mirrored in my teaching trajectory, which has its fair share of twists and turns. As each unfolds before me, I get a chance to drift in and out of my inner and public self. Sometimes, I feel like I am a spectator and at other times, an actor, so much so that I have unwittingly become a creator and co-creator of a living plot that is still panning out before my eyes, real-time. The plot's beginning is marked by the ushering in of the morning.

Morning — The Learning Phase

The whiteness of the sky ushers in the freshness of morning. My teaching career starts off in very much the same way. As a beginning teacher, I had many ideals to achieve and many aspirations to realise. A white canvas will not stay untouched in the care of an eager apprentice. The artist within me could hardly wait to transform the white canvas into an explosion and multitude of colours. Be it Van Gogh's *Starry Night* or Picasso's *Weeping Woman*, I wanted to surpass them all. I yearned to leave my mark somewhere, everywhere.

My fervour and enthusiasm reached white-hot intensity when I was appointed the school's Head of Department (HOD) for Information and Technology. This was half a year into my fledging teaching career. Having the audacity to appoint a rookie as a HOD, my Principal was relentless in driving a hard bargain. Procedures, new and old; staff, reporting to and reporting from; politics, conscious and subliminal, there was so much to learn. In retrospect, I certainly got what I had bargained for and perhaps, even more. My canvas was surely filling up quickly.

As a beginning HOD, I was mentored by two incumbent HODs who had covered my post prior to my appointment. One was the school's Mathematics HOD while the other was the Discipline Master. Both men were as bipolar in their dispositions as the east is from the west. From the start, I should have guessed from their appearance.

The Mathematics HOD often came to school wearing polo shirts that were hanging out of his over-sized work pants. Coupled with his unkempt hair, he cut a scruffy and sloppy figure. No one would guess that he was one of the most resourceful and helpful colleagues in the school. Furthermore, he endeared himself to many with his constant and affable smile that would cause his eyes to stretch into narrow slits, barely visible behind those thick glasses of his. The same man who moments ago appeared unkempt, now gave people a relaxed and approachable feeling.

In my mind, the bespectacled Mathematics HOD embodied the quality associated with his signature horn-rimmed glasses. He was a rare vintage, so unlike teachers of today. Many teachers nowadays have become so adept in multi-tasking that it is difficult to command their full attention once they have stepped out of the classroom. Ironically enough, they could be the same people demanding the undivided attention of 40 individuals earlier on throughout their lesson. But the Mathematics HOD would exhibit none of this paradoxical trait.

He was this omnipresent being who would drop everything in a flash to attend to people's requests or needs. It did not matter if he was in the midst of doing his work. No request was too troublesome and difficult for him. No need was too trivial and unimportant to him. By the time he had served your needs, you would feel sorry for him because the man would almost always have forgotten or forfeited what he was doing prior to your interruption. Always serving, never demanding. He stooped as a servant to fellow mankind but stood a giant in the eyes of many men. At this point, my regard for this man reached an almost deity-like proportion.

All this while, I could not comprehend this man's seemingly selfless disposition. It seemed all too unfathomable and illogical to me. From a young age, I was taught that there was no such thing as a free lunch. One had to work hard in order to earn it. However, here was a man who upon your order for a meal, not only offered it free but delivered it to you as well.

I once asked him how he could be so selfless in helping others, on top and sometimes at the expense of his own workload. For once, unsure of how to answer my enquiry, he scratched his head and in the process, knocked his trademark glasses askew. After a considerable pause, he re-adjusted his glasses and replied, "For things that don't kill, I do if I can. I wait, if I cannot." I was stunned by his almost riddle-like answer. "What do you mean?" I shot back. I wanted him to know that I was disappointed with his failing to meet my expectations of him.

Noticing my dissatisfied look, he quickly chipped in, "I just do my best so that at the end of the day, I can look forward to spending time with my daughter and reading my books."

The man had obviously tried his best. I had no heart to probe or interrogate him further. I looked at him with a forced smile. Thinking he had once again served yet another satisfied customer, he broke into his trademark smile before turning and disappearing down the corridor.

In all honesty, I was no more enlightened at the end of the conversation than I was at the beginning. One thing for sure was that a seed of discontent was sown as I struggled to come to terms with his nebulous responses.

Over time, I realised my dissatisfaction with him was the result of a deeper unmet need. He had not been the mentor I was looking for in terms of learning and honing my leadership skills. There I was, a young and freshly-appointed HOD, ready to explore uncharted frontiers and push for new boundaries. I was all set to become a dynamic, goal-oriented leader. However, all he had to offer to me was how to be a resourceful and people-oriented manager. If the Mathematics HOD had warmed my heart, he did not win it over.

On the other hand, the Discipline Master had the opposite effect on me. It was as if I had experienced first-hand the effervescent nature of tropical weather. The contrast was nothing short of a drama. If the Mathematics HOD was like an electrical switch on the wall, easily accessible to all, the Discipline Master would be the electricity current, hidden and looming ominously behind that switch. To the uninitiated, the current might present a nasty surprise if one's hands and fingers happened to be wet. Alternatively, it might be the very input needed to jolt a non-functioning machine into life.

With his hair always well-oiled and never out of place, the man's demeanour was equally uncompromising and unyielding. His icy stare behind those metallic-framed glasses was enough to convince anyone that if he ever asked you to jump, your only response was "How high, sir?" I was sure that it did not matter whether the respondent was a teacher or student. When it came to this man, compliance and submission were not a matter of choice but a given.

Strangely enough, people had this mixed sense of reverence and fear for him. Perhaps it was the high standard he set that earned him the respect of people around him. More crucially, people knew he would demand no lesser from himself than from them.

I recall one occasion where the school Principal was very keen on featuring video-conferencing as part of an important school function. However, the infrastructure of the school was unable to support such a technically and logistically complex set-up. The Principal was about to drop the idea when the Discipline Master stepped in. All this while, he had a penchant for anything to do with Information Communication and Technology (ICT). This was the chance for him to scale new heights and seal his reputation in immortality.

The gauntlet was thrown and the man accepted the challenge with much gumption and gusto. For the next few weeks, he was like a man-machine possessed and driven overtime. Summoning technicians, engineers and experts within and beyond the education fraternity, he started working, eventually transforming our humble school hall into an impressive hub of wires, cables and even one satellite dish! He spent so much time, including his weekends, to test-run and re-test-run the system.

Although on paper, I was the overall-in-charge, he was effectively Batman, the main character, and I, the sidekick, Robin. I witnessed first hand, how he was able to attend to details without losing sight of the big picture. It was a leadership course like none other I had attended. The impromptu lectures, just-in-time tutorials and live demonstrations were a refreshing change from the mundane workshops or table-top exercises I had undergone before. He was John Dewey in person, demonstrating "learning by doing" live. As far as leadership training was concerned, I reckoned I learnt more from him within those few weeks than all the years with the Mathematics HOD put together.

Surprisingly, the Discipline Master did have his soft side as well. I recall attending an IT-related management course with him which lasted for a few days. I remember I had a sleepless night before the first day of the course. I dreaded the thought of being alone in his company. Here was a man whom colleagues feared and fled from. But there I was, being thrown into the lion's den to fend for myself.

What happened over the next few days was yet again an unexpected twist, like the surprise "sun-rain" (literal translation of a phenomenon known in Mandarin as "太阳雨") we sometimes experience on a hot tropical afternoon. I saw an entirely different side of the man. The first sign of abnormality came when he turned up at the workshop venue wearing a collared polo-shirt and cotton pants, albeit his hair was still well-oiled and immaculately combed.

True enough, for the next few days, he was a totally different person from the one whom I knew in school. He enquired about my personal life and volunteered information on his. He also shared about his pet interest in ICT knowledge and offered me a glimpse of his leadership philosophy.

In his mind, an effective HOD is no different from an effective teacher. One leads teachers. The other, students. He used the analogy of flying a kite to illustrate his point. To first get a kite off the ground, one needs to exercise full control over the kite line, applying and loosening tension according to the prevalent wind condition. Once the kite catches the wind and begins to soar, one's control takes another form. The kite-flyer decides how high or low the kite flies by shortening or lengthening the line. In summary, by being in control, we can achieve our goals and, in his words, "get things done."

He had convinced me during the brief time that I had with him that he was not his normal self at the work place. Why then the need to put up such a façade? I find myself asking this question repeatedly.

Perhaps it was to allow him to maintain a distance so as to preserve the *status quo*. I suspected that his uncompromising drive towards excellence gave him the needed moral authority to continue his persona in school. His hard approach had been tried, tested and yielded results. It had been a winning formula for him.

At the same time, I attributed his almost obsessive need to control as a manifestation of a deeper need. I would venture to speculate that it could be a sense of insecurity. There could be unresolved issues or past hurts which would cause him to adopt such a defensive strategy in dealing with people. His behaviour reminded me of documentaries I had seen on animals in the wild. At the first sniff of threat, the ears would prick forward, the muscles would tense up and the body would strain forward to gain that extra inch in height. The animal would watch and listen intently, ready to launch a do-or-die counter-attack or to engineer a lightning escape. Until and unless the danger is perceived as passed, the animal would not stand down and relax.

At this point, it was inevitable for me to draw a comparison between my two mentors. I realised that both men were adverse to changes and wanted to maintain the *status quo* for different reasons. The Mathematics HOD worked hard to avoid and solve problems. In my mind, his thinking was that when there was no problem, there was no need to change. I resisted this line of thought as without change, there would be no possibility of progress.

As much as I liked the man, I felt increasingly trapped and stifled under his supervision. The only time I could find myself criticising him was when I hardened my heart and not let my emotions cloud my mind.

For all his helpfulness, he was not as altruistic as he appeared to be. As a manager, he kept everyone happy and ensured the house was in order. He neither took risks nor did he do anything that might rock the boat. His remark about doing things "that don't kill" now made perfect sense to me. His non-confrontational and ever-helpful disposition had provided him with the perfect alibi to maintain the *status quo*. Without the need to change, he could do what he had to do during the day, so that he could be free after work to pursue his real interests and priorities.

It was clear that both men had different working ethics and philosophies. I readily admitted that for all their good intentions, I felt constantly torn between choosing to be a people-oriented or task-focused leader. Unsure and unwilling to support one and risk offending the other, I chose to tread the middle ground. I side-stepped the need to make a choice by resorting to selective adoption.

My *modus operandi* was to size up my opposite number and depending on their personality, I would administer either a soft or hard approach. Essentially, whenever I was dealing with a colleague whom I deemed to be vocal and having a strong personality, I would use a soft approach. On the other hand, I would not hesitate to switch to a hard approach on colleagues whom I assessed as less vocal or more easy-going. In both scenarios, the end in mind was to get the work done.

Initially, the dilemma I felt in adopting this hodgepodge strategy bothered me. However, any sense of self-doubt was soon cast aside as colleagues and superiors alike praised me for my work efficiency and inter-personal skills. For a while, it seemed that I had harnessed the strengths of my two mentors, without the side effects of the lack of drive of one and the hawkish disposition of the other.

In truth, I was hiding behind a veil of deceit and blind mimicry. I was like a fickle-minded and almost irrational scientist experimenting and operating with a hit-or-miss mentality. My unsuspecting colleagues were nothing more than a collection of laboratory mice and guinea pigs on whom I was freely experimenting my leadership style on. While it looked like I was on a winning streak, surely it was a matter of time before one of my reckless trial-and-error attempts would go awry. In fact, I did not have to wait too long for it to happen.

My learning and training phases were over, or so I thought. I was eager to step out of both my mentors' shadows and strike out on my own. By this time, the freshness of the morning had come to pass. The simmering heat emitted from the overhead afternoon sun signalled impending trouble.

Afternoon — The Application Phase

In tropical Singapore, afternoons are often marked by scorching heat followed by heavy downpours. The two occurrences are neither fortuitous nor random. The early afternoon heat would accelerate water evaporation which in turn would trigger off a chain of atmospheric processes and culminate in a thunderstorm.

People generally do not take a liking to either occurrence. They cause disruption to one's daily routines and bring about much physical discomfort. Who would like to be soaked in perspiration one minute and be drenched by rainwater the next? This extremity challenges an urban dweller's ideal of living in comfort and style.

Unfortunately for me, I was unable to escape from both occurrences in the next stage of my career trajectory. A comedy of errors and misjudgements scorched and drenched me. A large part of it has to be accrued to the price I paid in my mismanagement of interpersonal relationships. Although there were petty conflicts and niggling friction along the way, all paled in comparison alongside the unprecedented altercation I had with a colleague.

Her name was Audrey*. The first time I met Audrey was when she turned up in our school to attend an interview session. Earlier on, she had applied for a vacancy in our school under the Ministry's open posting exercise. As she was applying for a management position within my department, my Principal naturally requested me to join her in the session.

She struck me as an unassuming and quiet lady. She was able to handle our questions in a professional and polite manner. She revealed that she was expecting her third child and wanted to move to a school closer to her mother's place. In this respect, our school's location was ideal. Throughout the session, she stayed poised and confident. Nothing belied her stoic demeanour or caused us to have second thoughts of accepting her application.

The first incident occurred within weeks of her first academic term with the school. I was recalled for my annual military in-camp training and she had to step in to cover my duties in my absence. During this time, students were sitting for their common tests and there were a number of administrative tasks which she had to monitor and supervise on my behalf.

There were obvious lapses on her part. However, I chose to give her the benefit of the doubt that she was still settling down and familiarising herself in a new environment. I decided to go with the soft approach. We had an open discussion to distill the learning points from the episode. It was all cordial and I had faith that she would learn from the experience and improve henceforth. Or so I thought.

A few months later, she was again put in charge of the department as I temporarily left school to attend a four-month professional development course. Again, this time round, she was found wanting. One lapse in particular, was so serious that I was actually called back by my school leaders mid-way through my course to manage the situation.

By this time, she had exhausted my patience and I had no further grace to offer her. I was furious with her as well as the school leaders whom I felt could have played a more active role in first, preventing and second, managing the incident. It was ironic that I had just undergone four months of training to be a better middle manager for the purpose of enhancing organisational effectiveness. There was no better opportunity than this to put my learning into practice. Sadly, the heart over-ruled the head. The knowledge I had gained during the course stayed very much at the cognitive level and remained unapplied. As much as I tried, I could not resolve the sense of indignation brewing within me. Justice had to be done. The wrong had to be put right. She, not I, had to pay the price for her incompetence.

To make matters worse, she had left for her maternity leave when I returned from my course. Grudgingly and reluctantly, I went about attending to the work she had left behind. While I appeared fine on the outside, however on the inside, I knew my dissatisfaction and vexation was growing with each unfinished piece of work I had to complete or unresolved matter I had to attend to. I could sense that the afternoon heat was reaching its boiling point.

Finally, I imploded. I fell like a heatstroke victim, with my sense of rationality and civic-mindedness knocked out. What happened next could only be described as a moment of madness. Discarding any sense of decorum, I initiated a series of messages on her mobile phone, raining my disapproval and disappointment over what I perceived to be her incompetence and mismanagement of work matters. The thunderstorm with its pent-up energy and stored-up moisture exploded across the text battlefield.

She did not take my barrage of criticism sitting down and returned fire with salvo from her own arsenal. To her, I was a dictator who stifled free-play and a slave-driver who spared no thoughts for others. At this point, whatever initial impression I had of her being a quiet and stoic person had vanished completely. At her end, whatever goodwill I had earned for being a patient and understanding Reporting Officer had all but vaporised. Accusations were thrown in both directions as we argued over who was right and who was wrong.

As suddenly as the war of words started, it ended just as abruptly. She texted me to say that she needed to attend to her new-born baby. Almost immediately, the raging storm was replaced by a deafening silence. Almost instantly, I regretted my actions of initiating the verbal fight. Unlike the rainbow that signals the end of an afternoon shower, there was no redemption offered at the end of this storm of mine. Like water that sizzles and fizzles on a white-hot metallic surface, I endured a prolonged and heightened state of emotional unrest.

After that disastrous virtual encounter, we had no contact whatsoever. She requested to extend her four-month maternity leave which was then followed by a successful request for a transfer of school. Initially, I was glad that the fight did not make headline news at the workplace. In my calculated mind, such a debacle would have had detrimental impact on my promising career and reputation as a caring and effective leader. However, the way the drama had turned out to be a non-event was becoming as much as a bane, as it was initially perceived to be a blessing.

As I was afraid that news of it may leak out, I spoke to no one in my workplace about it. If I had no confidante, it was expected as I had estranged many relationships with those junior in rank. As for my mentors, they had become my "peers" as I had risen through the ranks to earn my seat beside them in the school's Executive Committee. More importantly, my fast-growing reputation as a goal-getter had meant that the Mathematics HOD was avoiding me like the plague while the Discipline Master saw me as upstart who was outshining him. I could no longer seek their counsel or support.

For the longest time, I was tormented and torn by the conflicting need to confront or deny the cause of my troubled mind. This need to make a choice was a *déjà vu* feeling for me. As familiar as the feeling was, I was disappointed with myself that in certain aspects of leadership, I had not grown at all. Gradually, as I became mired in my own internal struggle, I became withdrawn from people. The growing nauseous sense of remorse and regret was slowing, creating an air of despair and resignation.

Like an ice-cream that melts in double-quick time in the afternoon heat, my self-confidence had taken a beating and my self-belief was thrown in doubt. No longer was I the strutting peacock ever ready to spread its feathered wings. I was more like a beaten and dethroned alpha-male lion who had to fade into the background with his tail between his legs. It would take me a long while before I regained my spiritedness and swagger of yester-years.

Evening — The Consolidation Phase

Nikki Giovanni, an American poet (1943), once said, "Mistakes are a fact of life. It is the response to error that counts." Many years had passed and I had plenty of time to sort out my thoughts. I figured that what I lost during the learning and application phases, I might never find. But what I had gained in the process, I would protect with my dear life. I was determined that my experience with Audrey would be the first and last.

Time is a good healer and an even better teacher. For one, I learnt that words have power. They can either build up or destroy a person. So I have learnt to guard my words closely and dispense them wisely. The second is that people are emotional beings. How well we manage their feelings will affect how receptive or resistant they are to us. So I have learnt to be more sensitive to people. The third and most important of all, is about me.

My mishandling of Audrey's case jolted me to critically review the years of tutelage I had under the two men. Just like any electrical appliance, the two men's approaches each came with an operating manual. Neither claimed to be superior over the other. They were functional to the extent of one's compliance with, first, the assembling and, second, the operating instructions. I did not care to read them, much less the fine print.

It was after many moments of reflection that I finally understood why I handled Audrey's case in the manner that I did. The problem was not in adopting any of the approaches. The problem was with the adopter. In truth, the problem was, simply, me.

As I reflected upon my prognosis of the two men, I realised my interpretation of their behaviour and disposition were really reflections of myself. Behind the two qualities of people-orientedness and task-orientedness which I ascribed to the two gentlemen, laid a latent motive to avoid trouble and an even deeper sense of insecurity. I, not them, was the insecure person.

As I was a rookie HOD, I was constantly insecure and needed people's affirmation of my ability. Thinking back further, seeking the approval of people, especially those close to me, has always mattered a lot. Perhaps it had to do with my upbringing in a typical strict and traditional Asian family.

Growing up in an environment where outward display of emotions was a rarity, I was constantly looking to earn them. I remember as a child, I would make a fool of myself so as to be able to draw a smile of approval from my stern and unsmiling dad. Also, my motivation for studying hard and doing well was to gain the approval of my teacher mother.

Looking back, the signs of this need for affirmation and acceptance were always there — telling of white lies, going along with the majority, joining cliques. I was just trying to fit in and well with everybody. My actions and more importantly, the consequential results would make my day and in my mind, more than justify my efforts, even if it means compromising my standards or even integrity. While this need had become the driving force for me to excel and achieve, it has also become my area of weakness.

Learning to accept myself as who I am has brought a new-found freedom for me. No longer am I afraid of making tough but unpopular decisions. People's opinions of me still matter. Criticism and unkind words still sting no less now than in the past. What has changed is that I no longer allow myself to feel down for long. I realised that we can only be truly and deeply hurt by people or matters that are of significance to us. Strangers can stir emotions within me but I have no emotional attachments to them. Hence, whoever bothered me in the first place had already intruded into my personal space long enough. The longer I allow myself to brood and sulk, the more undeserved attention I am giving to the person.

The next step was to accept others for who they are. Each person's story is a compilation of life experiences, crafted and carved within a distinct space, time and context. No person is any more important or less significant than another. When we can learn to respect one another's uniqueness, we can truly celebrate the richness and diversity of the human spirit. When I was attempting to account for the dispositions behind the Mathematics HOD, Discipline Master or even Audrey, I had unilaterally imposed my values system and passed judgments on them. They never consented to participating in the personality profiling exercise that I had forcefully put them through. Perhaps the only saving grace was that I have never shared the results with anyone until now.

Two years ago, Lim*, a trainee teacher, was posted to our school for her teaching practicum. Like Audrey, her subjects came under my purview and I was one of her supervising officers. She reminded me so much of myself in my morning phase of my career. Enthusiastic, energised and endearing, she had all the qualities of an outstanding teacher. Prior to her attachment to our school, she had already applied and had been accepted by her alma mater to start her teaching career upon the completion of her training at our school. I was undeterred as I saw so much potential in her, and wanted to have a chance to groom her. Using the people skills that I had learnt from Mr. "Nice Guy" and adopting the spirit of perseverance imbibed in me by Mr. "No- Nonsense Guy", I managed to persuade her to stay in our school. My success in keeping her gave me hope that I would find the fine balance between the two approaches of my mentors and finally be able to pay homage to them both.

Lim was like a fresh breath of air. Wherever she went, her liveliness rubbed off on people. The senior colleagues supported the initiatives she proposed while the younger ones rallied around her to see through those initiatives. It was no surprise that at the year-end ranking sessions for two consecutive years, I had no problem convincing the ranking panel to award her with the highest performance grade.

I sometimes asked myself whether through Lim, I had found my restitution in making amends for the mistake with Audrey. My effort in grooming her might not have been entirely altruistic. There might be some element of truth in the allegation but I am not the least bothered by it.

What matters is that nowadays, I feel happy seeing people succeed. But knowing that I have contributed somewhat to their success heightens my sense of achievement. Be they students or colleagues, I have learnt to celebrate successes, big or small. Even if my effort does not achieve the intended results, or worse, turns out to be a failure, I can pick myself up, taking heart that I have tried my best. What is important is to learn from one's mistakes and move on.

Just as the passing of a day heralds the start of another, the best day or worst day will come to an end. As long as we have a good rest, regroup and reenergise, there is always a new morning awaiting us.

As for the Mathematics HOD and the Discipline Master, I owe it to them for starting me on this journey of self-discovery. They have both taught me right things and taught me rightly. For all my misgivings about him, I acknowledge that the Mathematics HOD could have valued relationships far more than results. I had a new-found respect for him as he did not succumb to the pressure to change and continued to hold onto his priorities. In this achievement-oriented day and age, one's beliefs are continually tested by external influences and pressure, crying out for results and performances. But this man would have none of it. Behind the constant smile lay a resolve that was of no laughing matter. As for the Discipline Master, his spirit of excellence is a reason for celebration. His drive and energy should be models for aspiring officers to emulate. In this society that craves instant gratification, he shows that there is no short-cut to success. To mock or even speculate the motive behind his effort would surely be meaningless.

As for Audrey, seeing her at a recent promotion ceremony brought yet another closure to another day for me. It was good to know that she had sought and found greener pasture elsewhere. For a moment, our eyes met briefly. It was then followed by a mutual smile.

As for Lim, her good performance did not go unnoticed and she is now at Ministry of Education (MOE) headquarters under the Future Leaders Programme. Well, as they say, it is all in a day's work. Who knows? A day might come when I get to work under her. But that would be a story for another time.

*Pseudonym used.

Reference

Giovanni, Nikki. (1970) *Black Feeling, Black Talk, Black Judgment.* New York: W. Morrow.

Chapter 24
Becoming My Own Heroes

Thiam Chuan YAP

Introduction

"*A hero ventures forth from the world of common day into a region of super-natural wonder: fabulous forces are there encountered and a decisive victory is won: the hero comes back from this mysterious adventure with the power to bestow boons on his fellow man*" (Campbell, 1949, p. 30).

When we look at our own life at different points in time, we derive different perspectives and different meanings. More significant events in our lives last much longer in our memories and these episodes stringed through the stream of time, are not isolated events but connect to form a web of meaning unique to each individual.

I have chosen the metaphor of an adventure to link up the significant episodes of my professional life. I have quoted from this book, "The Hero with a Thousand Faces", written by Joseph Campbell in 1949, to provide the context of the metaphor. Campbell (1949) had very elegantly used the metaphor of the adventure of a hero to reflect human nature and aspirations, and also how one reacts to challenges. I saw a parallel between what was reflected by Campbell (1949) and my episodes.

In the Beginning

I have always enjoyed helping others figure out what they did not understand in lessons since my teenage years. I wanted to be a hero who could save the day. Teaching, naturally, is the perfect profession for me. It did not occur to me that it was a lot more complex than I imagined it to be.

After my training at the National Institute of Education (NIE), I joined my alma mater, a junior college (senior high school). Many things had not changed including my Principal and many of the teachers. The school culture was familiar to me. The students were from top secondary schools. Being high-achievers all their lives, they were highly motivated. The students and I shared a similar background in terms of educational experiences.

In the first year of teaching, life was exciting as I was doing everything for the first time. Having gone through the education system, the things that I was doing were so new yet so familiar. Sometimes, I felt like a student playing the role of the teacher. This feeling was especially strong when I joined the level meeting. I was not sure whether it was because many of my colleagues were my lecturers or because I was new to the discourse and the profession of teaching. I had yet to sufficiently develop the professional identity and pedagogical content knowledge to feel like part of the teaching community. Maclean and White (2007) stated that teacher identity included participation in the profession and more broadly "is linked to teachers' confidence in their own competence; to their commitment to their profession; and to the satisfaction they obtain from the continued practice of teaching" (Maclean & White, 2007, p. 48). This perspective was very useful for me to make sense of my professional development trajectory.

The second year was better for me as I began to get familiar with the work and discourse. It was still exciting for me as I constantly challenged myself to improve by doing my work better than the first time. This had provided me the motivation and satisfaction.

The Call to Adventure

"*'Call to adventure'—signifies that destiny has summoned the hero and transferred his spiritual center of gravity from within the pale of his society to a zone unknown*" (Campbell, 1949, p. 58).

For the first three years, I found great satisfaction without deliberately searching for challenges. I was very excited about everything that I did and spent great effort to improve my pedagogy. But boredom quietly crept in.

I began searching for more challenges such as taking over new Co-curricular Activities (CCAs). At the peak, I was taking care of four CCAs (usually teachers would only need to look after one CCA) and performing the role of an assistant coordinator at the same time. I was taking up new hobbies such as Taiji, inline skating, Aikido and Judo. I still found joy in teaching my students. But I needed challenges to excite me.

By taking on many new CCAs and projects, I realised that moving out of my comfort zone allowed me to discover new things. Many new assignments that I took on came with uncertainty, as I did not have any idea how it could be done. The uncertainty did excite me, as I perceived uncertainty to be creative space.

Very early in my career, I realised that the role of the teacher should not just be about academic achievements. I had many opportunities to help my students to develop cognitively and emotionally, especially through CCAs. However, I found that the profile of my students did not allow me to play "hero" very often. They were generally sensible and motivated. The time that I had with them was also very short, less than two years. This was a source of dissatisfaction for me.

A very significant event happened during this time. I became a father; my first son was born. Assuming a new role in life has significantly changed my perception of education. I was able to better appreciate the perspectives of parents. This greater empathy has allowed me to understand the anxieties of the parents and hence relook into how the school practices could be more sensitive to the feelings of parents.

Just before I left the junior college, I undertook one of my most memorable challenges. I led 18 students and 2 teachers to Laos on a Youth Expedition Project supported by the Singapore International Foundation (SIF) for 21 days. I spent three months planning for this project that normally took others six to nine months to plan and execute. This was the first project of this nature for the school; teachers and students did all the planning and execution without support from vendors. Our main objective was to help the villagers build a small library for an elementary school. The school was not well-equipped; there was no telephone line and only one power socket. There were no proper desks and chairs for the classrooms. Some classrooms did not have walls and the floor would be muddy during the rainy season. It was a very different school setting compared to what was familiar to most Singaporeans.

I was the most senior teacher and the team leader. The other two teachers had just been posted to the school. The students were about 17 years old. None of us spoke the language of Laos. In this unfamiliar country, we were equally helpless. We had to re-negotiate the power dynamics between teachers and students. Though I was the team leader, official power had little leverage in this situation as strong emotions were at play; there were conflicts among students, between teachers and students and among teachers. This experience made me rethink about human relationships and power dynamics. The concept of absolute superiority of the teacher, for example, was problematic. All of us stayed in the same classroom. The proximity caused discomfort among the team members, teachers and students alike.

When leading the team, I did not have the absolute authority in terms of knowledge or experience. This was very different from leading the students in the school context. I could not pretend that I knew what was going on as many things did not go according to plan. The uncertainty created tremendous amount of anxiety among the teachers and students.

Students needed to learn how to cook using a stove that used wood as fuel. Many students did not even cook in Singapore and hence cooking using such primitive method was even more challenging for them. Teachers had not used such stove before, but we demonstrated once how it could be done. The food turned out to be quite all right, but this had little comforting effect on the students. I felt that the challenge could be too much for them. In other words, there was a mismatch between the competencies and level of difficulty of the challenge resulting in high anxiety that could lead to disengagement (Csikszentmihalyi, 1997).

Being the team leader, I needed to provide emotional support. But I knew I could not deny how helpless I was too. I remembered that night I was in tears when I shared my helplessness. I knew many others were in tears too. It was a valuable teachable moment. At the end of that sharing, I assured all that I was determined to make sure we would pull through as a team; I was assuming the role of the hero. We were no longer teachers and students, but team members. With relationships that I had developed in Singapore, I was able to harness trust and cooperation from my team members. I saw optimism in my students the next morning. That was the turning point of the whole trip. Students began to appreciate the experience. Everyone was in tears when we left the village. Laos provided the trial we needed to grow.

After this event, my understanding of a hero changed. A hero is not a person with far superior knowledge, skills or competencies. With the support of others, he assumes the role of a hero and achieves with his team; heroic acts are acts of collaborative effort.

My request to be posted to a secondary school was approved. Many colleagues were shocked when they knew about my decision.

"Aren't you enjoying yourself here? Why change? You are much appreciated here," exclaimed one of my colleagues.

I replied," Yes, but I would like to try something different."

I wanted to be a hero who could make a greater difference in the lives of my students.

The Trials

"Once having traversed the threshold, the hero moves in a dream landscape of curiously fluid, ambiguous forms, where he must survive a succession of trials" (Campbell, 1949, p. 97).

I was posted to a secondary school as the head of Science department. I did not have any experience in secondary schools apart from my own secondary school days. During my Postgraduate Diploma in Education (PGDE) days, I was posted to a junior college for teaching experience and practicum. My first posting was a junior college too. I felt like a novice entering a secondary school even after spending five and a half years in the education service.

Being always in junior college before this, I had very naive views of the students in the different streams of secondary education. Most, if not all, were inaccurate. This was probably because of the profile of students that I taught in the junior college.

I remember the first day of school was a rude shock to me. I felt I was in a different world with a very different culture. I felt that I was not ready either mentally or technically to teach in a secondary school. I always wonder if new teachers feel the same way when they started teaching.

My first lesson with the Normal (Technical) class (the lower vocational technical stream) was memorable. When I first stepped into the class, I knew it was a very different class, so different that I did not have any past experience to draw from. What I could do, as I crossed my fingers, was to use what I had used for the past five and a half years. To begin the lesson, I had to power wrestle with one boy who was the ringleader of the class. (Unfortunately, I only found out after the lesson.) I managed to get him to settle down using teacher authority that I regretted on hindsight. I will call him M. It is quite customary for science teachers to talk about laboratory safety during the first lesson of the year. When I came to the issue of fire in the laboratory, I told the class that all would leave the laboratory in an orderly manner and let the teacher handle the fire.

"What if there is a student trapped inside?" shouted M.

I responded without much thought, "All of you would leave the laboratory, I would try to save the student."

"Try ah, people dying already and you only try to save them." M retorted. The whole class laughed and went in havoc. I stood there stunned. I was thinking to myself, "Where were these people from?"

I had never encountered such students in my life. I could not remember how I ended the lesson as I was in a daze already after that exchange. I went to my table exhausted and shocked. My fellow colleagues saw and came to console me. I was very thankful to them. They were generous with their time and their sharing of their experiences and strategies. My Principal, Vice Principal and Superintendent were very supportive. They had given the support needed for me to grow to meet the demand of the new job.

I lost six kilogrammes in the first two weeks and had several nightmares that woke me up in the middle of the night!

Family support was critical for me to pull through this period. In addition, what I learnt about my son made me reflect on my practice and students. When my son was old enough to interact with me, I was amazed at how a two-year-old child could have a mind of his own. Looking at my students, I began to reflect on the tension when parents' expectations did not match the aspirations and competencies of the students. The tension could undermine the relationship between parents and students. But underlying that tension could be the anxiety of the parents about the future of their children when they were not performing in school.

In my first school, my students were highly motivated. They were willing to put in extra effort to perform academically. Most students had very good family support. Even when they were playful like most teenagers, they were able to manage their impulse and work extremely hard for the national examination.

I thought that students from other academic streams were just weak academically. But academic performance was just a symptom of a myriad of problems.

I went around talking to other teachers asking about their experience with Normal (Technical) students. I also made informal observations of the lessons conducted by other teachers.

There was one experienced teacher in my department well known for his ability to manage Normal (Technical) classes. He was a member of the Discipline Committee. I went to him to seek his advice. Being very tough with the students, I was rather surprised when he shared with me the softer approaches such as being patient and resilient, and getting the students to understand that it was not in their best interest to oppose you. I also came to the realisation that I needed to face this alone, as I was going to be the only one in class.

I started with many tactics, as I would call them, such as worksheets to keep the students occupied. These seemed to work initially. When the novelty effects wore off, everything went to back to normal if not worse. I realised that I would need to strike a balance between long-term goals and short-term gains.

I recalled about my experience in Laos. I needed to work with the students, not against them. I began to talk to the students, one on one outside curriculum time. I relooked at my pedagogy including classroom management techniques. I came to many conclusions. For example, rules should be limited to the ones that really help in ensuring that learning takes place, as the students would not be able to remember all of them. Teachers would also have problems with enforcing too many rules. Enforcing the rules is important as it represents teacher authority; I persisted when facing constant challenges of the rules by the students.

Through six months of hard work, I managed to establish good relationships with many of the students in the class including M. It was through such relationships that I began to see my students beyond their academic competence. Many of the students were from less privileged background. As a result, many of them did not even acquire important literacy and numeracy skills. In addition, they seemed to accept the low expectation placed on them.

When I started remedial lessons with the class, the reactions from the students told me that they never expected any teacher to work hard for them. Providing remediation indicated that I would still expect them to achieve. Many expressed that they would turn up, but only four came. I was not discouraged and I carried on. The number remained at four, but I began to notice a considerable change in the attitude of my students towards me.

I was always wondering about why the students appreciated my effort to help them, but not many turned up. Could this be an issue of priority? Could it be that these students had already lost their motivation to learn? I did not pursue the matter further. On hindsight, I might have been able to gather more students for remediation if I could have identified the factors deterring the students from attending the remedial lessons.

To fully appreciate the improvement, we could compare the following lesson that was conducted six months after my first lesson of the year. I remember that I was teaching the topic of acids. I was already able to hold the attention of the students for a considerably long period of time for Normal (Technical) standards. One way that I discovered was to relate to the daily experiences of the students. I started the lesson with gastric problems and how acid was produced in our body. Suddenly, one boy, B, asked an important question.

"What does pH stand for?" B asked.

I was speechless, as I did not know what the answer was. I might be confident enough to say I did not know, but what would happen to the class when I said that? But I did and I said that I would find out and let the class know. The boy and the class accepted my response and remained silent waiting for me to carry on with the lesson. From that point on, I knew I had won the class over. The reaction from the class was very different from the first lesson.

During one of the remedial lessons, one student told me with great conviction "I want to be a doctor." I was astounded. I did not know what to say to her. It was going to be very challenging for her. How could a teacher be a deliverer of hope and optimism in this situation? Who was I to dish out "sound" advice that was essentially based on my own limited experience and knowledge?

That day, I went home with a heavy heart. I could have asked the student to do something within her reach and as a result dash the dream of a young girl. But does our system allow for people to make a significant switch later on in their lives? Do we even understand our students, their strengths and passions enough to guide them in making life decisions? Do we see our students as individuals or digits?

My greatest takeaway from teaching the first batch of Normal (Technical) students would be that I began to question the definition of a good teacher. I never thought that a good teacher was all about helping students to achieve academically, though it was one of the many aspects of a good teacher. I always thought a good teacher would also help students develop as a worthy person. This idea was not challenged when I was in the junior college, but after teaching different groups of students, I began to wonder what it means to be "worthy". My definition of a worthy person might be irrelevant or even totally meaningless to my Normal (Technical) students. What a hero would consider as a heroic act might not be much appreciated by the people, as they might not share the same beliefs and values.

Concurrent to this, I was a new leader. Head of the Science Department was my first official leadership appointment. My teachers looked up to me for leadership, but I was not only new to the school, I was also new to the secondary school system and new to leading a department. With the experience of working with my students and colleagues in Laos, I adopted a very open relationship with my teachers. Building a good relationship was my key strategy. Being a young officer, the more experienced teachers appreciated my humility. On occasions that I had to exercise my authority as the Head of Department, the relationship between my teachers and I provided the trust and respect needed for difficult decisions to be made.

Time passed very quickly, this class finally took the "N"-Level examination. I was more concerned about whether they found their lives meaningful and whether they saw hope in their future. I left the school shortly after they received their results. I went on to my third school. That was not the end. Three students from that class came all the way down to my third school to pay me a visit on the eve of Teachers' Day. I was surprised to see them.

The first thing they said to me was, "Tell us a story, Mr. Yap."

I knew from that instance that they had left a place in their hearts for me. I was very glad that stories I told in class to motivate them had left indelible impressions on them. I was sure that they would do well in the future.

As I went through this second phase of my professional life with the help of many others, I came to the conclusion that the formation of a teacher's identity is a collaborative effort. A teacher must not work alone.

The Next Phase

My third school was a typical neighbourhood secondary school. Just when I thought I was comfortable with dealing with students in a neighbourhood secondary school, I was proven wrong again. In my second school, there was only one Normal (Technical) class in the level that I was teaching. But in this school, we could have two Normal (Technical) classes in the same level. As a Vice Principal, I interacted with all these classes. I realised that when we had two classes in the same level, a different dynamics emerged. We tend to compare the two classes, but this comparison did not do any good to anybody. Students hated to be compared; they wanted to be unique.

This was a particular timely reminder as my second son was born. I had to remind myself that everyone is unique and it is impo tant to see every child's uniqueness. That would be the way that I would have to treat my two sons. In addition, I learned while teaching my Normal (Technical) class that it is important to understand the students without imposing one's values on them. I knew I needed to take the first step to understand the students and let them know that I valued each individual.

I realised that they were not given a lot of attention even from some of the teachers teaching them. I began going to the classes and talked to them during free periods or after school when I found them loitering in school. Initially there were a lot of resistance, but it disappeared after a year's effort. These students were very candid in what they said. One must be willing to accept their candid comments and accept them as who they are rather than trying to change them at first attempt.

From my interactions with them, I learnt that they had many beliefs about family, school and society that teachers usually could not accept. But understanding about their beliefs helped me understand their behaviours. Many seemed to think that they were impulsive. Yes, a lot of actions were carried out on impulse, but their beliefs about the world reinforced the impulse and influenced other decisions. A teacher educator in China, Chen (2008), commented that in order to change a student, we need to change his or her goals in life. Many students did not have concrete goals as they felt that they did not have many choices to choose from anyway. I constantly reminded them about hope and taking charge of their lives through stories that I told during assembly, in class and conversations beyond school hours.

One important incident during my stay in the third school was again leading an overseas trip. This time it was to Zhengzhou, Henan, China. I had 30 students and 3 teachers with me. This was the second time I led a group to Zhengzhou for an immersion programme.

This trip was significant because I had the mission to help the three teachers be familiar with the programme so that they could oversee the programme in the subsequent years. They were committed teachers. However, I thought they were not very sensitive to many issues, as they did not have the habit of reflecting. Throughout the trip, I had many conversations with them to get them think deeper into educational issues.

During the trip, we had reflection sessions almost every day. We wanted to deepen the learning of our students. This was the first time that I had Normal (Technical) students in the group. It was very difficult to get them to speak in the presence of others, but I constantly encouraged them to speak as I felt they have valuable views to share too. One night, after we visited the Ming Tombs in Beijing, we were talking about immortality and subsequently about death. I prompted many students to speak. One girl said that she had thoughts of ending her life as she found life meaningless. There were immediate reactions from other students and the teachers were very uncomfortable. I persisted and got her to speak a bit more about why she thought life was meaningless. A few students also echoed similar views on life. We knew that many teenagers have suicidal thoughts but we did not realise that even students who seemed optimistic, cheerful and extroverted could harbour such thoughts.

Later, I had a discussion with the teachers as I usually did to help them understand the facilitation techniques as I used during the group discussion. The teachers were shocked too after hearing from the students about their views on life. I took the opportunity to impress upon them that behind all the digits in the report book, we have individuals who yearned to be recognised as a valuable being in their own ways. Being a significant adult in this phase of their lives, a teacher must recognise the value of each student even when the students themselves had given up hope on themselves. Only in this way would we continue to be significant beings throughout the rest of their lives. It is our moral obligation. From the determined look in their eyes, I knew we were going to have three good teachers. A hero cannot have significant achievements by doing it alone or with a group of followers. He can only do it by inspiring more heroes. This was what I learnt working with all teachers in the school as a Vice Principal.

A significant event need not necessarily be a big event. I knew a female student shortly after I joined the school. She was not a bad girl, but she had a lot of issues with the school. Her family was not intact and she was looked after by her grandmother who was unable to control her. She got into trouble with the law but she re-joined the school after her probation. I could see how she had changed after being punished by the law, but her rebellious traits were still evident. When I talked to her, there was resistance.

During my farewell, she gave me a small note thanking me for helping her. This note reminded me about one disciplinary case that she was involved in after she re-joined the school. The Discipline Master came to me asking for advice on how to deal with her. At that time, I asked the Discipline Master to be more understanding when dealing with her. To me, it was just one of many conversations I had with my colleagues. To the student, it made a difference. We tend to go for the easiest and most efficient method and as a school leader,

I play the role of asking teachers to pause and think before reacting to their emotions. When we discipline a child for their mistakes, we need to be sure that we are helping them to learn from the mistakes. We could at times get carried away by our anger or disappointment. This would render the disciplinary actions ineffective.

Conclusions

After two and a half years, I left the school to pursue full-time studies at NIE. It was a great opportunity for me to consolidate what I had learnt for the past 10 years. Looking at my adventures in the three schools, there were common features. Firstly, my experiences seemed to suggest that I was going through a spiral curriculum: from novice to gaining competencies with the help of others and to novice again in a new context. I think it is important to join a new school with a novice mindset. Without baggage from the past, a novice is humble enough to learn from others. The challenge would be how to retain such mindset after becoming experienced; as more experience does not necessarily mean more wisdom.

Secondly, many different people can help us develop. We should not restrict these people to our colleagues. Teachers need to see their students as an important group of people that can help them grow. At times, surrendering teachers' authority would help the teachers see the education process more clearly. Without listening to the voices of students not only in the curriculum but also in professional development, we cannot truly be practicing student-centred education.

Thirdly, past experiences are valuable too. My past experiences provided me important resources that I could tap into in a new context. With the understanding that what I know is never final, I am open to new experiences that could challenge what I knew and shape my understanding of educational issues.

Fourthly, professional identity is important to professional development; the identity emerged from the professional development. While teachers engage the students in learning, the school needs to engage the teachers through professional development. Challenging teachers to renew their passion is important. More importantly, we need to help teachers make sense of the challenges. When this is not done, teachers' identity could be eroded, resulting in disengaged teachers.

Fifthly, personal life phases have important implications in shaping the beliefs of the teachers. It is unrealistic to demand teachers to be void of personal feelings when carrying out their duties; professional life and personal life are intertwined. Different phases of life can thrust a teacher into disequilibrium. Professional development that ignores the life phases that the teachers are in would be ineffective and insensitive, as it does not address the needs of the teachers.

Lastly, my narratives carried strong emotions. Emotions are not always negative. We need to learn to be in touch with our emotions in order to channel these energies to more constructive means. Education, being a social process, must be participated in by real beings with real emotions.

"Learning from experience is not inevitable. It must be intentional" (Barth, 2001, p. 65). During my short career in education, I was constantly reflecting on my practice, not just about the operational issues, but also deeper meaning of education, ethical and moral dimensions (Luttenberg & Bergen, 2008). Reflection is an important platform for me to make sense of the practice, in teaching, leadership and education.

I am a young officer still searching very hard for the meaning of a good teacher while I share my professional life episodes.

References

Barth, R. S. (2001). *Learning by heart.* San Francisco: Jossey-Bass.

Campbell, J. (1949). *The hero with a thousand faces.* London: Fontana Press.

Chen, Y. (2008). Building of excellent schools — Compilation of education speeches by Chen Yukun. Shanghai: East China Normal University Press. *Yi Liu Xue Xiao de Jian She. Chen Yukun Jiao yu Jiang Yan lu.* Shanghai: Hua dong shi fan da xue chu ban she.[1]

---

[1]陈玉琨 (2008)《一流学校的建设: 陈玉琨教育讲演录》上海, 中国: 华东师范大学出版社。

Csikszentmihalyi, M. (1997). *Finding flow: The psychology of engagement with everyday life.* New York: Harper Collins.

Luttenberg, J., & Bergen, T. (2008). Teacher reflection: The development of a typology. *Teachers and Teaching,* 14 (5), 543–566.

Maclean, R., & White, S. (2007). Video reflection and the formation of teacher identity in a team of pre-service and experienced teachers. *Reflective Practice,* 8 (1), 47–60.

Part 5:
Teacher Identity and Self

Overview

Yanping FANG and Sonia KHAN

While narratives in Part 3 are about teacher identity shaped dynamically by external factors (such as family upbringing, work assignments, colleagues and so on), narratives in Part 5 are concerned mainly with teacher identity examined from within the experiences of teachers themselves. Experience is central to narrative. As teachers looked inwardly in search of who they are, they do not only draw from their past experiences to make sense of their conceptions of teaching, their roles and responsibilities and their multi-faced selves, such as gendered and racial selves in the larger society. They also depend on the significance of their past in making decisions of what they want to be and assign meaning to their work and life (Connelly & Clandinin, 1990; Sachs, 2005). Needless to say, this inward gaze and the journey they travel on is deeply emotional (Johnson & Golombek, 2011), demanding courage to face, identify with and accept their other selves, which can often be darker and hidden or neglected.

Tin Hong's narrative takes us through the journey of a teacher who became a school leader but eventually chose to give up the role of a leader in order to live the "simple joys of spending time with students and just being their teacher." He looked into the initial difficulty for him to "let go of the prestige and merits of being a school leader." Burrowing through his experiences with "unteachable" students and his persistent efforts to guide his students, he could identify more with them and thus became more convinced of his wanting to be the teacher "sweating in the sun with students." He drew a parallel with the story of a Zen master, "I have let the maiden down a mile ago. Why are you still carrying her?" to help him in reaffirming his identity.

As a veteran English teacher, CHC had struggled with his own "jaded attitude" towards daily school activities. When joining a new junior college where his expertise was highly regarded by the school leadership, he started experimenting with mindfulness to "overcome some challenges by assuming a different persona" through which his mind eagerly seized every aspect of the new surroundings as "symbolic invitation for renewal." As he brought his full consciousness to experience every routine school activity — the morning assemblies, school meetings and parent–teacher conferences — they adopted new meanings as he began living the moment here and now. In the graceful style of his writing, one can appreciate his peace of mind at this serene stage of teaching when the intellectual nature of the work to "invigorate young minds" prevails.

As teachers grow in their respective work realities, they grow, too, as individuals. Emotions and a sense of the moral and ethical responsibilities for their students are usually the driving force for their knowing and becoming. Such "nested knowing" (Lyons, 1990, p. 162) and development can be seen through the classroom experiences with dishonest students that drove Andy's readiness towards developing himself in the area of character development. At a much later stage, he was "overwhelmed by questions of self-doubt, concerned about being a bad role model" for the younger teachers in his school so he decided to work at Ministry of Education (MOE) in the area of induction and mentoring of novice teachers. Andy claimed that he did not have anything extraordinary to narrate about his life as a teacher, so he dramatised the emotions and tensions he was experiencing in those 'ordinary' encounters by connecting them to dramatic words and scenarios.

This gives an interesting and enlightening twist to connote that our mundane daily existence can be filled with heroic encounters made so by our emotions and moral tensions.

The three narratives that follow represent the conscious racial identity struggles of minority Malay teachers in the mainstream Chinese Singaporean society. Such struggles permeate particularly throughout the narratives of N.B. Mizzy and Sabariah, who taught English, a subject in which Malay teachers are commonly considered weak. Both of them questioned why being Malay could have subjected them to discrimination and unequal treatment from the society and people around them both in their school days and in the early years as young teachers. By working hard, they wanted to prove their self-worth and while doing so, they grew in confidence and capacity. However, as a Malay language teacher, racial identity did not surface as strongly from Rina's narrative. She reflected towards the end, how, like N. B. Mizzy, growing up in the Malay community, being labelled as "poor and lazy", she wanted to prove from a young age that she was different, which was echoed by N. B. Mizzy, "I was determined, in my own quiet way, not to allow that same label to be stamped on my forehead." As a Malay language teacher, she always believes in caring for every student, regardless of his or her racial background. She worked hard for self-actualisation. Rina's trajectory is quite similar to that of many other capable and caring teachers, who achieve their potentials and utilise opportunities to grow through diligence and continued learning, taking up more important roles as curriculum officers at MOE and after that as key personnel in schools.

Last but not least, Vivian, an Indian Singaporean who, after her National Institute of Education (NIE) training days, taught first at a boys' school, then at a girls' school, and in more recent years, at an international school. Her narrative provides an interesting and unique example of one teacher in search of a more complete sense of self through negotiating a complicated array of multiple identities, a process she likened to putting together again "a life in its jigsaw pieces". She found herself a "minority" in many ways: being trained to teach a rare subject combination of English and Physical

Education (PE) at NIE, teaching PE in a boys' school staffed by mainly male teachers where "I had represented everything that was against what they were brought up to believe as tradition and culture." Her self-consciousness about being a piece that somehow did not fit into the larger jigsaw drove her to find her place in the larger scheme of things in a male world to obtain the same level of status and recognition (Olsen & Maple, 1993). As she put it, "I was indeed a boy like them but in a skirt, possessing strong qualities and was able to toughen up and get on with it." At the time of writing her narrative, Vivian, a successful, well-paid teacher in an international school, still found it hard to reconcile with her blue-collar parents who did not show much interest in her schooling as she grew up. Indeed, Vivian's struggle for a gendered, racial and social class identity has it all. Much to her fulfilment, she eventually attained a sense of whole when she found she had managed to put nearly all the jigsaw pieces together to form a complete picture and a sense of who she is and wants to become.

To conclude, the idea is that through these narratives and reflection the teachers have grown more aware of their strengths and weaknesses as well as their struggles and resolutions that shape their identities and their missions. All these determine to a great degree how they will answer the questions, "Who am I, and how do I reflect who I am?" (Korthagen & Verkuyl, 2002, p. 44). Through narrating and inquiring into their life stories, they have invariably achieved a sense of continuity in which their personal and professional development meet at the intersection of teaching. (Palmer, 1998)

References

Connelly, F.M., & Clandinin, D.J. (1990). Stories of experience and narrative inquiry. *Educational Researcher*, 19(5), 2–14.

Johnson, K.E., & Golombek, P.R. (2011). The transformative power of narrative in second language teacher education. *Tesol Quarterly*, 45(3), 486–509.

Korthagen, F., & Verkuyl, H. (2002). Do you meet your students or yourself? Reflection on professional identity as an essential component of teacher education. In C. Kosnik, A. Freese, and A. P. Samaras (eds.), *Making a Difference in Teacher Education through Self-Study. Proceedings of the Fourth International Conference on Self-Study of Teacher Education Practices*, pp. 43–47. Toronto: OISE/University of Toronto. Retrieved from http://resources.educ.queensu.ca/ar/sstep/index.html.

Lyons, N. (1990). Dilemmas of knowing: Ethical and epistemological dimensions of teachers' work and development. *Harvard Educational Review*, 60(2), 159–181.

Olsen, D., & Maple, S. A. (1993). Gender Differences among Faculty at a Research University: Myths and Realities. *Initiatives*, 55 (4), 33–42.

Palmer, P. J. (1997). *The Courage to Teach: Exploring the Inner Landscape of a Teacher's Life*. San Francisco: Jossey-Bass.

Sachs, J. (2005). Teacher education and the development of professional identity: Learning to be a teacher. In P. Denicolo & M. Kompf (Eds.), *Connecting policy and practice: Challenges for teaching and learning in schools and Universities* (pp. 5–21). Oxford: Routledge.

Chapter 25
The Heart of a Teacher

Tin Hong HON

In the most pensive of moods as I contemplate life and its meaning, the question — "Who am I?" surfaces often. I could define myself as a man, a son, a Singaporean, a Chinese; but none fits better than defining myself as a teacher. Yes, I am a teacher and proud of it! Of course, we know teachers teach subjects to students; I know I teach Physical Education (PE). But beneath the superficial features of what teachers *do*, who *is* a teacher? What does it really mean to be a teacher? What defines my identity as a teacher?

"By identity I mean an evolving nexus where all the forces that constitute my life converge in the mystery of self: my genetic makeup, the nature of the man and woman who gave me life, the culture in which I was raised, people who have sustained me and people who have done me harm, the good and ill I have done to others, and to myself, the experience of love and suffering — and much, much more" (Palmer, 1997, p. 17).

Indeed, what it means to me being a teacher is that it is a nexus which has been formed from a series of turning points through my 15 years of teaching. Each of the episodes in the following paragraphs contain tensions which are sensations I feel due to a lack of "balance between contending forces, contending views, and

359

contending personal impressions" (Connelly, Clandinin & He, 1997, p. 670). In resolving these tensions, personal reflection and illuminating stories[1] were instrumental in providing insights in each episode to help me think about what I should do and to make sense of what being a teacher really means to me.

Episode One: Every child matters. 28 April, 1997, 7.30 am. The school bell rang and the Head of Department (HOD) on duty screamed at the students to "SHUT UP!" before the Head Prefect gave the command to commence the flag-raising ceremony. The command started my first day of reporting for duty after graduating from teacher training at the National Institute of Education. Not knowing where I should stand, I stood at the back of the school while the anthem was being played. I tried to sing the anthem but could not really follow the music that was being drowned by the voices of talking students who seemed to pay more homage to their hairstyles and expensive designer bags than the rising national flag.

After the ceremony, many late-coming students streamed in and joined other students going to their classrooms in all directions — some criss-crossing other classes; some scuffling for space; others strolling leisurely and laughing loudly at their own private jokes, totally oblivious of others around. After some time, everyone left the parade square except for the cleaning uncle sweeping away a large amount of litter the students had left behind. This was the opening scene that gave me my first glimpse into the culture shock that was in store for me.

Lessons commenced right after the students got to their classrooms and I followed the HOD around for an orientation programme for the day. Then about five minutes before school ended, screams were heard. Apparently, a serious fight between two groups of boys had broken out in a school toilet! There was pandemonium as a few teachers tried to separate the rioting students, while others tried to shoo away the busybodies.

---

[1]These stories, written in italic as story segments for each episode, are restoried from those I have heard or read.

Days later, I found out that one of my students, Tom, had been involved in the fight. He was a student who often lacked focus in his work and would disturb others around him. And when he was not in a good mood, at the slightest provocation, he would unleash his rich vocabulary of swear words about which his English teacher once commented that if Tom would put his linguistic creativity to good use, he would be an outstanding poet.

My first interaction with Tom was during the third week since joining the school. It had started to rain just as I was about to start my PE lesson. So the lesson had to be conducted in class instead and I took the opportunity to conduct health education. As I was teaching, I saw, to my great disgust, Tom spitting onto the floor! Of course, I was disturbed especially when I was just there talking about the importance of personal hygiene. So I stopped the class, went over to Tom and confronted him:

"Tom! How could you spit in class? Do you do that at home too?"

"Yes," Tom replied.

Tom was not replying out of defiance. From the way he looked as he replied, I sensed that he was indeed telling the truth. I was speechless for a moment until I smelt the foul sweaty odour coming from the PE T-shirt he was wearing and asked:

"We did not even run today. How did your T-shirt get so smelly?"

"'Cher![2] My brother lah! He got PE yesterday, but forgot to wash it loh! You think I want to wear it, is it? I give you face because you say no T-shirt cannot play. If I know today rain, I won't come one."

"Why did you have to wear your brother's shirt? Where's yours?"

"You think everyone got money to buy so many shirts is it?" came Tom's reply before he rested his head on the desk and refused to talk anymore.

I was angry at Tom's insolence towards me. I was even angrier at myself for having the ill-fortune of being posted to the school

---

[2] 'Cher is a colloquial term used by students when addressing their teacher.

which had a culture totally opposite from that which I was educated in as a boy in a relatively well-regarded school. I had a lot of difficulties assimilating into and understanding a culture in which students did not take learning seriously and had little respect for teachers.

After class, I sought counsel from an experienced teacher — Mrs. Practical, who had taught Tom before, in the hope of getting advice on what I could do with the boy. She had very negative thoughts about Tom and other students, who were somewhat similar — not interested in school generally, only interested in playing or disturbing others, having poor social habits, and lacking respect for teachers.

Mrs Practical's advice for me was to focus on those who could learn rather than to waste time and energy, and risk feeling burned out, on those who were simply "unteachable". Besides, teachers were assessed on performance indicators like how well the classes performed during national examinations; how many awards their co-curricular activities could win; and how many large-scale or newsworthy events they could organise to bring fame to the school. But turning around a badly-behaving student was clearly not a performance indicator for teacher assessment. "So what's the point? You can't save them all, you know?" came the parting remark as the school bell rang for the next lesson.

What Mrs. Practical said seemed to make sense. After all, many students like Tom, who were placed on a vocational educational track, would get promoted or advanced to the next level as long as they did not do too badly in school. They would eventually go to the Institute of Technical Education even if they do not attend school regularly, but sit for and pass the final "N"-Level examinations. They would eventually get a technical certificate, work, and be useful citizens after that. So even if I just let Tom be his destructive self for the next few years, he would still somehow turn out alright.

Rational though it sounded, I felt a tension — it just did not feel right to ignore the needs of any child even if he or she seemed "unteachable". The thought of ignoring these "unteachables" could not resonate with the moral compass in me. Then the following story I came across brought forth some enlightenment and comfort in me:

A Zen Master was travelling with his disciple to visit another monastery in a foreign land. While walking towards the jetty along a beach, the disciple intermittently picked up starfishes, which were drying and dying on the beach, and threw them back into the sea. The master then asked his disciple:
"My dear disciple! I am pleased that there is kindness in your heart. But do you realise that you can never save them all?"
The disciple walked a few more steps, picked up another starfish, then replied: "I know I can't save them all nor decide which one to save and which one to let die, but …," he continued as he threw the starfish in his hand out to sea, "it mattered to that one. And that is good enough for me."

So while being fully aware that it is not possible to save every child who is crying out for help, what a teacher does or fails to do surely matters to each child that we come into contact with. Being unconcerned about studies or behaving badly might not always be the fault of someone like Tom who was in fact a victim of circumstances, as I found out later.

Tom came from a broken home. His mother had passed away while his father was in jail. So he and his brother had to live off pittance from his mother's three siblings who took turns weekly to house them. Tom and his brother were practically living off a suitcase moving week-to-week and from house to house.

Tom's plight was the dire reality that I slowly realised quite a number of students in the school faced. The more "unteachable" a student appeared to be, the sadder the story I tended to uncover when I probed into his or her circumstances. Initially, I got upset with these students whenever they refused to help themselves out of their difficult circumstances. But as I came to understand more and more of these students, I realised that many of them had learnt to resign to their fate and for some, the only way they could express their angst was through destructive behaviour. Many of them really needed adult guidance, which they lacked and even secretly longed for.

So every time Tom did something which I felt needed to be corrected, I took time to explain to him why it was important to do or not to do certain things. There were times when my painstaking explanation must have sounded like nagging to Tom's ears. But I persisted.

On graduation day, Tom shook my hand and said: "'Cher! I am sorry that I gave you a lot of trouble … and thank you for teaching me what is right and wrong!" I guess I could never really know whether my efforts would pay off later in Tom's life, but knowing that they meant something to Tom was all it took to convince me that all that nagging was worth it. The episode with Tom made me realise that a teacher must persist in teaching every "unteachable" student — every child matters to a teacher; a teacher matters to every child.

Episode Two: It takes a village to raise a child. 2 January, 2002, 7.30 am. It was the first day of school and five years had passed since I was posted there. The school bell rang and I was the HOD on duty for flag-raising ceremony. I walked up the dais and asked calmly and firmly through the microphone: "Are you ready?" The students, who were noisy from the joy of reuniting with their classmates after the vacation, quickly quietened down. The Head Prefect gave the command, and the ceremony started and ended promptly and solemnly. Some new teachers were introduced to the school, and announcements were made, before the classes were led orderly by the teachers to their classrooms. When the school left the parade square, the same cleaning uncle moved in to sweep away twigs and leaves shed from the big Angsana tree next to the parade square. There was no litter. Contrast this with the opening scene in Episode One. It would be difficult not to notice that much change for the better had happened in student behaviour and school learning culture over five years since my first appalling day in school.

I had been the HOD for Discipline, better known as the Discipline Master, for almost three years then. It was fortunate for me that the school leaders had enough faith to appoint a young teacher to oversee the important and problematic area of discipline.

A "dirty job" is how some would describe the work of a Discipline Master, as it is an emotionally draining role which entails dealing with the worst of students and sometimes their parents as well. Naturally, few people aspire to be Discipline Master, but I took up the challenge as it meant I could have the opportunity to reach out to more "unteachable" students like my dear Tom.

Perhaps the dirtiest job as a Discipline Master lay in the task of caning students. Caning was and still is used as a last resort when students, after repeated warning and counselling, refuse to make amends. During the earlier days when school discipline was lax and there were rampant fights and blatant truancy, there was an urgent need to restore a conducive learning environment and to establish a sense of order in school. With such widespread disorder and indifference in students' attitude towards education and discipline, "spare the rod and spoil the child" became the maxim to set the school back on the right path.

For the first few months, it was almost a weekly affair to have students caned in class. It became a dreadful ritual for me: the long walk with the Principal or Vice Principal to the class, calling the boys to the front of the class, reading out the serious and recalcitrant offences they have committed, caning the boys, warning the class of the consequences of ill-discipline, then moving on to the next class for another round of punishment.

Caning students had held great tensions for me. How would the parents feel when their children got caned in school? How could I bear to cane a student whom I had been teaching for years? Would the punishment even change juveniles who sometimes did things without thinking as their moral agency had not fully developed? But it *had* to be done in the interest of the greater good.

There is a Chinese saying — 殺一儆百 — which means "kill one to warn a hundred". Harsh as the use of caning as a tool for improvement might be, general discipline and school learning culture did improve as a result. Students became more aware of the consequences of their behaviour in class and outside school, and teachers got a better environment to teach in.

Even though I had misgivings about caning students, I was glad that it paid off when students started to become more serious in their work and behaved better. Of course, school tone and discipline could not be sustained by the constant threat of harsh punishment alone. Thus, I had to establish a system to reward students who displayed good or improving behaviour to counter-balance the harshness of punishment, so that the students would learn that good and bad behaviour each has its justified consequences.

To establish and enforce a sense of order throughout the school, I would patrol the school throughout the day to make sure that students were not skipping lessons. At times, I would step into a classroom and lecture the whole class when the students were not focused or became boisterous during lessons. I was working almost 12 hours a day.

Looking back, there were many stressors during my first two years of teaching while managing discipline and grappling, at the same time, with the steep learning curve as a beginning teacher. There were times when I wondered if I had become a policeman, a judge, or an executioner, rather than being a teacher. I had lots of energy but still I was really tired after slogging for a couple of years. But the most important reason why I was very emotionally drained was because I was working mostly alone as I did not feel good involving other teachers in the "dirty work" I had to do. Fortunately, I soon realised the importance of involving others[3]:

"I know one man's effort is insignificant, dear Master!" the disciple continued, "So I share with fellow disciples about why I continue to throw starfish back into sea no matter how futile my individual effort might seem. So when more join in the effort, though we still cannot save them all, with each of us doing just a bit more, many more could live."

Before boarding the boat for their destination, the Master bent down, picked up a starfish, threw it into the sea and said: "Yes, my young disciple! Together, we matter to more of them."

---

[3]The story continues from the previous story segment in Episode 1.

Like the Master in the story, I realised that teachers do not mind getting involved in discipline as long as they understand the significance of what they do. In fact, most teachers care about the behaviour of their students. Why the school discipline had deteriorated over the earlier years was because teachers were working mostly on their own when it came to managing the behaviour of students. They did not have much support when it came to the "what" and "how" of managing student discipline. So I gathered a few teachers who were keen to take on a greater role in discipline management and together we set up structures to give support to every teacher who needed help with discipline issues. When teachers saw the support given, more teachers got involved in managing their own students' behaviour. Success begets success. Soon, the school tone and discipline became every teacher's business as part of a school-wide approach.

The important lesson for me in this episode is two-fold. The first is that doing the "dirty job" of teaching the "unteachables" is what we ought to do as members of a noble profession. Who else is going to teach these children if we do not want to get our hands "dirty"? The second is that teachers should never work alone as more can be done when they feel supported and want to work together in teaching the students as one big family. After all, it takes a village to raise a child!

Episode Three: The threat to identity and the courage to let go. 2 January, 2007, 7.30 am. I was newly appointed as Vice Principal of a primary school and it was my first day in the school. The school bell rang and the familiar opening scene of each school year flashed across my eyes, but I no longer needed to get the school ready for flag-raising ceremonies. The HOD on duty did not have a hard time getting the ceremony started and the angelic primary school children sang the anthem loudly. After a brief introduction of myself to the school and some quick announcements, the students were led by their teachers back to the classrooms. For the first time in 10 years, I did not need to rush to get ready for my first PE lesson of the day. Instead, I was dressed in office attire and headed back to my air-conditioned room.

A typical day began with checking and sending emails. Then there would be a walkabout to ensure that students were engaged in lessons — the Discipline Master in me refused to fade away quickly even though that role was no longer relevant. After ensuring the school facilities were safe and everything else was functioning like it should, I would proceed back to do other administrative tasks. Paperwork and filing would need to be done quickly as teachers, parents, and sometimes students would soon start streaming in to talk with me over a myriad of matters.

Besides a big change in job scope as compared to that of a HOD, a Vice Principal also had to spend much more time away from school. There would be many briefings and meetings to attend with different ministerial agencies, and occasional evening and Saturday meetings with grassroots organisations for organising community events. Schools have been clustered as a group under the leadership of a Superintendent and each monthly cluster meeting would become the mother of all smaller cluster group meetings during the month, to work on various aspects of education and organise cluster events. Once, when I saw my desk full of papers to be read instead of a class full of students, I could not help but wonder if I could still be called a teacher? It then dawned on me: I had worked hard for all of 10 years to become an administrator!

The truth was that while being a school leader had kept me in the education fraternity, it had estranged me from teaching. I could no longer enjoy the "aha" moments when students learnt something. Lesson timetables had given way to meeting schedules spread across my table top. I never carried my handphone when I taught as I deemed it unprofessional to answer calls when my full attention should be on the students when I teach. But as a Vice Principal, the handphone was always in my shirt pocket just in case any emergency matters might arise. Weekends used to be family time when I was a teacher. But as a Vice Principal, I could expect calls or electronic messages for urgent matters that needed attention before school resumed the following Monday. It was hardly a year into the job when I started to feel a sense that I had lost my bearing of why I had become a teacher in the first place. In other words, my sense of identity as a teacher was threatened.

The loss of identity was a tension I could hardly bear. But at the same time, I would have to struggle with other tensions if I were to go back to teaching: Should I let go of the promotion which I had just been given? Would people think less of me or my abilities? Would I be disappointing people who had worked hard to support my appointment to school leadership? Would it be hard to go back to lesson planning and to managing a class of 40 students running wild during PE class? Would I be able to adjust to the heat in the classrooms after getting used to sitting in my cosy air-conditioned office? Or should I just stop worrying, let it all go, and return to teaching which I loved?

The master and disciple were at sea for a day before reaching their destination. As the boat docked at the jetty, a young maiden on the same boat asked the master to help carry her up the jetty as she was timid. The master obliged and carried her all the way to a dry spot of the jetty before bidding her farewell.

The master and disciple continued with their journey till about a mile away before the disturbed disciple asked: "Master! Please forgive my insolence! How could you carry the maiden when our strict code forbids us to have any physical contact with ladies?"

The master calmly replied: "My dear disciple! There are times when we need to do what it feels right doing, even if we worry about what others might think. I have let the maiden down a mile ago. Why are you still carrying her?"

I guess in Singapore and probably in many prosperous countries, people tend to judge a person's success by material possessions he has acquired like the house he lives in, the car he drives or the job title he holds. So the keeping up of appearances makes it difficult for many people to let go of worldly possessions.

Similarly, I also initially found it difficult to decide if I should let go of the prestige and merits of being a school leader. But even stronger was the pull of sweating in the sun with students. So, I eventually decided to let it go and stepped down. Like the disciple in the story, some friends questioned my decision to step down, while others felt sorry for my decision. But I never looked back or regretted my decision. For every loss I had as a school leader, I gained back double through the simple joys of spending time with students and just being their teacher.

Conclusion

If I should get into a pensive mood of contemplating what it means to be a teacher again, what can I conclude from the reflections on the three episodes over my career in education?

First, to be a teacher is to love each student regardless of who they are and what wrong they have done. Victor Frankl once wrote: "Love is the only way to grasp another human being in the innermost core of his personality ... By his love he is enabled to see the essential traits and features in the beloved person; and even more, he sees that which is potential in him, which is not yet actualized but yet ought to be actualized" (Frankl, 1984, p. 134). It is this love and the willingness to see beyond the façade of each seemingly "unteachable" student like Tom that continue to sustain my persistence in guiding students even though I can never know how much of a difference I can really make in the short four to five years they have in the school.

Second, being a teacher is being happy doing what is intrinsically satisfying about teaching. Lortie (1975) has found that the greatest satisfaction teachers look for is not in prestige, pay or promotion but the joys of caring for and working with children. Satisfaction thus comes in the form of what he called "psychic rewards". Working with Tom was satisfying as I see my effort being appreciated by him. Working with other teachers on the harsh and "dirty work" that needed to be done was satisfying as both students and teachers earned for ourselves, in the end, a better environment to teach and learn. But being a school leader for me was not as satisfying as being a teacher as I lost the daily interactions I had with students. So stepping down brought back the psychic rewards I craved for. Therefore, being a teacher is really about relishing the simple joys of teaching children.

Third, being a teacher is to have integrity which is about discerning "what is integral to my selfhood, what fits and what does not... [While] identity lies in the intersection of the diverse forces that make up my life ... integrity lies in relating to those forces in ways that bring me wholeness and life rather than fragmentation and death" (Palmer, 1997, p. 17).

The human soul within me would have fallen apart if I had not persisted with my nagging at Tom, if I had not caned students for the greater good, if I had not gotten other teachers to work as a village, and if I had not stepped down. Doing every one of those things felt right and integral to me as a teacher.

Finally, Eisner (1983) has likened teachers to craftsmen and artists who "tend to care a great deal about what they do [and] they get a great deal of satisfaction from the journey as well as from the destination" (p. 13). Thus, being a teacher is ultimately about enjoying the journeys of growth we share with our students and living a life with integrity to reach a destination which is really in the heart of a teacher.

References

Connelly, M. F., Clandinin, J. D., & He, M. F. (1997). Teachers' personal practical knowledge on the professional knowledge landscape. *Teaching and Teacher Education*, 13 (7).

Eisner, W. E. (1983). The art and craft of teaching. *Educational Leadership*, 40 (4), 4–13.

Frankl, V. E. (1984). *Man's search for meaning*. New York: Pocket Books.

Lortie, D. (1975). *School teacher: A sociological study*. Chicago: University of Chicago Press.

Parker, J. P. (1997). The heart of a teacher. *Change*, 29, 14–21.

Chapter 26
An "Upgraded" Consciousness

CHC

Renewal and Reinvention of the Self in a New College[1]

I am surprised to find myself *here*. I do not mean a place as much as an invigorated state of mind which has come rather late in the game. By conventional expectations, I should be jaded.

I started teaching 27 years ago but the last few years have been unprecedented years of experimentation. I have had the opportunity to play a larger role by being involved in North Zone[2] programmes, cluster projects, the professional development of new and senior teachers as well as a number of other educational initiatives. I have also immersed myself wholeheartedly in shaping the General Paper[3] (GP) curriculum in my college by devising new pedagogy and material. Despite being a painfully reserved person, I went out of my comfort zone to help teachers of other disciplines in my college, English teachers beyond my college and to help

---

[1] "College" here refers to Junior College, the equivalent of a senior high school.
[2] Singapore's school system is divided geographically into four zones and each zone is further divided into clusters.
[3] General Paper is a H1 academic subject, focused on English language and writing, for the "A"-Level examination in Singapore.

strengthen the network of senior teachers in my cluster. But this external influence was the expression of an inner change which is far more important. My real experimentation and activism has been on a deeper psychological plane.

Taking stock of my present situation, I am surprised to find a sense of fulfillment and optimism despite the heavier responsibilities and busier schedule. Like a re-serviced, upgraded old computer, I feel more equipped to deal with the work. I am less overwhelmed by negativity as if corrupt programmes have been purged and replaced by new ones. I cannot really pinpoint the exact time my attitude started changing. I can say with certainty that transferring to a new college in 2004 certainly helped. My Principal was fond of saying that our new college had no history and therefore no baggage. Personally I felt "new" and could easily pretend I was a different, more dynamic person than the emotionally burnt out teacher I used to be. Can such pretense become self-fulfilling through psychological suggestion? I do not have empirical evidence for it but am fascinated by the idea that we can overcome some challenges by assuming a different persona.

I have even been inspired to share this (admittedly half-baked) idea with my students, "Put on a different personality and your brain will follow". I know it sounds more like New Age fancy than cognitive science but perhaps it did work for me considering the new and unfamiliar endeavours I managed to undertake. The old me would have been petrified at the prospect of presenting at a North Zone seminar, conducting a workshop for senior teachers in my cluster or even sharing at an interdisciplinary meeting within my college. I had moments of embarrassed stuttering when my innate self-consciousness got the better of me. But I did become more confident because that was what I imagined myself to be. By a similar logic, I became a credible Senior Teacher (2006) and Lead Teacher (2011) because I succeeded in "playing" and appropriating the role my colleagues projected on me. The 'act' became fact. Perhaps what I needed most was an affective nudge to the cognitive domain. I suspect Physical Education teachers and sports coaches would agree with me because many of them are experts in using emotions to develop psychomotor skills and cognition. Perhaps we all have latent ability which is more easily brought to the surface through "pretense" than through painful effort. If this is true, I am tantalised by the peda-gogical implications. On a deeper level, I am curious if my present identity is the result of a desired alter ego superimposed on the old self. Has the old me been "written over" by new data?

Transferring to a college without history gave me a feeling of "lightness" and the chance to reinvent myself. I am not being flippant in speculating that perhaps a different physical environ-ment — including even a new cubicle with new office furniture — could have set the stage for change as it provided the psychological tipping point I needed. The mind works in devious ways; when we want something, we see omens and signs everywhere. Perhaps, des-perate for a change after years as a jaded teacher, my mind eagerly seized every aspect of my new surroundings as symbolic invitation for renewal. (Consider how many people relocate to start a new phase of life. Even physical belongings become unpleasant remind-ers of the old life.) I had amassed 11 boxes of pedagogical material in 13 years at my former college and five years in the college before that. But despite being a hoarder, I threw away most of the notes and books like someone moving unwanted files to the computer recycle bin. I rationalised that the syllabus was changing. In retrospect, I have to admit the act was more symbolic than pragmatic. Ironically, I miss some of the old notes which may still be relevant. At any rate, I have been inspired to devise new and better teaching materials for my college. This brings me back to a central point in my narrative — that professional growth is often catalysed by decisive inner change. This suggests — at least for me, since I do not have basis for generalising — that professional training of skills may be futile without emotional readiness.

Making Meaning out of Ordinary Challenges

I may seem perverse in not focusing on climatic events or extraordi-nary students in my narrative; there have not really been many dra-matic moments or larger-than-life people. My growth as a teacher and person has largely been shaped by very ordinary challenges and the cumulative impact of small but constructive choices I made along the way. These choices involved a very conscious change of mindset from negative perceptions.

Much of a teacher's work consists of having to deal with routine and rituals, some of which can be mind-numbing monotony. Marking (especially for an English teacher), endless rounds of consultation with students, examination invigilation, staff meetings, the daily assembly, talking to 20 sets of parents in one evening… All contribute to the impression of enforced drudgery about which one has no choice except endurance. These mundane events take up so much of school and personal time that I feel they have to be foregrounded in my story as a teacher. I used to count these as time lost. At a deeper level, the loss of time always implies a loss of personal power and autonomy. Do teachers feel like prisoners of the system? Ironically, even as adult professionals, we feel as if we have never left school because we are always informed that "attendance is compulsory". Certainly this feeling of being trapped is not unique to the teaching profession but teachers are arguably among the worst afflicted.

An Experiment in Mindfulness

At whole-school staff meetings especially, I dreaded the slow march of time because the agenda would invariably be full. We had to sit through so many 10–15-minute presentations about financial procurement procedures, work improvement teams, school administrative matters, student discipline, logistical preparation for upcoming events and other matters so mundane that people lose concentration after a while. For me, these were non-events at which my mind went blank — though I was careful not to let the boredom show on my face. A veneer of professionalism was still necessary even though I was not always interested in what was announced or discussed. I became a fragmented self. The self others could not see was an anxious clock watcher. I was equally uninspired at morning assembly. After all, how much enthusiasm can one summon up for daily attendance taking out in the morning sun? These were moments of suspended animation to be lived through without much conscious thought. Test or examination invigilation was likewise a monotonous routine to be undertaken in automatic mode. There was nothing to engage the mind, much less the spirit. My jaded attitude towards many school activities was ironic considering how teachers themselves are supposed to invigorate young minds.

More from desperation to reduce boredom than a desire to learn, I started to train myself to focus on what I heard. To be honest, I was not inherently interested in work improvement teams, financial procedures or college administrative matters, but could keep my attention from wandering by re-contextualising the information so that it became personally relevant. "How financially sound would I be if my own spending were so clearly anticipated and accounted for?" "How enhanced would my quality of life be if I had well-defined Areas of Improvements (APIs) like these work improvement teams?" Such questions were not just idle mind games. Through them I realised how little conscious planning and intelligence I had exercised in my personal and professional life. At the very least, the questions kept me curious and engaged at staff meetings where painful boredom used to be the norm. When I shared this with my Vice Principal (VP), she described it rather flatteringly as "self-mastery". I prefer to call it "self-preservation". Anything is preferable to three hours of mindless tedium. I remember a movie, *The Kiss of the Spider Woman*, in which the protagonist, a prisoner, occupied his time by spinning tales of fantasy because using his imagination was the only way to escape his cell. My way of coping was not to escape but to go deeper into what initially bored me. That was also an act of imagination but unlike in the movie, it gave me real freedom.

It sounds very gratuitous, but I brought a similar mindfulness to morning assemblies. I must have been really tired of going through the motions everyday singing the national anthem or the once-a-week college song in an insensible manner without registering the lyrics. As usual, I joined in the singing but tried to do it more contemplatively as if I were singing to myself. Since it was difficult to think about the whole song, I focused on one or at most two lines each time and was rewarded by a heightened sense of the ideals expressed in the words. Perhaps I will be laughed at for thinking while singing the national anthem, "What worthy sentiments these are! Of course, I want happiness for every Singaporean...". The prospect of my students (many of whom do not come from a privileged background) having a slice of that happiness gave the lyrics added poignancy. What a pity I had been desensitised to the lyrics after repeated exposure. They conveyed sentiment, not sentimentality. When I was more mindful of the words, I could sing the song with more sincerity. Patriotism aside, it was a way of making meaning for myself.

An Experiment in Slowing Down

Let me first say that I believe in the virtues of communicating and collaborating with parents. But appreciation can wear thin when one has to meet more than 20 sets of parents on the same evening. If one is not mindful, it becomes an assembly line — where parents and their children are "processed" in mechanical fashion at a relentless pace. I asked myself, "The meeting has to brief but must it be hurried? I have to attend to everyone, but can I be more empathetic?" Realising my own impatience, I consciously slowed down within the 10 to 15-minute slots allocated to parents. Within the time slots, my focus was entirely on the parents and student I was seeing. Slowing down must have helped me to **see** more. There is a huge difference between a fact and an emotional truth which hits us with real force. It sounds obvious but I had a stronger sense that I was talking to **parents**, people whose investment of hope in the child is total. They deserved my complete attention. I think it was not just the parents who benefitted from the extra attentiveness and sensitivity. I felt more aligned in spirit with a task which had previously seem like a pointless but compulsory public relations exercise.

An Experiment in Appreciation

Against habitual inclination to complain, I made it a point to take note of as many good things as I could that vindicated my decision to move to a new college. I was on a quest to justify the move. It was easy enough to like the campus; all the facilities were spanking new. It was even easier to like the five-day week and the Saturdays unmolested by college demands. I also liked my VP for giving me such a long personal audience of 1.5 hours as if speaking to me and hearing my views would make all the difference in the world to staff development and the GP results. I emerged from her office feeling important... which I also liked and committed to memory. You could say I was actively reprogramming myself to like as many things as possible. It was certainly not difficult to like the Principal whose choice of vocabulary spoke volumes. Whenever I talked to her about a project I was involved in, she would invariably ask whether it was "meaningful" — which implied a concern for deeper goals in contrast to mere "usefulness". I realised how important a leader's use of language is as it shapes the moral tone of our conversations and endeavours. I also made it a point to like the office staff who were undeniably helpful. Evidently, I had taken the clerical and technical staff for granted. It dawned on me how any teacher can walk down to the office and ask to be attended to for a wide array of needs. Everyone, not just the school leaders, can give them unanticipated work outside their jobscope. As support staff, they are very often treated like foot soldiers in someone else's war — most exposed but least likely to be decorated. My complaints as a teacher must be put into perspective and weighed against their contribution — which makes mine possible in the first place.

In my self-induced alertness to everything positive, it occurred to me that when I entered the GP classroom, a girl always cleaned the board without anyone asking her to, after which no one thanked her. And that a Burmese student, anticipating my Audio and Visual Aid (AVA) needs, would automatically come forward when there was a technical glitch. I remember thinking how unassumingly generous these students were and wondering why I had been oblivious to similar acts of goodwill from other students. There must have been many in the past. Acknowledging them would have made me more grateful to be a teacher.

Reassessment of my Obsession with Examination Preparation

In the past, I especially dreaded the pre-examination consultations which began in the morning and often extended to 8 or 9 pm with minimal breaks in between. There were times when so many students sought last-minute help that I would be talking between mouthfuls of food during my canteen break. With the examination looming near, it never occurred to me to refuse their request. Unwell one day, I went home early after 5.5 hours of consultation and continued consultation by phone for another 4.5 hours, while emailing individual advice to students. Many factors contributed to this seemingly insane, relentless examination preparation. In the second–year Pre-University programme, the time runway to the examination is short relative to the "O"-Levels or Primary School Leaving Examination (PSLE). Many students were genuinely weak despite remedial sessions and teachers' earnest attempts at pedagogical improvement.

This was undeniably hard work but examining my own motives, I cannot claim to be entirely noble. I certainly thought my students' grades reflected on my competence and that I would be held accountable if they failed. In a sense, their paper chase was my rat race. Furthermore, was my concern for students partly tainted by a saviour complex — a proud over-estimation of my own abilities? I certainly enjoyed boasting about my students' success as if it defined my worth as a teacher. In addition, perhaps my contribution in helping students pass the examination was only a short-term fix which created long-term dependence on the teacher — hardly a worthy preparation for university or for life. As a teacher, I question whether my work was compromised by self-interest and whether the help was indeed constructive in the final scheme of things.

While still heavily committed to helping students pass examinations, I have learnt to examine my motives to ensure that I am not doing the work out of anxiety or self-interest. I value the distinction that Nel Noddings made between "accountability" and "responsibility". Accountability results in anxious work driven by fear of negative judgement. Responsibility leads to wholehearted work inspired by students' well-being. I prefer the latter, not just for students' happiness, but my own. A balanced view of responsibility reminds me that students must rely first on their own effort. A healthy sense of responsibility liberates me from obsession with examination outcomes after I have done my human best to facilitate their long-term learning. Accountability is imposed by external authority; responsibility is owned by me. Facing work in the latter spirit gives me more dignity and autonomy.

Redefining Professional History and Engagement

Do historians ignore the texture of life as it is lived by ordinary people? One argument against the official history we read in books is the inherent bias. Historians have a preference for momentous events and dramatic upheavals. But the ordinary and mundane is where we spend most of our days. In crafting this narrative of my professional history, I wanted to foreground the daily demands which sap teachers' energy and sense of purpose. I also wanted to affirm the possibility of growing professionally by changing the spirit in which we face those daily challenges. When we consider the term "experimentation", we feel compelled to cite initiatives with measurable targets. In my case, initiatives of the spirit have led to more tangible renewal in the way I approach my job as a teacher. When we talk about professional development of teachers, we envision improved pedagogy. But my own experience shows me that an improved attitude is more fundamental.

More important than upgraded skills is an upgraded consciousness.

Chapter 27

Beyond Passing Them Knowledge and Skills — The Moral Dimension of a Teacher's Work

Andy TAN

I must admit that preparing for this narrative inquiry was quite a harrowing experience for me. After countless nights reflecting on my teaching career, I struggled to come up with the "more memorable" experiences that I would use for the narrative inquiry. Not that I dislike the work, but in the build up to writing, I had concluded that my teaching career story, if ever translated into a book or a movie, would be a dull one. No intriguing and subtle first chapter to begin my story or suspense and drama in the middle of the story to keep readers glued to the story. No twists, no conspiracies and most definitely no scandals in my story as well. Just the one plain simple plot — I am a teacher and I want to do my job well.

Then, someone told me that narrative inquiries are not always about narrating the spectacular events or turning points that happened in one's career. It is about how we can use our experiences to help us reconcile what is known with that which is hidden, to confirm and affirm, and to construct and reconstruct understandings of ourselves and our work as teachers. In fact, it was suggested that the "one plain simple plot" is, usually, not that plain or simple in reality.

With this in mind, I asked myself what had made me come up with the "one plain simple plot". Certainly, the sense of pride and professionalism I have of being a teacher. I noted that I had concluded this quickly but I knew that this had not been developed in isolation nor had it been something that came about from the day I joined teaching. There had been many professional development opportunities and interactions in my career (about nine years as a teacher in a junior college and another five years as a staff officer in Ministry of Education Headquarters (MOE HQ)) that had helped to shape the way I think, feel and behave as a teacher.

As such, I decided to share my story in the form of learning experiences that I have encountered over the years. I have used pseudonyms in place of the names of the real characters in my story. I hope that readers will be able to connect with my experiences, learning points and shape their own meaning out of them for their own learning.

I would like to start my story from my National Institute of Education (NIE) days in 1997. I had just been posted to a neighbourhood secondary school near my house then.

What it Means to Teach

"… our shields are down and Engineering reports that the last photon torpedo took out our port nacelle. Warp core breach is imminent! What are your orders, Captain?"

I stood stunned in class. On this "all so typical" day in my three-month practicum, I had scheduled a class test for my class of Secondary Three Express kids. It should have been an easy and relaxing period for any student teacher but for a moment, I felt like the good captain in my favourite *Star Trek* show. NIE certainly had not prepared me to face situations like this.

I had started my collection of test scripts right after the bell had gone. Uhura, the girl sitting in the middle of the third row, watched me as I picked up her script from her desk. Sensing something was amiss due to her "unusually weak" expression on her face, I stopped to ask her if she was alright. She hesitated at first but with tears slowing coming down her cheeks, she told me,

"Sir, I have a very bad headache and I am unable to move my lower body. I don't know what to do. Can you help me?"

There was silence initially but it was quickly interrupted by spontaneous murmurs from her classmates for all of us had heard what she said. It must have been at least a couple of seconds before I reacted because I knew I was stunned and really did not know what to do to help her. Before I realised it, I panicked and did the only thing that made sense to me at that moment. I ran.

I told Uhura that I will go get help and ran down a flight of steps to look for my Cooperating Teacher (CT). Fortunately, he was right where I thought he would be.

"Come quick!" I said. *"Uhura is paralysed and needs help! Should we call for a doctor?"*

My CT, a teacher with years of classroom experience, looked stunned initially but responded quickly by getting me to calm down and to tell him what has happened. By the time we got back to the classroom, Uhura was already feeling much better and she was able to call her father to come and take her to see a doctor. I collected the rest of the scripts before dismissing the class. In case you are wondering, this story is not about me needing to learn how to stay calm at a moment of crisis (well... that too) but really about what I found out a few days later.

Uhura stayed back after class one day and confided that a good number of her classmates had made use of the few minutes while I was out of class (looking for help) to "share" their test answers. Needless to say, I was devastated by their actions and I could not understand why they needed to cheat. I shall skip the part on how I punished the culprits but what I clearly remember about that day was that I was troubled and I had spent the better part of the week reflecting on the incident. More specifically, my thoughts were not on how I should have handled the incident in class better but rather more of what my role as a teacher is. I had always thought that "good teachers" are those who can get their students to do well in their examinations and, most definitely, I had planned on become a "good teacher". That was what I truly believed in when I signed up to become a teacher. But this incident had unsettled me because I realised that I was upset not because my students failed their tests. It was their dishonesty and lack of moral awareness. I could not help feeling vulnerable and confused in the sense that the compelling ideals I had of a teacher's professional identity were threatened. And what made it so frightening is how it seemed so wrong. What I had thought was the most important outcome in school, i.e. good grades, did not seem that important now.

It turns out that the most powerful lesson I learnt in NIE was not about what Piaget said or what different strategies of teaching we can use in class. It was about what teaching really is and what it is not. For the first time, I had come to the understanding that I need to do more than just teach well in class to be a good teacher. It was a scary thought but I wondered what kind of teacher I would end up as if I had persisted with the view that good teachers are about producing students with good grades.

Fullan (1993) had said that teaching at its core is a moral profession and we all have a moral purpose for teaching. Good teachers combine the mantle of moral purpose with the skills of change agentry. He explains this by saying that moral purpose keeps teachers close to the needs of children and youth; change agentry causes them to develop better strategies for accomplishing their moral goals. I did not read Fullan's article back then but what I felt then was not very far away from what he said. I knew I had the moral purpose to be a good teacher but I lacked the "know-hows" to help my students learn to become a better person morally. I remember asking myself why this was not covered in my NIE course. Was it because we were assumed to already have the "know-hows" or was it because NIE thought that there were other more critical things we had to learn?

Because of this experience with Uhura's class, I saw the need to develop myself in the area of character development and sought out my senior colleagues for assistance. Some were as clueless as me and a few offered suggestions using teachable moments in Co-Curricular Activities (CCAs) which I did not really think was what I needed at that time. What about the other students in my class but not in my CCA? Does it mean that classroom teaching is purely for covering the syllabus? I just could not find any satisfactory answers to my questions at the school.

Ms. Sato was my practicum supervisor from NIE. She had taught in a junior college (JC) for a good number of years and was doing the practicum work for NIE on a consignment basis. At the debrief after my final lesson observation, I told her my experience with Uhura's class and asked her if she could offer any advice. To my utmost horror, she dismissed it as a case of poor classroom management and suggested that I work harder at it! Almost immediately, I regretted telling her the experience with Uhura's class. "She'll probably give me a failing grade now," I thought to myself.

Turned out that it did not matter. Around two months after I finished my practicum, I found out that I had passed my practicum and was posted to a JC as a Mathematics teacher. Thinking back now, I now realise that the experience with Uhura's class had strongly influenced my choice of work in my later years of my teaching career (Student Development and Community Involvement Programme).

I would now like to continue my story at the school that would be my second home for the next eight years where I honed my skills as a teacher of both academic knowledge and character development.

The Important Things in Life...

"*Strange, isn't it? Each man's life touches so many other lives. When he isn't around he leaves an awful hole, doesn't he?*"

I was fortunate to be posted to a school with a positive learning culture after graduating from NIE. My colleagues were very helpful and collegial in my professional development. Professional learning for me in the first few years involved mainly learning on the job about how to teach my core subject well — the content, the pedagogies that work, classroom management and assessment. I attribute my learning to my colleagues who coached and mentored me to become the confident teacher that I have become. I was also motivated by my experience at practicum not to focus just on teaching the academic content but also to look at teachable moments for character development.

I was a hardworking and disciplined teacher. My work and students came first in terms of priorities. Staying back late and working in school on Saturdays became an acceptable norm. In 2001, I was given the opportunity to oversee student development in my school. Professional learning for me converged into core areas related to student leadership and volunteerism. The learning experience during this period was rich but it also made greater demands of my time. I did not mind that because I believed that it meant that I would have more influence on the character development programme for our students and of course, that my hard work had been recognised by my Principal.

Then, the unthinkable happened. George, a treasured colleague, passed away due to an unfortunate accident. He was, like me, just into the first few years of teaching, full of energy and had a positive attitude to work. Well-liked by his students because of his dedication and earnest approach to teaching, he was also well-respected by his colleagues as a role model for young teachers. In short, he had a bright future in front of him prior to the accident.

All of his colleagues were sad and those of us who had worked with him closely were devastated. On the day after the accident, the Emergency Behavioural (EB) standard operating procedures (SOPs) kicked in and we were all offered counselling help by our school's EB officer, Clarence.

"… *I would like to invite you to share your feelings* …", said Clarence before I interrupted him, saying "*I prefer to get back to work. It is probably the best way for me to deal with the grief.*"

He looked at me and allowed me to go before I could cite the work and the deadlines I had to meet. In truth, I had desperately needed the time alone and putting me in a room with my colleagues to share our grief was not going to help. I had not fully come to accept George's sudden demise. There were so many "why" questions in my head that no one could answer.

"Why did he have to die so young?"
"Why did he miss the pot hole?"
"Why him?" ...

Then out of the blue, came the "what" questions — "What if it had been me instead?" I was struck momentously by this wild thought and those that came quickly after the first.

"What would happen to my young family?"
"What have I achieved?"
"What have I done to deserve this?" ...

I had never entertained the thought that someone close to me could die at such a young age. Life seemed so much more fragile and precious after George had died. That day, I left school early, i.e., immediately after my last lesson. I wanted to be with my loved ones and not think about the work at school. The incident had forced me to reflect on what I have, my responsibilities and priorities in life. The notions of work–life balance and harmony suddenly meant a lot more to me.

I did not need to think twice when I left school early the next few days.

The next story took place when I was at the MOE HQ. After realising I had reached a plateau in terms of learning, I decided to make the leap from the classroom to MOE HQ. I wanted to see what was happening in the other parts of the education landscape and because of that, I decided to apply for a post at the MOE HQ. I was glad that I made the choice because this is the stage where my learning has been the greatest and also the steepest. My new job role involved planning professional development opportunities for teachers and that meant that the people that I now worked with were no longer students but teachers from schools all over in Singapore.

Our Role as Teachers

"He told me enough! He told me you killed him." Darth Vader, in his menacing voice, fist in the air, said, "No, I AM YOUR FATHER." Luke cried out, "No, no, that's not true, that's impossible!"

Leia stood at the back of the training room with her eyes wide open, not quite believing what she was seeing. She nudged me on the elbow and directed my attention to one of the teacher participants in the workshop who was playing with a PlayStation Portable (PSP) while the trainer was talking to her class.

In hushed tones but clearly agitated, she said, "… how could she (a teacher) do that! We get scolded whenever our teacher thinks that we are not listening in lectures and there she is, playing on a PSP under the table…" I started to go over to the "PSPing" teacher to give her a piece of my mind but I ended up walking over to alert the trainer instead. I had decided in those few steps that I should let the trainer, an ex-JC Vice Principal, handle the unsuspecting teacher so that I could calm down my young intern who was just about to release another round of controlled outburst. I took Leia out of the training room and told her that this was a "one-off" incident. I added that the teacher was a Beginning Teacher (BT) who was into her first few months of training and that she would become a better teacher as she progresses. At that time, I thought Leia did not look convinced but she decided to let it go as we were due for a meeting soon. I did not blame her because I was only half convinced myself.

"What is happening to our BTs?," I thought silently as I headed back to the office with Leia.

I am not sure why, but I thought about the incident on the way home that day. I had hoped that Leia would not be too affected by the incident. After all, the internship was aimed at encouraging students to take up teaching as a career. I could understand why she had reacted that way. Leia was an extremely well-disciplined JC student who had worked hard to get the grades that she deserved. I had had a few interns attached to me previously. They usually spent their breaks on Facebook or messaging on the phone. Not that there is anything wrong with that, but Leia would take out her Calculus notes to read. She was probably every teacher's ideal type of student.

"But the thing about teachers valuing discipline in students is that they quite often forget that it works both ways as well," I thought to myself.

Leia, like many other students, had a stereotyped perception of values and behaviours that came with the teaching job, of which one was discipline. I had no doubt that Leia had lost a bit of respect for the teaching profession this morning and I was wondering why the behaviour of BTs seemed to be getting worse by the cohort.

"They probably had 'bad teachers' when they were students..."

I froze at that thought as it occurred to me that I could have taught this cohort of BTs! I did a quick set of calculations in my head and yes, they would have been my fourth batch of JC students! Had I been one of those "bad teachers"?

It had never occurred to me to ask myself this question before when I was still teaching in the school. But was I a bad role model? I had always focused my work on the teaching aspect, both in and outside the classroom, but I had not consciously worked on the modelling aspect. But why so, I asked myself, when it was so obviously one of the key roles of a teacher?

Have I taken it for granted?
What else have I also taken for granted? ...

A few isolated incidents in school when I had missed out on the little things came into mind, and more questions followed. If I recall correctly, I remember finding it both a little amusing and sad to be overwhelmed by these questions of self-doubt after having left the school for more than two years. It was already too late to do anything. Having said that, it was still a meaningful lesson for me that day for I had come to understand that our actions or inactions may have unintentional effects on others even though the effects may not be evident till years later. At that time, I was leading my zonal team in my branch work. Evidently, I still had much to learn about leadership and I could not help wondering if I would ever find out whether I had been the role model that I thought I was.

Two years later, I thought I kind of got an answer to the last question. Two of my ex-students became teachers and joined my branch after a stint in their schools. On one of my last few days at work before I left for my studies, I told them that I had had a blessed stint at MOE HQ. Not only did I have the chance to work with wonderful colleagues, I also had the good fortune of having the two of them sit in the same work area as me.

"Because every time I feel down or discouraged by work, all I need to do is to stand up and look to my front and to my left (where you are seated). The sight of two highly successful and morally upright individuals (who were my students) would put me back in good spirits automatically," I said to them.

I will not be able to forget the intense feelings of joy when I received the two emotional hugs that followed immediately afterwards.

Conclusion

Bearing in mind that some of the incidents happened a long time ago, I have tried to be as authentic as possible in reconstructing my conversations and thoughts. After more than 13 years in service, I still believe in my one plain simple plot — I am a teacher and I want to do my job well. I hope my narrative inquiry has resonated with you and has helped you make sense of your own experiences like it has to mine when I started writing it.

I end here with two questions for you to reflect on.

Do you have a plot in your teaching career?

What would that be?

Reference

Fullan, M. (1993). The professional teacher: Why teachers must become change agents. *Educational Leadership*, 50 (6).

Chapter 28

Regardless of Race, Language and Religion — My Identity as a Malay Teacher

N. B. MIZZY

When I first put serious thought into the writing for this assignment, I felt quite empty. I knew that I had to delve deep into my memory and emotions and identify some sort of turning point, or significant event that has either shaped me, or at least my teaching philosophy. I do not have any heart-wrenching, tear-jerking or hair-pulling classroom experiences to write about. However, my journey towards being a teacher was filled with a lot of unexpected twists and turns on the academic and professional front. Astonishingly, most of the reflections that I have about my early and present education are enriched and enlightened by my Master of Education (MEd) journey. It was only recently that I could understand why I learnt what I had learnt and why I learnt the way I had learnt. Through the readings of Eisner, Freire and Apple in curriculum theory, and the lectures of Professor Gopinathan in understanding the curriculum in Singapore, I managed to excavate my educational journey and connect the dots that outline my cultural and intellectual identity as a student and, simultaneously, a teacher.

Article 152: Prior to my MEd journey, the term "Article 152" was quite insignificant. Until Nominated Member of Parliament, Viswa Sadasivan, was publicly "shot down" in Parliament in 2009 for his "highfalutin ideas", and when the topic of meritocracy was discussed, Article 152 of the Singapore Constitution was merely a political term to me. It reads,

"Minorities and special position of Malays

152. — (1) It shall be the responsibility of the Government constantly to care for the interests of the racial and religious minorities in Singapore.

(2) The Government shall exercise its functions in such manner as to recognise the special position of the Malays, who are the indigenous people of Singapore, and accordingly it shall be the responsibility of the Government to protect, safeguard, support, foster and promote their political, educational, religious, economic, social and cultural interests and the Malay language."

I did not realise the impact and influence it had on me in my critical years of development as a learner from a minority race. In fact, that realisation forced me to probe every step of my educational journey since the early 1980s. I asked questions like: Did I feel specially-treated as a Malay? Besides "enjoying" subsidies, were there any other benefits? Should I attribute all my successes to the provisions that I got as a Malay? Was the playing field altered so significantly that the path I took was smoother than those of the other races, or at least the other minority races?

Despite being in a state of internal anarchy, it was not so difficult for me to unabashedly come to a conclusion that I had made it thus far through my own hard work and merit. Yes, the government paid some of my fees. However, I did not want to accept any notions of being given the upper hand in any of my academic or social pursuits. As a young student in the 1980s and 1990s, I was aware of the rut that the Malay community was in. I started Primary One in 1981 — a year before that MENDAKI, a self-help group for the Malays, was established. Among the issues that it was tasked to tackle were the growing drugs problem, increasing divorce rates, and, most importantly, the high drop-out rate in schools. In primary school, I did notice that the monolingual stream had mostly over-aged Malay and Indian students but I had never questioned why. I did notice that the tattooed and golden-haired boys at the void deck of my flat lazing around with their guitars and cigarettes were mainly Malays. But it never occurred to me that there was a problem or that they were the problem.

In secondary school, when I was more aware politically and socially, I tried to distance myself from the problems that my race was facing. To me, the problems were a misrepresentation of the good work done by many individuals in the Malay community. Even as a teenager, I consciously looked for non-Malay friends to hang out with while trying to be a role model to my Malay friends. Whatever I did, be it in my studies or Co-Curricular Activities (CCAs), I did it with only one aim in mind — to be the best. I wanted to strongly dispel the notion that Malays are lazy, easily contented, overly-focused on their spiritual development, have short marriages but lots of children, are only good in football and playing the guitar at the void decks and use drugs as a pastime. There was this "anger" in me towards my own community for allowing ourselves to be labelled as such. I was determined, in my own quiet way, not to allow that same label to be stamped on my forehead.

Eventually, this resilience shaped my attitude towards everything that I did up till now. I grew up with the belief that, as a Malay, I must prove some sections of society wrong. I must prove the system wrong. I must prove that Article 152 did not in any way help me to gain an unfair advantage over my other peers. At the same time, somehow, I believed strongly in meritocracy. I believed in the system. I believed in Mr. Lee Kuan Yew's idea of a democracy. These tensions underlined my climb up the meritocracy ladder. I experienced several trials and tribulations that forced me to check my beliefs and values again and again. There was a point of time when I questioned if I had put my loyalties and beliefs in the right place.

I entered teaching after much "resistance". I went to the polytechnic first, motivated by the economic merits of obtaining an

Engineering diploma and also because I had set myself an ill-conceived "10 points or bust" standard for my General Certificate of Education (GCE) "O"-Level examinations. I had 13 points. I could have gone to any of the Junior Colleges near home in the east, but almost fearing for my future and the horror stories of those who did not get complete "A"-Level certificates, I took the obvious route, following my closest friends. Data and the talk on the ground during that time showed a high percentage of Malays who either obtained incomplete certificates or only scraped through the "A"-Levels and ended up in teaching or in the arts and social sciences faculty at the National University of Singapore (NUS). For me, then, it was Engineering or bust.

However, by the second year in the Electronics Engineering diploma course, I had lost interest in everything associated with Engineering. I loved the learning process, the discovery and the challenge but I hated the "dehumanised" nature of Engineering. I began to question the wisdom of my decision. I questioned my stubbornness in ignoring my strengths in the arts — I loved drama, I loved words and I loved literature. Back then, I did not realise that my potential (and interest) was stifled by the rigidity of the education system. To be able to do Arts in Junior College, one would have to be in the Arts stream in secondary school. The irony was that I was in the pure science stream but I also did Literature. My MEd lectures put those experiences in perspective. Looking back, I realised that my peers and I were caught in a rigid system that did not allow for any sort of inter-disciplinary mobility. Everything was just too clear cut.

The period after National Service was filled with a number of incidents and signs that indicated to me that I did not belong anywhere else but in education. First, I was rejected by the police force for being too short and too light in weight. I was rejected by the army for being a Malay (more about this in the next section). With the Engineering diploma in hand and a non-existent work experience, I readied myself for a series of four interviews in multi-national companies, no less. Unexpectedly, I was given a "take it or leave it" proposition during the very first interview session. I was staring at a life of 12-hour shift work, overtime, excessive attention to quality control, possibly clad in uniform that blends with the machines and having to start each work day with stretching exercises accompanied by Japanese words and songs.

So I took the job.

It was on a Friday.

I did not turn up the following Monday.

I then took up a job as an assistant store manager in a renowned bookshop at the airport. I enjoyed it but still, something was missing. I enjoyed interacting with tourists and travellers. I enjoyed the latest books that I could read for free. But I was not making any difference in anyone's life. I was just living for me. And the books.

Six months on, I finally succumbed and heeded the call of the teaching profession. I wanted to teach but more importantly, I wanted to teach Physical Education (PE) as I loved sports and the outdoors. When I signed my teaching bond, I resolved to make Ministry of Defence (MINDEF) and the police force pay for not accepting me. Their loss will be the Ministry of Education's (MOE) gain, I told myself. I was determined to be a damn good teacher. No, I was determined to be a damn good Malay teacher. Three key phases defined my journey.

Phase I: Sink, Float or Swim? All of the Above!

I started off as a contract teacher for six months. The words "hand-hold", "supervise" and "coach" came up quite often. But none of them were relevant to me. I was the only contract teacher in the school then. Yet, I was left to my own devices. So what did I do? I taught, all right. Oh yes, I did. I taught exactly the way I was taught — in primary school! Cooperative learning? Never heard of it. Differentiated learning? Yes, I taught different things everyday. Learning styles? Oh yes, my style was that the children must learn whatever I teach. Chalks and dusters flew across my classroom, just like they did when I was in primary school. Wrong words for spelling were to be corrected 10 times, just like what I had to do. And any indiscipline warranted writing line after line of empty promises not to repeat the offence.

On some days, I felt like Superman. On most other days, I felt like The Swamp Thing. Inside, I was screaming for help. Obviously, no one heard me. So throughout those six months, I sunk, floated and swam whichever way I knew how. I was expected to know how to teach. And if I did not, I was supposed discover it myself. Thankfully, there were a couple of familiar faces. They helped quite a bit but I needed more than advice and encouragement. I needed actual teaching skills — skills to facilitate actual learning, not just completion of workbooks and worksheets. I took all that in my stride, juggling three subjects — English, Mathematics and Science — while also lending my experience in soccer to the school soccer team. I even had to set a Primary 6 Science examination paper! I struggled at balancing the teaching and non-teaching responsibilities, managing the curriculum, understanding my students and understanding the school. Although not much damage was done, I knew not much learning had taken place either.

Six months on, I received a letter of admission from the National Institute of Education (NIE). I could not wait to leave behind a period of educational darkness. I just could not wait to be trained. To learn. To know.

Phase II: Finding the Voice

Being in NIE made me realise two things. Firstly, my critical thinking skills needed serious development. As a young student, the only times I felt like I had my own voice was during Literature class and when I was writing English essays. Even then, for the latter, there was always a voice telling me to play it safe — no alien or ghost stories are allowed; keep it simple but exciting enough to get an A1. I felt alive in Literature classes. Besides the fact that our teacher was pleasing to the eyes, I grabbed at the chance when I could critique Shakespeare, George Orwell and William Golding. I could relate to what they were trying to say through their protagonists and I embraced the experience wholeheartedly. I remember being peer pressured into buying the guides but I hardly used them. I got a B3 for it in the "O"-Levels but I did not care. That was the only subject that spoke to me. But like most good sons, I put Engineering and economic viability first. Literature became a hobby. A retreat. An escape.

To plug that gap in critical thought, I spent a lot of time reading and photocopying articles from journals. I spent countless hours in the library in my first semester at NIE which also translated into turning down many offers to play sports after lessons. I just felt the need to know more, even if I felt that I have had enough. I had to ask myself serious questions. How could I invoke strong feelings in my students, let them take different perspectives or hear their voices if I did not have the ability to do likewise?

The second thing that I realised was that I could not survive studying alone. Sure, I did well in my first year but I did not really enjoy the process. It was only in the second year that I managed to open up to my coursemates and through them, I felt I became a better student and person. I shared my notes willingly, started study groups, did assignments with less familiar classmates, and even engaged my lecturers in discussions beyond the subject area.

However, there was still this inability to problematise issues. I was frustrated at not being able to dissect issues and viewpoints and offer my own voice on it. Even if I could "say" it in my head, I could not verbalise my thoughts. This inability was exposed further when I started the MEd. In one of my assignments, I reflected upon this "handicap" when I read Freire. I wrote,

"He (Freire) made me ask questions about my conformity, my unquestioning acceptance of my education, my pedagogies and my philosophy in life in general. Have I been oppressed so effectively that I have retreated into a culture of silence, giving my oppressors (my teachers, my teachers' teachers, the government, the whole system!) more motivation to keep me in my oppressed state and them indulging in their oppressor mentality? I look at those who pine for more freedom and I ask why. But perhaps I should ask why I am not asking for more. Do I fear freedom? Or am I so limited in my knowledge of the world such that I could not care less what more the world could teach me?"

It was easy to blame the system in which I was educated but I believe the "culture" to inquire, challenge and probe just was not ingrained in me. When I was growing up, I was taught to understand and respect the Malay rituals and traditions. A teacher is a learned person who is to be respected and revered. You learn because you do not know. As a learner, you take in whatever you are taught from your teachers; no questions asked. If you ask, you give two impressions — one, that you are rude; and two, that you have not been paying attention and thus you are disrespectful towards the learning process.

My defining moment took place in mid-2000. This incident shaped my core beliefs and philosophies in life and education in general as it touched the very base of who I am as a teacher today.

It was during one of the mass induction sessions that pre-service teachers had to attend as part of our graduation "requirements". One of the topics was on Remaking Singapore, as part of the Singapore 21 series of discussions. The guest speaker was the young and upcoming Dr. Vivian Balakrishnan, who was then chairman of the Remaking Singapore Committee. His address touched on topics pertaining to citizenship, nationalism, racial and religious harmony and why we need to create a vibrant Singapore on all fronts. As I sat there listening to him talking about meritocracy and loyalty, something struck me. It brought me back to just two years earlier when I was serving in the army as an automotive specialist, or, in more modest terms, a vehicle mechanic.

The year was 1998. There were only six months left to my run-out-date (ROD). It was only six months since I limped out of the Officer Cadet School (OCS) after quite a serious injury. Circumstances in the family directed me towards signing up as a regular personnel in the army. While attending a vehicle maintenance course, I approached the career officer to tell him of my intention to sign-on and to switch from the automotive section to the electronics section to put my polytechnic diploma to good use. I was eager, and almost desperate. However, I did not expect his response, which, on the evidence that I could still remember his exact words till this day, changed some of my perspectives on what meritocracy is really like in my country of birth. He said, "Don't waste your time.

You're a Malay. Even if you can get in, you won't go far." At first, I thought that he had seen my polytechnic results, for it was delivered with nonchalance. No guilt attached. No sugar coating. It was an "in-your-face" moment for me. Despite the ongoing laments of the Malay community during that period of time, on the lack of Malays in key military positions, I refused to believe that my Singapore practised discrimination. What happened to rewarding those who worked hard? What happened to progression by merit? What happened to equal opportunities?

Fast-forward to the year 2000 at the Nanyang Technological University (NTU) Auditorium. During the question-and-answer session, I mustered enough courage to walk to one of the standing microphones along the aisle. I looked around me and estimated about 1,000 pairs of eyes were looking at me. The then-Director of NIE, Professor Leo Tan (one of my idols to this day), was sitting next to Dr. Balakrishnan and prompted me to say my name and the programme that I was in before asking my question or making my comment. My coursemates looked at me, wondering what was it that I was going to ramble on that time. Taking a deep breath, I started.

"Sir, before I get to my main point, let me share with you that I am a true blue Singaporean. I grew up following the speeches of Mr. Lee Kuan Yew and every year since I was five years old, I looked forward to his National Day Rally speeches, even though I could not understand most of the issues then. I feel it deeply if our neighbouring countries attack our sovereignty through their policies or their comments, or meddle into our affairs. However, Sir, an incident two years ago made me question if I have put my heart in the right place."

I recounted my experience with the army career officer. I then continued.

"Sir, in a few days' time, I will officially be given the license to teach. I will exercise my duties fairly and to the best of my abilities. However, as a teacher, one of the responsibilities that I would have is to teach my students the national anthem and the pledge. 'We the citizens of Singapore... regardless of race, language or religion ... so as to achieve happiness, prosperity and progress for our nation." Now, Sir, this is where my dilemma lies. If a Malay boy comes to me and says, "Teacher, I would like to be a pilot or an intelligence specialist!" Do I tell him what I was told: "Son, you're a Malay. Don't waste your time." Or do I tell him the story of *Animal Farm* (by George Orwell), where one of the commandments read, "All animals are equal but some animals are more equal than others."

After that last line, the whole auditorium ruptured with deafening applause. I was close to tears. My knees were shaking. I did not expect the reception that I got. It went on and on and on. I quickly scanned the aisle for an empty seat and rushed to it when I saw one. After the applause had died down, I braced for the backlash. Professor Leo Tan was all smiles. The auditorium fell silent, eagerly waiting for Dr. Balakrishnan's response.

But the response was a letdown.

It was a typical politically-correct response that made you forget what the initial question was. But that was secondary. As I returned to my seat, I received pats on the back, even from fellow trainee-teachers who were complete strangers to me.

At the end of the session, as we were making our way out, Dr. Balakrishnan's personal assistant approached me. He said, "Dr. Balakrishnan would like to have a word with you outside the auditorium." I half-expected the Internal Security Department (ISD) people to stand next to him, waiting to bundle me into a van and grilling me on my political orientations, if I had any. As I approached him, I was relieved that he was alone. He commended me for being brave enough to say what I had said. We then discussed meritocracy, the Malay community and my role as a teacher. He said that more like me should come forward. As we spoke, I could imagine myself wearing all white and being hoisted on shoulders of people also in white and chanting three alphabets repeatedly, punching the air with gusto, waving three-coloured flags and placards with my face on them. But I digress. We parted with a firm handshake, as if coming to an agreement that I would make a difference in the lives of my students, even if some animals will continue to be more equal than others.

Professor Leo Tan walked behind me, put one arm on my shoulder and offered a handshake with the other. "Well done," he said, "that's the kind of things we want to hear from our teachers." I was over the moon.

I felt that I had finally crept out of my shell, ready to face the world. I felt that I had finally found my voice. Things might not change too much in our military, but I did not really care that much. More importantly, I felt that what I said had to be said, not through any feelings of hatred or maliciousness, but buoyed by the ideals of meritocracy that we were so consistently reminded to uphold. M.M. Lee may have his reasons for his military policies, but there are so many other ways and avenues through which I could contribute. Education is my chosen battlefield. No, wonderland. And in this wonderland, I intend to welcome learners of all colours, languages and religions. *Majulah Singapura!*

Phase III: The Leadership Challenge

2002. The year that I graduated from NIE. It was almost a year after the 9/11 incident. The landscape for racial and religious harmony had shifted a little because of that tragedy. The Muslim community felt that it had to distance itself from the terrorists who claimed to be Muslims. It felt that it had to explain its stance and clearly define what Islam really is about. Sadly, though, it also had to reaffirm and re-establish its position in multi-racial and multi-religious Singapore. The term "moderate Muslims" splashed across all available media.

I was posted to an all-boys mission school. That year, a significant number of Malay/Muslim teachers were posted to either mission schools or clan schools. Somehow, we felt that we had a mission to accomplish. Perhaps the government felt that there was a need re-emphasise the assimilation of all races and religions in all educational institutions and, if need be, use us as agents for racial harmony, understanding and tolerance.

With 9/11 as the background, I stepped into my posted school, determined to put into practice what I had learnt. I did not really feel that my race and religion was important at all. I was, first and foremost, an educator. Being posted to a school as a trained teacher made people see you in a different light. You are no longer the inexperienced staff member. You have learnt about Vygotsky, Piaget and Bandura. You know the three-stage process of a good lesson. Thus, there are no excuses for not ensuring that learning takes place. You are now an official member of the teaching fraternity.

Although I was trained to be a PE teacher, I only had an hour of PE on my weekly timetable. I became a generalist, having to teach all three core subjects to a class of P3 boys. Naturally, I struggled with the pedagogical content, especially in Mathematics and Science. I struggled with the requirement to use Information and Communication Technology (ICT) at least once a week. I also struggled with the duties of a form teacher as well as membership of many sub-committees. Still, there were no mentors. There was an induction programme that lasted a mere one hour, mostly focusing on the school's directions and personnel. I was also not prepared to be faced with a class of 40 boys. I've never had that experience but since there was no mention of it during my NIE classes, I assumed I had to teach them the same way I teach a co-educational class. Sadly, within my first three months, nothing I learnt in NIE was applied. I went back to my untrained teacher mode. It seemed the safest way to go. Teacher-centred lessons were the order of the day.

Pedagogical challenges aside, what caught me off-guard was the culture shock of being in a mission school. Again, this was not something that you learn in NIE. My new school leaders, perhaps assuming that I would know, did not explain this aspect of the culture. So I was caught off-guard by the rituals, the language and the adherence to accepted norms and routines. I had to adjust my perceptions and misconceptions fast while also trying not to lose my identity and beliefs. I found myself naturally looking out for Malay/Muslim pupils and ensuring that they understood and knew when to draw the line between adherence to the school culture and exercising their right to their own religion. That became a path where I practised my leadership. Eventually, I became a source of consultation where religious matters were concerned. Malay/Muslim parents felt at ease knowing that someone was looking out for their children's spiritual well-being. Sadly, though, I had to grapple with misled colleagues who made comments to Malay/Muslim students like, "If you want to be in this school, then you'll have to follow whatever we do. Otherwise, go to a secular school."

Somehow, those sort of comments made me resolve to keep my head down and focus on my role as an educator. I recalled the speech I made in the NTU auditorium and resolved to maintain impartiality in my teaching. I focused on the process of turning all my boys into men, even though only 3–5% of them were Malay/ Muslims. Religious values, to me, can be universal. I centred my character and values education on simply being human — a good human being. I used the opportunity to share with my boys the concepts of race and religion, what Islam is and what it is not and to clarify whatever misconceptions that they had. Perhaps, I thought, that was what the government had wanted us to do. Clever.

Within my second year, I was thrust into a leadership position. No other Malay colleague, I noticed, was holding on to any leadership position. So I grabbed it. I was made a Sports Secretary and had to assist my Head of Department (HOD) PE in running the department. There were no schemes-of-work for PE, no proper structure of equipment management and the CCA programme was, at best, haphazard. Finally, I was in familiar territory. The tasks were arduous and challenging but it gave me, even in my second year in service, a renewed sense of purpose.

When I was officially appointed Subject Head for PE two years later, more responsibilities came with it. I sought to contribute as much as I could in steering the school towards its vision, never mind that it contained specific religious ideals. However, deep down inside me, something did not feel right. Despite being acknowledged for my leadership qualities and initiative, I still felt inadequate in shouldering many of the big decisions that affect the school. Being given the trust to make key decisions is good, but as a young leader, I felt that I was not given the proper development to sustain a high level of performance. Conversations during department meetings always centred on the daily operations; never on the soft skills of leadership, or the long-term directions of the department. In my six years there, I could only recall being observed formally twice and going through a proper appraisal session once. I pined for someone to mentor me.

As the years went by, I felt that I was becoming too comfortable where I was. My attempts to inject some innovative or unconventional ideas were not taken too well. If it ain't broken, don't fix it, they said. I was reminded again and again about the school's more-than-a-century-old tradition and history. I just could not convince them enough that our students had changed tremendously since then. I felt that there was a clash of ideologies. My heart was yearning for something more. I felt that it was time to go. While I appreciated the opportunity and recognition that the school had given me, I told myself that for the love of teaching, I needed a fresh environment. I needed a new challenge.

When MOE wanted to start a new concept school and advertised for a HOD for PE, I didn't have to think twice. I applied for it. I liked the challenge that it posed — a brand new primary school. It was an opportunity for me to contribute immensely in starting up a school. The idea was still ambiguous. Nobody, not even the principal, knew what the new concept school, leveraging on ICT, should look like. But I was at a place in my life where ambiguity was to be embraced; not avoided. The work of curriculum innovation, professional development and embracing change has become part and parcel of my daily activities. The challenge of being pathfinders in ICT-integration in schools has re-ignited the passion in my colleagues and I, who come from many different schools, equipped with many different experiences but sharing one common goal. I feel alive. The journey that I have taken thus far has forced me to make substantial revisions of my identity and my priorities. I found myself searching for answers while playing multiple roles in the school community. I looked for answers through my learning and the people around me.

How have my experiences helped me in my current work? I would not pinpoint to one particular experience or skill or incident. To me, the attitude that I carried along with me stems from the need to excel, to prove my worth and to prove people wrong. Does being a minority help? To a certain extent, it did imbue in me the resilience, that never-say-die spirit. I wanted so much to break the stereotypical view that my community has been stigmatised with. In the end, that quest for excellence has defined who I am as an educator, a leader, a father, a husband and a person — without having to sacrifice my identity and my ideals.

My search for leadership ended up with me taking charge of my own progress and development, taking charge of who I want to be in the context of my professional landscape and making a difference in the lives of the people whose paths I cross. It also taught me that leadership is not just about meeting targets, but also about forging and strengthening relationships. The moment you put yourself up on a pedestal, you simply stop being human.

The experiences that I had pertaining to my struggles as an indigenous citizen made me resolve to be impartial in my teaching and dealings with students and colleagues alike. Being colour-blind has always been second nature to me. Although there were occasions that tested my convictions, I was thankful that I did not succumb to them. This belief has helped me to see every student as they are, to see their talents unfold and to see them grow before my eyes — regardless of colour, race or religion. And I will continue to work hard to pass down these values to all my students.

Through the process of narrative writing, I have forced myself to not just recall what had happened in my journey, but to connect those discrete events into one big story. My MEd journey has definitely enriched and enlightened my view of my educational experiences. Previously, I used to look at those experiences as they were. Now, I look at them with new lenses. I am now able to appreciate them through multi-focal perspectives which are set against social, cultural, political and educational backdrops.

I do not know what the future holds. But I know that I will be all right. The past has given me the strength. The present supplements me with added vigour. The future is but the start of a new journey.

References

Constitution of the Republic of Singapore. Retrieved from Singapore Statutes Online website http://statutes.agc.gov.sg (accessed on 15 February 2010).

Orwell, G. (1947). *Animal farm.* New York: The New American Library.

Chapter 29

Re-Evaluating My Professional Trajectory: A Journey in Search of My Identity

Rina MIZZY

Introduction

Bruner (1990) believes that creating stories is a human and natural response for making-meaning or comprehending events in our lives. He argues that stories are often created around puzzling, surprising, confusing or frustrating episodes in our work. According to Conle (2003), the act of telling one's story is very important because we may come to understand our own story anew through the retelling. These two authors resonated well with me. I began to gain new insights into how I think, the conflicts that I experienced, the fears that I encountered, and the benefits I derived through the whole inquiry process. This chapter shares how the events and people in my life have impacted my growth and development as a person and as a teacher.

The Narrative

An assignment I thought was easy enough to complete and submit suddenly became difficult and heavy. It is not an easy task for me because writing about myself requires me to look at myself so objectively. Teaching is a passionate subject for me. What is funny is that I never once thought of teaching when I graduated from junior college. It was truly fateful that I signed the form my aunt shoved in my lap when she saw me moping around when I got my General Certificate of Education (GCE) "A"-Level results. It was a pretty good result but it did not land me a place in the one and only university on this island at the time.

Teaching was never my first choice but I knew that I wanted to work with people and put my creative juices to good use. I thought I would probably be a designer of some sort or work in an office in an advertising company. But obviously that did not happen. Writing my story, I thought, was just too personal, as I have to look deep into my emotions and personal experiences that have shaped me into who I am today. I did not know whether I could do justice to my valuable experiences and myself. But what came out strong as I finished school was the fact that I was searching for who I am, my true identity and how, as a student, I kept pushing myself to the limits, wanting to prove to the community, that I am Malay but I am different. I wanted to prove that with hard work, I would succeed unlike my cousins who were born with a silver spoon and whose future had already been guaranteed.

The Passionate Teacher

I decided to go ahead with submitting the application form my aunt had helped me fill out. I wanted to give a try because I did not want to enter the working life just as yet. I was still thirsty for knowledge and since I had the drive and the capacity, I wanted to continue studying, unlike my friends who were already working right after the last GCE "A"-Level paper ended. The three years I was in the then Institute of Education (IE) were a breeze. It was stress-free and full of fun and exploration. It was not so bad.

My first real job was as a Malay Language teacher in a school situated in the West of Singapore. Right out of IE in 1990, my batch was the last one to do a specialisation in Malay Language and a minor in English and Social Studies. When I was assigned to my first class, the first thing I did was to understand where my students came from and who they were. My school was in a poor neighbourhood. Most of them came from broken families; some had not met their parents before in their lives and regarded their grandparents as their parents. Drugs, gangs and fights reigned in that neighbourhood. It was not a good place to raise a child but ironically, the school was smack in between the housing flats. It was as if to signal that the school is their only hope, only chance of survival. I asked to be assigned to an EM3[1] class so that I could really help the children. My Reporting Officer (RO) smiled, clearly understanding my motivation, I thought. There were not many Malay pupils in the school. But I wanted to reach out to as many pupils as I could, so I asked to teach Art. I was given about seven art classes to teach besides teaching Malay Language and Social Studies. It did not matter that I lived in the East and had to travel to the West by bus every morning. The East–West Line (part of the MRT or subway) was only completed the following year.

What changed me from someone who was never interested in teaching, to this? It happened when I was walking from the bus stop to the school on that first day (and every other day) — I saw eager little children holding hands with their parents, grandparents, guardians, skipping to school with wide smiles on their faces. I heard them talk about the teachers, about their friends and about their activities in school with so much excitement. I heard their parents, grandparents and guardians telling them to be good in school and study well. And then I saw how they hugged the little ones goodbye, kissing them on their chubby cheeks and watched lovingly as their little ones skipped their way into school. It was a sight to remember. A sight enough to tell myself, "I must not fail them. They have such high hopes and I can make a difference in their lives and future." That was all I needed to see to reassure myself that I had made the right choice.

---

[1] A ability-based streaming in which only foundation courses were offered. It was replaced by subject-based banding in 2008.

Five years on, my spirit has not failed me. I have met so many children, all with different characters, needs and aspirations. Through language and art lessons, I brought little children into a different world — a world that their parents, grandparents or guardians could never give them. I gave them the experience of their lives when we put up skits on stage, or prepared for the end-of-year exhibitions and read countless books. We played games that required them to strategise and yet have loads of fun. We spent many hours under the rain tree, picking up pods, playing hopscotch or just talking about their favourite things. What mattered the most for me, as a Malay Language teacher, was that I was able to reach out to all students of different races, Chinese being the majority. There was no question about cultural difference or status. I spoke a universal language — love, compassion and care. These needs are no different from now. Children always get turned away from these things because adults simply do not have the time to shower them with love, compassion and care or simply do not find these important for children's development.

I remember Ah Teck. He was made my class chairman because I wanted to bring him on my side. Outside the school, he was part of a gang. His father was a gangster. He simply looked up to his father and the power he possessed. He was very difficult to deal with at first because of his abusive language. He also threatened to beat up teachers if they bothered him with the school rules. But one day, he changed. He did not mind being the class chairman because I said so. It happened when he accidentally tore his pants while playing with his friends in the field. Embarrassed, he hid in the toilet. His friends told me that he did not feel like coming to class. I looked for him and asked him what happened. After much coaxing, he told me about his pants. I smiled. He ran back into the toilet, cursing me, thinking that I was making fun of him. Minutes later, I came back with a needle and a thread. I sewed up the torn part and asked him to come back to class. Since then, he treated me like a queen. He would listen in class, do his homework, and play his role as the class chairman well. He said to me before he graduated to secondary school one day, "'Cher, you are the first person who was ever kind to me." It seemed, I had left an impact. I did not think a simple common sense gesture would matter to this young gangster wanna-be who had only known that violence begets violence.

I had aspirations too. I had always wanted to go to a university and earn a degree. My leave was approved for the following year. And that was when I met Ashraf. He was a Primary Two boy. He had bright eyes and a killer smile but he was not that bright. He was a struggling reader but he had such great determination. In the same class, was another girl who could read and write quite well. Yes, there were only two of them that year. Ashraf was always following me everywhere when school was over. He would stay to talk to me about the things that were written in the textbooks as he could not read fluently. He would ask many questions. He wanted to know about the world beyond his own. One afternoon, I sent him home, curious to know who his parents were. But I could find no one but another little boy who was waiting for him to come home so that he could eat his lunch. Every day, Ashraf would serve his brother his lunch and dinner, shower together and go to sleep while their mother worked two shifts back to back. They had no one else and even if they did, no one cared. That year, I told Ashraf's mother that I would like the two boys to stay with me during the school holidays every year as I could not imagine them spending the June and December holidays without anyone minding them. Today, they are in their 20s, doing well in their lives. Every month they visit my mother and me. They could not imagine what might have happened if I had not taken them into my home. They would have probably led different lives now, joining gangs and selling drugs. I shudder at the thought of it.

Bruner (1990, 2002) states that we construct an image of ourselves by telling and listening to stories of our own and others' so that we are formed and transformed by them and become who we are. I believed that I started to listen to the children's stories and they listened to mine. We had formed and transformed through the life experiences that we went through together, whether it was inside the classroom or outside the classroom. During the first five years of my teaching career, I had shaped my identity as a classroom teacher and found the answers to the question I asked myself seven years ago, "Why would I want to become a teacher?"

The Frustrated Graduate

Having spent four years overseas studying for my first degree, I felt it was long enough to have stayed away from teaching and children. I was immediately posted to a secondary school in the East — an all-girls school. It was a totally different environment. Again, the number of Malay students was small and my skills were tested to the maximum when I found out that 75% of the students who were offered Malay Language were non-Malays or of mixed parentage. But the students came from well-to-do families. All the girls needed to worry about was whether they were more popular than the rest every day of their lives.

It was July 1999. Masterplan 1 kicked in while I was away. Cooperative Learning, Brain-based Learning and many more new initiatives were introduced while I was away. After having spent four years away from the system, I found myself struggling to understand it. Teaching was not how I used to know it. Teachers spent hours planning lessons and marking their work. I observed that they were just happy to stay as long as they could in the staff room, away from the heat outside. Students had to peep through door cracks to look for their teachers.

As for me, I busied myself with the new teaching techniques that were deemed to improve students' learning. I read books on how non-native speakers learn a "foreign" language. I spent time knowing who my students were and how they felt doing a subject that was forced on to them because of the policy. The first two years teaching in a secondary school taught me a lot of things about myself and about teaching. I came to realise that teaching was not the only thing I had wanted to do. I realised that I did not want to be just a mere technician executing programmes that have been pre-packaged and prescribed by others. I did not want to feel any sense of helplessness about my role in an education system. I wanted to do more than just carry out a lesson plan in class. I wanted to have a say in the planning. But Malay Language was not the focus of the school. It had a very small role to play in the school. As a new teacher to the school, I was dying to burst into flames and make things happen. I remember suggesting to my Head of

Department (HOD) to introduce speech and drama for Malay Language students. Since most of my students were non-native speakers of the language, I thought that speech and drama would help them to express themselves fluently in the target language. I had read extensively from books and research papers on how to approach language learning for non-native speakers and experimented some of these in the classroom. It had been proven effective. My students would be able to expand on their vocabulary. They also could relate to the lessons as they found the simulations and scenarios given helped them to practise using the language in the real world. The speech and drama programme was not approved. It was just not the school's focus.

I was frustrated because the opportunity was not there for me in the school. I felt that with the Honours Degree in my hands and the experience I had gained, I was underutilised. I had so much to give but no one wanted it. But within those two years, I began to do more reflection about the education system, ranking process (students' and teachers'), the curriculum and its impact, testing and assessments. I expressed my thoughts to my RO and she told me to focus on students' results. Failing a subject would impact their overall opportunity to enter a junior college or polytechnic. I was crushed. Do not get me wrong; the school was a great one, under the leadership of a very vibrant leader who was ahead of her times, and a strong advocate of character development. I have learnt so much from her, especially when it comes to being innovative and compassionate. She was a visionary.

In January 2001, I received a call from the Curriculum Planning and Development Division (CPDD). I was invited for a chitchat session. I was asked about how I feel about the current education system and the Malay Language Curriculum. I was asked to compare between the Primary Curriculum and the Secondary Curriculum. Two weeks later, I got a letter that said that I would be posted to CPDD in June. Just like that. Thinking back, I wondered what was it that I had shared that resonated well with the panel of interviewers. I certainly had a lot to say about the curriculum gaps between primary and secondary. I remember mentioning that I did not like the idea of language learning only amounting to pen and paper assessments. Even though the curriculum intent did advocate that the majority of the time should be dedicated to developing oracy skills, in reality, it was not so. Teachers were still very much traditional in their practices. Language is about expressing oneself, not just in the written form. I thought these beliefs hit home with the CPDD panel of interviewers. I was elated. Perhaps more of my ideas would be heard there.

The Enthusiastic Specialist

I thought being in CPDD was the height of my career. I wrote a total of 30 units for the Malay language textbooks, translated numerous articles, wrote speeches for Guests of Honour, attended countless meetings and organised work plan seminars and workshops. The plumpest job of all was when I sat in the Secretariat in the curriculum review committee that also gave me the opportunity to travel on study trips.

The first year in my job as a curriculum planner was a breeze. Most officers would call it the honeymoon period. I had time to plan how I wanted to contribute in the organisation. As a teacher, I know I can influence my practices in the decision-making. I became aware of who I am as a teacher and the limitations I faced. As a teacher, I could not do as much as I wanted to improve the overall teaching and learning from the bottom. Into my second year, as I sat in countless critique sessions, I realised the root of all problems in the schools, started here. This ivory tower has long separated the ideal from the current reality on the ground. I focused so much on how I could contribute and make the difference when the whole deal of being a curriculum planner was to conform. Policies were already there and as an officer, my job is to be able to translate these into bite-sized practices for easy digestion by teachers in school. Most of the time, I ended up explaining the policy, explaining why things are being done that way and how teachers should implement them the way they were supposed to. At the end of the day, I was defensive about the actions and thoughts of the Ministry.

Until I met her. She was one of the directors of a unit. She was different. She did not conform. She was firm but she knew the ground so well. She shook up everyone who had been in the ivory towers since yonder years. I admired how different she was from the rest I had worked with. I was inspired. She was a school principal before this. I was under her in one of the committees. She brought us back to reality — that schools will still function and innovate even without the help from CPDD. She got us to bring the message back to our units to start recognising the efforts that schools are doing to customise their curriculum to suit the needs of their students and how we must always make students and teachers as our focal points in whatever we do.

The passion that I felt when I first started teaching was re-kindled. I no longer just looked at students. Now I looked at teachers. Often, educational reforms have been authorised without input from the teachers who must implement them. Consequently, some teachers have experienced feelings of alienation and isolation because they have been asked to implement changes they have had no part in shaping. As an officer, I felt that way too. But I was proactive in taking control of my working life. As the situation in CPDD started to change and move forward, I felt empowered to decide and engage in a more systematic reflection about my work by thinking, writing and talking about the curriculum, teaching and learning, observing the acts of my own and others' and by gauging the impact of the instructional materials on students learning. This has helped me to locate myself within my profession and start to take more responsibility for shaping my own practice as a teacher and a curriculum planning officer. Through this act of reflection and experience, I felt that my own professional growth was certain (Dewey, 1993/1958).

Whenever I got the chance to conduct workshops with teachers, apart from sharing strategies, I would never fail to remind teachers about the importance of being reflective. Reflective teachers make a point of becoming aware of the factors that affect their practice so that they can improve their teaching and thereby, positively influence the educational systems they work in. I wanted them to learn the word "contextualisation", a word that I have come to understand throughout my stint in CPDD, which somehow did not really reach the schools. I wanted teachers to look within their classroom, and choose what is best for the students, not just merely 'copy' good practices without thinking. Most often, I observed how teachers are happily innovating while knowing that it would be just a passing fad, just to satisfy the school leaders.

The Learning Leader

After five years in CPDD, it was time for me to go. Even though there were talks about extending my term in CPDD to oversee a certain project, it was inconclusive. I, for one, wanted to go with the flow. Unlike most of my colleagues who went scrambling for schools of their choice and ensuring that they got a key personnel (KP) post, I left my fate to Personnel Division. Firstly, I did not have the time to scout for schools. Secondly, it did not really matter where I was sent because work is work. As a civil servant, I should be able to work in any school and show the same passion and attitude towards teaching and learning. Little did I know I would be posted out as KP and promoted to a senior grade. I was partly disappointed at not knowing. I just wanted to be more prepared.

I had no idea what my job scope was really like. Frankly, I felt that I was thrown into the deep blue sea and I was expected to learn how to swim — on my own. At this point of time, the question of who I am became even stronger. It would not have happened that way if I were not constantly reminded, in a subtle way, of the fact that I was the only Malay with a KP position or the fact that I should reach out not only to the Malay teachers and students but all students because one day, I might be posted out as a Vice Principle and that kind of impact is needed in a school leader. But not once was I offered a mentor nor was I being coached. As a leader, I was left alone. But I did not want to disappoint my team of able and extremely dedicated Malay Language teachers. I studied the Enhanced Performance Management System (EPMS) thoroughly and asked a lot of questions though sometimes I would not get any answers. With the experience in CPDD, I led my team of teachers into customising the curriculum, aligning assessments, developing frameworks and deliberating on a lot of teaching and learning matters. We clicked so well. We could get into hot arguments in our discussions and at the end of the day, we could still have coffee and laugh at ourselves.

Was I a good leader? I led my teachers with my heart. I wanted my small department to be a flat organisation and not something hierarchical. Happy teachers will produce happy students. I dirtied my hands and worked as hard as my teachers to achieve our targets. For five good years, we met our targets. My department was commended for two consecutive years for having the best practice.

When I asked my teachers to evaluate our success, this is what they wrote, "… in any great department or organisation, we need leaders with courage and capacity to build new cultures based on trusting relationships. It requires a leadership that goes far beyond improving examination results. Only in this kind of setting can teachers develop and flourish."

The lack of mentorship had actually forced me to learn to find my own style and develop my own personal vision. I was faced with many challenges that shook my confidence as a leader. What kept me going were vision and passion: vision that I had for the school and students, passion for learning and knowledge — for the students and the teachers under my charge.

The school I was posted to is like any neighbourhood school. With an average Primary School Leaving Exmination (PSLE) T-Score of 199, it was definitely a challenge to teach my students who had very colourful family backgrounds. Teachers were constantly thinking of ways to engage students from the word "go" till the end of the period. As a teacher I was not spared from this. Like everyone else who is caught up in the life of teaching, I didn't have the time to stop and reflect on why I approached things as I did. Only when I allowed myself the luxury of reflection and began to realise how critical it was did I really look at what I do on a day-to-day basis.

Looking at the weaknesses in my teaching, the abstract random nature of my organisational skills and my way of managing things,

I also was able to confront the strengths of my teaching. I teach the student, not the content. I relate well to young people. I care deeply and lay bare my feelings about what I teach and those who are learning it and I draw my students together into small learning communities. Most of my school day is spent talking to students individually. I listen and develop relationships with them that are nurturing and encouraging. Roaming the school corridors, I found it important to include as many students as I could into the school culture. I will seek out those who hide in the corners and try to connect with those who might not connect easily to anyone. The personal nature of schooling is my main priority. The phrase "safe and caring schools" to me is the most apt description of what all schools should be and that is what I attempt to do.

Learning about hidden curriculum in my postgraduate studies, I began to wonder why I taught this way. It was not necessarily the way I was taught to teach. Most secondary school teachers do not approach things as I do and many do not think that what I do is rigorous. In my journal writing when I was doing my Management for School Leaders Course (MLS) in 2010, I spent a lot of time writing about my experiences as a teacher, I began to make connections between teaching and learning and my students being the central focus point. Living heartfully in teaching opens up ways of seeing the self outside the planned curriculum (Aoki, 1983). By putting myself outside the planned moment of teaching, I was able to view the implications for knowing the self as an engaged teaching being as I asked myself: What is the significance of the other party (students) in the pedagogic situation? Pinar (2004) pointed out that living wholeheartedly in pedagogy connects the teacher to the human subjects in the classroom.

There are situations in my school when students come to class not ready for learning. Their personal world experiences affect their learning. There were students who came to school feeling the trauma after their parents had a fight right before their eyes. Some faced food and shelter scarcity. Some lacked the security and faced other kinds of suffering as they entered the classroom. It was heartbreaking for me as a teacher. But it angered me when I was told that it is my duty as a Malay KP, that I should look into the matters that are affecting some of the Malay students: one of the issues was smoking and the other was the lack of motivation. Again, the issue arises once more. This made me question, "Has teacher education failed to teach teachers of any race to reach out to students of any race?" Should not that be the job of all teachers, to reach out to all students no matter what their colour is? Smoking is a national issue and lack of motivation — should it not be the responsibility of all teachers to be as engaging as possible? Eisner (2002) pointed out that "ultimately, the growth of students will go no farther than the growth of those who teach them" (p. 384).

From my experiences in school, I cannot help but look at myself as a leader in my own family. How my students' experiences in their own lives have shaped my identity as a mother of three young toddlers. When I was a young student, I ensured that I studied and worked very hard to prove to myself that I would succeed on my own merits. And thus, I worked hard as a working mother to ensure that my children will have the best love, care and education. From there on, I feel I am unable to separate my personal identity from my career identity. This is who I am and I cannot lead separate lives. I cannot tell my students that it is too bad that they are not able to make it in life while I ensure that my own children will.

In school, I am a teacher first to my students, a coach and friend to my colleagues. I only put my HOD hat on when I am dealing with administration matters and having to make decisions. Otherwise I am what I am.

The Inquiry

What matters is that lives do not serve as models; only stories do that. And it is a hard thing to make up stories to live by. We can only retell and live by the stories we have read or heard. We live our lives through texts. They may be read, or chanted, or experienced electronically, or come to us like murmurings of our mothers, telling us what conventions demand. Whatever their form or medium, these stories have formed us all; they are what we must use to make new fiction, new narratives (Heilbrun, 1988, p. 37).

Narrative inquiry is an approach to understanding human experience (Clandinin & Connelly, 2000). In understanding my own experience, I draw at least three emerging themes in my narrative: the first, the role of self-identity in shaping the pupils under my charge. Second, the struggle to reconcile the importance of academic results and character development and the third, leadership. In the inquiry portion, I would use two approaches: (i) personal reflection and self-study as a methodology in my personal sense-making quest, and (ii) co-learning. Personal reflection and self-study allow me to look deep into myself while "moving away from self" (Loughran *et al.*, 2004). Co-learning happens when I discover that the role of who I am, my own self-identity has helped to shape me as a teacher, as an educator. My own personal beliefs have helped me to be the teacher that I want to be. As I looked deeper into myself, I discovered that what I had gone through as a child has impacted me a lot in shaping the person that I am today. I grew up in a mixed parentage environment. My mother is of Arab descent. She had the support of her rich and influential family. Her father was a philanthropist and well-known among not only the Malay/Muslim community but also among Singaporeans. Her marriage to my father, an Indonesian Malay, was not approved by the family. Thus, they were ostracised by my mother's family. As I was growing up, I understood the situation as this: Malays are poor, lazy and unsuccessful, because that was the impression I got. I was confused as to what I should call myself. I was even confused because my father was neither poor nor lazy. He was a successful businessman. I certainly did not want to be ostracised. I did not do anything wrong and the only way to prove to myself and my mother's family that this notion was not true was for me to excel in whatever I did. I studied really hard and I made sure I got into the express stream and eventually into a junior college. When I came to my first school, the first people that I wanted to work with were kids like me who thought that they were not given a place in the society simply because their families were falling apart, or because they lack the cultural capital. That was why I was driven to help Ah Teck and

Ashraf. Kindness can change people. It touches people's heart. When my father died when I was 14, my mother refused my grandmother's help. She wanted to make it on her own. But my mother was a kind person. She helped others who sought her help with the very little that we had. The people whom she has helped have talked about her kindness and how it had changed their lives.

The second theme was about how I struggled to reconcile between the importance of academic results and developing character. I had never been posted to a premium school. The first and the current school I am in are similar in profile. 80% of the student population comes from disadvantaged families. The current Singapore system measures success in the form of percentage of students who passed the GCE "O"-Level exams and those who scored distinctions. I am wondering why schools cannot define what success means to them, especially in today's context where a university degree is not equivalent to success. Looking at my students, I felt that I was a liar, telling them every day that they would go to the polytechnic when I knew, the four-year runway is too short for them to prove anything. What I wanted to tell them was that it is all right to take a longer route to success and after all, life is not about possessing the piece of paper in their hands, but who they are and the values they acquire that will help them live life happily and meaningfully. No doubt that as a teacher, our job is to motivate and set targets but not all students possess the same learning style and interest.

The third theme centres around leadership. I felt that because there was a lack of mentorship, I was drawn to the leadership track. The most important aspect is the fact that I know my role well in developing others and filling the void.

In analysing myself, I felt that comments from significant others helped me to discover and deconstruct my story. Through the group discussions, the tensions and difficulties that I have been facing throughout my career trajectory were better identified, and that released some of the tensions. One such example that surfaced during the discussions was that the lack of confidence in me was because of the lack of mentorship.

Conclusions

Narrative inquiry has contributed to new insights about how a teacher perceives the teaching career, how important it is to have a vision and how important it is to build personal beliefs about education. Getting inside the narrative allowed my identities as a classroom teacher, leader and person come together. It enabled me to monitor my own learning journey so that I can be more attuned to the challenges of my own career trajectory, and to the fact that what the prospective KPs need the most is the support in their pursuit to balance the demands of the classroom and the students and the demands of getting the education policy right.

References

Aoki, T. T., Carson, T. R., & Favaro, B. J. (1983). Understanding situational meanings of curriculum inservice acts: Implementing, consulting, inservicing. Department of Secondary Education, Faculty of Education, University of Alberta.

Bruner, J. (1990). *Acts of meaning*. Cambridge, MA: Harvard University Press.

Bruner, J. (2002). *Making stories: Law, literature, life*. Cambridge, MA: Harvard University Press.

Clandinin, D. J. & Connelly, F. M. (2000). *Narrative inquiry: Experience and story in qualitative research*. San Francisco: Jossey-Bass, Inc. 211 pages.

Conle, C. (2000). Narrative inquiry: Research tool and medium for professional development. *European Journal of Teacher Education*, 23(1), pp. 49–63.

Dewey, J. (1958). *Experience and nature*. New York: Dover Publications.

Eisner, E. W. (2002). *The arts and the creation of mind*. Yale University Press.

Heilbrun, C. G. (1988). *Writing a woman's life*. New York: Ballantine Books.

Loughran, J. & Russell, T. (2004). *Improving teacher education practices through self-study*. New York: Routledge.

Pinar, W. F. (2004). *What is curriculum theory?* Lawrence Erlbaum Associates.

Chapter 30
My Life in (Jigsaw) Pieces

Vivian RODRIGUES

My Pre-Service Days

From the moment I took the teachers' pledge in Lecture Theatre 2 in the old Teachers' Training College at Bukit Timah, I knew my life had changed but I was not too sure if it was for the better. Back then, I was the only student in my year to take Physical Education (PE) with Literature and so I found that my classmates in PE were different from my classmates in Literature. Not only were they a physically different set of people, they were also different socially and psychologically. The differences were as varied and interesting as oil is to water. Whilst I seemed to be a part of this overall "jigsaw puzzle" that constituted my life as a trainee, I still had not determined where exactly I fit and could see my future lying ahead in pieces.

Geographically, the old teacher training facility was built on a hill that had also segregated the PE campus from the general academics campus. The students had a special name for it. The PE students were called the ones from "downhill" and the general academic students were called the ones from "uphill". All the classes held for PE were in the campus closest to the main road back in the day. It was also where all the PE facilities lay. The PE students seemed to be on the fringe. Held apart. Staying aloof.

The impact on me personally was that it set the tone of self-reliance throughout my teaching career. I showered and changed quickly instead of gossiping in the shower rooms and rushed straight to the Literature class, when everyone was off to their Sciences or Mathematics classes together. And after Literature classes I walked back to the PE campus alone as all the Literature students had classes within the same "uphill" campus. I found my lonely trudge a task to be repeated, day in and day out. It was neither something that I had chosen for myself nor one that I enjoyed. It was out of my control. Added to this, sometimes my lunchtimes would not coincide with my PE classmates whom I most enjoyed being with and I would spend hours apart before I saw them again.

But life went on and I managed to come to terms with it. To be alone with myself was valuable thinking time. I had friends in class when I was "in class" and that would have to do. I learnt more about myself than I had in my previous years as a student. Too many a time had the class been asked to group up with others and I looked around to find myself without a partner. The students who found instant solidarity and support were ones who had been sharing classes and group work from the very beginning of their tenure at the Institute. I knew where I was weak and was determined to be stronger. I came to the conclusion that I needed to work on interpersonal and communication skills in order to fit instantly and anywhere like a generic jigsaw puzzle piece. Humour was a great asset in every sense; it placed me well in any initial interactions with someone new. I had to be, if I wanted to survive the next four years.

Further, I learnt that if I wanted to work well, especially in a group, I had to be vocal and make connections with others quickly. I had to be dependable and even more so because the others did not know me quite so well. I had to be affable and treat others in a way that was accommodating so that people were willing to work with me. On their parts, I sampled and experienced a multitude of different, and sometimes rather trying personalities but they educated and matured me in a rapid way. I grew up quickly in those first few months at the National Institute of Education (NIE) and found "friends" in classes I attended quickly. Despite the odds, my new-found set of skills brought me associations quicker than ever. There was seldom a moment where I would walk into the room and not know someone's name. But the knowledge of the people around me was sadly very superficial. It was here that I started to nurture a not-so-friendly disagreement with the old adage of "quality versus quantity". If it were true, my short interactions with other trainees would have been absorbed at a deeper level. As I had revealed in the earlier paragraphs, I was never around one group long enough to be able to develop lasting relationships. Comparatively, it was easier for my course mates to develop such permanent connections with each other as they were taking more common courses. I had numerous acquaintances but no real friends and though I had someone to sit with if I wanted to, I still felt inferior and lonely in a crowd. Though I was a part of this superior jigsaw, I was out of place and kept trying to fit in. Should jigsaws not have pieces that naturally have a place to fit? I was at a loss to find mine. There was this deep cavity where a sense of security should have been. This would manifest as a recurring theme throughout my teaching career.

On reflection, I wonder just how much of the actual me my classmates knew. I was so wrapped up in trying to achieve a harmony between the worlds that I wonder if I had become something or someone else unconsciously. Soon, the other "me" became so natural that the change was unnoticeable. Was I the poster girl for the self-determination theory? Had my motivations internalised this active need for external accomplishment such that I transformed into something that I was not meant to be? I now realise that those certain behaviours and personal values of the time, though I doubt reflected the real me, had ensured my survival and very possibly came at the right time in my life. Previous incidents of my past had developed me into an immature and impatient girl who felt as though she could do everything on her own. I didn't despise the loneliness then. NIE taught me that I could not be that girl anymore. I needed people.

My Survival Stage

When I started to work in my new school upon graduating, I had hoped (and perhaps too deeply) that this sense of disjointedness and loneliness would change. I was finally in a school, with a set timetable, with a set department and a set way of doing things. I was looking forward to fitting into the rote of mundane working life just so I would have the more stable relationships that were absent in my training life. I knew the school I was assigned to was an elite school and was known for its academics as well as sports. In addition, it was steeped in Catholic tradition and was an all-boys school (I got along better with boys than I did with girls). I had hoped for these two qualities in my naiveté, thinking it was simply the best combination for me. I could hardly contain my excitement and counted down the days till my start.

All my hopes and dreams for a fulfilling work life slowly dissipated as water does in a dry Saharan desert. I eventually found that my very new and my very first professional attachment soon promised none and I felt cheated. In my new predicament, there were neither relationships to be found nor deeper contacts. I had looked around for new teachers to feel some sense of support and camaraderie but could not initiate an iota as the others were too wrapped up in their own pressures and were trying to swim as desperately as I did in the deep end that we were thrown into. Why were all of us drowning when we should have been in a thriving nurturing environment? The answer lay in the absence of a mentor programme and new teacher support. But why did a school of such high repute not have an adequate support system for its beginning teachers? Why were so many of us sinking and left to our own devices to muddle our way through?

The school, as mentioned before, was a strict Catholic all-boys school and in that sense it explained why it was so resistant to changes. We, Catholics, have been known to be rather stubborn in our ways. Even the New Testament version of the Bible that was approved by the Pope himself was not accepted till the latter half of this century! The school had been forced to accept more female teachers when previously it was predominantly male (which was unusual in the Singapore context where most teachers were women). Added to this, most teachers were old boys of the school who had had a rigorous Catholic education in those same hallowed halls. Support was a reward and not a given, in their chauvinistic opinions. I was a female teacher, routinely, who taught PE, making me the most atypical sort of female in the education service that they had come across or experienced.

The majority thought me to be rather bizarre. Remember that most of my colleagues were in their 40s or 50s in addition to being male — they had come from a time when women were a lot more repressed in terms of outlook and freedom. I represented everything that was against what they were brought up to believe as tradition and culture. The Asian orientation and opinions of women in the mid-1990s added more salt to the wound and they would not budge from their beliefs. We still seemed, at least to me, to be behind the Western way of thinking. Thus, in a show of "xenophobia", they stayed away and would not interact.

When I would ask one where a certain resource was, they would wave me off, without looking up from marking students' notebooks, in the direction of the resource room, believing that either I did not have the gumption to try looking for it myself before asking or that I needed to be spoon-fed the solution. The one situation that had the greatest effect on me was when I had returned from maternity leave. Many administrative procedures had changed when I was away and I had not been told of the new developments upon my return. I was asked to be in charge of booking buses for the whole school to travel to the nearby Sports Stadium for Sports Day, which I had thought I had done to the letter. Unbeknownst to me, the system of booking buses for outside events had changed.

The day before the event, when I started to go through my checklist to make sure everything was completed for the event, I realised to my absolute horror, that the booking had not gone through to the administration or been approved. Instead of working on finding a solution to the sudden discovery with me, my Vice-Principal (VP) chose to discipline me with a vociferous tirade that lasted ten minutes for all of the office to hear. He did not want to listen to any explanation. In his mind, I should have known the changes although I was away and done the job well. It was as if to him a simple slip up, though easily rectified, had labelled me inefficient and confirmed that I was not worth as much as the men in my department.

There are many ways that situation could have played out after the debacle but I chose for it to further frustrate and anger me to the point that I would imagine walking into the VP's office and throwing my resignation form in his face. I looked around at the so-called "men" in my office and none of them, not one, stood up for me or corrected the VP to remind him that I had indeed been away for three months and many things had changed within that time.

Again, when I pause to reflect at this part of my journey, I am suddenly aware that I may have been a bit too sensitive. I felt like an outcast yet again and perhaps even more so after such an embarrassing and public humiliation. My desperate need to finally find true connections with people had already heightened my senses to an unusual point and then to be faced once again with such a situation, where I was on the outside looking in, was all in all just too much to bear. With the "bus incident", whatever meagre hopes I had were thoroughly squashed. In my despair, I may have been unreasonable and perhaps too quick with my assessments of the old boys. They treated me as they would a new male teacher, which was fair now as I think about it in hindsight, allowing me to struggle and endure the shelling I received. It was the only treatment they knew.

I may have been harsh in writing off the other new teachers as well. There may have been critical turning points in the early part of my career, which I may have been blissfully oblivious to in my despondency. How I wish this present epiphany had taken hold of my senses then. It would have saved me a lot of heartbreak!

So here I still found myself years on, running around in shorts and tennis skirts, making myself heard amongst the boys and teachers as real as can be. In front of the students, I was excitable, full of energy and was constantly in a run instead of a walk. I guffawed.

I did not laugh pretty. My skin was as dark as night, as not only did I teach under the sun most of the time, I trained and coached others during my off hours. I was the grim reaper with a smile and I seemed to toll the death knell for the old ways. I did not fit the world that was their jigsaw. They did all they could to make me more acceptable and break my spirit to accept the old ways, the way things were and the ways they did not want to change. But a puzzle piece cannot be forced into a certain part of the jigsaw that it is not meant to be placed in. There is a natural place for such things.

Soon, the pressure to conform was starting to swallow me in ways that caused me to silently and internally combust. I would be upset most days and more often than not, rue the day I put ink to paper where I signed my soul off to the Ministry of Education (MOE). I had years more of this. I could not bear going into school. I did not know how I was to ever survive.

My Discovery Stage — The Turning Point

Academically, I was given subjects to teach that I had little training in. Some elements of Science and Mathematics escaped me as they did when I was myself in school as a student. I never felt a kinship for those subjects and I possibly never will. Those subjects were everything I was not. I was more tactile and emotive. Expressive and unpredictable. The English language was no challenge in my hands. The Arts will always be something that inspire me to do better, to go bigger. I was never at a loss of imaginative and resourceful ideas when it came to such subjects. The combination of such natural talent and true affinity to English and Drama encouraged me to want to teach others. But I was not given that opportunity to touch lives in a way I wanted to. Instead I struggled with the "black and white" binds of Science and Mathematics teaching. I made a lot of mistakes along the way and what frustrated me was that this could all have been avoided from the beginning with some support from the school.

On the upside, I learnt a lot along the bumpy trails of my tribulations and my old self-resilience kicked in, that is, only after I stopped feeling so sorry for myself. I now knew where within the resource room I could find materials, after much diving into the dusty corners and rusty shelves on my own. I befriended the administration office and made no further errors when it came to paperwork. Through much trial and error, I started to enjoy Mathematics and Science teaching. I endeavoured to take my post-graduate diploma in Life Sciences and found that I indeed had the aptitude for Science and was thoroughly enjoying the course. Yes, I was disappointed that I had not found what I wanted from this school and did not quite fit perfectly but I was forced to find my own way, which is probably what the "old boys" had wanted to see. Still, the cavity of insecurity existed. And though I was finding a better fit now that I knew and understood the inner workings of my professional environment, I still did not fit perfectly.

The turning point came when I was assigned a facilitator's role for co-operative games at a staff retreat. A role which I performed, to the best of my abilities, being the one for which I was trained. Moreover, I had had many years of experience in youth and school camps. I showed the "old boys" through my successful activities facilitation that I was as good as my laugh, which was neither weak, indecisive nor deceptive. I was indeed a boy like them but in a skirt, possessing strong qualities, and was able to toughen up and get on with it. I called a spade a spade and was sincere with my words as well as with my resolute actions. Suddenly I deserved their attention. I deserved their help. From that point I got exactly that. My learning journey in that school then went on overdrive. I started to accomplish work at superfast speed and got things done. The work done showed quality that the "boys" expected to see and that I unpredictably and surprisingly now expected of myself. I had proven that I was indeed good in my job and had worked hard to get there. As a result, I finally started to build the connections I had longed for. There was a much stronger possibility of fitting than ever before.

With the benefit of hindsight, I am able to personally attest to the fact that with enough perseverance and persistence, eventually things do turn out for the better. This situation brings to mind my early days at NIE where I was the original misfit. It was there that I learnt how to identify skills to survive and get through the hard times. I managed to come out on top with little scarring. It was the same case here a couple of years after my graduation. Eventually, I got on my feet and got on with my work. I found my own feet again, albeit a couple of battle wounds on the way but it felt good. I was stronger than I thought I was and found light at the end of a tunnel, which I thought would never end.

My Stabilisation Phase

Five years on, I was in an excellent position in the school. I was being trained to be Head of Physical Education. I was a mentor (we started a mentorship programme finally) and was helping others. In addition, I was training other new teachers and was a supervisor for trainee teachers from NIE, twice to thrice a year. I had promised myself that no one would go through what I did. I was successfully seeing this through with a mentorship programme and a handbook which I designed. I felt good about what I was doing and had a deep sense of purpose. I finally had a voice and instead of wanting to become one of the "boys", I could be myself in my own right.

Further, there were more females on staff and there was a second woman on the PE team. The greater influx of females had toned down the male testosterone in the environment. More than that, these women brought ideas and initiatives that softened the outlook of the staff and the austere surroundings to the school. There was greater community spirit amongst the staff and everyone seemed to be helping one another a lot more than in the days when I first started. Physically, the staff room was feminised, with regular tea and cake times in the lounge area accompanied by cheerful staff banter, colourful soft toys and jovial family portraits at desks. My old PE teacher (and one of my favourites) from junior college, Mr. Tong, was the new Principal and he knew me well enough to know what I was capable of. He was too an "old boy" of the school but was in no way like the old boys that were teaching there. Firstly, he was in his late 30s, which made him a very young principal. He was a breath of fresh air and made everyone feel like they had an important role in the school. Mr. Tong had an open-door policy in his office where anyone and everyone could walk in and air their grievances. He took it all in his stride with a genuine smile and oftentimes, a teacher would leave less upset than when he or she had first walked in. If he knew you were struggling, he did not wait for you to get into a fix, but gently nudged you in the right direction and made you feel like you had done it all by yourself at the same time. The framework of the "jigsaw" that seemed to exist in the forefront faded in the background with Mr. Tong. No one needed to fit into such constrictive confines. We suddenly wanted to teach here and do well, not only for ourselves but also for him. What the power of allegiance! As the jigsaw piece that never found a fit, a sudden perfect fit did not seem so important anymore.

My Head of Science was a lovely woman, who was very motherly and looked after us like we were her own, always making sure we were well-prepared and that we understood our subject. She would often accidentally meet you alone in the staff lounge every few weeks to ask how you were doing and if things were going on well in the classroom. When a parent had any queries about teaching, she would be the one to make the call to the parent and quell any fears. She was always there for us and stood by us to work out problems and find solutions. And she did this all with a gentle and reassuring voice. I felt important and I belonged somewhere finally. I had a family! Things looked like they were finally on the up. I was doing well and felt connected to my job, the people and the place I worked in. Despite all this, the old feelings of wanting more started to stir again within me and when I realised what they were, I was taken aback. What was wrong with me? Did I not have most of the things I had wanted initially? Why did I feel like I was left with an ever-widening hole once again?

Stumbling Blocks to Stabilisation

Upon reflection I now realise that this was also around the time that my first marriage started to break down and I needed to feel a sense of worth. My struggles with the school initially emerged out of a pure desire at having to feel like I belonged and that I was doing well at what I was trained for. That did not exist any longer. I did belong! I was doing well! But with a divorce looming, little by little, the drive and newfound energy I had at school was drained out of me with what I had to face at home. Despite working so hard to be accomplished at work, I was quite the opposite at home. Regardless of the hard work at home, things did not fit and fall into place like it did at work. My "home" jigsaw was falling apart! My personal issues were exactly that deep dark hole, which I had discovered. I desperately wanted to feel like I was still empowered and could still hang on to the whole happy picture that was my life. At home, I was powerless to do anything to prevent this awful thing from happening despite my best efforts at saving my marriage. But I knew what I could do was change the course of my career. At least, I had the power to change this part of my life for the better. I thought I had found the answer, when abruptly, something else rendered me powerless to stop it from happening.

My Science Department Head, Annie, developed a highly aggressive form of liver cancer. The fact that this disease riddled her body in the most grievous ways brought a lot of agony to many of us who deeply respected her. In my last year in that school, I watched her grow from a woman that totally encompassed you in her uplifting personality, to one who was a shadow of her former self. Bravely, she kept coming to school in between her lapses with the disease, stoically trying to belie the outward regression. As a department, we segmented bits of her workload to make it easier for her to handle. We were happy to do so as she had taken such good care of us and now it was our turn to help her. We hoped. We prayed. But Annie lost her fight very quickly and it took her eight months to waste away. So many of us went to her funeral and we paid our respects by laying flowers as she lay in state. I could not bear the thought of being in the school any longer and having so many memories of her and our conversations in the different sections of the school. I had lost again and my "work" jigsaw puzzle was in pieces. Without Annie, we all felt broken up.

The professional and social comfort that I had fought so hard for slowly dissipated in the ensuing months. The pleasant working environment had not changed — I still had the respect of my colleagues and the support of the other women but the small and recognisable important pieces that made life at this school satisfying were slowly disappearing. As my jigsaw started to dislodge with the bumps and humps I now faced, so did the hole start to widen further.

The hole could not merely be closed with passage of time, unfortunately. I had to make a change if I wanted to survive divorce and death.

My Experimentation and Activism Stage

I applied and successfully got the job of Head of Department, Physical Education, at an all-girls Catholic school. Maybe it was here that I would feel at home. Maybe it was here that I could get empowerment and the new family I was seeking for. Upon my arrival though, I faced yet again a situation that was out of my control. Internal shuffling meant that I lost the Head of Department post, even before I got there. Yet again, the "power" I was seeking was wrested away from me and I found myself unhappy and discontented from the very beginning.

I did try to make the best of it. I was ready for this new environment having taught now for six years. I knew what to expect and my strengths in the job. It needs to be said that the environment was a much more supportive one and was made up mainly of women. However, the new Head had no experience, not having taught the subject before. I found that I had to babysit her through some modules and it felt like I was doing the job of two people. The other two women in my department were wonderful but had no voice when it came to taking decisions on important things. When I dared to show initiative to get a project moving forward, I was generally frowned on as I had overstepped my boundaries. There existed a highly feminised approach to hierarchy.

Had I gone "from the pan and into the fire"? Why did the women in my school seem to be so highly sensitised to my methods?

As I reflect on it now, I come to another realisation that I was probably desensitised to general female insecurities as a result of working with a large group of men for the longest time. I had ignored my feminine side and wiles to get things done and had approached my teaching in a very masculine way. What had I become? Could I change into something that I was meant to be? Was I meant to be more "feminine" in the first place? How had this affected my teaching and my approach to my new set of colleagues? I recalled my first metamorphosis as a trainee. It had happened again without me knowing! It took a while but I eventually realised that this was not the place where "empowerment" could be found. The power needed to come from my own self-realisation and I needed to look nowhere else but within. I came to understand that self-knowledge of my skills and abilities as well as the definition of power was all up to me. It did not matter whether or not I was the Head of any department. I knew what I could do and I knew my attributes well. I knew that in the struggle for empowerment in a place that provided none, the only loser of the battle was myself. I did not need power. Once again, I was in search for connections with people who understood me and who would fit into my life at a deeper level. I could not find that here. I simply did not fit yet again.

My "Taking Stock" and Final Stabilisation

I tolerated a year and a half before I applied to an international system and successfully secured a place. I have been here for the last six years teaching the International Baccalaureate (IB). There have been ups and downs that come naturally with any job but I have found a place that has accepted my masculine approach to teaching. I have also found the freedom to be myself when I needed to be. I found that in this new place, I could lean on my prior strengths at being independent and self-reliant but still have a support system that welcomed weaknesses and inexperience as something to be improved upon and not punished. They took mistakes in my subject area as indications to the lack of knowledge with IB and the mistakes were not a focal point in my work appraisals. Rather they took it as an opportunity to diagnose and send me for training to upgrade myself. When I had returned to teaching after my second and third child, they made sure my relief teacher was still in class with me for an additional week to do an accurate and concise handover. If you were ill and notified the school, the staff believed that you were truly ill and the administration did not require a doctor's certificate to say you were so. We were treated like mature adults.

In addition to finally finding a system that I enjoyed, I have carried on board the lessons I have learnt in my prior schools. I know my abilities and I know my strengths. I know that self-empowerment comes from within. I know sometimes, as the French say, "C'est la vie", such is life that one can be knocked down often but what is important is that one gets up every single time.

Finally, in retrospect, my teaching life seemed to revolve around finding a place that I could be happy at and, like a jigsaw puzzle piece, to fit in. Till this day, I regard my school, the place where I spend most of my waking hours in away from my true family, my second home. It meant more than dearly to me that I was settled and got on well with the people and schematics within the school environment. Despite espousing qualities of self-reliance, self-actualisation and independence on the surface, underneath it all, I seem to have this profound need for human contact and relationship. What engineered me this way? The only answer lies in the finger-pointing blame directed squarely at my blue collar parents who were never really around to support my learning in school, my progress academically or my sporting career. Yes, because they worked hard to put food on the table and ensured that I was clothed and fed, I am eternally grateful. But in my formative and growing up years, I was mainly left to my own devices when they could not and sometimes would not be there, though I desperately wanted them to. Case in point was the instance where I filled out my own Primary School Leaving Examination (PSLE) schools nomination form myself. My parents did not even want to know my choices. They never understood why I wanted to play a variety of sports when one would do. Once, I had broken my foot at a football game and my father refused to take me to the hospital, saying that I had chosen to play the sport and would pay for the consequences myself. My classmate took me there in the end. Not once did they even attend any of my concerts when I played in a military band. Neither school ceremonies nor sports days where I won awards annually, though I pestered them to. I was proud of my achievements and wanted them to be proud as well. It is highly probable that I sought recognition and love from people other than my parents so as to feel like my existence was justified. With some shame, I admit I was rather attention-seeking in this respect and it may have affected my career somewhat. I was never anywhere long enough to create much of an impact or develop in the way my classmates, who graduated with me, had. They went on to become Vice Principals and Heads of Department way before I did and well within their first 10 years at a school. I do take responsibility for this part of my life, which is of my own doing.

Experimentation and the Future

Every now and then, I do doubt that I would ever cease to feel the need to keep searching for something better. My 14 years of searching have ingrained a rather undesirable trait of "itchy feet". After six years in the international school system, happy with where I am and what I have, I have once again started to feel stirrings in my undisciplined podiatric extremities as I had with my first professional attachment in a local school. As it is for now, I am embarking on another new stage in my teaching to a learning phase with further education. What I want from this, I am not entirely sure as yet. What has changed are the choices I make with respect to my career advancements. If I were to make a change, it will not be in search for relationships and a sense of security anymore. The support and love I was seeking at the outset from outsiders, all those years, I have realised is right here at my own home, from my loving husband and extraordinary children. Everything else is just secondary. I, finally, am at peace because I fit. I fit perfectly.

Part 6:
Research on the Narrative Inquiry Practice of Course Participants and Instructors

Overview

Yanping FANG

Part 6 presents three studies on the narrative experiences of the teacher participants. The first two were written respectively by David and Sonia, members of the book's editorial team, who attended my postgraduate class in 2012 and 2013, respectively. They each provided a reflective narrative of the collaborative restorying experience in their Group Projects, a major course component requesting group members to read, provide feedback to each other's narratives and analyse them with a goal to identify patterns and make meaning in light of the course readings. (Refer to the Epilogue for more details about the Group Project.) The third chapter, an academic research paper, was written by the course instructors on the emotional work of teachers in interacting with their students based on analysis of the narratives written by a class of 33 participants in 2011. The authors took a step back and looked at the teachers' narrative experiences again from "outside in" to describe them and understand their importance to teacher learning and teachers' work in Singapore.

David's group began their Group Project with a feeling of uncertainty. They were trying to figure out what the Project expected them to do exactly as they needed a structure not only in analysing their narratives in light of the course readings but also in analysing the group discourse, beyond simply retelling. Meanwhile, he feels that this uncertainty had led his group to unexpected richness in learning. With different and sometimes contradictory views shared on each other's narratives, tensions and discomfort arose in the group. It was, he believes, the group members' strong sense of community and mutual trust developed over time as they took courses together that enabled them to negotiate and embrace the differences, and eventually reconsider their own narratives from others' perspectives. In doing so they reached new understandings of their long-held beliefs and came to terms with their own long-harboured painful memories. This reflective process is captured by Jackie's (Part 3) and Ting Ting's (Part 2) narratives in this book. They showcase the meaningful collective retelling experience which has eventually liberated each of them and taught them to let go.

In developing a narrative of her Group Project, Sonia went back to the very first day of the course when she chose to sit with four familiar former course mates who learned more about one another through drawing their individual symbolic tokens on their "name cards" as a way to introduce themselves to the class. She then introduced the group members by presenting their career cycles and the critical incidents from their narratives. This serves as a context for the exploratory journey the group travelled in finding their common metaphor, a poem by Lord Tennyson, to tie up their meaning-making process in the Group Project. The five Brooks flowing with one purpose stand for the dynamics of her group's discourse and decision-making processes in which five teachers from four different races, teaching different subjects at different school levels, tried to come up with a group metaphor. The poem blends together the lyrical notes of the five Brooks flowing down merrily, taking twists and turns against all odds in celebrating the lives of teachers, filled with rewarding adventures in learning and growth.

Fang and Yeo[1] reported findings from their analysis of 33 teacher narratives written by participants who attended the postgraduate course on curriculum and teacher learning through narrative inquiry in 2011. They situated the emotional work of individual teachers in managing teacher–student relationships in the social, cultural and institutional contexts of Singapore, a high-performing and highly demanding education system. They captured the emotional understanding of the teachers through their encounters with students by focusing particularly on three key areas of the emotional work: grappling with the physical distances between teachers and students created in the pursuit of academic performance; finding hope and commitment by bridging the social–cultural differences with students; and deriving the ethical and moral meanings of teaching and understanding the nature of teacher–student nested knowing (Lyons, 1990). The findings, in many ways, reflect the emotional work of all teachers who have attended the postgraduate course over the years. They further suggest that building inquiry through sharing and writing life narratives can lead to deepening of teachers' personal practical knowledge (Clandinin, 1985) and self-understanding (Kelchtermans, 2005), which are critical to bringing about continuous professional learning for teachers.

References

Clandinin, J. (1985). Personal practical knowledge: A study of teachers' classroom images. *Curriculum Inquiry*, 15 (4), 361–385.

Kelchtermans, G. (2005). Teachers' emotions in educational reforms: Self-understanding, vulnerable commitment and micropolitical literacy. *Teaching and Teacher Education*, 21, 995–1006.

Lyons, N. (1990). Dilemmas of knowing: Ethical and epistemological dimensions of teachers' work and development. *Harvard Educational Review*, 60 (2), 159–180.

---

[1]It was a joy to co-teach this course with John Yeo from August 2010 to November 2011 and write this piece together. John's energy, enthusiasm to learn and caring for the students were inspirational.

Chapter 31

The Collegial Factor in Narrative Inquiry — How Group Meaning-Making Helps Let Go Deep-Seated Traumas

David Yean Sin LIEW

As part of the requirements for our master's module on narrative inquiry, we formed groups of four to five in order to act as reflective agents for our teammates' narratives. In our team, there were five members with very varied backgrounds in terms of experience. There was one member who taught at primary school level, two secondary school Mother Tongue teachers, one mathematics and physical education teacher who had done a stint in an international school in Thailand, and the last being a junior college history and art teacher who had spent the last five years teaching in a polytechnic. Four of us had taught for 13 years and one had taught for six years by the time we took the course in 2012. Save for one, all had worked at managerial levels in their respective jobs. All had been involved in curriculum development.

The task at hand was to firstly develop our respective individual narratives about our lives as teachers. These narratives would then be examined and analysed as raw data for our team assignment, with the aim of understanding how these narratives were formed and how they represented a growth trajectory for the teacher. What transpired in the course of development can best be described as "organic". There were very few "rules of engagement" that were thought out at length, apart from the general agreement that all involved treat the provided narratives as data, as a reminder to ourselves not to make immediate and unconscious assessments based on our own predilections. Perhaps the only "rule" that was set was to adopt a spirit of providing "feedback" or "critique" through the lens of restorying by someone other than the narrator. Thus, questions were not meant to challenge or seek justification, but instead, to clarify and by extension, strengthen the narrative by situating our group inquiry within what Clandinin & Connelly (2000) called "a three-dimensional narrative inquiry space" and creating "meditational spaces" for reconstructing a collective knowing (Golombek & Johnson, 2004).

We lacked agreed mechanisms pertaining to resolutions of any potential conflicts. This had not even occurred to us until it was raised during a much later class session. By then, the team had already met a few times, shared our stories, and even had at least one revision each for our respective narratives after discussing it with each other. On reflection, this was something we put down to the fact that our team members were hardly strangers to each other. We had been in the same master's programme since January that year and while everyone had not worked together on the same team before, we had worked with each other in other groups in the course of the year. As such, there was already a familiarity that helped reduce the inhibitions that may have existed in the case of sharing personal narratives with strangers. The formation of the team itself was somewhat based on this sense of comfort with each other. We joked that we five formed a team largely on the basis that we happened to be sitting in that cluster in the classroom when the call for group formation was made. However, when examined further in light of the collegial aspect of our team's work methods, the "convenience of location" that seemed to underscore our team's formation also speaks to this sense of collegiality. As our seating positions in the classroom were not fixed, we tended to choose seats with people we knew and had good rapport with. When projected onto the assignment procedure, it became a critical cornerstone for the strength of the work that emerged.

The collegiality and good relations among the team members thus tempered all the discussions and reflection that transpired. Examined in context, it helped defuse any potential apprehension and vulnerability towards sharing personal stories and by extension put the queries that came as part of restorying in a non-confrontational or judgmental manner. This was evidenced by one narrative that the group came across as rather "disengaged", with a group member most bluntly describing it as being "unfeeling and indifferent". Without the constructive spirit of discussion that prevailed, the writer could have understandably felt seriously threatened by what seems to be an attack on her personal story.

On the contrary, in the process of forming this chapter, the narrator of that particular story reflected, at that juncture, that she felt no threat in terms of criticism of her story content, recognising that the critique was due to her own style of writing. Yet, in the middle of developing a group-based analysis, the narrator shared that she did feel some initial disappointment that most of her team, save one, appeared not to have grasped the deeper feelings embedded within her narration. In fact, this aspect seemed to be the most explicit area of contention. Some team members' first reaction to the narrative indicated that its tone distanced the narrator from the story, almost making it bland and emotionless. Initially, the narrator was reluctant to try her teammates' suggestion to bring herself closer to the narrative by citing specific incidents with more detail, while giving more credence to the expression of emotions. She believed, however, the existing mode of expression was more natural and therefore, more authentic a voice. It was in the meditational space that she was able to engage in the negotiation between herself and the group members as researchers on each other's narratives and establish a better understanding of who she was as a professional and how she viewed herself.

Given the positive atmosphere of the group discourse, she was able to reflect on her story in an attempt to understand why she had chosen to depict the incident in the way she did. In the end, she did not restructure the story but rather reconceptualised it. She recognised that her almost third person account was her own way of coping with the very painful episode of her experience of being a young teacher who had been maligned by a senior colleague. As a younger teacher newly posted to the school, she was enthusiastic about doing her best for her students and also contributing to the teaching and learning of the Chinese Language (CL). However, she was baffled and later hurt deeply by the fact that what seemed to be something so right to her was not readily accepted by her fellow CL teachers, especially so by the Head of Department (HOD) herself. The situation worsened as she gained her footing in the school and started to be recognised and affirmed by colleagues and superiors beyond the department. Her efforts to push for progress in the department's work were met with much resistance and apathy from the CL teachers, and eventually she was ostracised by them. This situation escalated to a breaking point when the HOD deliberately made her work on an item for a language camp, then cancelled it suddenly just when she was ready to present the item during the camp. She was deeply hurt and decided to approach the principal for help. Thereafter, the HOD's hostility towards her worsened and continued until the HOD retired at the end of the year. In the context of the narrative inquiry process, she sensed the discomfort in being too close to the story and its very powerful negative memories had the potential to distort the narrative, thus the need for distancing.

As an important outcome at the end of the exercise, this teammate had a near epiphany: becoming able to understand the events from the perspective of the perpetrator. The HOD's hostility and machinations had arisen from her own sense of insecurities and discomfort, for instance, the inability to use English effectively in the work setting and feeling challenged by much younger colleagues who are equipped with new ideas and are quick to learn. On a personal level, it allowed the narrator to bring the story out of a wholly personal level and review it within a holistic framework of teachers' lives. With the enlarged canvas offered by the narrative inquiry (NI) exercise, the narrator developed a far greater understanding and appreciation of the lives of Mother Tongue Language teachers, both her own and that of her counterparts in the field. Her perspective was no longer that of someone looking back, but instead someone who used her present to relook her past and by extension get a better understanding of that same present, albeit with a much broader scope of vision.

In the case of the narrative from the team member whose last tour of duty was in a polytechnic, sharing the story was an important aspect of his development. Recounting a difficult episode involving a former colleague and a student within an inappropriate relationship, the narrator was able to regain control of his part of the story as a result of the non-judgmental environment in which the group process took place. In that narrative, he had to investigate the case where a student he was going to fail for non-performance in a module had cited that her lack of performance was caused by the fact that she was involved in a relationship with a staff member, the one that he was assigned to investigate. He had to walk a very delicate tightrope when tasked by his superiors to investigate the allegedly inappropriate relationship between this colleague and the failing student. Up until that moment of restorying of this experience, this group member had held a nagging perception for years that he was somewhat responsible for the resignation of that colleague who, up to the point of the investigation, had been believed to be innocent of the charges.

In the course of the investigation, he uncovered the reality that this alleged relationship was known to many other staff members who chose to keep quiet. The accusing student had apparently repeated her story of the affair to almost anybody who came into earshot for such a long period that the idea of it being an illicit relationship had become difficult to hold, that is, this relationship had been seemingly acknowledged. On one hand, even though the narrating group member also felt that the student was deluded and his colleague was a victim of youthful misunderstanding, he had to face hostility from his colleagues for his seeming interference into the issue. On the other hand, he also had a debate with his own ethical premises over what seemed to be the institution's reluctance to act in defence of one of their own staff whose professional integrity was being challenged. From the outset, the student's track record of poor academic performance and social immaturity had made her accusation unsubstantiated, a flimsy attempt to divert attention from her academic failings. While coming forward to reveal their knowledge of the student's "revelations" did expose them to criticism of not investigating the claims, it was a lesser infraction letting a colleague go through the pain of official inquiries and investigations by the higher management over a seemingly trumped up charge. The eventual investigation by the external inquiry board exonerated the colleague but he resigned from service thereafter, leaving the narrating teacher (the group member) to wonder for years whether his own investigative action, driven by a firm adherence to his belief in professional ethics, had inadvertently caused the loss of a good teacher for the school. A central issue was addressed during the restorying among his group with varied experiences and backgrounds — whether his, the narrator's judgment call, made on what he believed to be ethical perceptions, had been a mistake. Without having to negotiate varied interpretations of the story from a third party perspective, the group had uniformity in the restorying — that the central issue of the narrative was that the narrator's sense of professional ethics was challenged not so much by the incident itself but by the manner in which it resolved itself, something that had not been within his own purview.

This aspect resonates with the belief within narrative inquiry that a valuable source of restorying comes from an "other" expert (Golombek & Johnson, 2004). In this instance, there was not only a single "other" but four others in the group to strengthen the value of the process. An added aspect for consideration is the fact that even though the narrator himself has had a long track record of experience in counselling, he was unable to resolve his own "demons", not for the want of ability, but rather the very basic fact that in situations like this, self-reflection can be overshadowed because a central player in the narrative is the analyser himself. This is in line with the practice of many medical practitioners who would actually seek treatment for themselves or their family members from other practitioners, even though they could enact this treatment themselves. Professional ethics aside, the underlying understanding is that this distancing is to allow for a more effective intervention due to the objectivity granted by decreased proximity.

Do Not be the Trapped Monkey and Let Go

In the course of preparing the project for presentation, one of the group members offered this story on how African tribesmen trapped the wily and elusive monkey. The hunters would take a hollowed-out gourd with a neck just large enough for a monkey's hand to reach in. Inside this gourd they would place tasty morsels highly prized by the simians, and then the gourd is left in an area frequented by monkeys. When the passing monkey investigates the gourd, it reaches in to grasp its prize, only to have its hand trapped inside as the fist closed around the titbit is too large to exit the narrow neck. Despite its vulnerability, the monkey continues to hold on, making it an easy pick for the waiting hunter.

This became the metaphor for the power of restorying for the group as we realised that the narrated incidents were very much like the morsels within the gourd for us. We inadvertently held onto them, grasping them tightly for the very ironic reason that the pain associated with the narrated experiences made them something not easily forgotten. By extension, despite being afflicted by the painful memories of their negative experiences, the narrators could not let them go, just like the monkey bent on obtaining the morsel in the gourd. In the case of the project team, restorying these experiences that had hitherto "trapped" the narrators actually allowed them to reconceptualise them and reintegrate them as learning points for growth rather than as painful scars that haunt them. Drawing on the adage that what does not kill you would actually make you stronger, the narrative inquiry process as explored by the project team allowed the members to see these experiences as milestones of their growth as professionals, rather than as millstones dragging them into despair. Ultimately, they came up with their own motto reflecting a contemporary parody of a wartime propaganda poster encouraging resilience in the face of adversity:

"Let go and grow".

References

Clandinin, D. J., & Connelly, F. M. (2000). *Narrative inquiry: Experience and story in qualitative research.* San Francisco: Jossey-Bass.

Golombek, P. R., & Johnson, K. E. (2004). Narrative inquiry as a mediational space: Examining emotional and cognitive dissonance. *Teachers and Teaching: Theory and Practice,* 10 (3), 307–327.

Hargreaves, A. (2000). Mixed emotions: Teachers' perceptions of their interactions with students. *Teaching and Teacher Education,* 16, 811–826.

Chapter 32
Five Brooks One Purpose

Sonia KHAN

Different contexts,
Different cultures, different stages,
Different emotions at different times,
Different subject specialisations,
Different challenges yet we criss-cross at some point.
So much is "Different"
Yet as teachers, our passion makes us one!
Our paths converged here and now.
Like a brook, we flow,
We "bicker", "babble", "chatter,"[1]
We keep moving on
Taking all in our stride in re-storying our own growth trajectories,
And facing the challenges that strike.
We interact with our past, present and future,
We interact with our own self or with others,
We try finding answers to a handful of questions,
We try braving the odds around us,
We are inexhaustible as we merge,

---

[1]Words taken from the poem "The Brook" written by Lord Alfred Tennyson (1865).

Not just among us five,
But with the community of teachers ...

S. Khan (June, 2013)

Five different people came together under one roof through a course module that introduced using narrative inquiry for teacher learning and development in the graduate programme in Curriculum and Teaching at National Institute of Education, Singapore. Nanban, a Tamil Singaporean teaching Chemistry; Peng You, a Chinese Singaporean teaching Mathematics; Dost, an Indian Singaporean teaching Physics; Kawan, a Malay Singaporean teaching Art; and I, Mitr, an Indian living in Singapore and teaching English Language and Literature in an international school.[2]

Even though the five of us taught different subjects and came from different cultural backgrounds, we felt connected as we all had one passion — passion for teaching. We shared the same concern — the betterment, progress and growth of our students and the same values — openness and respect for others. This gave us the rudder to flow together from any direction and share views even if contradictory, and most importantly, to be truthful in expressing our own opinions.

Sailing Inwards

On this journey, we were not looking outside to find answers to our teaching practices, or getting right into the critical aspects of a theory. We were not "conduits" who state their purpose as "flowing down to them from others" (Connelly & Clandinin, 1994, p. 147), from curriculum development, board policies, school restructuring. We were, for the first time in this Masters programme, venturing into the self. We were the landscapes of making a difference by ourselves, making a difference in our own understanding, thereby leading to transformations in students' lives. The most important

---

[2]All our names are pseudonyms and bear the same meaning, *friend*, in five different languages. All the four, except Mitr, taught in Ministry of Education schools.

questions were: Who am I? What do I know of myself? How do I make meaning of my actions? How do I interpret others' actions? How do I reinterpret my story and re-interpret it through the triggering questions posed by my friends, friends who are knowledgeable others and also teachers? As Connelly & Clandinin (1994) say, "if a teacher understands (can tell) the story of her own education, she will better understand (tell the stories of) her students' education" (p. 150).

Card writing: Peeping into the inner worlds

The first step to start on this meaningful journey was to ask what defines me as a teacher? What has been a key thread that has woven my entire journey as a teacher? Thus, we were triggered to look inside, to think, go back into the past, search and find a metaphor, the quintessence of self as a teacher. We could see the shift from a teacher as a conduit that follows to a teacher as an interactive landscape that creates.

We were given small cards to draw and write on. Kawan, an Information Communication and Technology (ICT) teacher and now a Head of the Department (HOD) with 12 years of teaching experience, identified herself as steadfast, the one who had spent 15 years in total in teaching. Peng You, a high school Mathematics teacher with seven years of teaching experience, had an artistic streak. She drew smileys and stated her interest in photography and use of symbols in her work. The most experienced was Dost, with almost two and a half decades in the profession. She has continually done different courses to upgrade herself so far and continues to do so. She gave credit to her students who let her keep going. I, Mitr, with 10 years of teaching experience, drew a road embedded in the heart. I had chosen this profession with all my heart and thus, tread it with all my heart and courage. It is pertinent for me to touch the hearts that I teach or meet in this beautiful and satisfying journey. "Touch the heart" is my motto and my life line. Our fifth member of the group, Nanban with 13 years of teaching experience, joined us in the next session. He was aware of the activity through Kawan, so he quietly placed his card among other cards displayed on the table. However, Peng You, Dost and I, the curious lots, inquired and learnt that he believed in symbiotic relationships, "it is very important to build relationships," he said.

No doubt, by now, we had peeped into our inner selves and also shared metaphors with other groups and learnt about theirs. We were exposed to take a glance of a few other landscapes and gaining an understanding of agendas that are closer to us as teachers. For instance, a fellow teacher from another group said, "I teach Physics. It is taken as a serious subject and so it is assumed that a teacher will also be the same. But when I enter the classroom, I exude happiness and smile like a ray of sun, fresh and comforting. So my students find it refreshing and not only connect well with me but also with the subject." Yet another teacher stated, "I value friendships. It is very important that we build trust and strong friendships to be able to seek help and give some when required."

Huberman's Trajectory: A Common Vocabulary

During the course, we read and discussed recent research on teacher development, some very thought provoking literature. Resting ourselves on Huberman's (1992) Professional Life Cycle, A Schematic Model, we tried to relook at our teaching trajectories from an angle alien to us. The most experienced amongst us, Dost, skipped the survival stage and went straight into the discovery stage (Huberman, 1992, p. 123). This was because prior to joining teaching she had worked as a relief teacher for six months during which she had experienced the survival phase. At the discovery phase, she consolidated her expertise and built bonds with her pupils and colleagues.

This was followed by the stabilisation phase (Huberman, 1992, p. 124) during which she held the responsibility of a subject co-ordinator and shortly after as a department head. Here she experimented both at the departmental and school level. She had moved from serenity to conservatism to disengagement (Huberman,

1992, p. 125–6). She felt less energetic, less fire in her than 10 to 15 years ago. However, she had confidence given her wealth of experience. Currently, she holds on to certain beliefs and principles and does occasionally resist changes and plans, which in her opinion are not well thought through or which do not benefit her clients, the students. Even today her enthusiasm is intact and she neither questions nor thinks of changing her profession despite obstacles and problems that come in her path.

While Dost had skipped the survival phase, Nanban had faced it twice, the first being during his stint at his alma mater when he had no formal teacher training. He had taught by instinct, drawing from his past experiences as a student and from the advice of his school teachers, who had then become his colleagues. He then entered the discovery phase. He had started to like the profession and wanted to pursue it as a career. And so, had enrolled himself in a teacher training course. Backed with formal training and experience as a relief teacher, he set foot in his new school "only to be greeted with issues and concerns of a different dimension" that brought him back to the survival phase again. For him, the three phases — responsibility, experimentation and stabilisation (Huberman, 1992, p. 124) — had all come at the same time in this new school. He was tasked with school-wide responsibilities while he was still finding his footing as a stable classroom teacher. He was not given the time to "cultivate" his garden, and instead very ambitiously undertook the task of "reforms" (Huberman, 1992, p. 130). His experience thus raised a pertinent question — Does this mean that he was destined for bitter disengagement? (Huberman, 1992, p. 128–9), which somewhat explains his next stage where he decided to seek renewal by signing up for the Masters in Curriculum and Teaching.

My career path revolves around two stages till date and is entering the third, which is also quite close to the first two stages. The first stage, that is the initial two years of teaching after the requisite professional teaching course, was marked with confidence in teaching due to a command in the subject, strong pedagogical skills and commitment to the profession. This was due to the fact that I formerly entered into teaching after my Masters of Philosophy in

English and with a prior experience of teaching as an intern in higher education. My level of mastery in the subject, new approaches to teaching, good pupil result and intense teacher–student relationship won me appreciation and shouldered me with responsible positions in the school I worked. For me, "Experimentation" and "Stabilisation" (Huberman, 1992, p. 124) went hand in hand. The second stage included "Reassessment", "Experimentation" and "Stabilisation" (Huberman, 1992, p. 124–7) followed by continual assessment of instructional strategies, building relationship with peers and creating a network of support both within and outside the organisation.

Moving on to Kawan, she is currently in the "Experimentation" stage after having been through the "Survival" and "Discovery" (Huberman, 1992, p. 123–4) stages in her teaching career. Having taught in the same school for 12 years, she decided to apply for a study leave to complete a graduate course as she felt a need to take stock (Huberman, 1992, p. 125) and improve her craft so as to contribute better to the service. She hopes to proceed on to the serenity stage, with some aspects of the "Experimentation" (Huberman, 1992, p. 124) phase as, according to her, the field of education is always evolving and would require her to always keep up with the latest trend.

And last, but not least, Peng You, with seven years of teaching experience, believes to be currently in the phases of "Stabilisation" and "Experimentation"/"Activism" (Huberman, 1992, p. 124). She has been through the first few years as a Beginning Teacher and has moved on to a phase where she is a little more confident in her classrooms in displaying different sets of teaching skills at different scenarios. She is a part of a Professional Learning Team or an ICT Mentorship Programme that she believes will improve her teaching capabilities. In future years, she believes she will move on to the "Serenity" (Huberman, 1992, p. 125) phase in which she will not whip herself for not being perfect (Huberman, 1992, p. 126) and plans to ward off stagnation by drawing on the diversity within the teaching profession, a kind of "slight, spontaneous role shift when one began to feel stale" (Huberman, 1992, p. 131). Thus, she hopes to end the last years of her teaching career in the "Serenity" (Huberman, 1992, p. 125) phase.

Having viewed our respective trajectories, two things were clear by now and in consensus. First, we were all, to a very large extent, influenced by and depended on social dynamics, the "quality of colleagues or experts to whom teachers turn spontaneously in the course of their private tinkerings and experimentation in their classrooms" (Huberman, 1992, p. 137), that was available to us during our teaching journey. Second, none of us wanted to land up as "Disengaged (Bitter)" (Huberman, 1992, p. 127) and that was the reason for us to review our teaching, to learn new approaches to teaching and learning, to understand the complexities involved and to be able to view the situations that arise in teaching from varied lenses, and above all to understand — Who Am I?

The more I re-read our narratives and re-visit our interactions, the more similarities I find. All of us had some teaching experience with us. We had been exposed to a traditional way of teaching, either through experience as a student or from experience gained in teacher training programmes. A lot has changed over the last decade in this profession. New approaches to teaching have come to surface, incorporation of technology in teaching has shifted the teaching paradigm, and so it also requires us as experienced teachers to revive ourselves. It is not that these new things have not been known to us. We have been incorporating the traditional with the new approaches of teaching and learning. Discarding traditional approaches only because new ones have come makes not much sense. Our past results have proved the efficacy of old and tested methods, but we also know that change is just around the corner and is inevitable. And so, we have been upgrading ourselves through collaborative efforts in our respective schools and also, by taking up such a fresh course that has opened up more vistas for us to choose from, and to experiment and further modify our teaching. We are at a place in our trajectories where we are blending or taking the best of both worlds — traditional and progressive.

Bruner's Narrative Structure: Our Own Narratives

An understanding of our context helped us in making meaning of our teaching practices when it came to writing our own narratives of our professional growth trajectories. Meaning is construed not event by event or sentence by sentence but by putting it in larger structures/frames that provide a context and can be understood in context (Bruner, 1990, p. 64). From our teaching experience, we recall the past, delve into our memories and pick critical events in our trajectories that have impacted our work and have made all the difference. While we were recollecting our specific critical events, we also constructed and re-constructed our stories and interpreted and re-interpreted our understanding both within the situated and distributed selves (Bruner, 1990; Golombek & Johnson, 2004). Sharing the critical events of our teaching profession in narrative form was challenging, interesting, unusual and helped us see the dissimilarities and similarities among us five. Initially, we felt that we were very different from each other in terms of what we believe in, in terms of our metaphors and also in terms of our subject specialisations, but towards the end of the module we gave this thought a second thought.

Restorying by Sharing our Own Narratives

Our narratives, when shared and recounted, helped us reflect on some essential questions that are already raised at the very beginning and provided us opportunity to venture into the "mediational spaces" (Golombek & Johnson, 2004) that each of us had created and utilised to learn and reflect further.

Dost's story

Dost wanted to move from Lower Secondary to Upper Secondary and shared her interest with her HOD. Having gotten the nod, she was given a Secondary Five class, that is, from Lower Secondary straight into a graduating class and a notoriously difficult one. She was a little sceptical initially about whether she would able to make it, but decided to take on the challenge. On the very first day, which continued on the second day as well, she faced a chaotic class that was least bothered by her presence. This shook her confidence in classroom management. She felt miserable and very disturbed but determined to find a way. Amidst all the commotion, what went in her favour was that she neither shouted nor scolded the students who were accustomed to being treated in such ways. A turn of events followed while she observed the commotion silently mostly not knowing what to do. One of the boys, popular amongst them appreciated her treating them differently with no yelling or scolding. Dost grabbed the opportunity and solicited his help that led to her successfully negotiating with the class for peace during lessons and slowly things started to change. A few months later, she became the form teacher of the class. However, her battle did not end here. She took initiatives and organised meetings with the subject teachers of the class but nobody was willing to review and renew their relationship with the class that they so disliked. Moreover, in doing so, she faced a direct confrontation with her colleague, an experienced Mathematics teacher who believed that Dost had been asking her students to only listen to her. At that point in her career, Dost lacked the courage and feared being penalised as the Mathematics teacher was much senior and on very good terms with the senior management. Even though she wanted to clear the wave of misunderstanding, she remained silent. To her it was important that her students learn; it did not matter what others thought. Being in an indifferent context, especially in relation to her interactions with the indifferent "distributed Self" (Bruner, 1990, p. 117), she decided to keep silent and continue her efforts. She faced the hostile environment for a year and then applied for a transfer as she found the environment too stifling.

Nanban's story

Similar to Dost, Nanban also faced a chaotic class. On the first day, students were all scattered and on the second, he found that a few students in the class had skipped his lesson. All his aspirations as a teacher waned as he felt he was facing students who did not even have the basic value system in place. On the other hand, even the commitment of the other teachers was at question. The teachers also felt relieved that, with a few students skipping their lessons, managing the class would not be an issue. As days went by, Nanban was offered the post of Discipline Coordinator which he accepted rather reluctantly as he could not refuse his Principal. He knew that more problems were to come his way. Four girls from Secondary Two had earned notoriety in the school and he could do nothing but hope these girls would graduate in two years for his torment to end.

However, an incident changed his perception of things. The girls were caught shoplifting at a beauty store. Their parents, with whom all previous attempts to connect failed, were informed and called in. The fear of their children being arrested for shoplifting made them rush down to the school. Utilising the opportunity, both Nanban and his Vice-Principal (VP) explained to the parents about their daughters' behavioural issues. The revelation was as startling for parents as was for Nanban and his VP. All the four girls came from dysfunctional families. Their parents were divorced. The mothers of two of the girls had abandoned their families. The custody of the girls were granted to their fathers who had little time to supervise their daughters as they had to hold more than one job to make ends meet. Life for them at home was tough, and they had no one to share their conceerns with. Filled with guilt and regret, Nanban realised that students carry an "emotional baggage" with them and learnt the invaluable lesson from the entire episode that it is important to connect and build relationship with students.

Kawan's story

In the contexts that we teach and interact, it requires a consistent and persistent effort in trying not to become bitter. Reading Kawan's story, one comes across such effort. She went through feelings of betrayal when she was asked to step down from the post of Head of Department, Information Technology, a post which she originally was not keen on taking but was convinced by her Vice Principal to take the leap. She gave it her time, devotion and juggled well between teaching and higher responsibilities, even at the expense of coping with her family life, only to hear one day that a new Head of Department would soon take over. She was confused as nothing was transparent. She was put in an awkward situation, to declare this to her family and to face colleagues' reactions. But she maintained her calm and continued with her work as a subject teacher. She tried her best to develop a rapport with the new Head of Department, and learnt new things; most importantly, she learnt to sail in such situations. She was offered the post once again after several years. With steadfastness as her particular strength, she had definitely acquired the skills the post demanded, and had learnt to run short races.

Peng You's story

In the times when there was a concept of inclusion in mainstream schools, but provisions to aid them were less and teachers were not prepared to handle such situations, it can be challenging to have special needs students in class. Though now, seven years on, the situation has changed for the better as there is enough support for teachers in place.

Peng You knew that teaching entailed an extremely heavy workload; however, she had no knowledge that the mainstream education included children with special needs such as Attention Deficit Hyperactivity Disorder and Asperger's Syndrome. She did not expect that she would have to handle two special needs students at the start of her career. Many a time, her lessons would be disrupted by either of the boys' mischief or frenzied behaviour. To add to her work load, Peng You had to learn to work with their parents and lend a listening ear to the other subject teachers. Though there were counselling sessions to help the two children learn to interact with their classmates, these were inadequate. She often felt that both the boys were victims of their own circumstances. Both of them wished to be a part of the class, and in turn, the classmates and teachers wished that they would play their roles in creating a conducive learning environment.

My (Mitr) story

My critical event revolved around establishing constructive and communicative approaches in teaching under the new guidelines from the central government of India as opposed to a lecture method that was followed for generations. In doing so, I received extreme opposition from dominant teachers in school and also initially from the Principal. But in all this, when I reflect, I tried to interact with other teachers and gain their views. I found some teachers had become bitter in the past, in the process of trying to put in similar efforts. This forced me to visualise myself 10 years from then. And seeing myself as a recluse, bitter, doing work only for the heck of it gave me a shiver. The best part of my entire experience was my relationship with my students, even though I was battling to establish new approaches of teaching and learning in my class. I was following the government's initiative, an initiative that took away focus from teachers and brought students to the core and was trying to change passive learning to active learning. Keeping the moral stance, I took courage to follow my heart and God blessed me in my venture.

God here is not an end in itself in the sense that whatever happens, happens for a good reason or is bound to happen. God is representative of holding one's spiritual connection as a prominent part of self with whom one interacts. It does not matter if you look inside to interact or upwards to interact. What remains crucial is interaction with self and interaction with others, and reflection.

Searching Our Collective Metaphor — To Build Shared Meaning

When I ponder over our stories yet again, I realise that when teachers make decisions whether small or big, a lot depends on the context. How much is the teacher at ease with the Principal and other teachers? What are the repercussions of her taking a stand or standing firm on her understanding of situation or standing firm on her beliefs? How much can she share and who is the right person to share with? How will his/her words be measured and interpreted? What other elements apart from individual self will define an individual's entity? All this and more shapes the quality of our interactions with our students, colleagues, seniors and others.

We were not only bound by reflecting upon such questions but also by the metaphor that runs in each of our stories. With five different metaphors, we grappled with finding a suitable metaphor shared by the group, a metaphor that defines and binds us all through our group project. In our enthusiasm, we put forth a lot of ideas. So Peng You suggested, Five Narratives, Five Teachers. Each of us will be represented by a cartoon character that we like. Then I suggested using *Avatar* as our theme. This proposal started with light humour about how we had depicted a real world of conflict and tensions and our intentional states just like the protagonist of the movie who was simultaneously in the cubicle in the research lab and in the forest. But the discussion did not lead anywhere, so we kept it for another day. From *Avatar*, we picked the forest as a common theme as Nanban suggested, which sent Peng You and me to the heights of our imagination, while Kawan, the quieter one, was listening to our bickering with amazement. Yet Dost kept silent. Observing her and realising that in our enthusiasm we had inadvertently failed to involve her. She was the most senior among us five, and we were all very talkative juniors; definitely there was a gap. The point was to bridge the gap. So I asked her what her view was with regards to a metaphor of our group story. She consented to the forest but still the smile was missing. So I continued asking for her suggestions. And finally, after some hesitation she asked, "Is it ok if I still keep unpolished diamonds as a metaphor of my story?" I probed further and after some conversation, could see her eyes sparkle like diamonds just on the mention of her students. She knew them well. She still remembered their names and some of their mischief. And now, actually talking to herself aloud she was confident of keeping what she had decided as the metaphor of the story.

In the meantime, the other three had already captured some images in their minds depicting their respective metaphors in the metaphor of Forest. So finally, "Forest" as a metaphor echoed with us all. It covered Symbiotic Relationships (Nanban), Short Races (Kawan), Tapestries of Life (Peng You), Unpolished Diamonds (Dost), and Heart Within and God Overhead (Mitr). But we all felt something still missing. And yes, by the end of the day, Dost was

smiling and fully involved, speaking her mind without our requesting her to do so. We were a team now.

Flowing Together Towards the Final Metaphor

By the end of this session, we had established a wonderful camaraderie, replete with mutual trust and respect. This aspect of restorying merged our individual themes into one and brought forth a key
aspect of constructing meaning together (Bruner, 1990, p. 32). Our
stories at once achieved the transactional aspect as these became "a
joint product of the teller and the told" (Bruner, 1990, p. 124) and
included not only a part of an "immediate private consciousness"
but of a "cultural historical situation as well"(Bruner, 1990, p. 107).

To continue with such a transaction, we met again for discussion
at Dost's residence. This time it was more of a planning and assign-
ing of tasks. We did this without any problem of ego. All aspects of
presentation were important. So we readily took our parts. Now we
started to think of the concepts to be included in each of our slides.
While we were doing so, after a little hesitation, I sought their permission to share something that came to my mind. In fact I had
been thinking of this since our last discussion, but the answer came
at that moment. I said, even if I thought it was too late for any such-
decision, "I recall a poem by Lord Alfred Tennyson, The Brook...
I think it suits and fits each one of us." "A poem...we know you are
crazy about a poem as a metaphor!" they all spoke together in
amazement and giggled. But while laughing, they said let us hear
the poem as though they were the nobility and I a minister whose
duty was to please them with my art. Even the setting added charm
to this mood. We were sitting in the garden and felt the pleasant
cool breeze fanning our poetical temper. After a little fun and
humour, I started the recital and explained the interpretation of
certain stanzas that I thought echoed with us. Bingo! That's the
metaphor...Finally, all of them gave their consent. No doubt, no
more questions. That was the trust we shared.

Using a poem as a metaphor is innovative and also challenging
and we were not sure if that would be accepted. But that was the

essence of this teamwork — we were standing together in this innovative idea. It belonged to all of us. And so we assigned ourselves
parts by mutual consent. Each part of the presentation was crucial,
so each one was equal. There was no debate about whether this
could be two minutes or five minutes of time. Usually people are
seen bickering over trivial matters and in the process lose track of the
goal. We were constantly after it for self-development and learning.

The Final Metaphor

Thus, we are Five Brooks with One Purpose. Just like the Brook, a
stream, we all have different starting points — different school contexts, different subjects, different cultural background, and differ-
ent beliefs. We go through different emotions at different times. We
chatter, we babble, we bicker, making different sounds at different
times — times of joy, resentment, pain, concern, apathy — in short,
different emotions, different sounds. Yet, each one of us continues
the unbending flow of our lives, sailing through new destinations
and challenges. In this way we take our past along, to impact our
present and future.

Each one of us has been treading our respective journeys as
teachers, moving in and out of schools, within schools, classrooms,
staff rooms and within the white free space of our self-reflection.
Dost identifies herself with "graylings" and "trouts":

> "... wind about and in and out,
> With here a blossom sailing,
> And here and there a lusty trout,
> And here and there a grayling" (Tennyson, 1865).

To her, "graylings" and "trouts" are symbolic of students that
personify life in the classrooms, just as fish symbolises life in the
poem "The Brook" (Tennyson, 1865). The students are different from
one another, they may be disciplined or undisciplined, may be high
scorers or low scorers or at mid-levels or in between, they have different personality traits, but they are like unpolished diamonds to

Dost. She considers it her duty to help polish these unpolished diamonds.

Kawan and Nanban's metaphors echo with the following lines of the poem.

> "By thirty hills I hurry down,
> Or slip between the ridges,
> By twenty Thorpes, a little town,
> And half a hundred bridges" (Tennyson, 1865).

For Nanban it is about building relationships on our journey, relationships with our students, their parents, colleagues, and with the community. To take everybody along is his motto. For Kawan, it is all about running short races, taking one goal, one challenge at a time and moving on.

Peng You believes in creating tapestries of lives in connection with her students.

> "I make the netted sunbeam dance
> Against my sandy shallows…" (Tennyson, 1865).

When the light of the sun falls on the surface of the brook, it forms a net as it passes through the trees that block its way. And the "netted sunbeam" seems to dance on the brook's surface. Peng You tries her best to create such beautiful pictures for herself and her students and help them rejoice in the journey of their learning.

Lastly, I, Mitr, believe in the key role that interaction plays in learning. I enjoy listening and interacting with my students and trying to understand the meanings they make during interaction in the process of learning. I believe we learn best through interaction. There should not exist an element of fear but comfort that supports learning. My heart lies in their smiles and their conversations.

> "I chatter over stony ways,

In little sharps and trebles,
I bubble into eddying bays,
I babble on the pebbles" (Tennyson, 1865).

And so, just like the Brook, each of us continue our respective journeys,

"And out again I curve and flow
to join the brimming river,
For men may come and men may go,
But I go on forever" (Tennyson, 1865).

By this time, our thinking was transformed; we realised that even though we are different with different metaphors, we are one. We are like a brook that has one purpose, which is to move on. We are like a brook as we have to take people along; we have to keep trying the endearing efforts to facilitate our students; and we have to continuously take challenges. We converge as our goal is one, well-being and progress of our students. Another awakening that struck us all was that we all come from different cultures, yet no culture binds us, akin to the Brook that is not bound by any culture. We all were joined in the beautiful journey of Teacher Learning and Development through the phenomenon of Narrative Inquiry, and joined further along together through reflection and…

"And out again We curve and flow
to join the brimming river" (Tennyson, 1865),

For challenges may come and challenges may go,
But We go on forever.

We may be a small part but are definitely a significant part in nation building. Just like the Brook bends itself according to its context, becoming narrow and then, at another time comes wide out, at times hidden and quiet and at times known, similarly we as teachers mould according to our contexts and continue doing the noble and complex work. All of us were in consensus that though our respective metaphors belonged to our particular selves, yet all the five metaphors belonged to all five of us. All five of us believed in symbiotic relationships, in running short races, in polishing the unpolished diamonds, in weaving a colourful tapestry of our students lives into our lives, and all of us have a heart, courage within and almighty overhead. We are all willing and open to make significant and "worthwhile changes" in ourselves and our teaching practices and to develop as teachers (Johnson & Golombek, 2002, p. 309).

References

Bruner, J. S. (1990). *Acts of meaning*. Harvard: Harvard University Press.

Connelly, F. M. & Clandinin, D. J. (1994). Telling teaching stories. *Teacher Education Quarterly*, 21 (1), 145–158.

Golombek, P., & Johnson, K. E. (2004). Narrative inquiry as a mediational space: Examining emotional and cognitive dissonance in second language teachers' development. *Teachers and Teaching: Theory and Practice*, 10 (3), 307–327.

Huberman, M. (1992). Teacher development and instructional mastery. In A. Hargreaves and M. G. Fullan (eds.), *Understanding Teacher Development*, pp. 122–142. New York: Teachers College Press.

Johnson, K. E., & Golombek, P. R. (eds.) (2002). *Teachers' Narrative Inquiry as Professional Development*. Cambridge: Cambridge University Press.

Tennyson, L.A (1865). The Brook. *Poetry Archive*. Retrieved on 9 May 2015 from http://www.poetry-archive.com/t/the_brook.html.

Chapter 33

Understanding the Emotional Work of Singapore Teachers in Interacting with Students[*]

Yanping FANG and John YEO

This chapter reports findings from analysis of 33 teacher narratives written by participants who attended our postgraduate course on curriculum, teaching and teacher learning through a narrative inquiry approach in 2011. This study focuses on the emotional work of individual teachers in managing teacher–student relationship in the social, cultural and institutional contexts of Singapore, a high performing and highly demanding education system. It also attempts to capture the emotional understanding that the teachers gained from those critical experiences as a result of learning more about themselves and their professional roles, particularly, in three key areas: grappling with the physical distances between teachers and students in the persistent pursuit of academic performance; finding hope

[*]The authors are grateful to the teachers who participated in our postgraduate course and who willingly give us permission to use their written narratives for our analysis to inform the continuous improvement of our teaching and contribute to knowledge building.

and commitment by bridging the social–cultural differences with students; and deriving the ethical and moral meanings of teaching and understanding the nature of teacher–student nested knowing. The findings further suggest that building inquiry through sharing and writing life narratives can lead to deepening of self-understanding and personal practical knowledge that are critical to bring about continuous professional learning for teachers.

Introduction

The journey of discovery consists not in seeking new landscapes, but in seeing them with new eyes.

Marcel Proust

While the McKinsey & Company report (2007) rated Singapore as one of the top performing educational systems that recruits some of the best teachers, little is known of the emotional trials they go through in their learning to cope with a demanding and changing system, particularly in interacting with students. School Climate Surveys in recent years have turned out a decreasing level of staff engagement across Singapore schools (Hanson & Ward, 2010). Substantial investment has subsequently been made to train school leaders' leadership skills to improve the situation. While a Staff Wellbeing Committee has also been set up in each school, teachers' psychological and emotional dimensions of their work, which constitute their general sense of wellbeing, engagement and productivity, have hardly been studied. Hargreaves (2000) reminded us of "the disturbing neglect of the emotional dimension in the increasingly rationalised world of educational reform" (p. 811). Teacher emotions constitute teacher cognition and a sense of wellbeing (Day & Gu, 2011); understanding them and their impacting factors in the social, cultural and political contexts of teachers' work will inform the effort to improve teacher engagement in substantive ways. This chapter represents an initial yet serious effort to describe and examine the emotional work of teachers in Singapore through teacher-authored narratives focusing on the interaction with students with a goal to help schools, policymakers and researchers attend to, understand and support teachers' emotional work.

Findings are reported from a focused analysis of 33 narratives written by teachers who attended our postgraduate course on Curriculum, Pedagogy and Teacher Learning through Narrative Inquiry at National Institute of Education, Singapore in 2011. In these narratives teachers mapped out their personal and professional learning and growth trajectories, searched from their work experiences the most memorable events and people that have impacted on their learning and shaped who they are as educators. A detailed coding analysis of the narratives has revealed that interactions with students, colleagues and opportunities to learn by playing different roles are the most frequently narrated. This echoes what Lortie (1975) and other studies of teachers and teaching attribute to the nature of teacher's work as "people work" in which teachers gain "psychic rewards" from interactions with students and those later studies that emphasise the importance of collegial work to the well-being of teachers. Yet, such interactions and rewards are also highly contextualised — they are shaped by the social–cultural context of an educational system as well as the social and political expectations of teachers' work. In a multi-racial and multi-cultural society that has traditionally held education in high esteem and in which teachers are held accountable for delivering results in teaching diverse and highly streamed students, what would the patterns of people interactions and rewards or lack of them look like in Singapore? In this chapter we focus on reporting findings from the teachers' narratives related to interactions with students. What do these stories entail and in what ways do they characterise teaching, teachers and their identity making uniquely pertaining to Singapore?

Emotional work of teachers

Lortie (1975) in his classic sociological study of school teachers found that a key purpose of teachers in his study was reflected in the pride they took in building bonds with and creating change in attitudes and behaviours of their students. Such psychic rewards, as he identified, are a key motivation drive for many teachers to choose teaching as a career, including the teachers in our study. More specifically, teachers, in our study, tend to take pride in sharing how they succeeded in changing a problematic child to a good student. This is similar to the long list of prideful cases in Hargreaves' study (2000), such as "teaching a very disadvantaged student life skills; being perceptive enough to identify a student with a learning disability and successfully modifying their learning; and so on" (p. 818).

As teaching "demands a high level of investment of oneself as a person," the process of achieving such rewards involves intensive emotional labour when teachers are dedicated to what works "in the best interest of the students" (Kelchtermans *et al.*, 2011, p. 218). Teachers' emotional work in interacting with students varies across different career stages based on Huberman's model (1992). They struggle for survival in their early years of teaching, become stabilised and more confident with more instructional mastery, then start experimenting with building a rich repertoire of teaching to meet different students' needs, and feel either serene or bitter in their late career stage depending on whether they are at peace with themselves. In addition to life stage, contextual factors, such as the school culture, the students and subjects they teach, the roles they play, the parents they work with, all invariably affect the feelings and emotional state of teachers. Broadly speaking, the social, cultural, and political environment all impact on the emotional work of teachers by placing high expectations on their work and holding them accountable for what they do. So our teachers' stories carry the special "flavour" since they respond to the "barometer of the local cultural weather" (Bruner, 1990), which is results-driven and adores governance by meritocracy. Such cultural expectations and the rapid educational reform climate both locally and globally have given rise to teachers' emotionally charged growth trajectories. As "emotional engagement" and "strong and continuous relationship between teachers and students" (Hargreaves, p. 815) are required in achieving the very purpose of teaching and learning, teachers' narratives of their work, especially, in interacting with their students, are naturally an outlet of their rich emotional encounters. Capturing these encounters and understanding the characteristics of and factors that impact their emotions will help us identify issues with teacher engagement and provide better support.

Emotional geographies and the social, cultural and institutional contexts

Hargreaves's concept of emotional geographies refers to the "... spatial or experiential patterns of closeness and/or distance in human interactions and relationships that help create, configure, and colour the feelings and emotions we experience..." (Hargreaves, 2000, p. 815). Although the concept was developed to examine teacher–parent interactions in Ontario, Canada, we find it useful to analyse the Singapore teachers' emotional geographies in their interactions with students captured in their narratives particularly in three dimensions — the physical, social–cultural, and moral. In the following, we detail these three dimensions by casting them in the context of Singapore.

Physical geographies

Singapore school education achieves its success through "a very tight coupling between the high stakes summative assessment system and classroom instruction" (Hogan & Gopinathan, 2008). Many teachers, like those in our study, were caught in running the race for raising examination scores, particularly for the high-stakes exams geared towards promoting students for higher levels of schooling.[1] They find it difficult to have time to attend to students as emotional

---

[1] These high-stakes exams include the Primary School Leaving Exams (PSLE) which determine which secondary school a student will go to; the General Certificate of Education (GCE) "O"-Level Exams which determine which junior college (senior high school) a student will attend; and the GCE "A"-Level Exams for university admission.

and thinking beings. This can give rise to distanced "physical geog-raphies" (Hargreaves, 2000) and infrequent interactions with stu-dents and parents causing lack of understanding or misunderstanding between them. In such cases, as our analysis shows, teachers can sometimes encounter intense emotional struggle questioning the real purpose of education and their own beliefs in education.

Social–cultural geographies

In the meantime, the teaching force is increasingly young, with the median age of trained teachers falling to 34 years in 2006 from 43 years in 1996. The McKinsey & Company report (2007) high-lighted that Singapore recruits the best candidates to be trained to enter the profession with one in every six applicants selected from the top 30% of their age cohort based mainly on academic results (McKinsey & Company, 2007). Indeed, from the narratives, teachers often wrote about their diligence and academic success in their school days and the challenges for them to understand their stu-dents who had remarkably different social, economic and ethnic backgrounds, aptitudes, interests and learning styles. Such social and cultural distances (geographies) between teachers and students become a reality shock for beginning teachers.

Students are grouped by their academic results in the Primary School Leaving Exams (PSLE) into academically oriented express streams and the lower streams, including the technical streams (Kang, 2005) in lower secondary schools. The different academic learning backgrounds between teachers and students is also what leads to conflict and misunderstanding, when teachers start teaching students in lower streams. In our study, the teacher participants in our graduate programme often report the painful struggles that even-tually aroused their sense of care, calling them to help the disadvan-taged students with their academic learning and to make the effort to close the sociocultural gaps (Hargreaves, 2000) between them and their students.

With policies that support students with special needs to join mainstream schools in recent years, an increasing number of teachers face challenges in terms of lacking the knowledge and skills to understand and meet these children's learning needs.

Moral geographies

In a Chinese heritage culture, teachers are seen as the authoritative source of knowledge while students are expected to be obedient and good listeners (Fang & Gopinathan, 2009; Paine, 1990). Students who display resistant behaviour can be perceived as violating norms and rules and may subject themselves to punishment. In Singapore schools, more severe disciplinary cases may result in the students being caned publicly. We found that teachers face intensive emotional labour when confronting such situations. In certain cases, they see themselves unable to bridge the "moral geographies" (Hargreaves, 2000) with their students and find it hard to condescend themselves to listen to the voices of these students. But when they manage to bridge such gaps, they find hope and harvest more emotional understanding.

More subtle and detailed than what Lortie and Hargreaves had found through teacher surveys and interviews, these teacher narratives reveal teachers' struggles when they were caught in the entanglement of the above emotional geographies as well as in their effort to close these distances between themselves and the students. Stories of success are easily shared but it is those of failure that have led to sombre ponderings and at its best, more nuanced understanding of students and their varied lives and needs. This chapter, drawing on careful analysis of the narratives authored by a group of Singaporean teachers and our teaching experiences as course instructors, provides details of teachers' emotional encounters with students and their effort in building connections with them and developing emotional understanding in the process.

The Study

Narrative inquiry has long been used as a research method in many fields and disciplines but not until the 1980s has it been adopted by researchers in studying teachers' life and personal practical knowledge (Clandinin & Connelly, 1988, Connelly & Clandinin, 1990). Narrative inquiry has also been used in teacher education coursework as a vehicle for building inquiry and reflective practice. Researchers examining teacher narratives found that they can constitute powerful resources for teacher learning (Conle, 2000; Golombek & Johnson, 2004). In our teaching, we adapted narrative inquiry as a tool for teacher learning, for studying our teaching and lives of Singapore teachers.

We asked the course participants, who are teachers from different educational institutions, to map out, share and write narratives of their own professional growth and learning trajectories. Such narratives serve as a mediational means with which teachers articulate, inquire into, and make meaning of their own concrete professional learning experiences. They also engage in group projects by retelling their life and career stories, get different peer perspectives to their own narratives and analyse group learning patterns informed by course readings. See more details about the course in the book's Epilogue. Here we present some of the restorying experience to allow us to examine teachers' personal practical knowledge within the school context which bears upon the emotional nature of teachers' work and their learning in interacting with students as well as the emotional understanding they have achieved.

Of the 35 teachers in that cohort, 33 teachers (8 males and 25 females) were teaching in Singapore public schools. The average number of years of teaching experience was 10.45 with the youngest having taught for 4 years while the most experienced teachers served for up to 23 years. Spanning across a spectrum of 29 different schools in Singapore, 13 of the teachers taught in primary schools, 19 in secondary schools, and one in a junior college. In other cohorts, we also had nursing educators from institutions of technical education (ITEs) and polytechnics as well as art and engineering educators from polytechnics.

We adopted critical incident analysis approach (Harrison & Lee, 2011), taking a critical incident as the unit of analysis. To draw out more details of the teachers' experiences, the context, scene, plot and implications for learning were analysed for each incident.

A total of 117 key incidents were counted from the narratives with a third (46) about various dimensions of interactions with students, 40 on interactions with colleagues and supervisors and the rest on miscellaneous topics. To allow for a more in-depth examination of these incidents, we chose to focus on themes related to interactions with students in this chapter.

Findings

As the narratives were analysed with an openness to examine the meaning constructed from teachers' experiences, we found it insightful to understand how the boundaries overlapped between the way teachers articulated their own knowledge construction process, often in search of the authentic connection between what is "personally acceptable" and what is "professionally accepted". Teachers' emotional and cognitive dissonances are often found in those overlapping boundaries where conflicts and meaning making thrive.

Grappling with teacher-student physical distances in the single-minded pursuit of academic performance

Hargreaves (2000, 2001) considers how physical geographies are created when possible interactions between teachers and students become disconnected, fragmented, infrequent and formalised. Encounters with such characteristics frequently appear in the narratives that we examined. They typically took place in schools that are obsessed with student academic performance or rank teachers by a checklist of teachers' competences, which tends to create a rift between the teachers' beliefs and their actual practice. For instance, Ms. YL[2] struggled between her care for students' mathematical understanding and her need to maintain high scores:

> "My focus of drilling and practicing to prepare my students for PSLE has dumbed down the importance of students' mathematical

---

[2]Names of teachers are in pseudonyms, except for those whose narratives appear as chapters in this book.

thinking. My students were not exhibiting metacognition when solving a problem as they were merely memorising and regurgitating steps without giving much thought to the process. I have lost the focus of allowing my students to think about their thinking which will deepen their learning. Since my students were weak in mathematics, all the more I must spend time providing opportunities for them to think about their thinking. ..."

Mdm. BH felt she had to choose between serving the psychological and social needs of a problematic child and meeting the competitive demand for ensuring that he performs well academically, as she wrote,

"I had mixed emotions. I was angry with him but I also wanted him to do well in his examinations so that his future would be somewhat secured. ... I broke down and cried continuously as I was emotionally exhausted which I did not realise at all."

From her confession, one cannot help but sense the pressure to teach to the test and question whether teachers are really able to bring out the best in all students, without compromising on the grades. These trying situations often require the teachers to take a stand between their "value choices and engagement of one's person" (Kelchtermans, 2005, p. 1005). They often have to redefine what success meant to them as teachers, confronting their own perception or misperception of the child either as an individual with learning needs or as a student who needs to perform well due to school and parental expectations. More significantly, the teachers specifically wrote about how, in their early years as beginning teachers, their expected roles to help students excel academically could often discourage them from opportunities to make mindful decisions about the students' needs. So a distinct theme emerging from the narratives was the challenges these teachers faced in balancing their professional roles as teachers. As we encouraged teachers to reflect on their own practice and articulate their understanding in an increasingly critical light, Ms. CC wondered aloud when the shocking secret of a boy in her class who had been suffering from severe family abuse became known while she and her colleagues had been, unknowingly, after him for missed work:

"Have we been so engrossed in our pursuit of our As that we were unable to detect B's unhappiness? Or was B only willing to show us his indifferent attitude as we had not really tried to understand him as an individual and our focus had always been on academic performance? What students present to us in school are what they want us to know about them and that is the only one façade visible to us."

Ms. JT wrote vehemently with a similar but more determined note:

"... I wonder if the culture of academic excellence in our education system provides the best for our students. Is the system too rigid? ... I feel that the active process of imparting values to our students is even more important than coaching them to score A1s for their exams."

In the above quote JT voiced how such demands unavoidably created an attention conflict between how teachers rigidly adhere to Ministry of Education's (MOE, 2010) expectation that "Schools will equip students with the necessary knowledge, skills and values for living and working as adults in the 21st century" and how they perceive the students' learning needs as individuals.

From their narratives, some teachers commended that Singapore's curriculum reform crouched in the national initiative of "Teach Less, Learn More" helped to free up "white space," a "free hour" for teachers to learn together. Others lamented that the excessive technical or administrative matters in schools often squeeze out whatever little time is left for teachers to explore creative teaching, relationship building or other things that help to fuel the passion to teach. Most of the teachers also shared the lack of support and guidance for them to reconcile the tension between the high expectations of the profession and the complex work of caring for the students, individually. As Mdm. SM wrote,

"However, with such a system of ranking and over-emphasis on results, it removes the joy of teaching. Teaching becomes mechanical, using often the tested formulas for good results. Any move to try new innovative strategies was under scrutiny in case a wrong move would bring down the results. There were lots of drill and practice just to perfect the answering skills and to help pupils remember the huge amount of content."

Given these contradictions, it is understandable that some of the teachers would often experience intense emotional labour when they helped their "weak" students deal with the incredible fragmentation in their lives. Clearly, the secondary school system compounds this fragmentation even further by "boxing up" students to many different subject teachers who may make little or no effort to establish a safe learning relationship (Hargreaves, 2000).

Many teachers, however, also shared how they rose against the odds. They narrated how they developed the students' beliefs in their own ability to achieve better academic performance. Quite a few also realised that they needed to help students manage anxiety as the "weaker" students often demonstrate apprehension with learning a particular subject. They had to invest time and find extra resources to re-build students' self-concept in the subject before helping them gain some self-confidence with the subject. The emotional labour was further evidenced when Ms. SC celebrated what she considered as more gratifying when she learnt to define success as addressing the individual needs of her students and concluded that "teaching is more than just teaching academic subjects." She chose to build a trusting relationship first before re-engaging her students with their new learning strategies by drawing out their emotions through writing journals.

Finding Hope and Commitment by Bridging Social–Cultural Differences with Students

As mentioned earlier, in lower secondary schools, the academically-inclined and better-performing students go to Express streams, while the lower-achieving students join the Normal Academic (NA) and Normal Technical Technical (NT) streams based on their results in the Primary School Leaving Exams (PSLE). Teachers who are recruited from the top 30% of school achievers have experienced schooling in very different contexts from those academically less motivated students in the "tail-end" classes of the NA and NT streams (forming 30% and 15% of each cohort respectively in the lower secondary schools) (Thuraisingam, 2007). In primary schools, students weak in the English language used to be placed into the lower EM3 stream at the upper primary level, a practice which has been replaced by subject-based banding since 2008. A great number of the teacher narratives recollected the stressful days when they started teaching in those tail-end classes. Given a choice, some teachers would shun teaching these classes at all cost. While research on the practice of streaming in Singapore has been largely concerned with students, teachers' perceptions and discourse about streaming have been generally unexplored and a comparison of their views against those of the students is noticeably absent (Ng, 2004).

In fact, the sociocultural geographies in the classroom indicate that the teacher and students view each other from different "worlds", as Mdm. BT observed:

> "I notice that the phenomenon of the 'emo' (pessimistic and depressive) students is prevalent in my Normal Academic class. There are many of them who are stressed, have low self-esteem and they vented their frustration by self-inflicting pain. They feel hopeless and sad. To them, school is pointless and life is depressing. The implication is that when they perceived themselves with so many emotional issues, it is not surprising that they are not interested in Mathematics or English."

Being unfamiliar with the background and traits of these students heightens the emotional strain of teacher–students relationship, which could be made worse when teachers' work is organised to focus on academic work. This is reflected in Mdm. WP's concerns, when she shared:

> "I found myself spending most of my time on marking and neglecting the more important subject — that is, the students. ...
> I found that the students did not relate to me and I could not

motivate some of them to improve their attitude and effort in their work. I felt emotionally and physically drained."

Unsurprisingly such tensions are numerous in their beginning days in dealing with rebellious students. Most of the teachers described how their authority was threatened leaving them feeling deflated, such as in Mr. SL's case:

"… my tightly clenched fists, my body shivering with anger, my mind working furiously to defuse the situation contending with the indignation I felt at the student's gall. The explosive encounter that I had with this particular student started from something as innocent as me asking the student to tuck his shirt in as he walked past me. The student blatantly ignored me and walked on. I raised my voice and asked him to stop. … I think it goes back to recognising that students have bad days, and sometimes, we just need to give them a break."

Narrating and re-living those experiences would invariably strike these teachers with a sense of guilt and a growing awareness of the space that the students fought for themselves against the overbearing teachers. Similar to SL, Mr. CP's encounter was also an opportunity for him to reflect:

"These comments provoked the "meanest" boy in the class, FC, to want to fight with me, saying that I had no right to insult them. I was shocked, followed by more anger that someone would actually threaten my authority as a teacher. Reflecting deeper, I felt ashamed. FC was right. No one has the right to insult another, no matter what circumstances or situation. … I believe my apology forged the first and strongest bridge that slowly mended our relationship."

In our study, some of the more spectacular individual cases of challenging students came from those teachers who struggled to meet these students' socio-emotional needs. While recognising that learning to be better teachers is a process that takes time, they would also realise that unresolved conflicts and negative emotions in dealing with students might hurt all parties and therefore, they would emerge from those encounters with important lessons of humility. While bitter regret has remained in a few cases in which the teachers ignored or neglected such students, it is encouraging to note that nearly all of them also cited sources of positive emotions when they managed to help these stigmatised students turn around against the odds. It is such experiences that created a deep sense of psychic rewards as they found they were able to mediate the sociocultural differences with their students. Such cases include: rescuing students who were neglected or abused at home; helping a child to seek professional care and treatment from sexual assault; identifying a student with learning disability and successfully modifying learning for him; creating engaging teaching resources to help students become more motivated to learn; inspiring 37 out of 40 students in a poor performing "tail-end" class to score distinction in the national examinations; going out of her way to help a graduating class of Malay students improve from a U-grade (ungraded) to a pass in their PSLE; helping a student who returned from the Boys' Home to once again believe in himself; encouraging a teen to believe in his dreams and pursue his passion despite the family's objection; and allowing a boy with anger management issues who punched the teacher to make peace with her years later.

While the above teachers shared experiences of much emotional labour with the "tail-end" classes, the following narrative calls attention to the dilemmas of a teacher who was transferred to teach what the system labelled as gifted, the top 5%, cream of the crop students. Ms. CC started her narrative inquiry with the heading, "Gifted Students — A Misunderstood Race?" In her struggles, she learnt to understand the sociocultural geographies of her "misunderstood" students, and learnt something more valuable about herself, as she wrote:

"They (children in gifted classes) thrive on embarrassing their teachers and reducing them to tears to prove that they are the stronger race.... X antagonises on purpose to get a reaction from his teachers and peers on a daily basis. He will purposely be defiant towards teachers in school to challenge their authority with the intent of creating chaos. ... Is it also fair to his teachers when the emotional hard work we put in reaps little effort on his part to improve? Our emotional labour is becoming negative and draining as we mask and manufacture our emotions to remain unruffled when confronted by his defiance in class. ... I have to look beyond to see that the child in front of me wants to be acknowledged and accepted as a child, not just as a smart kid labelled 'gifted'."

She concluded that through her years as a teacher, she has gained a better understanding that her role in a gifted classroom is to facilitate students' learning by imparting skills to enable them to be aware of their own thinking and skills to apply the vast amount of knowledge they bring with them. She has learnt to create opportunities for students to stretch their minds and be open to feelings and understand issues from different perspectives.

For these teachers, stepping into a child's reality requires them to make conscious decisions. They admit that the lack of a personal understanding of the child has created negative emotions in the classroom when they feel that students do not know them. This creates an emotional rift between teachers and students. In a sincere confession, Ms. SP wrote, "Perhaps I have not tried to understand the students enough because I do not come from that kind of background and I cannot identify with their experiences. I have been using my lenses to look at their problems and using strategies that I see as applicable to them.... The students indeed were very different." While she realised that everything worth learning comes with a price, Mr. MC learnt the same lesson differently when he openly connected with his rebellious student with this honest admission, "Yes, you are right, I come from a neighbourhood secondary school, just like you." MC was then able to enter into the student's inner world when the student confessed how he hated teachers because he felt "none of the teachers understand the life of a neighbourhood secondary school boy... since you all are up there; we all bottom one!"

In more recent years, students with special learning needs are placed into mainstream schools. Many teachers also wrote about their struggle with teaching these students because of lack of knowledge about their problems and skills in differentiating instruction to cater to the learning needs of these students. Ms. SS shared, "I had never felt so helpless before. I was totally clueless how to help this child, as I, myself had never encountered someone with selective mutism. ... How I wished there was someone to handhold me and to provide me with some form of professional guidance. I confess, I could not read her mind and did not know what made her cry."

As Hargreaves (2000) best put it, such an emotional geography "helps us identify the supports for and threats to the basic emotional bonds and understandings of schooling that arise from forms of distance and closeness in people's interactions or relationships" (p. 815). What resonates with those who are purposeful in their vision is to teach from the heart and to find their moral compass. From the narratives above, the emotional work, once properly attended to, would often lead to a change in the way the teachers viewed teaching and the actions they subsequently took. Again it goes well with what Hargreaves (2000b) put it, "it seems, while teachers expend their energies on their classes, they continue to invest their hopes in individuals" (p. 818).

Deriving Ethical and Moral Meanings of Teaching — Teacher–Student Nested Knowing

Out of the 15 teachers who have taught for more than 10 years, 12 wrote in their narratives about significant experiences that brought emotional understanding when working with students. These senior teachers in Singapore's education system would echo what Hargreaves (2003) considered as well-developed teachers who "display much self-confidence and openness in their professional relationships with adults as do with children" (p. 48). As he further noted, it is the emotional understanding that they need to draw on in developing mature, caring and respectful relationships.

The journey in developing such emotional understanding is one full of "dilemmas of knowing" (Lyons, 1990) in which constant teacher decision-making involves ethical and moral implications and their sense of self and professional identity in working with students.

Mdm. BH credited her prestigious Caring Teacher Award to a "forsaken" child, KL, who has been badly hurt by peers, family and even some teachers. While wrestling within herself how much care is sufficient for this individual student, she found a deeper truth that sustained her purpose for teaching.

> "I expressed negative emotions on KL because I felt that he was being irresponsible for not coming to school… By engaging my emotions sentimentally, I may not help him to survive and succeed in the new global landscape since I have been focusing on his intellectual and emotional aspects. KL also needs to have the values and skills to cope with the changing times. …. In teaching, there must be love, which comes along with care. Both are powerful to transform the lives of our students. I have seen it. I have tasted it myself too. Some of my students have changed their behaviour and attitudes toward their work when they feel that they are being loved and cared for. I believe there are many great teachers out there who also have great love for their students."

From the narratives, instances of teachers navigating across such moral dilemmas include: being overwhelmed with students' dishonesty when they cheated collectively as a class in an exam with their lack of moral awareness, leaving the teacher with a sense of despair; living with a guilt when regrettably scolded students with hurtful words and wishing he had never spoken; blaming students for terrible behaviour without any consideration of the heavy baggage they shoulder; and learning to reach out to students who were looked down upon by other teachers.

In these narratives, our teachers' ways of knowing was situated in the tensions and contentment of different student–teacher relationships. It came as no surprise with many stating that there is no "overnight success" pertaining to such emotional work of teachers and they have to live with the reality that there is uncertainty to whether their actions would lead to good result (Lyons, 1990). Just when one feels he/she has achieved progress with a student, another incident may upset the equilibrium of "feeling good". This process is well demonstrated in Ms. LX's case, a young teacher on her journey to develop such emotional understanding in working with a notoriously rebellious student, Ryan, in her school.

Through much effort, LX grew to believe that she had helped to transform Ryan and a sense of pride and inspiration surged.

> "Instantly, I felt good. I sensed the goodness in him. Somehow, I felt he was different from what the teachers had made him out to be ... Every chitchat session with him was enjoyable and I got to see him in a different light.... Even till today, that conversation keeps me motivated. I want to be the best teacher I can be for my students. Trusting myself and believing in my students empower me to contribute more to their learning."

This sense of initial success ignited a young teacher's passion to believe in her students and advocate for them. It was this emotional connection that made the teacher feel that she was obligated to mediate misunderstandings between the child and other teachers, even though she was not the form teacher of the boy's class. As she continued,

> "Needless to say, I was constantly entangled between some of the teachers and Ryan. I had to double up as 'Aunt Agony' for both parties, providing suggestions and making sure that the relationship between them would not be strained. It was frustrating for me. I had to be politically right to my colleagues, and at the same time be that of a nurturing and understanding figure to Ryan. I felt as if I had a split personality!"

This emotional turmoil sometimes became draining as she was trying to manage her dilemma of how far she was able to reach as she wondered aloud: "Here I have a student who has so much belief in himself and myself. And yet, as a teacher, I have doubts about my own capacity and will to help him to scale greater heights in the language." While the student turned into a motivated learner with promising academic progress under her care, once out of her charge two years later, she found herself caught again in an unfortunate clash between the boy and another teacher, feeling vulnerable and defeated again.

> "Sitting beside Ryan, I felt helpless. I looked at him. In my eyes, he had not changed much since I first knew him in Secondary Two. Flashbacks of past years' encounters began to blur my eyes … It was an emotionally stressful week for Ryan, his parents, his auntie and myself. My mind was frantically searching for the answers needed. I did not know how else to help him. All I knew was that he stood a high chance of being suspended or caned. And all the teachers in the staffroom will probably laugh their heads off and drown me in their sarcasm."

Through such emotional trials, however, the teacher demonstrated a clearer conviction about her moral responsibility to understand and stand up for problem students. She concluded her narrative with a higher sense of such moral and ethical understanding: "Students today yearn to be heard. They wish to be understood. And they are crying out silently for the need to be respected!" Such emotional understanding manifests the personal practical knowledge that LX has gained from her encounters with students and is shaped by her purpose and values she held as a teacher (Clandinin, 1986).

Mdm. SG cherished the trust she gained from a student who shied away from everyone else in the school. It was after months of constant encouragement and caring, the girl learnt to open up. Similar to Ms. LX, it was her sincerity to love and protect the child's basic physical well-being despite not knowing how best to connect with the hurt and pain of the child. In SG's words, "it was very traumatic because now I realise what I had seen in her pain. There were times that she will casually tell me all the things the man had done to her. It was cruel and heartless and evoked strong emotions in me so much so that I felt like shooting him dead... It was a traumatic experience for me but after months later when I could see slight improvement in her behaviour it gave me immense satisfaction that I have done something... It was this child who had reopened my wounds, nursed them..."

Both of the teachers above showed consistent effort to care for their students who could sense the "safe" environment that their teachers created for them. Both spoke about how these experiences provided them "magic", "purpose", "passion" and "strength". From the narratives of these teachers, we can see that when their actions were based on what their students needed, they each found the calling for hope and purpose. What was more significant was that both teachers found these poignant experiences integral to their own learning while acknowledging the child's role in helping each of them reach for higher social and moral goals.

While the above cases find teachers' effort in improving students' sense of well-being and protecting children's rights, the reverse is also true — in which a teacher could be "rescued" by the students when she felt lost and powerless. In Mdm. GP's narrative, as a Chinese Language teacher who felt marginalised in the mainstream Chinese culture where English is the official working language and instructional media in schools, she made sincere effort to help her unmotivated students appreciate the learning of Chinese and gain their acceptance as a Chinese Language teacher. In doing so, she let go of her professional self as her way of showing care in exchange for pleasing the students — she said okay to students when they found excuses for being unable to submit their homework. This subsequently led to her being bullied and blamed by students, parents and even her reporting officers when she scuffled to put together students' assignments for file check. A clearly passionate teacher for her love of the subject, she lamented how "I had never really felt the discrimination for Chinese Language to be this intense." It was an incident in which a student spoke up that made her realise about her "blind" personal weakness that she struggled with for years. In her words, "I sought to be every student's dream teacher... by garnering 'popularity vote' from students." She sought out different ways to help students appreciate her lesson, even at the expense of ridiculing herself. However, a stinging experience in class made her realise that she herself was one of the causes of students' poor perception of the subject.

> "Then came the enlightenment one day. As I was teaching some Chinese vocabulary to my Secondary 4E students and as usual, cracking some age-old demeaning jokes about myself to illustrate the meaning of these words, a student by the name of Yuan Qing retorted, "Teacher, can you stop that crap out of you? Stop belittling yourself!" Time seemed to come to a standstill. There was awkward silence in the class and I felt my face burning. Suddenly I realised what went wrong."

Thanks to the above student, she not only took a more proactive stance when it comes to the promotion of Chinese Language but is now more "self-assured in my role as a Chinese Language educator, I have to take extra care not to come across as a self-indulging Chinese narcissist as Singapore is still a multi-racial society with English being the first language."

For these teachers, their growth and learning happens as what Lyons (1990) termed, the "nested knowing", "the interdependence of students and teachers as knowers in learning" (p. 173), more specifically, "teachers and students influence and are influenced by each other's knowing — they are nested knowers" (p. 174). Such "nested knowing" not only helps us understand how Hargreaves (2003, p. 48) argued for the moral mandate of teaching beyond the knowledge society where teachers view their calling as a "personal path towards greater professional integrity and human growth." It also enabled us to better appreciate the psychic rewards the teachers obtained from students who returned to thank them years later. They draw inspiration and motivation from such cases to reconnect with their purpose of teaching and sense of commitment and wellbeing (Day & Gu, 2011). A classic example of a real classroom story of a "villain" turned "hero" revolves around Mr. CP who clashed and nearly fought with a student in his early days teaching a Normal

Technical class. When the teacher was later transferred to another school, the many upheavals he experienced led him almost to resign from the service. Yet, it was the same boy that helped CP change his mind.

> "Yes, he was from the 4NT class that I taught in my first year at my previous school. I was really touched, as he had taken pains to track me down. He was studying in Central ITE (a vocational and technical school taking in students graduating from the Normal stream) at that time and he told me that he was very grateful to have had a teacher like me, for the things that I had done and for all the fun that we had in class. ... It was this comment and show of gratefulness that explains why I am here today. His presence brought me back to the days when all I wanted was the best that I could give to my students and made me realise what I had become."

Discussion and Conclusion

While our teachers learn to develop an inquiry stance (Cochran-Smith and Lytle, 2001) through writing their narratives, they start to create for themselves opportunities to interrogate their practice by considering the unique needs of their students and the context of their schools and communities. As we examine these teacher narratives more closely, we find that recollecting and narrating their lived experiences has helped them articulate their struggles as a balancing act of teaching in an attempt to both value individual students and meet expected academic goals as teachers. Behind these struggles lies what Kelchtermans (2005) called the "inescapable vulnerability in teaching", the embracing of which helps teachers develop their self-understanding, a resource for personal and professional growth which "ultimately constitutes the very possibility for teachers to 'educate' and to teach in a way that really makes a difference in students' lives" (p. 1005).

Meanwhile, by locating ourselves in the act of teaching through restorying, we have learnt how teachers deepen their own pedagogical understanding through their shared learning experiences with students as part of their construction of knowledge-of-practice. Our findings lead us to believe that teachers develop stronger emotional understanding when they are committed to their students and their learning. Many, in their attempt to build more trust and stronger rapport with students, begin to use the subject matter content they teach in more creative ways to reach students more effectively. From these heartfelt narratives, we also grow more aware that it is through writing and sharing their stories that they weave in their thoughts, emotions and dilemmas, a process which has helped bridge the psychological and social perspectives in heightening their sense of professional identity. The restorying process makes prominent the significance of teachers' role enactment within the school milieu.

In fact, the findings we have illustrated above resonate across the teacher narratives over the years of our teaching. We have been convinced by the power of teacher narratives in building teachers' inquiry stance and as a tool for knowledge building. The teachers feel strongly that this narrative inquiry experience has allowed them to reflect systematically on their practice and regain the meaning of their work. Using teacher narratives in capturing teachers' and students' ways of knowing would echo Lyons' (1990) words, "it keeps at bay a simplistic rendering or a reductionist categorisation of either teachers' or students' epistemological perspectives as a non-linear relationship emerges in the intersubjectivity of teachers and students as knowers and potential constructors of knowledge." (p. 174) This knowledge building forms teachers personal practical knowledge with a critical component of emotional understanding which is absent in the dominant research on teacher knowledge, skills and dispositions. Teacher narratives not only enable us to see what is entailed in such emotional understanding but also how and where it is developed. They demonstrate how ethical and moral dimensions of teachers' work guide teacher's daily practices in working with students.

Just as the Singapore's Ministry of Education (2010) strives to effect change for teaching and learning in the 21st century, this study serves as a timely reminder that we need to re-examine the relationship between teachers and students, to redefine what counts as success for students' holistic education, and to better support teacher engagement in Singapore's schools.

References

Bruner, J. (1990). *Acts of meaning*. Cambridge, MA: Harvard University Press.

Clandinin, D. J. (1986). *Classroom practice: Teacher images in action*. Lewses: Falmer Press.

Clandinin, D. J., & Connelly, F. M. (1988). Studying teachers' knowledge of classrooms: Collaborative research, ethics and the negotiation of narrative. *The Journal of Educational Thought*, 22 (2A), 269–282.

Cochran-Smith, M., & Lytle, S. (2001). Beyond certainty: Taking an inquiry stance on practice. In A. Lieberman and L. Miller (eds.), *Teachers caught in the action: Professional development that matters*. New York: Teachers College Press.

Conle, C. (2000). Narrative inquiry: Research tool and medium for professional development. *European Journal of teacher education*, 23(1), pp. 49–63.

Connelly, F. M., & Clandinin, D. J. (1990). Stories of experience and narrative inquiry. *Educational Researcher*, 19 (5), 2–14.

Day, C., & Gu, Q. (2011). Teacher emotions: Well-being and effectiveness. In P. A. Schutz and M. Zembylas (eds.), *Advances in teacher emotion research: The impact on teachers' lives*. New York: Springer.

Fang, Y. P., & Gopinathan, S. (2009). Teaching in schools in eastern and western countries. In L. J. Saha and A. G. Dworkin (eds.), *The New International Handbook of Teachers and Teaching*, pp. 557–572. New York: Springer.

Golombek, P. R., & Johnson, K. E. (2004). Narrative Inquiry as a mediational space: Examining cognitive and emotional dissonance in second language teachers' development. *Teachers and Teaching: Theory and Practice*, 10, 307–327.

Hanson, D., & Ward, C. (2010). Staff engagement in the Singapore school system: Leadership training strategies for the development of Singapore principals. Paper presented at 2nd International Conference on Education and New Learning Technologies, Barcelona, Spain, 5–7 July, 2010. In EDULEARN10 Proceedings.

Hargreaves, A. (2003). *Teaching in the knowledge society.* New York: Teachers College Press.

Hargreaves, A. (2001). Emotional geographies of teaching. *Teachers College Record,* 103 (6), 1056–1080.

Hargreaves, A. (2000). Mixed emotions: Teachers' perceptions of their interactions with students. *Teaching and Teacher Education,* 16, 811–826.

Harrison, J. K., & Lee, R. (2011). Exploring the use of critical incident analysis and the professional learning conversation in an initial teacher education programme. *Journal of Education for Teaching,* 37 (2), 199–217.

Hogan, D., & Gopinathan, S. (2008). Knowledge management, sustainable innovation and pre-service teacher education in Singapore. *Teachers and Teaching,* 14 (4), 369–384.

Huberman, M. (1992). Teacher development and instructional mastery. In A. Hargreaves, & M. G. Fullan (Eds.), Understanding teacher development (pp. 122–142). New York, Teachers College Press.

Kang, T. (2005). *Creating educational dreams: The intersection of ethnicity, families and schools.* London: Marshall Cavendish Academic.

Kelchtermans, G., Ballet, P. Piot, L. (2011). Surviving diversity in times of performativity: Understanding teachers' emotional experience of change. In P. A. Schutz, & M. Zembylas (Eds.) *Advances in teacher emotion research: The impact on teachers' lives.* Springer.

Kelchtermans, G. (2005). Teachers' emotions in educational reforms: Self-understanding, vulnerable commitment and micropolitical literacy. *Teaching and Teacher Education,* 21, 995–1006.

Lortie, D. C. (1975). *Schoolteacher.* Chicago: University of Chicago Press.

Lyons, N. (1990). Dilemmas of knowing: Ethical and epistemological dimensions of teachers' work and development. *Harvard Educational Review,* 60 (2),159–180.

Mckinsey & Company (2007). How the world's best-performing school systems come out on top. Retrieved from http://www.mckinsey.com/clientservice/social_sector/our_practices/education/knowledge_highlights/best_performing_school.aspx. (Accessed on 28 April 2011)

Ministry of Education (2007). Ms. Seah Jiak Choo, Director-General of Education, 27 January. The purpose of teaching. Retrieved from http://www3.moe.edu.sg/purposeofteaching/ (accessed on 28 April 2011).

Ministry of Education (2010). Nurturing the young for our future: Competencies for the 21st Century, March 2010. Retrieved from http://www.moe.edu.sg/ (accessed on 28 April).

Ng, I. (2004). Perspectives on streaming, EM3 pupils & literacy: Views of participants. Paper presented at the Centre for Research in Pedagogy and Practice conference, Singapore, May 3–June 1.

Paine, L. W. (1990). The teacher as virtuoso: A Chinese model for teaching. *Teachers College Record.* 92 (1), 49–81.

Thuraisingam, P. (2007). Engaging the Normal Technical stream learner in the English language classroom. Paper presented at the Centre for Research in Pedagogy and Practice conference, Singapore, May 26–30.

Epilogue: Narrative Inquiry for Teacher Education and Professional Development — An Instructor's Journey

Yanping FANG

I close the book with some reflection on my own experience in designing and teaching this postgraduate course from which the narrative writing and research in this book are derived. Since 2006, I had taught a course on teacher learning and professional development in a canonical mode featured by readings, seminars, academic essay writing and a group project to redesign professional development initiatives. For a long time, I had wished this course to create an impact on teacher participants' personal and professional lives and had been quite aware that by teaching it in a generic way, it would be impossible to achieve such an impact. In June 2009, I attended a conference on Schwab's *The Practical — An East-West Curriculum Dialogue* at Beijing Capital Normal University. It was when Professor Michael Connelly and his doctoral students, who were teachers and school leaders from Hong Kong, shared how they grew as persons, educators and researchers as they journeyed through their narrative inquiry research that it dawned on me that teacher narratives and narrative inquiry would be the way to go.

My experimentation has thereafter undergone continuous redesign and improvement and has been filled with many challenges as well as important learning points. Here, as I review this arduous learning journey, I am very much indebted to the teacher participants — when things get tough, I regain a sense of purpose inspired by how these teacher narratives reconnected us to the fundamental purpose of teaching, and I am truly humbled by their commitment to the profession against all odds. It is through this experience that teaching, learning and research have finally been united to become an integral part of my life, constitutive of the very meaning of my existence. In the following, I first present a few learning points and then share both challenges and ideas to sustain continuous improvement as I continue with the journey.

Three mutually reinforcing levels of inquiry

To break new ground using narrative inquiry means more space has to be created for the teachers to tell and retell, write and rewrite their stories of learning and growth across their own personal and professional lives as an alternative way of learning and development (Conle, 2000; Connelly & Clandinin, 1994; Golombek & Johnson, 2004; Johnson & Golombek, 2011). At Pennsylvania State University, reflecting on their teaching using narrative inquiry, Johnson & Golombek (2011) felt strongly about the importance of "the parameters of narrative activities" and "how they (teachers) engage in narrative activities will fundamentally shape what they learn" (p. 8). I think of our own narrative activities in terms of creating three levels of mutually reinforcing inquiry.

Level one inquiry encourages teachers to map out their personal and professional trajectories or "chronicles" (Connelly & Clandinin, 1990, p. 9) with which to mediate their learning, to tell and retell the critical events or impactful people shaping who they are as teachers at the major turning points of their lives. Huberman's (1992) career-stage model has structured this experience by giving teachers a common vocabulary to articulate their experiences as they revisit their career stages both individually and through pair and group work. For instance, in Part 6, Sonia Khan shared her group members' narratives of their individual career chronicles and how this narrative activity shone light onto the darker or hidden corners of their past experiences. The process of externalisation, inviting self-doubt and emotional struggles in defining or redefining one's identify and self, is a profound inquiry in and of itself (Johnson & Golombek, 2011). More explicitly, the group's retelling of one another's stories helped "make their understandings explicit to themselves and others and their thinking is laid open to social influence. Their spoken or written words ... self-regulate their behaviours and control their own worlds, constituting an initial step in cognitive development" (p. 6).

Parallel to the first level of inquiry, Level two inquiry occurs in the process of writing personal narratives in which peer feedback has allowed the narratives to be read, interpreted, revised and reconstructed by considering multiple perspectives. For Sonia's group, "[S]haring the critical events of our teaching profession in narrative form was challenging, interesting, unusual and helped us see the dissimilarities and similarities among us five..." "While we were recollecting our specific critical events," she continued, "we also constructed and re-constructed our stories and interpreted and re-interpreted our understanding both in situated and distributed self" (Bruner, 1990; Golombek & Johnson, 2004). This group reconstruction experience has prepared the groups to take on researcher roles in their Group Projects.

Level three inquiry takes place in the final Group Project, a task to observe the group restorying experience and analyse the patterns emerging from group members' narratives using a set of conceptual tools developed from the core readings, such as Bruner's pentad features of narratives, metaphors, Connelly & Clandinin's notion of continuity between the past, the present and the future, and the three-dimensional model of narrative inquiry. In addition, the social–cultural tradition behind the course design has guided teachers to examine the roles played by their agency and the activity context in shaping their narrative and narrated experiences. The Group Project helps teachers externalise their narrative experience, verbalise their everyday concepts using the "scientific" concepts and "re-examine the everyday understandings of experience through the explicit, systematic, and connected knowledge that scientific concepts afford" (Johnson & Golombek, 2011, p. 7).

Meanwhile, the Group Project encourages group members to capture the metacognitive processes of team work by keeping track and recording their own discourse patterns in an effort to think about their thinking and see how and why it shifts and affects each of them along the way. David Liew's chapter in Part 6 captures, in powerful ways, important lessons in learning to let go, assisted by this metacognitive dimension of his Group Project. Putting together, these narrative activities suggest an emerging narrative pedagogy for teacher education and professional development that aims at engaging teachers in "systematic examination of themselves, their teaching practices, and the historical, social, cultural, and political contexts that constitute their professional worlds in particular ways" (Johnson & Golombek, 2011, p. 9). Such systematic examination can give voice to teachers, return the knowledge building power to teachers and empower them to build knowledge from their lived experiences in their daily practices.

Challenges and lessons learned

This redesigning process has been filled with numerous challenges for both the instructor and the participants. Accustomed to theory-based teacher education programmes, many teachers coming to class do not recognise the value of their own stories. Sharing, writing and analysing their own personal narratives have inevitably exposed them to the vulnerability of facing the past and thus require them to have courage in examining personal setbacks or professional pitfalls in learning to teach or seek better engagement, in teaching. For the instructor, replacing external expert knowledge with teachers' own experiences as a central resource for meaning-making requires a new pedagogy with different activity design and class facilitation rather than merely conducting seminars or lectures. Unlearning the generic mode of organising a postgraduate course around readings and essay writing demands learning new knowledge and instructional skills. It took nearly three semesters to gradually let go of my favoured classic readings on teacher knowledge, teacher learning and professional development that have informed my teaching and research. I constantly need to manage the time conflict between the need for facilitating understanding of the readings and for scaffolding the narrative activities. The iterative process of designing, redesigning and continuously improving the course and its class facilitation is captured below, using the Group Project as a case for illustration.

Emphasis on negotiating meaning and learning to let go

The iterative improvement is informed by research on teaching and teacher-authored narratives. Take the cycles of improvement in the Group Project as an example. Over the years, I have experimented with finding a balance between having too little or too much structure. For instance, in January 2012, to enable learning to emerge in the process, very little structure was given except that the groups were expected to share their own narratives to get different perspectives and analyse the group discourse in light of the course readings. Uncertainty arose against this lack of structure, as narrated by David in Part 6. However, he found that this uncertainty had led his group to unexpected richness in learning. When the group members had different and even contradictory views on each other's narratives, tensions and discomfort arose but the group members' familiarity with one another promoted mutual trust during the group conversations, which eventually helped them negotiate the differences and reconsider their own narratives from the others' perspectives. In doing so, they came to new understandings of their long-held beliefs and painful memories. The collective retelling had eventually liberated each of them and taught them to let go.

Emphasis on metaphors as resources of teacher creativity

In August 2012, with a smaller class of 12 participants, more time and space were made available to facilitate the narrative writing and the Group Project. The drafted narratives were amazingly rich in metaphors, which enhanced the meaning-making in both individual and group narrative experience in that semester. A few of these narratives are found in the book: Say Pin's "passing of a day", CHC's "upgraded consciousness", Li Meng's "being tested", Annie's "germinating process", Vivian's "jigsaw puzzle" and Hwei Fang's "box of chocolates". Inspired by the power of metaphors, in the following semester, January 2013, I organised the Group Project to have each group come up with a group metaphor, one that enables each group member to relate to his or her own narrative experience.

In choosing their metaphor, Sonia's group, as detailed in Part 6, made up of five teachers from different races and teaching different subjects and grade levels, moved from a tree, *Avatar*, a forest to eventually arriving at their metaphor from a poem by Lord Tennyson in praise of a joyfully flowing brook joined by different streams and braving the journey down to the river and sea. They all felt that the metaphor captured every member's individual metaphor, character, and belief very well. Yet at the end of the semester, I felt, when tied to the purpose of finding a single shared metaphor, the Group Project became a bit too structured leaving inadequate space for group members to negotiate their differences and learn from multiple perspectives. Nevertheless, the groups, including Sonia's, found more similarities than differences among group members. By identifying their similarities, they reconnected themselves to their purposes of teaching that initially drew them into the profession. For Sonia's group, after the emotional journey of examining their past, they reclaimed the heart of a teacher and came to terms again with who they are and what they want to achieve in teaching. While such deep learning might not have occurred to all the groups across the past four years, it nonetheless convinced me of the power in using narrative inquiry to create space for teachers to reconstruct their lived experiences and build personal practical knowledge.

Shifting emphasis to incorporating narrative inquiry as research

The current approach to the Group Project pays more attention to how the group members adopt researcher roles in systematically analysing their own narratives as a collaborative meaning-making process with the help of the course readings and theories. The Group Project, while still less structured, has been injected with more analytical rigor and depth of inquiry when mediated by the conceptual tools built from the core readings for analysis and reflection. The advantage of structuring around research could allow the course participants to be more aware of narrative inquiry as a research method in studying teachers' personal practical knowledge and enable them to theorise the narrative journey they experience both individually and collaboratively. To achieve this pedagogical purpose, I have started to scaffold research from the beginning of the course, for instance, by infusing narrative interview through pair work into the career mapping and narrative telling and retelling. Every new element to the narrative activities sets me on the way to learning new knowledge and facilitating skills and a new path with both risks and potential to learn and grow (Day & Lietch, 2001).

Beyond teaching — In pursuit of coherence, liveability and adequacy

The above reflection on certain dimensions of my teaching speaks to the "transformative power of narrative" which "lies in its ability to ignite cognitive processes that can foster teacher professional development" and "legitimate teachers' knowledge generated from teacher inquiry" (Johnson & Golombek, 2011, p. 19). The book calls for education institutions to value and capitalise on teacher and student narratives as resources for their own learning and development and for knowledge building. Through narrative inquiry, we are able to move beyond teaching and our professional world to create, as

Bruner (1990) puts it, a sense of "achievement of external and internal **coherence, liveability, and adequacy**" (p. 112) for teachers, students, and teacher educators alike. As shared by Aristotle Motii Nandy, a former Principal of a Jakarta-based International School, who took the course and contributed his work to the book and served on the editorial team:

> *What I personally learnt from the NI (Narrative Inquiry) class was that to actually benefit in the education process, we need to have the willingness and humility to learn from others, either from their feedback or from the sharing of their learning journeys. And it is for this reason I feel that if Singapore is to be a caring and progressive society, the use of NI as a research and educational tool is vital for all teachers and school leaders. In addition, I have learnt that we also need to look at issues from the perspectives of others, and consider our own shortcomings. To me, NI represents a progressive path of education, as we make our self (the subject) the object of our study. It helps us connect to a deeper level of our existence, and gently prods us forward while broadening our perspectives...*

To contribute to future narrative inquiry teaching and research, we are committed to a book series of teacher narratives in Singapore and to continue sharing the instructor's experience in developing a more rounded narrative inquiry pedagogy for teacher development. Future research will also expand to comparative studies of teachers' lives and professional trajectories in other cities in East Asia, such as Taiwan, Hong Kong and Shanghai, to understand the unique teacher learning patterns in Singapore and the importance of using narrative inquiry in teacher education in the East Asian context.

References

Bruner, J. (1990). *Acts of Meaning*. Cambridge: Harvard University Press.

Conle, C. (2000). Narrative inquiry: Research tool and medium for professional development. *European Journal of Teacher Education*, 23(1), 49–63.

Connelly, F. M., & Clandinin, D. J. (1990). Stories of experience and narrative inquiry. *Educational Researcher*, 19(5), 2–14.

Connelly, F. M., & Clandinin, D. J. (1994). Telling teaching stories. *Teacher Education Quarterly*, 21(1), 145–158.

Day, C., & Leitch, R. (2001). Teachers' and teacher educators' lives: The role of emotion. *Teacher and Teacher Education*, 17 (2), 4, 403–415.

Golombek, P. R., & Johnson, K. E. (2004). Narrative inquiry as a mediational space: Examining emotional and cognitive dissonance in second-language teachers' development. *Teachers and Teaching: Theory and Practice*, 10 (3), 307–327.

Huberman, M. (1992). Teacher development and instructional mastery. In A. Hargreaves and M. G. Fullan (eds.), *Understanding Teacher Development*, pp. 122–142. New York: Teachers College Press.

Johnson, K. E., & Golombek, P. R. (2011). The transformative power of narrative in second language teacher education. *Tesol Quarterly*, 45 (3), 486–509.

Index

Abuse victims, 23, 35, 36, 42, 56, 484, 489

Academic performance 4, 5, 37, 341, 447, 454, 475, 483, 485, 486

achievement and SES, 26

beyond, looking, 32, 38, 82, 88, 101–102, 110, 111, 113–114, 116, 129, 145, 152–154, 157, 159, 190, 205, 219–221, 224, 226–228, 233, 239, 245, 248, 251, 267, 273, 310, 311, 322, 331, 341, 348, 366, 385, 398, 403, 406, 421, 425, 430–432, 453, 458

    compared with race, 13, 26, 27, 53, 74, 115, 135, 138, 155, 164, 179, 190, 218, 338, 345, 368

    excellence and medical condition, 52

    focus only on, 260

    motivation for, 262, 331

    perceiving person's worth based on, 178

    physical distances with students in pursuit of, 447, 475, 483

    remedial lessons, 342, 343

    student's behaviour and, 5

    tactics to improve, 40, 476, 490

Accidental leader, 157, 161–164

Accidental teacher, confessions of, 5, 61–67, 82

"Accountability" *vs.* "responsibility," 380

Achievement, teacher's, 179, 180, 192, 193, 205, 206, 335, 336, 349, 443, 509

'Act' becoming fact, 374

Administration *vs.* teaching, 261, 296, 298, 423, 434, 440

    leadership as HOD, 94–98, 324, 407

    management of people, 112, 113, 127, 128

    misgivings in leadership, 333

Adopt-A-Park collaboration, 201

Adventure and uncertainty, of teaching profession, 337–339

Adversity Quotient (AQ), 272

Ahmad, L. B. S., 101

Allowing students to explore, discover and mature, 312

Alternative teaching methods, 106, 223, 224

Ambition, stress of, 24, 90,190

Ang, J. C. C., 207

Anger management issues of student, 10, 489

    closer look, 70, 74, 237, 327

    colleagues view, 5

    continuous issues and refuge, 12–14

    height of conflict, 13, 30, 333, 469, 487

    helpless, feeling, 9, 16, 36, 66, 92, 114, 140, 141, 148, 154, 158, 231–233, 236, 338, 339, 416, 491, 494

    initial apprehensiveness, 10, 11, 96

    issue, 10

    motivation to be the best, 13

    problem solving, 184, 248, 252

    quitting, 14

    right *vs.* wrong in conflict, 17

    standing firm in beliefs, 16, 18, 468,

    student's language proficiency, 10

    trust between student and teacher, 13

Animal Farm (George Orwell), 404

Anyon, J., 27

Apple, 28, 395

Appreciation, 58, 67, 143, 148, 161, 378, 453, 462

    experiment in, 376–378

    from colleague, 82, 141

    students', as the best gift received, 72

Areas of Improvements (API), 377

Asynchronous development, issues in, 30

Authority teachers', students personal space, 9–18

    succumbing to, 194

"Bad" teacher, 223, 238, 391

Balakrishnan, V., 402–404

Backgrounds of teachers, 170

Band (school), in charge, 198, 199

    indoor and outdoor performances, 199, 200

Beginner teacher, experience, 10, 62, 139, 180–183, 223, 244–247, 284–288, 310–315, 320–328, 338, 366, 462, 484

Beyond passing knowledge and skills, 383–393

Bloom's taxonomy, 248

Bourdieu, P., 26, 259, 263

"The Brook," 457, 470–474

Bruner, J., 3, 6, 155–156,169, 175, 260–263, 279, 411, 415, 463–465, 470, 474, 478, 499, 505, 509, 510

Bruner's narrative structure, 463, 464

Budding school culture, 300

Bull and Leopard, 5

'Call to adventure,' 337–339

Cambridge International General Certificate of Secondary

Education (IGCSE)
examinations, 303
Campbell, J., 335, 337, 340, 349
Caning students as punishment,
18, 365, 366
Care, 19–28
Certification process, 253
Challenges in teaching, 62, 70, 71,
226, 338, 375, 381, 421, 506
Change
growing and learning from
teaching different students
in context of, 69–77
of school, culture etc,
experience, 342, 343
Characteristics of ideal teacher,
223
"Charlie and the Chocolate
Factory," 92
Clandinin, D. J., 3, 6, 228, 260,
263, 274, 277–279, 317, 353, 356,
360, 371, 424, 447, 450, 456,
458, 459, 474, 482, 494, 499,
504, 505, 510
Classroom teaching, 75, 135, 387
Co-Curricular Activities (CCA),
64, 161, 171, 193, 199, 337, 387,
397
Collective metaphor, 468–474
Collegial factor in narrative
inquiry, 449–456
Comfortable environment equals
productivity, 103–105
Comparison of students, 345
Competitive society, 42
Complaint against a teacher,
handling, 121–124
Confessions of accidental teacher,
5, 61–68

Conflict
anger management issues of
student, 10, 11, 18, 489
with HOD, role of friends in,
148–152
right *vs.* wrong in, 17
specialisation, 140
tackling parent–teacher, 298,
354
Confucius, 28
Conle, 318, 411, 482, 499, 504, 510
Connelly, F. M., 3, 6, 274, 277, 279,
317, 353, 356, 360, 371, 424,
450, 456, 458–459, 474, 482, 499,
503, 504, 505, 510
Constraints for teachers, 23, 143
Constructivist pedagogy, 247
Context, teachers as part of larger,
3, 4, 69–77
"Contextualisation," 420
Cooley, 101, 109–111, 113, 116
Courage, tenacity and care, 4,
19–28
Critical learner, 189
Cultivation, 277
Cultural capital, 4, 26–28, 239, 424
Culture in difference in schools, 73
Curriculum leadership, 98
Curriculum Planning and
Development Division (CPDD),
106, 225, 417

Dahl, R., 92
Dai, D. Y., 29, 44
Death, dealing with, 388, 389
Defiant students, 108
Derogatory language usage, 120,
283
Developing own materials, 246

Dewey, J., 254, 255, 323
Dickens, C., 276
Differentiated instruction/
   teaching, 41, 77, 126, 186
Difficult student, narrative,
   231–234, 239–241
DiMaggio, P 28
Dimensions of learning, Robert
   Marzano's framework of, 245
Discipline committee, 38, 288, 342
Discipline Master, 64, 109, 320,
   322–324, 330, 332, 333, 347, 364,
   365, 368
   "dirty" tasks of, 365, 366, 367
   as mentor, 260, 320
Drug affected family, emotional
   effects of, 24

Eagles Award, 205
Eco Award, 205
Eco-Friend Award, 204
Education, joining world of, 19
Educational psychology, 105
Education professionals, qualities,
   xiii
Educator compared to book, 220
Educator's journey through door
   of mentorship, 295–307
Educator to researcher, from,
   98–100
Eisner, W. E., 371, 395, 423
Emotional geographies and social
   cultural and institutional
   contexts, 479–481
Emotionless teacher 6, 73, 74
Engaging *vs.* disengaged learning,
   223
English programmes and
   effectiveness, 96

Enhanced Performance
   Management System (EPMS),
   108, 208, 420
Environmental Education, 203,
   204
Environment Education Advisor
   (EEA), 203
Equal treatment to schools, 268
   avoiding demoralising, 270
   crisis tackling, 273
   perceptions and perspectives,
      265, 271, 275, 277
   rationale and situation of
      MOE, 271
   site/building planned for one
      school awarded to another,
      268–271
Examination
   driven teachers, 185–186
   preparation for, 376, 380
   pressure, 24, 34, 83, 104, 134,
      155, 178, 190, 234, 294, 333,
      401, 430, 433, 484
   setting, 104, 183–185
Experiences
   failure, 185
   faith in students, 59
   inquiry into, 43, 44, 356
   narratives and, 356, 445, 451,
      463, 482, 504,
   pupils motivating teacher, 51,
      53, 177
   shaping beliefs, 47, 48
   sharing of resources and
      teaching, 183
   as student, 32, 77, 355
   students absence, effect of, 55
   as teacher, 4–5, 23, 37, 42,
      47, 82, 84, 89, 94, 178, 181,

201, 228, 353, 368, 384, 390–392, 449, 459, 471, 475, 486, 497, 504

Experimentation, teaching, 373, 381, 462, 504

Express stream, student shifting, 62, 63, 191

Extra Co-curricular Activities (ECA), 199. *see also* Co-Curricular Activities (CCA), 171, 193, 199, 337, 387, 397

Facilitating learning, 250–252

"Facilitation display," 252, 253

Failure, experiencing, 145, 276, 288, 354

Family over teaching, choosing, 61, 69, 186, 187, 217, 219

Fang, Y., 353, 445, 475, 503, 499, vii

Financial Assistance Scheme (FAS), 26

"Foreign" language, 416

Forrest Gump, 157

'Fountain of Hope' in school, 265, 275

Fragment (Chinese poem), 278

Freire, 395, 401

Fullan, M., 307, 393

Gamoran, A., 28

General Certificate of Education (GCE) Examinations, 61, 232, 398, 479,

"Gifted achiever," 29, 30, 44

Gifted Education Programme (GEP), 27, 31, 179

Gifted Self strand, 44

Gifted student(s), 29–45

abuse of, 35, 36, 42

apprehensiveness in handling, 10, 32, 33, 63, 66, 95, 96, 244

assumptions about their abilities, 181

complex social–emotional needs, 30

dealing with difficult child, 37–39, 88

idiosyncrasies of, 31

indifference towards exam, case of, 35

knowledge authority in class, 33, 34

misconception, 30, 76, 188, 406, 407

notions on gifted education teachers and, 32

one student *vs.* class, care, 38–40

performance pressure, 333

presentation of lessons, 31, 374

reflection and discussion, 40–43

trauma in a, 5, 113, 191, 422, 449

Giovanni, N., 330

Goh, L. M., 170, 177–192

Golding, W., 400

Golombek, P. R., 156

Goodson, I. F., 316

Good/great teacher, defining, 231, 492

Green Club, 201–205

Groom, W., 157

Ha, M. E. L., 19

Hall, V., 307

Handling, lies of teacher, 285

Hargreaves, A., 6, 7, 40, 44, 129, 131, 172, 175, 217, 228, 241, 259, 263, 279, 303, 307, 456, 474, 476, 478–481, 483, 486, 491, 496, 500, 511
Hating subjects, reason, 48–49
Head of department, 286–290, 310, 314, 320, 344, 360, 407, 416, 438, 452, 466, 467
    mentoring, 297, 316, 317, 332, 354
    working along with, 416, 417
    role, 184, 259, 289–293
    rookie HOD experience, 261,
Helping individual, instance of, 321, 322, 324, 325
"Hero," 335–337
    achievement as, 347
    changed perspective of, 337, 402
"The Hero with a Thousand Faces," 335
Hoban, G. F., 302
Hoge, R. D., 29, 44
Hollingworth, L., 30, 41, 45
Home–school relationships, 26
Hon, T. H., 359
Hope
    and commitment by bridging social–cultural differences with students, 447, 476, 486,
    in midst of despair, 70, 71
Huberman, M., 131, 228, 241, 279, 307, 474, 500, 511
Huberman's model/trajectory, 478
Human potential, 29

Ibrahim, N. S. M., 309–318
Ideals challenged, 73–77
Ideal teacher, characteristics, 223

Ideas and strategies, sharing, 146
Identity
    formation as on-going process, 173–176
    as Malay teacher, 395–409
    as teacher, 363
    threat to, 367
Illumination, stagnation and, 115–116
Improvement, constant, 81
Indian musical instruments, 54
Informal atmosphere, managing students in, 88
Information and Communication Technology (ICT), 54, 186, 406
Inquiry into experience, 43–44
Inspiration
    from pupils, 4, 19–28
    vs. disincentive, teacher as, 69–70
    from working with low ability upper primary pupils, 19–28
Integrated Programmes, 27
Interactions with students and colleagues, professional identity from, 101–103
Inter-personal relationships, 111

Johnson, K. E., 44, 130, 156, 228, 241, 263, 279, 356, 456, 474, 499, 511
Journal (personal) writing 21, 26, 45, 57, 58, 89, 90, 99
Journey of developing prototype problem-based curriculum, 243–255

Kaliamoorthy, S., 47–60
Khan, S., 259, 353, 457
Kindergarten education, 26

Knowledge
    authority, teachers *vs.*
        students, 33, 34, 54, 55
    and skills, beyond passing,
        383-393

Lareau, A., 28
Lau, L., 69
"Leader-resistors or leader
    managers," 301
Leadership, 83–85, 94, 97, 98, 105,
    117–131
    attribute of leader, 261
    belief and philosophy of
        leadership, 117–118
    challenge, 405–409
    change in time table, reactions
        to, 98–99,109,152
    curriculum leadership, 98
    disadvantage of power, 99,
        110, 439
    essentials in leadership, 99
    ethics in, 117, 126–130
    existing programme
        reviewal, 97
    experience, reflecting on,
        94–97
    handling trips, 338, 346
    HOD position at young age,
        96, 136
    Language Support
        Coordinator and 95–96
    learning points 126–129, 384,
        455, 502
    learning leader, 420–423
    letting go, 455
    mentors, opposite natured,
        295–307
    misgivings in leadership, 333,
        366

    new reading programme,
        95–96
    opposition to programme,
        134, 468
    relationship with other
        teachers and, 110, 172, 327,
        342, 344, 409, 421, 475
    reviewing current English
        programmes, 96–97
    tension between power
        stations, 127
    tensions and cracks, 123–125
    true affirmation of leadership
        with heart, 122, 123
    updating to higher
        authority and handling
        issues, 122–124
Leaders making or breaking your
    career, 207–218
    bad leader narrative, 207–228
    good leader narrative,
        212–217
    handling students' family
        issues, 18, 213
"Learning character," 171, 251
Lee, T. T., 145–156
Letting go, 455, 456
    leadership, 369, 370
    Zen master and rescuing
        maiden tale, 354, 363
Liaozhai Huapi, 272
Liew, D. Y. S., 449
Life's lesson from a student,
    90–92
Li Shunren, encounter with,
    40, 41
Listening to students *vs.* adhering
    to lesson plans, 314
Literature, enjoying, 50
"Live" reflection-on-action, 253

"Looking Glass" theory, 82,
101–116
Lortie, D. C., 370–371, 477, 481,
500
Low ability upper primary pupils,
inspirations from working with,
4, 19–28

Maclean, R., 350
Malays in Singaporean
educational, breaking down
stereotypes of, 309–318
being a minority beginning
teacher, 408
bridging gap between
administrator to beginning
teacher, 315–317
relating and interacting with
fellow colleagues, 313–315
Malay teacher
identity as, 395–409
Language teacher, 413–415
Marzano, R., 245–247
Master of Education (MEd)
journey, 395
Mathematics
acceptance of the subject, 180,
181, 187, 188
model teacher, 221
teacher impression, 49, 50
Mature/sensible pupil, abuse story
behind a, 21–23
McLaren, P., 27
MENDAKI, 396
Mental processes in student, 76, 77
Mentorship. *see also* leadership
educator's journey through
door of, 295–307

issues in the mentorship cum
friendship, 298–302
mentor teacher, 89–91
resignation, 18, 191, 302–304,
330, 432, 453
Metaphor, collective, 470–476
Mindfulness, 354, 376–377
Ministry of Community
Development, Youth and Sports
(MCYS), 37
Ministry of Defence (MINDEF),
213, 399
Ministry of Education (MOE), 70,
76–78, 102, 103, 107, 115, 119,
120, 122, 128, 131, 160, 179,
186, 205, 211, 215, 216, 221,
225–227, 265–270, 286, 334,354,
355, 384, 389, 392, 399, 408,
433, 485, 500
Headquarters, 107, 160, 225,
334, 384
Ministry of Education
Regional Language Centre
(MOE RELC) Scholarship, 286
Minority, ethnic identity as,
311–313, 355
conscious struggles, 373
Misunderstood student, 489
Mizzy, N. B., 355, 395–409
Modus operandi, 326
Moral dimension of teacher's
work, 349, 383–393
Morning assemblies lead duty, 234
"Mothers," two. *see* same-sex
couples parentage
Moulding students, teachers' role
in, 47
Multiculturalism, 309, 315

Naipaul, V. S., 311, 312
Nandy, A. M., 3–7, 81–86, 295
Narrative inquiry, 6, 44, 130, 144,
    145, 156, 228, 229, 239–240, 260,
    263, 265, 277, 279, 306, 318,
    356, 383, 392, 424, 426, 443–447,
    449–475, 477, 482, 489, 498, 499,
    503–511
    collegial factor in, 449–456
    as teachers' voice, xi
National Environment Agency
    (NEA), 203
National Institute of Education
    (NIE), vii, viii, 10, 15, 17, 20, 98,
    105, 106, 115, 135, 161, 164,
    174, 220, 225, 284, 336, 348,
    355, 362, 384, 386, 388, 400,
    403, 405, 406, 429, 434, 435,
    460, 479, 503
Negativity, power of, 112–114
Netball coaching, experience, 171,
    194–198
"Never give up" policy, 14
"Nice" *vs.* "no- nonsense"
    mentorship, 332–334
Noddings, N., 28
Novice teacher experiences, 82,
    87–90, 243–245
152 (Article) of Singapore
    Constitution, 396

Ong, J. L., 9
Ong, R., 243
Opposite natured mentors, 323–328
    adopting best of, 326
Orwell, G., 409
Overloading to breaking point,
    209–210,

Parker, J. Palmer, 292
Pedagogy, 28, 68, 170–174, 180,
    188, 191, 211, 216, 223, 247,
    253, 337, 342, 373, 381, 422,
    501, 506, 510
    approaches in, 50, 467
    challenges, 30, 62, 81,
        204–206, 221, 226, 234, 260,
        285, 287, 312, 315, 337, 375,
        381, 457, 506
    constructivist, 247
Peer pressure, 234
Perfect profession, teaching as,
    336
Performance pressure, 37, 41
Person's worth in terms of his/her
    scholastic successes, 178
PE teacher, narrative, 103, 104,
    106
Philosophical role as teacher, 23
Physical Education and Sports
    Science (PDCM), 115
Piaget, J., 386
Picasso's Weeping Woman, 320
Politics, 101, 111, 112, 137
Positive and personal connections,
    power of, 74, 75
Power and responsibility of
    teachers, 239
Power of teachers, 50, 51
Power relationships, complexities
    of, 110, 111
Power struggle, 143
Primary One registration system, 27
Primary School Leaving
    Examination (PSLE), 24, 34, 58,
    90, 119, 170, 186, 223, 234, 267,
    380, 440

"Principle of equal misery," 70
Problem-based curriculum,
   journey of developing prototype,
   243–255
Problem-based Learning (PBL),
   171, 247
      facilitation processes, 254
      philosophy of, 41, 117, 118,
         122, 128, 248
      staff developers, 253, 254
Problems
      crafting, 227, 249, 381
      engaging with and
         confronting, 247–250
Productivity, comfortable
   environment equals, 103–105
Professional and social
   comfort, 438
Professional growth attribution to
   my mentor and my students, 87
Professional identity, 101–116,
   169, 171, 172, 174–176, 336, 348,
   357, 386, 492, 498
      from interactions with
         students and colleagues,
         101–103
Professionalism, teaching, 72–76,
   376, 384
Proud of student's development,
   93
Proust, M., 476
Public speaking, 205, 235–236
Punishment
      caning students as, 18, 365,
         366
      corporal, 38
Pupil Development Department,
   162, 289

Pupils motivating teacher, 59–60

Quality *vs.* quantity, 429

Rare awakenings, stories, 4
Reading programme, 95–97
Reality check, journey of, 290–294
Rebel in school, 287
Re-evaluating professional
   trajectory, 411–426
Reflective process, 276, 446
      teachers, 421
      on teaching career, 133–144
      on teaching practice,
         245–246
Reinventing oneself, 418
Relationship
      with and perception of
         supervisors and colleagues,
         172
      with students, responses from
         and, 172, 173
Remedial lessons, 342–346
Renzulli, J. S., 29, 44
Research experience, 100
Responsibilities, school, 84, 118,
   297, 461
"Responsibility" *vs.*
   "accountability," 380
Result oriented teaching, 226
Retrained teacher, 186–189
Rodrigues, V., 427
Roeper, A., 44–45
Role model teachers, 354, 388

Said, S. A., 219
Sambwani, V. D., 82, 87–100
Same-sex couples parentage, 23

Scheme of Work (SOW), 104, 146

Scholarship based university education, 61, 62

Schon, D., 253

School Advisory Committee, 27

School culture-building model, 300

School Staff Developer (SSD), 122

Scrutinised, feeling, 10

Seeing students beyond academic competence, 342

"Self-preservation," 377

Seng, A., 170, 193

Shakespeare, W., 50, 271, 400

Sharing of resources and teaching experiences, 136, 183

Silverman, L. K., 45

Singapore Institute of Management, 53

Sirin, R. S., 28

Sit, B. K. S., 61

Site/building for school, issues/confusion over, 267, 268

Slowing down, experiment in, 378

Social class
    disparity and education, 27
    and students education, 26

"Social Class and School Knowledge" (1981, paper), 27

Social–cultural differences with students, hope and commitment by bridging, 486–491

Social inequality, 24, 25

Social relations, 101

Social stratification, patterns, 27

Socioeconomic status (SES), 26, 28, 189

Song, H. F., 157

Specialisation conflict, 135, 138–140

Spiral curriculum, 348

Stabilisation stage, teaching career, 230

Staff developer, becoming, 253, 254

Stagnation and illumination, 115, 116

The Starfish Story, 67–68

Stereotypes, managing, 309–317

Stories as meaning of our lives, xi

Stress level of job *vs.* teaching, 133, 134

Stress of ambition, 24

Student centred education, 243

Students
    interaction experiences, 5
    learning attitudes of, assumptions, 178–181
    as learning experiences, 90–92
    optimism inspiring teacher, 50–51
    personal space, teacher authority and, 9–18
    potential of, teachers' role in realising, 64
    teaching student, 153, 184, 271, 480

Studying, purpose of, 180

Subject Head for Citizenship Education and Social Studies, 162

Subject strengths, 135–136

Success, defining, 230

Sun, H. M., 169, 265
Sungei Buloh Wetland Reserve
(SBWR), 201, 202, 205
Support network, importance,
107–116
Survival and discovery, 81, 83, 117,
284–286
Swearing. *see* derogatory language
usage

Tackling parent–teacher conflict,
119
Talent, concepts as, 29
"A Tale of Two Cities," 276
Talktive girl reputation, 48
Tamil language teaching, 6, 48, 53,
54, 59
Tan, S. P., 260, 319
Targets in terms of percentage of
passes, 184
Tayler, G. M., 278–279
Teacher Advisor, 162
Teacher career cycle, schematic
model of, 230
Teacher–student interaction, role
of, 5, 67–68
Teacher training, ups and downs
of, 105–107
Teaching, decision/purpose to
take up, 3, 136, 159–161, 222
Teaching career, reflection on,
133–144
Teaching competition, 183
Teaching materials
developing own, 375
Teaching *vs.* leadership, 214, 228
Tennyson, A., 457, 474
Teo, C. C., 29
Teo, S. K., 281

Thinking Schools Learning
Nation, 247
Tomlinson, C. A., 41, 45
Transformation, journey of
281–294
Trials, 340–345
"Tuned-in" to learning of students,
249
Tutorial classes, beginning, 243

Uncompromising and unyielding
teacher, 322–325
Underclass, student from, 20
Understanding of teaching,
186–189
Understanding students, 50,
347–348
Unpleasant dimensions, 4
'Unteachable' students, 354, 362,
363, 365, 367, 370
Unusual parentage. *see* same-sex
couples parentage
"Upgraded" consciousness,
373–382

Van Gogh's Starry Night, 320
Vice Principal, 83, 98, 99,164, 210,
214, 260, 282, 292, 298, 302,
305, 345, 347, 365, 367, 368
Victims
abuse, 5, 35–37, 42, 56
teachers as, 43
Vygotsky, L., 254

Ways, teaching, 223
White, S., 350
"Why" and "What" questions, 389
Work allocation, 83,104
Work disappointment, 83,110

Work Improvement Team Scheme
(WITS) tool, 287
Working with colleagues and
supervisors, xiii (xix)
"Worthy" person, 344

Xianyi, Y., 278

Yap, T. C., 335
Yeo, J., 475

Youth Expedition Project, leading,
338–339
Laos trip experience, 260,
338–339, 342, 344
providing emotional support,
40, 57, 141, 339

Zen master and rescuing maiden
tale, 354, 363
Zhilin, B., 278

www.ingramcontent.com/pod-product-compliance
Lightning Source LLC
Chambersburg PA
CBHW050622280326
41932CB00015B/2492